Information Theory and Coding

Information Theory and Coding

Muralidhar Kulkarni
Professor, Department of ECE
National Institute of Technology Karnataka (NITK)
Surathkal, Karnataka, INDIA

K S Shivaprakasha
Associate Professor, Department of ECE
N.M.A.M. Institute of Technology
Nitte, Karnataka, INDIA

WILEY

Information Theory and Coding

Other Wiley Editorial Offices:
John Wiley & Sons, Inc. 111 River Street, Hoboken, NJ 07030, USA
Wiley-VCH Verlag GmbH, Pappellaee 3, D-69469 Weinheim, Germany
John Wiley & Sons Australia Ltd, 42 McDougall Street, Milton, Queensland 4064, Australia
John Wiley & Sons (Asia) Pte Ltd, 1 Fusionopolis Walk #07-01 Solaris, South Tower, Singapore 138628
John Wiley & Sons Canada Ltd, 22 Worcester Road, Etobicoke, Ontario, Canada, M9W 1L1

First Edition: 2015

Reprint: 2018
ISBN: 978-81-265-5305-1
www.wileyindia.com
Printed at: Nice Printing Press

Preface

The twentieth century is referred to as the century of information, just as nineteenth century was the century of industrialization. The twenty-first century will go beyond the radio, television, telephone, computer, Internet and will change the way of life much more significantly than we have seen so far. The massive amount of information that can now be stored, transmitted and processed, with amazing speed, and accuracy will see further developments. All this has been made possible because of strong theoretical knowledge that has been built over the last two centuries particularly in the way information has been represented, stored and processed leading to information revolution. Information Theory and Coding has evolved over the last several years leading to several research fields and practical applications such as error control coding, data storage, cryptography, wireless communications and networking. The main goal of this book is to present the various aspects and results of Information Theory and Coding in a unifying and coherent manner particularly targeted to a first course for the undergraduate and possibly postgraduate students of Electrical/Electronics and Communication/Telecommunication Engineering departments. This book is an outcome of our experience gained in teaching Information Theory and Coding for the last few years and the difficulty faced by the students in grasping the abstract nature of the subject.

A brief rundown of the eight chapters will give a better idea of what is dealt with in this book.

Chapter 1 contains the mathematical prerequisites, with brief concepts of groups, vectors, random variables and probability theory.

Chapter 2 introduces Shannon's information measures detailing the properties of entropy and developing mathematical models to measure entropy.

Chapter 3 highlights the need for source coding in communication systems, provides a detailed study of the various source codes and validates the performance of the coding algorithms in terms of their efficiency.

Chapter 4 presents an overview of the channels used for communication and also introduces the concepts of various entropies.

Chapter 5 gives an insight into error control coding, detailing the mathematical modeling of linear block codes and binary cyclic codes.

Chapter 6 contains the need for burst error correcting codes and introduces some of the important classes of burst error correcting codes.

Chapter 7 highlights the encoding and decoding of convolution codes. Also an introduction to trellis coded modulation is presented.

Chapter 8 details the concepts of cryptography and introduces some of the most popular cryptographic algorithms.

The book contains a large number of worked examples along with exercise problems in all the chapters. MATLAB codes for some of the important algorithms have been included as Appendix, enabling the readers to run the programs for better understanding of concepts.

The book can be used as a textbook for undergraduate and postgraduate students of Electronics and Communication Engineering, Computer Science and Engineering, Information Technology, and Telecommunication Engineering. Just like any other document or book, this book being the first edition is bound to have some errors and omissions, which may please be brought to the notice of the authors or the publisher to come up with an errata or improvisation in the next edition. All suggestions and critical comments are welcome.

We wish to thank all our colleagues and teaching fraternity for their inputs at various stages of writing the book including the feedback from our students. We pledge our sincere sense of gratitude to our parents and all our family members for their constant support and encouragement. We are indebted to Wiley (India) for bringing out the book in record time.

Authors

Contents

1 Mathematical Prerequisite

'Nature's great book is written in mathematics.'

–Galileo

Learning Objectives

After reading this chapter, you will be able to:

- Recall the concepts of groups, vectors and probability theory.
- Define groups, fields, vector spaces, probability and random variables.
- Understand the process of evolution of vector spaces from groups.
- Demonstrate the practical significance of the mathematical functions in the field of information theory and coding.
- Compare and interrelate sets, groups, fields and vector spaces using the bottom-up approach.

1.1 Introduction

Engineering is a study of applied mathematics. Thus, recalling some preliminary mathematics becomes an essential task before we start our actual discussion. Two important branches of mathematics that serve as the basic foundations for information theory and coding are probability theory and modern algebra. This chapter deals with an introduction to these concepts so as to facilitate the readers to have an insight into mathematical prerequisite on the subject.

1.2 Groups

A group G is a set of elements associated with a mathematical operator * that satisfies some properties. It is generally denoted as $\langle G, *\rangle$, where G is a group with an operator *.

Definition 1.1: A set G associated with an operator * is said to be a group if

1. The operator * is associate, that is,

$$a*(b*c)=(a*b)*c \quad \forall a,b,c \in G$$

2. For every element $a \in G$, there exists a unique element e in G such that $a * e = a$. Here, the element e is called the identity element of the group G and is unique.
3. For every element $a \in G$, there has to be an inverse element b such that $a * b = e$. Here, 'b' is called the inverse of a and is generally denoted as 'a^{-1}' if the operation * is multiplication and as '$-a$' if the operation is addition.

Although the commutative property is not mandatory for a group, if the group satisfies the commutative property, it is called an Abelian group.

Definition 1.2: A group G is said to be an Abelian group if it satisfies the commutative property, that is,

$$a * b = b * a \quad \forall a, b \in G$$

EXAMPLE 1.1

Examine whether $G = \{0, 1, 2, 3, 4\}$ is a group under operation * – max( ).

Solution: Closure and associative properties are satisfied as seen from Table 1.1.

Table 1.1 | Construction table for G in Example 1.1

*	0	1	2	3	4
0	0	1	2	3	4
1	1	1	2	3	4
2	2	2	2	3	4
3	3	3	3	3	4
4	4	4	4	4	4

The identity element is 0 as $\max(0, a) = a \ \forall \ a \in G$. Therefore, an identity exists.
But inverse for any of the elements does not exist as zero entry is not present in Table 1.1 except for the first row. Therefore, the set G is not a group for the given operator.

EXAMPLE 1.2

Consider $G = \{0, 1, 2, 3, 4\}$. Test whether G is a group under addition modulo 5 and multiplication modulo 5.

Solution: The function tables can be constructed for both operations as shown in Tables 1.2 and 1.3, respectively.

Table 1.2 | Function table for ⊕5

⊕5	0	1	2	3	4
0	0	1	2	3	4
1	1	2	3	4	0
2	2	3	4	0	1
3	3	4	0	1	2
4	4	0	1	2	3

From Table 1.2, it can be seen that closure, associative and commutative properties are satisfied. 0 is the identity element, and inverses for 0, 1, 2, 3 and 4 are 0, 4, 3, 2 and 1, respectively. Therefore, *G* is an Abelian group under addition mod 5. On the contrary, from Table 1.3, it can be seen that inverse for 0 does not exist. Therefore, *G* is not a group under multiplication mod 5.

Table 1.3 | Function table for ⊙5

⊙5	0	1	2	3	4
0	0	0	0	0	0
1	0	1	2	3	4
2	0	2	4	1	3
3	0	3	1	4	2
4	0	4	3	2	1

It can be easily shown that $G - \{0\}$ or $G \setminus \{0\}$ forms an Abelian group under ⊙5. Proof of the same is left as an exercise for the readers. Also, sets of integers $\langle Z, +\rangle$ and $\langle Z - \{0\}, *\rangle$ are groups.

Theorem 1.1: The identity element of a group *G* is uniquc.

Proof: Let us consider that there are two identical elements e_1 and e_2 in *G*. Therefore, $e_1 * e_2 = e_1$ as e_2 is an identity. Also, $e_1 * e_2 = e_2$ as e_1 is an identity. Therefore, $e_1 = e_2$. Hence, the identity element is unique.

Theorem 1.2: The inverse of an element in group *G* is unique.

Proof: Proof of this theorem is left as an exercise for the readers.

EXAMPLE 1.3

Prove that all groups of three elements are Abelian.

Solution: Let the group $\langle G, *\rangle$ be $G = \{a, b, e\}$, where *e* is the identity element. Consider $a * b$, the value of which can be neither *a* nor *b*. It can be made clear by the following justification: If $a * b = a$, we get $b = e$, which is a contradiction.

Similarly, if $a * b = b$, we get $a = e$, which is again a contradiction. Therefore, $a * b$ has to be *e*. Similarly, it can be shown that

$$b * a = e$$

Therefore, it has been proved that $a * b = b * a$. Hence, group *G* is an Abelian group.

Definition 1.3 (Cyclic Group): If all elements of a group can be constructed using an element in the group, such groups are called cyclic groups and the element is called a generator. Cyclic groups can be better explained by taking the following example. Consider $G = \{1, 2, 3, 4\}$ and the operation is multiplication mod 5. Let us examine whether 2 is a generator. We know that

$$2 = 2$$
$$2 \cdot 2 = 4$$
$$2 \cdot 2 \cdot 2 = 8 \bmod 5 = 3$$
$$2 \cdot 2 \cdot 2 \cdot 2 = 16 \bmod 5 = 1$$

Thus, we can construct set G from element 2. Hence, G is a cyclic group and 2 is a generator element. Similarly, it can be proved that 3 and 4 are also generators of group G.

EXAMPLE 1.4

Determine the generators of $G = \{0, 1, 2, 3\}$ under modulo 4 addition.

Solution: Let us start with 1. We know that

$$1 = 1$$
$$1 + 1 = 2(1) = 2$$
$$1 + 1 + 1 = 3(1) = 3$$
$$1 + 1 + 1 + 1 = 4(1) \bmod 4 = 0$$

Therefore, 1 is a generator. Now consider 2:

$$2 = 2$$
$$2 + 2 = 0 \bmod 4$$
$$2 + 2 + 2 = 2$$

Therefore, 2 can generate only a subgroup of G and it is not a generator of G. Again, it can be shown that 3 is a generator of G.

Definition 1.4 (Order of a Group): Order of a group, sometimes also defined as the cardinality of a group, is the number of elements in the group.

EXAMPLE 1.5

Find the order of the group $\langle G, \oplus 5\rangle$.

Solution: It is given that $\langle G, \oplus 5\rangle$, which implies $G = \{0, 1, 2, 3, 4\}$. The order of the group G is 5.

Definition 1.5 (Order of a Group Element): The order of a group element 'a' is defined as the smallest positive integer n such that $na = 0$ if the operation is addition and $a^n = 1$ if the operation is multiplication. In Example 1.5, the order of 1 is 4 and that of 3 is also 4.

1.2.1 Subgroup

Let G be a group with operator $*$. A set H is said to be a subgroup of $\langle G, *\rangle$ if it satisfies the following properties:

1. The set H is a subset of G.
2. H is a group in its own right.

Consider a set of integers over the addition operation, $\langle Z, +\rangle$; clearly, Z is a subgroup of the set of real numbers, which in turn is a subgroup of the set of complex numbers C. It can be denoted as follows:

$$\langle Z, +\rangle \le \langle R, +\rangle \le \langle C, +\rangle$$

EXAMPLE 1.6

Consider the group of integers over the addition operation $\langle Z, +\rangle$. Prove that $H = 3Z$ is a subgroup of Z.

Solution: It is given that $Z = \{\ldots, -3, -2, -1, 0, 1, 2, 3, \ldots\}$ and $H = 3Z = \{\ldots, -9, -6, -3, 0, 3, 6, 9, \ldots\}$.
Hence

1. Clearly, H is a subset of Z.
2. Closure and associative properties need not be proved as they are inherited from the larger group Z. '0' is the additive identity. Also, $\forall a \in H$, '$-a$' exists, which is its inverse. Therefore, H is a subgroup of Z.

In general, it can be stated that for a group $\langle Z, +\rangle$, $\langle nZ, +\rangle$ is a subgroup.

Definition 1.6 (Coset): Let $\langle G, *\rangle$ be a group and H be a subgroup of G. Then for an element 'a' $\in G - H$, the right and left cosets of H can be constructed as $H * a$ and $a * H$, respectively. It is obvious that for a commutative group, left and right cosets are the same.

EXAMPLE 1.7

Consider the group $\langle G, +\rangle$ as Z_{16} over mod 16 addition. Let $H = \{0, 4, 8, 12\}$. Find the cosets of H over G.

Solution: It is given that $G = \{0, 1, 2, 3, 4, 5, 6, 7, 8, 9, 10, 11, 12, 13, 14, 15\}$ and $H = \{0, 4, 8, 12\}$. It can be shown that H is a subgroup. Consider $a = 1$. Then the coset of H over G is $1 + H = \{1, 5, 9, 13\}$. Similarly, we can construct two more cosets of H over G as follows:

$$2 + H = \{2, 6, 10, 14\}$$

and

$$3 + H = \{3, 7, 11, 15\}$$

EXAMPLE 1.8

Consider an integer group $G = \{0, 1, 2, \ldots, 31\}$ under mod 32 addition. Show that $H = \{0, 4, 8, 12, 16, 20, 24, 28\}$ forms a subgroup of G. Decompose into cosets with respect to H.

Solution:

1. To prove H is a subgroup of G:

- It is closure under + mod 32.
- 0 is the additive identity.
- $\forall x \in H$, $(32 - x) \in H$ is the inverse.
- Associative property is satisfied.

Therefore, H is a subgroup of H.

2. Cosets of H:

$$1 + H = \{1,5,9,13,17,21,25,29\}$$

$$2 + H = \{2,6,10,14,18,22,26,30\}$$

$$3 + H = \{3,7,11,15,19,23,27,31\}$$

Also,

$$G = H \cup (1 + H) \cup (2 + H) \cup (3 + H)$$

Theorem 1.3: All cosets of a group G have the same number of elements.

Proof: By the definition of the coset, for an element 'a' $\in G - H$, the corresponding coset is $a * H$. Let

$$H = \{e, h_1, \ldots, h_{n-1}\}$$

Therefore,

$$a * H = \{a * e, a * h_1, \ldots, a * h_{n-1}\} \tag{1.1}$$

In order to show that all cosets have the same number of elements, we need to just prove that all elements in Eq. (1.1) are unique. To prove this, assume the contradictory statement. Let

$$a * h_i = a * h_j$$

Multiplying both sides by a^{-1}, we get

$$a^{-1} * a * h_i = a^{-1} * a * h_j \Rightarrow h_i = h_j$$

which is a contradiction as every element in H is unique and distinct by the definition. Therefore, every element in a coset is uniquely identified by an element in the set H. Hence, the number of elements in every coset is the same as that of the subgroup H.

Theorem 1.4: Two elements a and b belong to the same coset of H over G if and only if $(a^{-1} * b)$ belongs to the subgroup H.

Proof: Let H be a subgroup of G. Then we get

$$H = \{e, h_1, h_2, \ldots, h_{n-1}\}$$

The coset $a * H$ can be constructed as follows:

$$a * H = \{a * e, a * h_1, a * h_2, \ldots, a * h_{n-1}\} = \{a, a * h_1, a * h_2, \ldots, a * h_{n-1}\}$$

Therefore, $a \in a * H$. Let

$$b = a * h_i \in a * H$$

Multiplying both sides *by* a^{-1}, we get

$$a^{-1} * b = a^{-1} * a * h_i \Rightarrow a^{-1} * b = h_i$$

Therefore, we can conclude that two elements a and b belong to the same coset if and only if $a^{-1} * b = h_i \in H$.

Theorem 1.5: The distinct cosets of H in a group G are disjoint.

Proof: Consider a group G with operation * $\langle G, *\rangle$. Let $\langle H, *\rangle$ be its subgroup = $\{e_1, h_1, h_2, \ldots, h_{n-1}\}$. To perform the coset decomposition, first consider an element $a_1 \in G$ but not in H, that is, $a_1 \in (G - H)$, and construct the first coset C_1 as follows:

$$C_1: a_1 * H = \{a_1 * e, a_1 * h_1, \ldots, a_1 * h_{n-1}\} = \{a_1, a_1 * h_1, \ldots, a_1 * h_{n-1}\}$$

Similarly, to construct the next coset, consider a_2, such that $a_2 \in G - H - C_1$ and C_2 is constructed as follows:

$$C_2: a_2 * H = \{a_2 * e, a_2 * h_1, \ldots, a_2 * h_{n-1}\} = \{a_2, a_2 * h_1, \ldots, a_2 * h_{n-1}\}$$

Now assume the converse of the statement, that is, elements in C_1 and C_2 are not disjoint. Let

$$a_1 * h_i = a_2 * h_j$$

$$a_2^{-1} * a_1 * h_i = h_j$$

$$a_2^{-1} * a_1 = h_j * h_i^{-1}$$

As H is a group in its own right, we have

$$h_j * h_i^{-1} \in H$$

Therefore,

$$h_j * h_i^{-1} = h_e$$

Hence,

$$a_2^{-1} * a_1 = h_e$$

From Theorem 1.4, $a_2^{-1} * a_1 = h_e$ implies a_2 and a_1 belong to the same coset. But it is a contradiction and is evident from the construction. Therefore, our converse assumption is incorrect. Thus, all elements of distinct cosets of H are disjoint.

Theorem 1.6 (Lagrange's theorem): Let G be a group of finite order and H be its subgroup. Then ord (H) divides ord (G). That is $|H| \mid |G|$.

Proof: Lagrange's theorem can be proved with the help of Theorems 1.3 and 1.5. Let ord (H) = K, and let there are 'm' cosets of H, that is, $C_1, C_2, \ldots, C_m$. From Theorem 1.3, all cosets of H in G have the same number of elements as of H; also, from Theorem 1.5, all elements of distinct cosets of H are disjoint; thus, we get

$$|H| + |C_1| + |C_2| + |C_3| + \cdots + |C_m| = |G| \tag{1.2}$$

But from Theorem 1.3, we have

$$|H| = |C_1| = |C_2| = \cdots |C_m| = K \tag{1.3}$$

Therefore,

$$(m+1)K = |G|$$

$$(m+1)|H| = |G| \Rightarrow |H| \mid |G| \tag{1.4}$$

1.3 Rings

Unlike groups, a ring is associated with two operations, namely addition (+) and multiplication (·).

Definition 1.7: A ring R is a set with two operations (addition and multiplication) with the following properties being satisfied:

1. R is an Abelian group under addition.
2. Closure under multiplication:

$$\forall (a,b) \in R, \quad a \cdot b = c \in R$$

3. Associative under multiplication:

$$\forall (a,b,c) \in R, \ (a \cdot b) \cdot c = a \cdot (b \cdot c)$$

4. Multiplication is distributive over addition:

$$a \cdot (b + c) = (a \cdot b) + (a \cdot c)$$

1.3.1 Properties of Rings

1. A ring is said to be a commutative ring if the multiplication operation is commutative, that is,

$$a \cdot b = b \cdot a$$

2. A ring is said to be a ring with an identity if there exists a multiplicative identity.
3. Elements in a ring that possess inverses for multiplication operation, are called units.

EXAMPLE 1.9

Investigate whether $\mathcal{R}$, a set of real numbers, forms a ring.

Solution: We have

$$\mathcal{R} = \{-\infty, \ldots, 0, \ldots, \infty\}$$

1. $|R$ is an Abelian group under addition.
2. Closure property under $\cdot$ is satisfied.
3. Associative and distributive properties can also be verified.
4. '1' is the identity element.
5. Commutative property is also satisfied.

Therefore, $\mathcal{R}$ is a commutative ring with an identity. All elements except 0 have inverses and hence are called units.

EXAMPLE 1.10

Let R be a ring with an identity. Denote this identity as 1. Prove the following:

(a) The multiplicative identity is unique.
(b) If an element a has both a right inverse b and a left inverse c, then $b = c$.
(c) If a has a multiplicative inverse a^{-1}, then $(a^{-1})^{-1} = a$.
(d) If $c = ab$ and c is a unit, then a has a right inverse and b has a left inverse.
(e) In a ring, a non-zero element a such that $ax = 0$ for $x \neq 0$ is said to be a zero divisor; show that if a has an inverse, then a is not a zero divisor.

Solution:

(a) Consider e and e' are two identity elements. Therefore,

$$a * e = a * e' = a$$
$$ae = ae'$$
$$a(e - e') = 0$$

As $a \neq 0$, we get

$$e - e' = 0 \Rightarrow e = e'$$

Thus, the multiplicative identity in a ring is unique.

(b) Given $ab = e$ and $ca = e$. So

$$ab = ca$$

Now

$$a^{-1}(ab) = a^{-1}e \Rightarrow b = a^{-1}$$

Also, we have

$$(ca)a^{-1} = e \cdot a^{-1} \Rightarrow c = a^{-1}$$

Therefore, $b = c$.

(c) Let $b = a^{-1}$. We have

$$ab = e \Rightarrow a \cdot b \cdot b^{-1} = e \cdot b^{-1} \Rightarrow a = b^{-1} \Rightarrow a = (a^{-1})^{-1}$$

(d) As c is a unit, c^{-1} exists. Consider $c = ab$. Then, we get

$$cc^{-1} = abc^{-1}$$

$$\Rightarrow e = a(bc^{-1})$$

bc^{-1} will lead to another element in the ring d. Thus, we have $e = ad$. This means d is the right inverse of a. Similarly,

$$c = ab \Rightarrow c^{-1}c = (c^{-1}a)b \Rightarrow e = fb$$

This implies b has the left inverse.

(e) Consider $ax = 0$. Then, we get

$$a^{-1} \cdot a \cdot x = a^{-1} \cdot 0 \Rightarrow e \cdot x = 0 \Rightarrow x = 0$$

But $x \neq 0$ from the data. Therefore, it is a contradiction. Hence, $ax \neq 0$ if a^{-1} exists.

1.4 Field

A field F is a set of elements associated with two operations, + and ·, satisfying the following properties:

1. F forms a commutative group under addition.
2. $F - \{0\}$ or $F\backslash\{0\}$ forms a commutative group under multiplication.
3. The operations + and · are distributive:

$$a \cdot (b + c) = (a \cdot b) + (a \cdot c)$$

$$(a + b) \cdot c = (a \cdot c) + (b \cdot c)$$

A field with a finite number of elements is called a finite field. They are also referred to as Galois fields (GF).

EXAMPLE 1.11

Examine whether $F_3 = \{0, 1, 2\}$mod 3 forms a field.

Solution: Tables 1.4 and 1.5 present the construction of F_3. Clearly, F_3 is a commutative group under addition:

Also $F_3 - \{0\}$ is a commutative group under multiplication. Therefore, F_3 mod 3 is a field.

Table 1.4 | Addition operation mod 3

⊕3	0	1	2
0	0	1	2
1	1	2	0
2	2	0	1

Table 1.5 | Multiplication operation mod 3

⊙3	1	2
1	1	2
2	2	1

1.4.1 Order of a Field Element

Consider a finite field with 'q' number of elements. Let

$$\beta \in F_q$$

$$\beta^2 \in \beta \cdot \beta \in F_q$$

which is as per closure property:

$$\beta^3 \in \beta \cdot \beta \cdot \beta \in F_q$$

As the field has a finite number of elements, sooner or later there has to be a repetition, that is,

$$\beta^m = \beta^k \quad \text{for} \quad m > k$$

that is, $\beta^m = \beta^k$. Let β^{-1} be the multiplicative inverse of β. Therefore, $(\beta^k)^{-1} = \beta^{-k}$ is the multiplicative inverse of β^k. Hence,

$$\beta^m = \beta^k$$

$$\Rightarrow \beta^{-k} \cdot \beta^m = \beta^{-k} \cdot \beta^k$$

$$\Rightarrow \beta^{m-k} = 1 \tag{1.5}$$

Therefore, from Eq. (1.5), we can conclude that for a finite field F_q, there exists a smallest number 'n' such that $\beta^n = 1$, $\forall \beta \in F_q$. Then n is called the order of the field element β in F_q.

Theorem 1.7: If $t = \text{ord}(\beta)$ for some $\beta \in F_q$, then $t|(q-1)$.

Proof: Let $F_q = \{0, 1, \alpha, \ldots, \beta, \ldots\}q$ elements. Consider $F_q - \{0\} = \{1, \alpha, \ldots, \beta, \ldots\}(q-1)$ elements. Also, $\beta^t = 1$ (given ord$(\beta) = t$). $F_t = \{\beta, \beta^2, \beta^3, \ldots, \beta^t = 1\}$ forms a group in its own right; also, it is evidently a subgroup of $F_q - \{0\}$. Therefore, F_t with 't' elements is a subgroup of $F_q - \{0\}$ with $(q-1)$ elements. Hence, according to the Lagrange's theorem, we get $t \mid (q-1)$.

Theorem 1.8: Let α and β be elements in F_q such that $\beta = \alpha^i$. If $\text{ord}(\alpha) = t$, then

$$\text{ord}(\beta) = \frac{\text{ord}(\alpha)}{\gcd(i,t)} = \frac{t}{\gcd(i,t)}$$

1.4.2 Primitive Element in a GF(q)

An element with order $(q - 1)$ in F_q is called the primitive element of F_q.

EXAMPLE 1.12

Determine the primitive elements for $F_5 = \{0, 1, 2, 3, 4\}$ under mod 5.

Solution: To find the primitive elements, we need to compute the order of all elements in $F_5 - \{0\}$, that is, $\{1, 2, 3, 4\}$. This is shown in Table 1.6.

Table 1.6 |

1	2	3	4
ord(1) = 1	$2 = 2$	$3^1 = 3$	$4^1 = 4$
	$2^2 = 4$	$3^2 = 9 \bmod 5 = 4$	$4^2 = 16 \bmod 5 = 1$
	$2^3 = 8 \bmod 5 = 3$	$3^3 = 27 \bmod 5 = 2$	ord(4) = 2
	$2^4 = 16 \bmod 5 = 1$	$3^4 = 81 \bmod 5 = 1$	

Therefore, ord (2) = 4, ord (3) = 4. Hence, 2 and 3 are primitive elements as their order is 4.

Primitive elements are important in the perspective of field construction. If a primitive element is identified, the whole field can be constructed as all elements in F_q can be represented as a distinct power of the primitive element.

Consider the primitive element 2 in the previous example. It can be shown that all elements in F_5 can be represented as a power of 2:

$$1 = 2^4 \bmod 5$$

$$2 = 2^1 \bmod 5$$

$$3 = 2^3 \bmod 5$$

$$4 = 2^2 \bmod 5$$

Definition 1.8 (Euler's totient (ϕ) Function): Euler's totient (ϕ) function $\phi(t)$ for an integer t is the number of elements in the set $\{1, 2, 3, \ldots, (t - 1)\}$ that are relatively prime to 't'.

For example, consider $\phi(8)$ that gives the number of elements in set {1, 2, 3, 4, 5, 6, 7} that are relatively prime to 8. Therefore,

$$\phi(8) = |\{1,3,5,7\}| = 4$$

Hence, $\phi(8) = 4$.

Properties:

1. $\phi(p) = (p-1)$ for p being prime
2. $\phi(p_1 \cdot p_2) = (p_1 - 1)(p_2 - 1)$ for distinct primes p_1 and p_2
3. $\phi(p^m) = p^{m-1}(p-1)$
4. $\phi(p^m r^n) = p^{m-1}r^{n-1}(p-1)(r-1)$ for distinct primes p and r

EXAMPLE 1.13

Compute $\phi(284)$, $\phi(440)$, $\phi(699)$, $\phi(788)$ and $\phi(1024)$.

Solution: For $\phi(284)$, factors are $2 \times 2 \times 71$. Therefore,

$$\phi(284) = 2^{(2-1)}(2-1)(71-1) = 140$$

For $\phi(440)$, we have

$$440 = 2 \times 2 \times 2 \times 5 \times 11$$

Therefore,

$$\phi(440) = 2^{(3-1)}(2-1)(5-1)(11-1) = 160$$

For $\phi(699)$, we have

$$699 = 3 \times 233$$

Therefore,

$$\phi(699) = (3-1)(233-1) = 464$$

For $\phi(788)$, we have

$$788 = 2 \times 2 \times 197$$

Therefore,

$$\phi(788) = 2^{(2-1)}(2-1)(197-1) = 392$$

For $\phi(1024)$, we have $1024 = 2^{10}$, therefore,

$$\phi(284) = 2^{(10-1)}(2-1) = 512$$

Theorem 1.9: Consider a GF(q). For an integer t, if $t \nmid (q-1)$, there exists no element in GF(q) with order t; else there exist $\phi(t)$ elements with order t. The number of primitive elements in F_q is exactly equal to $\phi(q-1)$.

1.4.3 Characteristic of a Field

Consider a field $F_q = \{0, \alpha, \alpha^2, \ldots, \alpha^{q-1} = 1\}$, with '$\alpha$' being a primitive element. Consider the following:

$$1$$
$$1+1=2(1)$$
$$1+1+1=3(1)$$
$$\vdots$$

As the field is finite, sooner or later there has to be a repetition. Therefore, it can be stated that there always exists a smallest integer m such that $m(1) = 0$, and 'm' is called the characteristic of the field.

Theorem 1.10: The characteristic of a field is always a prime number.

Proof: Consider a field F_q. Let m be its characteristic, that is, $m(1) = 0$. Let us assume the converse statement, that is, let m be non-prime. Therefore, 'm' can be represented as a product of two integers l and k, as follows:

$$m = l \times k$$

Clearly, l, $k < m$. Thus, we have

$$m(1) = l(1)k(1)$$
$$0 = l(1)k(1)$$

This implies that either $l(1) = 0$ or $k(1) = 0$, which is a contradiction with the definition that 'm' is the smallest integer such that $m(1) = 0$. Therefore, 'm' has to be a prime number.

Theorem 1.11: The order of a GF F_q is a power of prime.

1.4.4 Polynomials over a Finite Field

GF(q)[x] is defined as the set of polynomials whose coefficients are coming from the field F_q, that is,

$$a_0 + a_1x + \cdots + a_nx^n$$

where $(a_0, a_1, \ldots) \in F_q$ and there will be no restriction over the degree of the polynomial. For example, GF(2)[x] is a set of polynomials whose coefficients are either 0 or 1, say, $(x^2 + x + 1)$, $(x^5 + 1)$, $(x^{10} + x^8 + x + 1)$ and so on.

1.4.4.1 Irreducible Polynomials

A polynomial $g(x) \in F_q[x]$ is said to be irreducible if its roots are not present in $F_q(x)$. In other words, a polynomial $g(x)$ is called an irreducible polynomial if we cannot represent it as a product of two polynomials, say, $a(x)$ and $b(x)$. Obviously, the degree of $a(x)$ and $b(x)$ is less than that of $g(x)$. For example, consider a set of real numbers as follows:

$$\mathcal{R} = \{-\infty, \ldots\ 0, \ldots\ \infty\}$$

Consider the following polynomial:

$$x^2 + 1 = 0 \Rightarrow x = \pm\sqrt{-1}$$

But $\pm\sqrt{-1}$ is not included in the set $\mathcal{R}$. Therefore, $(x^2 + 1)$ is an irreducible polynomial over $\mathcal{R}$. However, it is reducible in the set of complex numbers $\mathcal{C}$.

EXAMPLE 1.14

Determine whether $(x^2 + x + 1)$ is an irreducible polynomial over $F_2[x]$.

Solution: We have

$$f(x) = x^2 + x + 1$$

Clearly, 0 and 1 are not roots as $f(0) \neq 0$ and $f(1) \neq 0$. Let us consider if x, $(x + 1)$ divides $f(x)$:

$$\begin{array}{r|l} & x+1 \\ \hline x & x^2 + x + 1 \\ & x^2 \\ \hline & x + 1 \\ & x \\ \hline & 1 \end{array}$$

Therefore, $x \nmid f(x)$.
Also,

$$\begin{array}{r|l} & x \\ \hline x+1 & x^2 + x + 1 \\ & x^2 + x \\ \hline & 1 \end{array}$$

Therefore, $(x + 1) \nmid f(x)$. Hence, $f(x)$ is an irreducible polynomial over $F_2[x]$.

1.4.4.2 Primitive Polynomials

An irreducible polynomial $f(x) \in F_p[x]$ of degree 'm' is said to be primitive if the smallest integer n such that $f(x)|x^n - 1$ is $n = p^m - 1$.

EXAMPLE 1.15

Determine whether $f(x) = x^4 + x^3 + x^2 + x + 1$ is primitive over $F_2[x]$.

Solution: It can be easily shown that $f(x)$ is irreducible. To check whether $f(x)$ is primitive, keep checking whether $f(x)|x^n - 1$ for $n = 5, 6, 7, \ldots$, as $m = 4$. For $n = 5$, since field is over binary, we have

$$x^5 - 1 = x^5 + 1$$

$$\begin{array}{r|l} & x+1 \\ x^4+x^3+x^2+x+1 & x^5+1 \\ & \underline{x^5+x^4+x^3+x^2+x} \\ & x^4+x^3+x^2+x+1 \\ & \underline{x^4+x^3+x^2+x+1} \\ & 0 \end{array}$$

Therefore, $f(x)|x^5 - 1$ but $5 \neq p^m - 1$ ($p = 2$, $m = 4$). Hence, $f(x)$ is irreducible but not primitive.

EXAMPLE 1.16

Determine whether $f(x) = x^3 + x^2 + 1$ is primitive over $F_2[x]$.

Solution: It can be shown that the minimum value of n, such that $f(x)|x^n - 1$, is $n = 7$, where

$$p^m - 1 = 2^3 - 1 = 7$$

Therefore, the given $f(x)$ is primitive.

Theorem 1.12: The roots $\{\alpha_j\}$ of an mth-degree primitive polynomial will be of the order $p^m - 1$.

1.4.4.3 Extension Field

As discussed in Section 1.4.4.2, a primitive polynomial is an irreducible polynomial of the order $p^m - 1$. Thus, the roots of primitive polynomials are not found in $F_p[x]$ but in some extensions of $F_p[x]$. The field $F_p^m[x]$ being constructed using the primitive polynomial of mth degree over the ground field $F_p[x]$ is called an extension field over $F_p[x]$.

As the order of the root of the mth-degree primitive polynomial $\{\alpha_i\}$ is $(p^m - 1)$, it will be a primitive element in F_p^m. Thus, the field can be constructed in terms of $\{\alpha_i\}$. Therefore, the resource required for the construction of an extension field F_p^m over F_p is an mth-degree primitive polynomial over $F_p[x]$. Let

$$p(x) = a_m x^m + a_{m-1} x^{m-1} + \cdots + a_1 x + a_0$$

Let α be one of its roots. Therefore,

$$p(\alpha) = 0 = \alpha^m + a_{m-1}\alpha^{m-1} + \cdots + a_1\alpha + a_0$$

$$\alpha^m = -a_{m-1}\alpha^{m-1} - a_{m-2}\alpha^{m-2} - \cdots - a_1\alpha - a_0$$

Now, the extension field F_p^m can be constructed as

$$0$$
$$\alpha$$
$$\alpha^2$$
$$\vdots$$
$$\alpha^{m-1}$$
$$\alpha^m = -a_{m-1}\alpha^m - \cdots - a_1\alpha^2 - a_0\alpha = -a_{m-1}[-a_{m-1}\alpha^{m-1} - \cdots - a_1\alpha - a_0]\cdots - a_1\alpha^2 - a_0\alpha$$
$$\vdots$$
$$\alpha^{p^{m-1}} = 1$$

EXAMPLE 1.17

Construct F_2^3 as an extension field over F_2.

Solution: To construct F_2^3, we need a primitive polynomial of degree 3. Thus, we can consider either $x^3 + x + 1$ or $x^3 + x^2 + 1$.

Consider $p(x) = x^3 + x + 1$

Let α be a root of $p(x)$. Therefore,

$$p(\alpha) = \alpha^3 + \alpha + 1 = 0$$

$$\Rightarrow \alpha^3 = \alpha + 1$$

Therefore, the extension field will be

$$0$$
$$\alpha$$
$$\alpha^2$$
$$\alpha^3 = \alpha + 1$$
$$\alpha^4 = \alpha^2 + \alpha$$
$$\alpha^5 = \alpha^3 + \alpha^2 = \alpha + 1 + \alpha^2 = \alpha^2 + \alpha + 1$$
$$\alpha^6 = \alpha^3 + \alpha^2 + \alpha = \alpha + 1 + \alpha^2 + \alpha = \alpha^2 + 1$$
$$\alpha^7 = \alpha^3 + \alpha = \alpha + 1 + \alpha = 1$$

The polynomial, power and m-tuple representation of F_2^3 over F_2 are shown in Table 1.7.

Table 1.7 | Extension field for F_2

Power	*Polynomial*	*m-Tuple*
0	0	0 0 0
α	α	0 1 0
α^2	α^2	0 0 1
α^3	$\alpha+1$	1 1 0
α^4	$\alpha^2+\alpha$	0 1 1
α^5	$\alpha^2+\alpha+1$	1 1 1
α^6	α^2+1	1 0 1
α^7	1	1 0 0

1.4.4.4 Conjugacy Class

Let $\beta \in F_q^m$. The conjugates of β w.r.t. subfield F_q are $\beta, \beta^q, \beta^{q^d}$, …. The list has to be finite as the field is a finite field.

EXAMPLE 1.18

Find the conjugacy classes in F_2^3 over F_2.

Solution: We have

$$F_2^3 = \{0,1,\alpha,\alpha^2,\alpha^3,\alpha^4,\alpha^5,\alpha^6\}, \qquad q=2, \qquad m=3$$

where α is a primitive element. Let $\beta = \alpha$. Then the conjugacy class includes

$$\alpha,\alpha^2,\alpha^{2^2}=\alpha^4,\alpha^{2^3}=\alpha^8=\alpha,\{\alpha,\alpha^2,\alpha^4\}$$

As α^2 is already included in the first class, the next permissible value for β will be α^3, as follows:

$$\alpha^3,\ (\alpha^3)^2=\alpha^6,\ (\alpha^3)^{2^2}=(\alpha^3)^4=\alpha^{12}=\alpha^5,\ (\alpha^3)^{2^3}=(\alpha^3)^8=\alpha^{24}=\alpha^3$$

Therefore, $\{\alpha^3, \alpha^6, \alpha^5\}$. Thus, the conjugacy classes of F_2^3 with respect to F_2 are

$$\{0\}$$
$$\{1\}$$
$$\{\alpha,\alpha^2,\alpha^4\}$$
$$\{\alpha^3,\alpha^6,\alpha^5\}$$

We can make out the following inferences with the above conjugacy class decomposition:

1. All elements in the set F_q^m will uniquely lie in one of the conjugacy classes.
2. The cardinality of the conjugacy class is a factor of m.
3. Conjugacy class is always defined with respect to a field.

1.4.4.5 *Minimal Polynomial*

A minimal polynomial defined for an element β belonging to F_q^m is the smallest-degree non-zero monic polynomial $p(x) \in F_q[x]$ such that $p(\beta) = 0$.

Theorem 1.13: Let $p(x)$ be the minimal polynomial of $\beta \in F_q^m$. Then the other roots of $p(x)$ will be the conjugates of β.

EXAMPLE 1.19

Obtain the minimal polynomials for all elements in F_2^3 over F_2.

Solution: We have

$$F_2^3 = \{0, 1, \alpha, \alpha^2, \alpha^3, \alpha^4, \alpha^5, \alpha^6\}$$

We have already obtained the conjugacy classes in F_2^3 as follows:

$$\{0\}, \{1\}, \{\alpha, \alpha^2, \alpha^4\}, \{\alpha^3, \alpha^6, \alpha^5\}$$

From Theorem 1.12, all elements in a conjugacy class will have the same minimal polynomial. Therefore,
Minimal polynomial for $\{0\} = M(x) = (x - 0) = x$
Minimal polynomial for $\{1\} = M_1(x) = (x - 1)$
Minimal polynomial for $\{\alpha, \alpha^2, \alpha^4\}$ is

$$\begin{aligned} M_2(x) &= (x-\alpha)(x-\alpha^2)(x-\alpha^4) = (x+\alpha)[x^2 + (\alpha^2+\alpha^4)x + \alpha^6] = (x+\alpha)(x^2+\alpha x+\alpha^6) \\ &= x^3 + \alpha x^2 + \alpha^6 x + \alpha x^2 + \alpha^3 x + \alpha^9 = x^3 + x + 1 \text{ (from Table 1.7)} \end{aligned}$$

Similarly, the minimal polynomial for $\{\alpha^3, \alpha^5, \alpha^6\}$ is

$$\begin{aligned} M_3(x) &= (x-\alpha^3)(x-\alpha^5)(x-\alpha^6) \\ &= (x^2 + (\alpha^3+\alpha^5)x + \alpha^8)(x+\alpha^6) = (x^2 + \alpha^2 x + \alpha)(x+\alpha^6) \\ &= x^3 + x^2(\alpha^6+\alpha^2) + (\alpha^8+\alpha) + \alpha^7 \\ &= x^3 + x^2(\alpha^6+\alpha^2) + (\alpha^8+\alpha)x + \alpha^7 = x^3 + x^2 + 1 \end{aligned}$$

It is evident that all minimal polynomials obtained belong to $F_q[x]$.

1.5 Quotient Ring

A polynomial ring R consists of an infinite number of polynomials whose coefficients are coming from the ground field F_q. In order to analyze them, we need to quantify them into a finite set of equivalence classes. This can be done by considering a $GF_q[x]/x^n - 1$ which does the division of every polynomial by $x^n - 1$ and assigns it to an appropriate set of remainder. Then by constructing the addition and multiplication tables, one can decide whether the given $F_q[x]/x^n - 1$ is a field or a ring. This can be explained by considering an example. Consider

$$F_2[x] = \{0, 1, x, x+1, x^2, x^2+x, x^2+x+1, x^3, x^3+1, x^3+x, x^3+x^2, x^3+x^2+x, x^3 + x^2+1, x^3+x^2+x+1, \ldots\}$$

Now let us decompose the set of polynomials into equivalence classes by considering $F_2[x]/x^3 + 1$. Let s_0 be the set of polynomials giving remainder 0 when divided by $x^3 + 1$. We get

$$s_0 = \{0, x^3+1, x^4+x, \ldots\}$$

Similarly, let s_1 be the set of polynomials giving remainder 1 when divided by $x^3 + 1$. We get

$$s_1 = \{1, x^3, x^4+x+1, \ldots\} = 1 + s_0$$

Continuing with the same procedure, we can end up with the following equivalence classes giving remainders x, $1 + x$, x^2, $x^2 + x$ and $x^2 + x + 1$, respectively:

$$s_2 = x + s_0 = \{x, x^3+x+1, x^4, \ldots\}$$

$$s_3 = (1+x) + s_0 = \{(1+x), x_3 + x, x^4+1, \ldots\}$$

$$s_4 = (x^2) + s_0 = \{x^2, x^3+x^2+1, x^4+x^2+x, \ldots\}$$

$$s_5 = (x^2+1) + s_0 = \{(x^2+1), (x^3+x^2), (x^4+x^2+x+1), \ldots\}$$

$$s_6 = (x^2+x) + s_0 = \{(x^2+x), x^3+x^2+x+1, x^4+x^2, \ldots\}$$

$$s_7 = (x^2+x+1) + s_0 = \{(x^2+x+1), (x^3+x^2+x), (x^4+x^2+1), \ldots\}$$

Let us label the equivalence class with the first element at each set, that is,

$$s_0 \to 0$$

$$s_1 \to 1$$

$$s_2 \to x$$

$$s_3 \to 1+x$$

$$s_4 \to x^2$$

$$s_5 \to x^2+1$$

$$s_6 \to x^2+x$$

$$s_7 \to x^2+x+1$$

The corresponding addition table is shown in Table 1.8.

It is clear from Table 1.8 that $F_2[x]/x^3 + 1$ forms an Abelian group under addition. Similarly, a multiplicative table can be constructed by performing the following operation:

$$(s_i \cdot s_j) \bmod x^3 + 1$$

A multiplicative table can be constructed following the same procedure and is shown in Table 1.9.

It is evident that multiplicative inverse does not exist for s_3, s_5, s_6 and s_7. Thus, we can say that $F_2[x]/x^3 + 1$ forms a ring but not a field.

Table 1.8 | Equivalence class

		0	**1**	x	$x+1$	x^2	x^2+1	x^2+x	x^2+x+1
	+	s_0	s_1	s_2	s_3	s_4	s_5	s_6	s_7
0	s_0	s_0	s_1	s_2	s_3	s_4	s_5	s_6	s_7
1	s_1	s_1	s_0	s_3	s_2	s_5	s_4	s_7	s_6
x	s_2	s_2	s_3	s_0	s_1	s_6	s_7	s_4	s_5
$x+1$	s_3	s_3	s_2	s_1	s_0	s_7	s_6	s_5	s_4
x^2	s_4	s_4	s_5	s_6	s_7	s_0	s_1	s_2	s_3
x^2+1	s_5	s_5	s_4	s_7	s_6	s_1	s_0	s_3	s_2
x^2+x	s_6	s_6	s_7	s_4	s_5	s_2	s_3	s_0	s_1
x^2+x+1	s_7	s_7	s_6	s_5	s_4	s_3	s_2	s_1	s_0

Table 1.9 | Multiplicative equivalence class

		0	**1**	x	$x+1$	x^2	x^2+1	x^2+x	x^2+x+1
	+	s_0	s_1	s_2	s_3	s_4	s_5	s_6	s_7
0	s_0	s_0	s_0	s_0	s_0	s_0	s_0	s_0	s_0
1	s_1	s_0	s_1	s_2	s_3	s_4	s_5	s_6	s_7
x	s_2	s_0	s_2	s_4	s_6	s_1	s_3	s_5	s_7
$x+1$	s_3	s_0	s_3	s_6	s_5	s_3	s_6	s_3	s_0
x^2	s_4	s_0	s_4	s_1	s_5	s_2	s_6	s_3	s_7
x^2+1	s_5	s_0	s_5	s_3	s_6	s_6	s_3	s_5	s_0
x^2+x	s_6	s_0	s_6	s_5	s_3	s_3	s_5	s_6	s_0
x^2+x+1	s_7	s_0	s_7	s_7	s_0	s_7	s_0	s_0	s_7

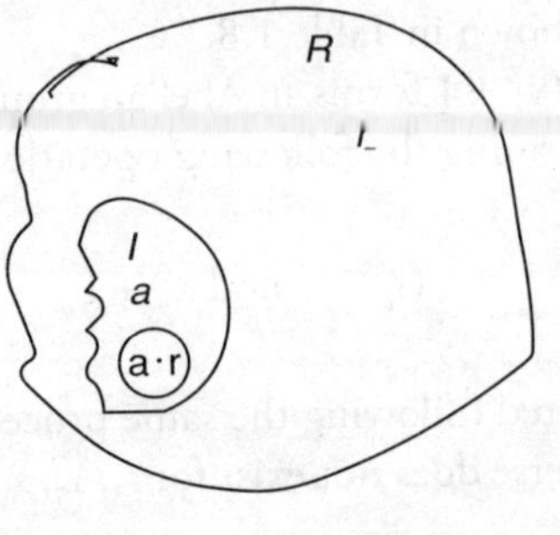

Figure 1.1 | Ideal for a ring.

1.5.1 Ideals in a Ring

Let R be a ring. A non-empty subset $I \subset R$ is said to be an ideal in R if it satisfies the following conditions:

1. I forms a group under addition operation in R.
2. For every $r \in R$ and $a \in I$, $a \cdot r = b \in I$.

It is as depicted in Fig. 1.1.

Note:

1. For every ring R, {0} and {R} are called its trivial ideals.
2. Ideals are of great interest in error control coding as cyclic codes form an ideal over a ring of polynomials.

EXAMPLE 1.20

Let R be a ring. Show that {0, 4, 8, 12} forms an ideal in the ring of integers R = {0, 1, 2, ..., 15} under mod 16 '+' and '.'

Solution:

1. To show that I is a group under $\oplus 16$:
   - Closure and associative properties hold good as integer addition is closure and associative.
   - 0 is the identity element.
   - $\forall x \in I$, there exists $(16 - x) \in I$, which is the identity element.

   Therefore, I is a group.
2. $I = 4x \bmod 16\ \forall x \in R$. Therefore, $\forall a \in I$ and $\forall r \in R$, $a \cdot r = b \bmod 16 \in I$.
   Hence, I forms an ideal.

EXAMPLE 1.21

Let A and B be ideals in a ring R. The sum $A + B$ is defined as $A + B = \{a + b, a \in A, b \in B\}$. Show that $(A + B)$ is an ideal in R.

Solution:

1. To prove $(A+B)$ constitutes a group under +:
   - Closure:

$$\forall (a_i + b_i) + (a_j + b_j) = (a_i + a_j) + (b_i + b_j)$$

$$a_i + b_j = a_k \in A \quad \text{since } A \text{ is an ideal,}$$

and

$$b_i + b_j = b_k \in B \quad \text{since } B \text{ is an ideal.}$$

Therefore,

$$(a_k + b_k) \in (A+B)$$

   - Associativity:

$$\begin{aligned}(a_1 + b_1) + [(a_2 + b_2) + (a_3 + b_3)] &= (a_1 + b_1) + (a_2 + a_3) + (b_2 + b_3) \\ &= (a_1 + a_2 + a_3) + (b_1 + b_2 + b_3) \\ &= (a_1 + a_2) + (b_1 + b_2) + (a_3 + b_3) \\ &= [(a_1 + b_1) + (a_2 + b_2)] + (a_3 + b_3)\end{aligned}$$

   - Identity: $\forall a_i \in A$, an identity exists, say, e_1. Similarly, $\forall b_i \in B$, an identity exists, say, e_2. Therefore,

$$(a_i + b_i) + (e_1 + e_2) = (a_i + e_1) + (b_i + e_2) = (a_i + b_i)$$

Hence, $(e_1 + e_2)$ is the identity.

   - Inverse: $\forall a_i \in A$, an inverse exists, say, $(-a_i)$. Similarly, $\forall b_i \in B$, an inverse exists, say, $(-b_i)$. Therefore,

$$(a_i + b_j) + (-a_i - b_j) = e$$

$$[a_i + (-a_i)] + [b_i + (-b_j)] = (e_1 + e_2)$$

Hence, $(A+B)$ is a group under +.

2. To prove $a \cdot r = b \in I \; \forall a \in I$ and $r \in R$:

$$(a+b)r = ar + br$$

$$ar \in A \quad \text{as } A \text{ is an ideal,}$$

and

$$br \in B \quad \text{as B is an ideal. Therefore,}$$

$$(ar + br) \in (A+B)$$

Hence, $(A+B)$ is an ideal in R.

1.5.2 Principal Ideals

An ideal I in a ring R is said to be a principal ideal if there exists an element g in I such that every element $a \in I$ can be represented as a product $a = mg$ for some $m \in R$. The element 'g' of the principal ideal is called the generator element. In the ring of polynomials, the polynomial $g(x)$ is called the generator polynomial and can be used to construct a cyclic code.

Theorem 1.14: Let I be an ideal in $F_q[x]/x^n - 1$. Then

1. There is a unique monic polynomial $g(x) \in I$ of minimum degree.
2. I is a principal with a generator $g(x)$.
3. $g(x)$ divides $x^n - 1$ in $F_q[x]$.

Proof:

1. Let us assume a converse statement. Let $g(x)$ and $g^1(x)$ be the minimum-degree monic polynomials in I:

$$g(x) = x^r + g_{r-1}x^{r-1} + \cdots + g_1 x + g_0$$

$$g^1(x) = x^r + g_{r-1}^1 x^{r-1} + \cdots + g_1^1 x + g_0^1$$

$$g(x) + g^1(x) = (g_{r-1} + g_{r-1}^1)x^{r-1} + \cdots + (g_1 + g_1^1)x + (g_0 + g_0^1)$$

As I is an Abelian group under addition,

$$g(x) + g^1(x) \in I$$

Therefore,

$$(g_{r-1} + g_{r-1}^1)x^{r-1} + \cdots + (g_1 + g_1^1)x + (g_0 + g_0^1) \in I$$

whose degree is x^{r-1}, which is less than the degree of $g(x)$ and $g^1(x)$. Thus, there is a contradiction as $g(x)$ and $g^1(x)$ are monic polynomials with the minimum degree in I. Therefore, the monic polynomial with the minimum degree is unique in I.

2. $g(x)$ is the monic polynomial with minimum degree. For I to be a principal ideal, every element in I, $f(x)$, has to be represented as $m(x)g(x)$ for some $m(x)$ in R. In other words, every $f(x)$ in I has to be divisible by $g(x)$. (**Note:** Subtraction can be replaced with addition as we are dealing with binary algebra.) Let us assume the converse statement, that is, there exists some $f(x)$ in I that is not divisible by $g(x)$. Therefore,

$$f(x) = q(x)g(x) + r(x) \tag{1.6}$$

where $q(x)$ is the quotient and $r(x)$ is the remainder. Clearly,

$$\deg\{r(x)\} < \deg\{g(x)\}$$

From Eq. (1.6), we can write

$$r(x) = f(x) - q(x)g(x)$$

$$\Rightarrow q(x)g(x) \in I$$

as I is an ideal. $f(x)$ also belongs to I. Therefore, $f(x) - q(x)g(x)$ also belongs to I, which implies $r(x) \in I$. But

$$\deg\{r(x)\} < \deg\{g(x)\}$$

which is a contradiction to the assumption that $g(x)$ is the minimum monic polynomial. Therefore,

$$r(x) = 0 \Rightarrow g(x) \mid f(x) \tag{1.7}$$

3. To prove the next part, again assume the converse statement, that is, $g(x)$ does not divide $x^n - 1$:

$$x^n - 1 = g(x)q(x) + r(x)$$

$$\deg\{r(x)\} < \deg\{g(x)\}$$

$$r(x) = [x^n - 1] - g(x)q(x)$$

As RHS belongs to I, $r(x) \in$ I, which is again a contradiction. Therefore, $r(x) = 0$. Hence, $g(x) \mid x^n - 1$.

Note: Theorem 1.14 has an important implication over the selection of the generator polynomial for a cyclic code. Generators for the cyclic code have to be the divisors of $(x^n - 1)$.

Thus, finding the factors of $x^n - 1$ for a given value of n becomes an important issue in the selection of the generator polynomial.

1.5.3 Factoring $x^n - 1$

It is given that every element in the field F_q is a root of $x^q - x = 0$. To factor $x^n - 1$, we can have two possibilities. n can be either of the form $n = q^m - 1$ or $n | q^m - 1$.

1. **Case (i):** $n = q^m - 1$.
   As every element of F_q^m is a root of $x^{q^m} - x = 0 \Rightarrow x(x^{q^m-1} - 1) = 0$ or every non-zero element of F_q^m is a root of $(x^{q^m-1} - 1) = 0$ or $x^n - 1 = 0$, the factors of $x^n - 1$ will simply be

$$x^n - 1 = (x - 1)(x - \alpha)(x - \alpha^2)\cdots(x - \alpha^{q^m-2})$$

2. **Case (ii):** $n|q^m - 1$. We have

$$f(x) = x^n - 1$$

   Let β be a root of $f(x)$. Then

$$0 = \beta^n - 1 \Rightarrow \beta^n = 1 \tag{1.8}$$

   that is, β is the nth root of unity. Thus, to factorize $x^n - 1$, the extension field F_q^m has to be considered. Then the element β in F_q^m has to be identified such that $\beta^n = 1$. Once β is identified, it can be proved that $\beta^2, \beta^3, \ldots, \beta^{n-1}$ will also satisfy the relation presented in Eq. (1.8), that is,

$$(\beta^2)^n = (\beta^n)^2 = 1$$

   Similarly,

$$(\beta^3)^n = (\beta^n)^3 = 1$$

   and so on.

Therefore, the term $x^n - 1$ can be factored as

$$x^n - 1 = (x-\beta)(x-\beta^2)(x-\beta^3)\cdots(x-\beta^{n-1})(x-1)$$

To simplify, we can group the terms into their conjugacy classes and then we can replace them with the corresponding minimal polynomial.

EXAMPLE 1.22

Factorize $x^7 - 1$ over $F_2[x]$.

Solution: We have $n = 7$, which can be written as $2^3 - 1$. Therefore, $q = 2$ and $m = 3$. Hence, it can be factored by just considering the elements of the field F_2^3:

$$x^7 - 1 = (x-1)(x-\alpha)(x-\alpha^2)(x-\alpha^3)(x-\alpha^4)(x-\alpha^5)(x-\alpha^6)$$

To simplify further, we can group the elements according to their conjugacy class and they can be replaced by their corresponding minimal polynomials. Also, the negative sign can be treated as + as the operation is binary:

$$x^7 - 1 = (x-1)\{(x+\alpha)(x+\alpha^2)(x+\alpha^4)\}\{(x+\alpha^3)(x+\alpha^6)(x+\alpha^5)\}$$

$$x^7 - 1 = (x-1)(x^3 + x + 1)(x^3 + x^2 + 1)$$

EXAMPLE 1.23

Factorize $x^5 - 1$ over $F_2[x]$.

Solution: Clearly, $n = 5$ is not of the form $2^m - 1$. Therefore, we need to consider case 2. First, we need to identify the extension field F_2^m such that

$$5 \mid 2^m - 1$$

From trial and error method, we get $m = 4$. Therefore, roots are present in $F_2^4[x]$:

$$F_2^4 = \{0, 1, \alpha, \alpha^2, \alpha^3, \alpha^4, \ldots, \alpha^{14}\}$$

Next step is to find β in F_2^4 such that $\beta^5 = 1$:

$$\alpha^5 \neq 1$$

$$(\alpha^2)^5 = \alpha^{10} \neq 1$$

$$(\alpha^3)^5 = \alpha^{15} = 1 \quad \text{in } F_2^4$$

Therefore, $\beta = \alpha^3$. The remaining roots can be obtained as

$$\beta = \alpha^3$$

$$\beta^2 = (\alpha^3)^2 = \alpha^6$$

$$\beta^3 = (\alpha^3)^3 = \alpha^9$$

$$\beta^4 = (\alpha^3)^4 = \alpha^{12}$$

$$\beta^5 = (\alpha^3)^5 = 1$$

Therefore,

$$x^5 - 1 = (x-\alpha^3)(x-\alpha^6)(x-\alpha^9)(x-\alpha^{12})(x-1) = (x+1)\{(x+\alpha^3)(x+\alpha^6)(x+\alpha^9)(x+\alpha^{12})\}$$

$$x^5 + 1 = (x+1)(x^4 + x^3 + x^2 + x + 1)$$

1.6 Vector Space

Let V be a set of vectors and F be a finite field. The operation '+' called the vector addition is defined between the vectors in set V and '·' operation called scalar multiplication is defined between the elements F and V. Then the set V can be qualified as a vector space if it satisfies the following conditions:

1. Set V forms a commutative group under vector addition.
2. For any element $f \in F$ and $\underline{v} \in V$, the scalar product $f \cdot \underline{v} \in V$.
3. The operations '+' and '·' have to be distributive, that is, $\forall f_1, f_2 \in F$ and $\underline{v}_1, \underline{v}_2 \in V$

$$f_1 \cdot (\underline{v}_1 + \underline{v}_2) = f_1 \cdot \underline{v}_1 + f_1 \cdot \underline{v}_2$$

$$(f_1 + f_2) \cdot \underline{v}_1 = f_1 \cdot \underline{v}_1 + f_2 \cdot \underline{v}_2$$

4. Associativity: that is,

$$(f_1 \cdot f_2) \cdot \underline{v} = f_1 \cdot (f_2 \cdot \underline{v})$$

5. Multiplicative identity 1 in F will also serve as a multiplicative identity for scalar multiplication.

EXAMPLE 1.24

Determine whether $\mathcal{R}^3$ forms a vector space.

Solution:

1. Closure and associative properties hold good for $\mathcal{R}^3$.
2. (0, 0, 0) serves as an identity. For every vector (x, y, z), there exists $(-x, -y, -z)$ in $\mathcal{R}^3$. Also, commutative property holds good. Therefore, $\mathcal{R}^3$ is an Abelian group under vector addition.

3. For any element r from $\mathcal{R}^3$, the product $r \cdot \underline{v} = \underline{v}, \in \mathcal{R}^3$.
4. Distributive and associative properties can be verified.
5. $\forall\ \underline{v} \in V, 1 \times \underline{v} = \underline{v}$. Therefore, 1 is the multiplicative identity.

Hence, $|R^3$ is a vector space.

EXAMPLE 1.25

Determine whether V_2^n is a vector space.

Solution: Here the field is a binary field:

1. Closure property is satisfied for vector addition. Vector addition over F_2 is analogous to component-wise binary addition. Therefore, associative and commutative properties are satisfied:

$$V_2^n = \underbrace{\begin{bmatrix} 1 & 1 & 1 & 1 & 1 \\ \vdots & \vdots & \vdots & \vdots & \vdots \\ \vdots & \vdots & \vdots & \vdots & \vdots \\ 0 & 0 & 1 & \cdots & 1 \\ 0 & 0 & 0 & \cdots & 1 \\ 0 & 0 & 0 & \cdots & 0 \end{bmatrix}}_{n\text{-tuple}} \Bigg\} 2^n \text{ vectors}$$

   Every vector will serve as its own inverse. [0 0 0 · · 0] will be the identity element. Therefore, V_2^n is an Abelian group under vector addition.
2. We have $F_2 = \{0, 1\}$

$$0 \cdot \underline{v} = \underline{0} \in V \quad \text{and} \quad 1 \cdot \underline{v} = \underline{v} \in V$$

3. Associative and distributive properties can be verified.
4. Clearly, 1 will serve as the multiplicative identity as $1 \times \underline{v} = \underline{v}$.
   Therefore, V_2^n is a vector space.

Definition 1.9 (Linear Combination of Vectors): Let $\underline{v}_1, \underline{v}_2, \ldots, \underline{v}_n \in V$ and $f_1, f_2, \ldots, f_n \in F$. Then the linear combination $f_1\underline{v}_1 + f_2\underline{v}_2 + \cdots + f_n\underline{v}_n$ also belongs to V.

Definition 1.10 (Spanning Set): Spanning set is a collection of vectors $\{\underline{v}_1, \underline{v}_2, \ldots, \underline{v}_k\}$ whose linear combination can generate all vectors in the vector space.
For example, vectors (1, 0, 0), (0, 1, 0) and (0, 0, 1) can serve as a spanning set for $\mathcal{R}^3$ as any vector $(x\ y\ z)$ can be generated as

$$(x \quad y \quad z) = x(1 \quad 0 \quad 0) + y(0 \quad 1 \quad 0) + z(0 \quad 0 \quad 1)$$

Definition 1.11 (Basis of a Vector Space): A spanning set with a minimum number of vectors is called a basis set.

Definition 1.12 (Linearly Independent Vectors): A set of 'm' vectors $\{v_1, v_2, \ldots, v_m\}$ are said to be linearly independent if the combination $a\underline{v}_1 + b\underline{v}_2 + \cdots + m\underline{v}_m = 0$ only when $a = b = \cdots = m = 0$.

In other words, if no vector in the set can be generated by the linear combination of other vectors, then such vectors are called linearly independent vectors.

EXAMPLE 1.26

Determine whether (1 1 0 1 0), (0 0 1 1 1), (1 0 1 0 1), (0 0 0 1 1) and (1 0 0 0 1) are linearly independent.

Solution: The given vectors are not linearly independent as the vector (1 0 0 0 1) can be expressed as

$$(1\ \ 0\ \ 0\ \ 0\ \ 1) = (0\ \ 0\ \ 1\ \ 1\ \ 1) + (1\ \ 0\ \ 1\ \ 0\ \ 1) + (0\ \ 0\ \ 0\ \ 1\ \ 0)$$

Note:

1. It is evident that the basis set contains the set of linearly independent vectors.
2. Also, the basis set for a vector space need not be unique, but the cardinality of the basis set has to be unique.

Definition 1.13 (Vector Subspace): It is a subset of the vector space V, which is a vector space in its own right. A vector space is shown in Fig. 1.2.

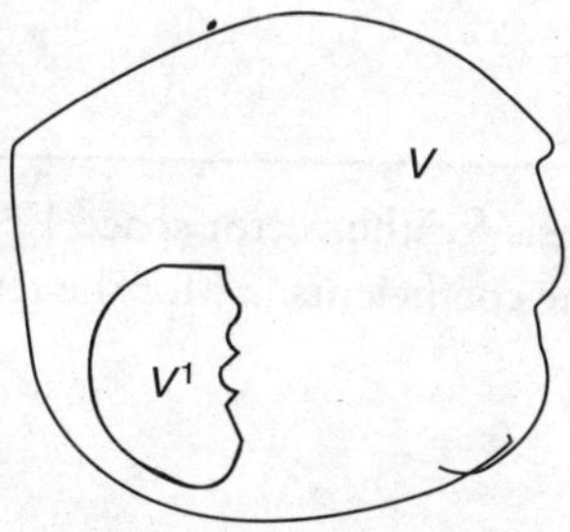

Figure 1.2 | Vector space.

V^1 is a subspace of V if V^1 can qualify as a vector space.

Definition 1.14 (Dimension of a Vector Space): The cardinality of the basis set determines the dimension of the vector space. For example, for $\mathcal{R}^3$, a canonical basis set would be {(100), (010), (001)} whose cardinality is 3. Therefore,

$$\dim(\mathcal{R}^3) = 3$$

In general, the dimension of V_q^n would be 'n' and the total number of vectors in V_q^n will be q^n.

EXAMPLE 1.27

Show that the set of binary polynomials with degree less than or equal to r forms a vector space over GF(2) with a dimension $(r + 1)$.

Solution: The binary polynomial with degree r includes $(r + 1)$ binary digits. Therefore, vector space includes

$$V = \begin{cases} \overset{\leftarrow (r+1) \text{ bits} \rightarrow}{[0 \ \ 0 \ \ \cdots \ \ 0]} \\ [1 \ \ 0 \ \ \cdots \ \ 0] \\ \vdots \\ [1 \ \ 1 \ \ \cdots \ \ 1] \end{cases}$$

Therefore, spanning set may include the vectors

$$\left.\begin{matrix} [1 \ \ 0 \ \ \cdots \ \ 0] \\ [0 \ \ 1 \ \ \cdots \ \ 0] \\ \vdots \\ [0 \ \ 0 \ \ \cdots \ \ 1] \end{matrix}\right\} (r+1) \text{ vectors}$$

Therefore,

$$\dim(V) = (r + 1)$$

EXAMPLE 1.28

Let $S = \{V_1, V_2, \ldots, V_n\}$ be an arbitrary basis for the vector space V^n, and let V be an arbitrary vector in V^n. Derive an expression for computing the coefficients $\{a_i\}$ for the representation $v = a_1 V_1 + a_2 V_2 + \cdots + a_n V_n$.

Solution: Let

$$V = [V^{(1)} \quad V^{(2)} \quad V^{(3)} \quad \cdots \quad V^{(n)}]$$

$$V_1 = [V_1^{(1)} \quad V_1^{(2)} \quad \cdots \quad V_1^{(n)}]$$

$$V_2 = [V_2^{(1)} \quad V_2^{(2)} \quad \cdots \quad V_2^{(n)}]$$

We have to find the coefficients a_i such that

$$\begin{aligned} a_1 V_1^{(1)} + a_2 V_2^{(1)} + \cdots + a_n V_n^{(1)} &= V^{(1)} \\ a_1 V_1^{(2)} + a_2 V_2^{(2)} + \cdots + a_n V_n^{(2)} &= V^{(2)} \\ &\vdots \\ a_1 V_1^{(n)} + a_2 V_2^{(n)} + \cdots + a_n V_n^{(n)} &= V^{(n)} \end{aligned}$$

There are n equations and n unknowns from which we can compute $\{a_i\}$.

Definition 1.15 (Inner Product): Let $\underline{u} = \{u_0, u_1, \ldots, u_{n-1}\}$ and $\underline{v} = \{v_0, v_1, \ldots, v_{n-1}\}$ be two vectors in the vector space. Then the inner product $\underline{u} \cdot \underline{v}$ can be defined as

$$\underline{u} \cdot \underline{v} = u_0 v_0 + u_1 v_1 + \cdots + u_{n-1} v_{n-1} = \sum_{i=0}^{n-1} u_i v_i \tag{1.9}$$

The inner product satisfies commutative, associative and distributive properties, that is,

$$\underline{u} \cdot \underline{v} = \underline{v} \cdot \underline{u}$$

$$f_1 \cdot (\underline{u} \cdot \underline{v}) = (f_1 \cdot \underline{u}) \cdot \underline{v}$$

$$\underline{u} \cdot (\underline{v} + \underline{w}) = \underline{u} \cdot \underline{v} + \underline{u} \cdot \underline{w}$$

EXAMPLE 1.29

Prove the following properties of inner product:

(a) Commutative property.
(b) Associativity under scalar multiplication.
(c) Distributive with vector addition.

Solution:

(a) Commutative property: To prove $u \cdot v = v \cdot u$ with respect to $u = (u_0, u_1, \ldots, u_{n-1})$ and $v = (v_0, v_1, \ldots, v_{n-1})$. Now

$$u \cdot v = u_0 v_0 + u_1 v_1 + \cdots + u_{n-1} v_{n-1}$$

As $u_i v_j$ are scalar products, they are commutative. Therefore,

$$u \cdot v = v_0 u_0 + v_1 u_1 + \cdots + v_{n-1} u_{n-1} \Rightarrow u \cdot v = v \cdot u$$

(b) Associativity under scalar multiplication: To prove $a \cdot (\underline{u} \cdot \underline{v}) = (a \cdot \underline{u}) \cdot \underline{v}$.
Consider

$$\begin{aligned} a \cdot (\underline{u} \cdot \underline{v}) &= a[u_0 v_0 + u_1 v_1 + \cdots + u_{n-1} v_{n-1}] = a u_0 v_0 + a u_1 v_1 + \cdots + a u_{n-1} v_{n-1} \\ &= (a u_0) v_0 + (a u_1) v_1 + \cdots + (a u_{n-1}) v_{n-1} \end{aligned}$$

So

$$a \cdot (\underline{u} \cdot \underline{v}) = (a \cdot \underline{u}) \cdot \underline{v}$$

(c) Distributive with vector addition: We have

$$\underline{u} \cdot (\underline{v} + \underline{w}) = \underline{u} \cdot \underline{v} + \underline{u} \cdot \underline{w}$$

Consider

$$\underline{u} \cdot (\underline{v} + \underline{w}) = u_0 (v_0 + w_0) + u_1 (v_1 + w_1) + \cdots + u_{n-1} (v_{n-1} + w_{n-1})$$

$$= u_0 v_0 + u_0 w_0 + u_1 v_1 + u_1 w_1 + \cdots + u_{n-1} v_{n-1} + u_{n-1} w_{n-1}$$
$$= [u_0 v_0 + u_1 v_1 + \cdots + u_{n-1} v_{n-1}] + [u_0 w_0 + u_0 w_1 + \cdots + u_{n-2} w_{n-1}]$$
$$= (\underline{u} \cdot \underline{v}) + (\underline{u} \cdot \underline{w})$$

Definition 1.16 (Dual Space of Vector Space): A *k*-dimensional subspace S of V is said to have a dual space $S^{\perp}$ in V if $\forall\, \underline{v} \in S$ and $\forall\, \underline{u} \in S^{\perp}$

$$\underline{v} \cdot \underline{u} = 0 \tag{1.10}$$

The subspace S and its dual space $S^{\perp}$ need not be disjoint.

Note: Dual space is also a vector subspace. It is shown in Fig. 1.3.

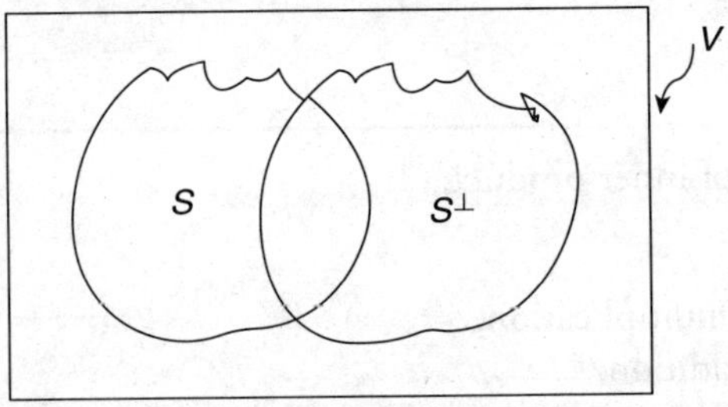

Figure 1.3 | Vector space and dual space.

Theorem 1.15: Let $\underline{v}_1$ and $\underline{v}_2$ be any two arbitrary vectors in the subset S of the vector space V. The subset S is a vector space if and only if the linear combination of $\underline{v}_1$ and $\underline{v}_2$ also belongs to S. That is, $\forall\, \underline{v}_1, \underline{v}_2 \in S$, $a\underline{v}_1 + b\underline{v}_2$ also belongs to S.

Proof: Let us assume that $a\underline{v}_1 + b\underline{v}_2 \in S\ \forall\, \underline{v}_1, \underline{v}_2 \in S$. Then

1. Closure and associative properties are satisfied. If $a = -1$ and $b = 0$, $(-1)\underline{v}_1$ will also belong to S $\forall\, \underline{v}_1$. Therefore, inverse exists. 0 is the identity element. Therefore, it is an Abelian group under vector addition.
2. Commutative, distributive and associative properties will hold good in S as S is a subset of V and thus these properties are inherited from V.
3. For all $f_1 \in F$, $f_1 \cdot \underline{v} \in S$ as per our assumption. Therefore, S is a subspace if $a\underline{v}_1 + b\underline{v}_2 \in S\ \forall\, \underline{v}_1, \underline{v}_2 \in S$.

Theorem 1.16: The dual space $S^{\perp}$ of a vector subspace S is a subspace in its own right under V.

Proof: Let $\underline{u} \in S$ and $\underline{v}, \underline{w} \in S^{\perp}$. According to the definition of the dual space, we have

$$\underline{u} \cdot \underline{v} = 0$$

$$\underline{u} \cdot \underline{w} = 0 \Rightarrow a \cdot \underline{u} \cdot \underline{w} = 0$$

and

$$b \cdot \underline{u} \cdot \underline{w} = 0$$

Therefore,

$$\underline{u}(a\underline{v} + b\underline{w}) = 0$$

This implies that $a\underline{v} + b\underline{w}$ also belongs to $S^{\perp}$. As $a\underline{v} + b\underline{w} \in S^{\perp}\ \forall\ \underline{v}, \underline{w} \in S^{\perp}$, it follows from Theorem 1.14 that $S^{\perp}$ is a subspace of V.

Theorem 1.17 (Dimension Theorem): Let S be a subspace and $S^{\perp}$ be the corresponding dual space of S in the vector space V. Then the sum of the dimensions of S and $S^{\perp}$ gives the dimension of the vector space V. That is,

$$\dim(S) + \dim(S^{\perp}) = \dim(V)$$

Proof: Let $\dim(V) = m$ and $\dim(S) = k$. Therefore, there are 'k' linearly independent vectors in the basis set of S. That is,

$$B_S = \{\underline{g}_1, \underline{g}_2, \ldots, \underline{g}_k\}$$

and each of these vectors is of n-tuple:

$$B_s = \begin{bmatrix} g_1 \\ g_2 \\ \cdot \\ \cdot \\ \cdot \\ g_k \end{bmatrix} = \begin{bmatrix} g_{11} & g_{12} & \cdots & g_{1n-1} \\ g_{21} & g_{22} & \cdots & g_{2n-1} \\ \cdots & & & \\ \cdots & & & \\ g_{k1} & g_{k2} & \cdots & g_{kn-1} \end{bmatrix} = G \tag{1.11}$$

Each of the rows in G is a vector in the basis set. As the rows of G span the entire set S, any vector $\underline{v}$ belonging to $S^{\perp}$ will satisfy the condition

$$G \cdot v^T = 0 \tag{1.12}$$

As $S^{\perp}$ is also a vector subspace, a basis for $S^{\perp}$ can also be obtained. Let us assume that $\dim(S^{\perp}) = t$. Then, we get

$$B_S^{\perp} = \{\underline{h}_1, \underline{h}_2, \ldots, \underline{h}_t\} \tag{1.13}$$

It is clear that all vectors in $B_S^{\perp}$ are linearly independent vectors of V. Thus, the basis set for the vector space V can be obtained by extending the set $B_S^{\perp}$, which implies

$$B_V = \{\underline{h}_1, \underline{h}_2, \ldots, \underline{h}_t, \underline{d}_1, \underline{d}_2, \ldots, \underline{d}_{n-t}\} \tag{1.14}$$

As the rows of G give a set of linearly independent vectors, row rank of G is k. As the row rank and column rank of a vector space are same, columns of G span k-dimensional vector space. Therefore, every k-tuple vector can be represented as

$$\underline{v} = G \cdot \underline{x}^T \quad \text{for} \quad x \in V \tag{1.15}$$

Also, every vector $x \in V$ can be represented as a linear combination of basis vectors of V:

$$\begin{aligned} x &= a_1\underline{h}_1 + a_2\underline{h}_2 + \cdots + a_t\underline{h}_t + a_{t+1}\underline{d}_1 + a_{t+2}\underline{d}_2 + \cdots + a_n\underline{d}_{n-t} \\ &= a_1[h_{10}h_{11}\ldots h_{tn-1}] + a_2[h_{20}h_{21}\ldots h_{2n-1}] + \cdots + a_t[h_{t0}h_{t1}\ldots h_{tn-1}] \\ &\quad + a_{t+1}[d_{10}d_{11}\ldots d_{1n-1}] + \cdots + a_n[d_{n-t0}d_{n-t1}\ldots d_{n-tn-1}] \end{aligned}$$

$$\begin{aligned} x = [&a_1h_{10} + a_2h_{20} + \cdots + a_th_{t0} + a_{t+1}d_{10} + \cdots + a_nd_{n-t0}a_1h_{11} + a_2h_{21} + \cdots + a_th_{t1} + a_{t+1}d_{11} + \cdots \\ &+ a_nd_{n-t1}\ldots a_1h_{1n-1} + a_2h_{2n-1} + \cdots + a_th_{tn-1} + a_{t+1}d_{n-1} + \cdots + a_nd_{n-tn-1}] \end{aligned}$$

This implies

$$x^T = \begin{bmatrix} a_1h_{10} + a_2h_{20} + \cdots + a_th_{t0} + a_{t+1}d_{10} + \cdots + a_nd_{n-t0} \\ a_1h_{11} + a_2h_{21} + \cdots + a_th_{t1} + a_{t+1}d_{11} + \cdots + a_nd_{n-t1} \\ \cdots \\ \cdots \\ a_1h_{1n-1} + a_2h_{2n-1} + \cdots + a_th_{tn-1} + a_{t+1}d_{1n-1} + \cdots + a_nd_{n-tn-1} \end{bmatrix}$$

$$x^T = a_1\underline{h}_1^T + a_2\underline{h}_2^T + \cdots + a_t\underline{h}_t^T + a_{t+1}\underline{d}_1^T + \cdots + a_n\underline{d}_{n-t}^T \tag{1.16}$$

Substituting Eq. (1.16) in Eq. (1.15), we get

$$\begin{aligned} \underline{v} = G \cdot \underline{x}^T &= G[a_1\underline{h}_1^T + a_2 + \cdots + a_t\underline{h}_t^T + a_{t+1}\underline{d}_1^T + \cdots + a_n\underline{d}_{n-t}^T] \\ &= a_1[G\underline{h}_1^T] + a_2[G\underline{h}_2^T] + \cdots + a_t[G\underline{h}_t^T] + a_{t+1}[G\underline{d}_1^T] + \cdots + a_n[G\underline{d}_{n-t}^T] \end{aligned}$$

But

$$[G\underline{h}_1^T] = [G\underline{h}_2^T] = \cdots = [G\underline{h}_t^T] = 0$$

Therefore,

$$\underline{v} = a_{t+1}[G\underline{d}_1^T] + a_{t+2}[G\underline{d}_2^T] + \cdots + a_n[G\underline{d}_{n-t}^T]$$

But $\underline{v}$ is a k-tuple vector as it is spanned by the column space of G. Therefore, $n - t = k$ or $t = n - k$. So

$$\dim(S^{\perp}) = \dim(V) - \dim(S)$$

$$\Rightarrow \dim(V) = \dim(S) + \dim(S^{\perp}) \tag{1.17}$$

1.7 Introduction to Probability Theory

In the analysis of communication systems, we often encounter random signals whose behavior cannot be predicted exactly. The output of information sources and noise are random in nature. Random signals cannot be expressed as explicit functions of time. However, when examined over a long period, a random signal may exhibit certain regularities, which can be described in terms of probabilities and statistical average. The main objective of this section is to develop probabilistic models for random signals.

1.7.1 Probability Theory

The performance of a communication system primarily depends on the external disturbances/noise signals that affect the signal and results in degradation of the signal-to-noise ratio (SNR). A comprehensive knowledge of the external disturbances/noise signals helps combat these effects to improve the reliability of the system. In this section, we briefly study some principles of probability theory so that these concepts can be used to calculate/determine the performance parameters of the digital communication system. Before we define probability, we define certain related parameters:

1. **Experiment:** An experiment is a process conducted to get some result.
2. **Outcome:** An outcome is the result obtained after performing the experiment.
3. **Event:** An event is a combination of outcomes.
4. **Sample space:** The set of all possible outcomes of an experiment is called sample space.

Let us consider a simple example of rolling a single die. There are six possible outcomes, 1–6. The sample space will be $S = \{1, 2, 3, 4, 5, 6\}$. The total number of outcomes in a sample space is defined by $n(S)$. In the above example, $n(S) = 6$. There can be many possible events. An event could be that an even number is obtained, $\{2, 4, 6\}$. Another possible event would be that 1 is obtained, $\{1\}$. This event has only one element in it and hence known as an *elementary event*. Let us now define probability of an event.

If an experiment is performed 'N' number of times, where 'N' is very large, and for 'n' out of these N experiments, the outcome belongs to a particular event, the probability of this event is defined by the ratio n/N (i.e., it is the fraction of times an event has occurred). The probability of an event A that occurs n_A number of times in N performances of the experiment is given by

$$P(A) = \lim_{N\to\infty} \frac{n_A}{N} \tag{1.18}$$

It may be noted that this probability always lies between 0 and 1, that is,

$$0 \le P(A) \le 1 \tag{1.19}$$

If we consider the example of tossing a coin as an experiment, the outcomes of this experiment are either head or tail. Let A represent an event with an outcome 'head'. If the experiment of tossing a coin is repeated, say, 1 million times, then the probability of occurrence of event A (head) is about 1/2, that is, in the 1 million tosses of the coin, half of them would show heads, that is,

$$P(A) = \frac{\text{Number of possible events } A \text{ (head)}}{\text{Total number of outcome } S \text{ (head or tail)}} = \frac{1(\text{head})}{2(\text{head} + \text{tail})} = \frac{1}{2} = 0.5$$

That is, the ratio of the number of heads to the total number of flips would approach 1/2. If an event is not possible, then the probability will be zero. Suppose we consider two different events A and B with probabilities

$$P(A) = \lim_{N\to\infty} \frac{n_A}{N}, \qquad P(B) = \lim_{N\to\infty} \frac{n_B}{N}$$

If the two events A and B do not occur at the same time, they are termed disjoint. For example, in a die throwing experiment, the events 'an even number of dots' and 'an odd number of dots' are definitely disjoint events, whereas 'an even number of dots' and 'two dots' are not disjoint. If A and B are disjoint,

$$P(A \text{ or } B) = \lim_{N\to\infty} \frac{n_A + n_B}{N} = P(A) + P(B) \tag{1.20}$$

If the two events are disjoint, the probability of their sum is the sum of their probabilities.

EXAMPLE 1.30

A die is thrown. Determine the probability that an even number comes up.

Solution: The sample space of throwing a die is given by

$$[S] = [1, 2, 3, 4, 5, 6]; \quad N = 6$$

If an even number is to come up as the desired outcome, then $A = [2,4,6]$, that is, $n_A = 3$. Now

$$P(A) = \frac{n_A}{N} = \frac{3}{6} = 0.5$$

EXAMPLE 1.31

If a coin is flipped twice, determine the sample space and obtain all possible probabilities of the various events.

Solution: The possible outcomes are [HH, HT, TH, TT], where H and T denote heads and tails. If the experiment is performed several times, each of the four possible outcomes would have a probability of 1/4. It is quite possible that any of these outcomes can be obtained. For example:

1. No outcome: $\{\phi\}$
2. One outcome: {HH, HT, TH, TT}
3. Two outcomes: {(HH, HT), (HH, TH), (HH, TT), (HT, TH), (HT, TT), (TH, TT)}
4. Three outcomes: {(HH, HT, TH), (HH, HT, TT), (HH, TH, TT), (HT, TH, TT)}

$$P[\phi] = 0$$

This implies that the zero event does not have any possible outcome (null event); in addition,

$$P[\text{HH}, \text{HT}, \text{TH}, \text{TT}] = 1$$

This is a certain event as the event is made up of all possible four outcomes. Then

$$P(\text{HH, HT}) = P(\text{HH, TH}) = \cdots = P(\text{TH, TT}) = \frac{2}{4} = \frac{1}{2}$$

$$P(\text{HH, HT, TH}) = P(\text{HH, HT, TT}) = \cdots = P(\text{HT, TH, TT}) = \frac{3}{4}$$

EXAMPLE 1.32

For the rolling of two dices, obtain the probability of obtaining the sum 10 and also the probability of obtaining a sum greater than or equal to 10.

Solution: For the rolling of two dices, the sample space consists of 36 points, (1, 1) (1, 2), …, (6, 6). The probability of obtaining the sum equal to 10 is given by

$$P\{(6,4),(5,5),(4,6)\} = \frac{3}{36} = \frac{1}{12}$$

The probability of obtaining the sum greater than or equal to 10 is given by

$$P\{(6,4),(5,5),(4,6),(6,5),(5,6),(6,6)\} = \frac{6}{36} = \frac{1}{6}$$

1.7.2 Properties of Probability

Equations (1.18)–(1.20) are the basic properties of probability (repeated here):

1. $P(A) = \lim_{N\to\infty} \frac{n_A}{N}$

2. $0 \le P(A) \le 1$:
   - $P(A) = 0 \to$ null probability
   - $P(B) = 1 \to$ certain event probability

3. $P(A \text{ or } B) = \lim_{N\to\infty} \frac{n_A + n_B}{N} = P(A) + P(B)$

   For disjoint events (also called mutually exclusive events).
   The other properties are summarized as follows:

4. $P(\bar{A}) = 1 - P(A)$

   $\bar{A}$ means the complement of A.
   If the sample space consists of two disjoint events A and $\bar{A}$, we get

$$S = A + \bar{A}$$

Then

$$P(S) = P(A) + P(\bar{A})$$

The probability of a certain event = 1. If the sample space contains all the events, then

$$P(S) = 1$$

Therefore,

$$1 = P(A) + P(\overline{A})$$

or

$$P(\overline{A}) = 1 - P(A)$$

5. If there are mutually exclusive events $A_1, A_2, \ldots, A_m$, then

$$S = A_1 + A_2 + \cdots + A_m$$

$$P(A_1) + P(A_2) + \cdots + P(A_m) = P(S) = 1 \tag{1.21}$$

If all the events $A_1, A_2, \ldots, A_m$ have the same probability of occurrence or equally likely events, then

$$P(A_1) = P(A_2) \cdots P(A_m) = \frac{1}{m}$$

6. If events A and B are not mutually exclusive events, then the probability of the union of A and B is given by

$$P(A + B) = P(A) + P(B) - P(AB) \tag{1.22}$$

where $P(AB)$ is the probability of both A and B occurring simultaneously.
This probability $P(AB)$ is shown as the joint probability defined by

$$P(AB) = \lim_{N \to \infty} \frac{n_{AB}}{N} \tag{1.23}$$

If events A and B are mutually exclusive, then $P(AB) = 0$.

7. If one random variable has any effect on the other, then we define conditional probability. Let A and B be two events; then the probability of event A given that B has occurred is given by

$$P\left(\frac{A}{B}\right) = \frac{P(AB)}{P(B)} \tag{1.24}$$

where $P(AB)$ is the joint probability of A and B.
Similarly, we can define $P(B/A)$, which is the probability of event B given that A has occurred and is given by

$$P\left(\frac{B}{A}\right) = \frac{P(AB)}{P(A)} \tag{1.25}$$

From this, it can be concluded that

$$P\left(\frac{A}{B}\right) P(B) = P\left(\frac{B}{A}\right) P(A) \tag{1.26}$$

It is quite possible that in the large number of experiments involving events A and B, the events A and B may occur jointly or independently. Let n_{AB} be the number of times events A and B occur jointly. n_A is the number of times the event 'A' occurs independently. n_B is the number of times the event 'B' occurs independently.

It is clear that n_A includes n_A and n_B includes n_{AB}. Hence, the event A occurs more number of times (either independently or jointly with B) compared with the joint occurrence of events A and B.

Therefore,

$$n_A = n_{AB} \quad \text{or} \quad 1 \geq \frac{n_{AB}}{n_A} \quad \text{or} \quad \frac{n_{AB}}{n_A} \leq 1$$

This ratio basically indicates the frequency of occurrence of B given that A has occurred. For large number of trials in $N \rightarrow \infty$, we can write

$$P\left(\frac{B}{A}\right) = \lim_{N\to\infty}\left(\frac{n_{AB}}{n_A}\right) = \lim_{N\to\infty}\left(\frac{n_{AB}/N}{n_A/N}\right) = \frac{\lim_{N\to\infty}(n_{AB}/N)}{\lim_{N\to\infty}(n_A/N)}$$

that is,

$$P\left(\frac{B}{A}\right) = \frac{P(AB)}{P(A)}$$

Similarly, we can state that

$$P\left(\frac{A}{B}\right) = \frac{P(AB)}{P(B)}$$

8. Two events A and B are said to be statistically independent if

$$P\left(\frac{A}{B}\right) = P(A)$$

This is because knowing that B has occurred does not tell anything about A since A and B are independent. Therefore,

$$P\left(\frac{A}{B}\right) = \frac{P(AB)}{P(B)}$$

or

$$P(AB) = P(A) \cdot P(B) \tag{1.27}$$

(If A and B are independent, $P(A/B) = P(A)$.)

9. Bayes' rule: If $B_1, B_2, B_3, \ldots, B_n$ are mutually exclusive events and event A occurs only when anyone of $B_1, B_2, B_3, \ldots, B_n$ occurs, then as per Bayes' rule

$$P\left(\frac{B_i}{A}\right) = \frac{P(B_i) \cdot P(A/B_i)}{\sum_{i=1}^{n} P(B_i) \cdot P(A/B_i)} \tag{1.28}$$

EXAMPLE 1.33

Determine the probability of a 5 turning up at least once in two tosses of a fair die.

Solution: Let A be the event of getting a 5 on the first toss and B be the event of getting a 5 on the second toss. Then $P(A \cup B)$ is the event of getting 5 at least once. Therefore,

$$P(A \cup B) = P(A) + P(B) - P(AB)$$

Now

$$P(AB) = \frac{1}{6} \times \frac{1}{6} = \frac{1}{36}$$

Therefore,

$$P(A \cup B) = \frac{1}{6} + \frac{1}{6} - \frac{1}{36} = \frac{11}{36}$$

EXAMPLE 1.34

A coin is flipped twice. Two events A and B occur, where A is the event of a match between the two flips and B is the event of a head on both flips. Determine their individual probabilities $P(A)$ and $P(B)$ as well as the conditional probability $P(A/B)$. Are they independent?

Solution: The events A and B are defined as follows:

$$A = [\text{HH}, \text{TT}], B = [\text{HH}, \text{HR}], AB = [\text{HH}]$$

Therefore,

$$P(A) = \frac{1}{2} \quad \text{and} \quad P(B) = \frac{1}{2} \times \frac{1}{2} = \frac{1}{4} = P(AB)$$

Also

$$P\left(\frac{A}{B}\right) = \frac{P(AB)}{P(B)} = \frac{1/4}{1/4} = 1$$

$P(A/B) = P(A)$ if A and B are independent. But here $P(A/B) = 1$ and $P(A) = 1/2$. Hence, the two events A and B are not independent.

EXAMPLE 1.35

Three students Swati, Suraj and Srikar studying in Bal Bharati Public School apply for admission to NITK and the probabilities of their selection are 0.5, 0.2 and 0.3. The probability that Swati, if selected, will join NITK is 0.3 and the probability of Suraj and Srikar joining NITK if selected are 0.5 and 0.8. What is the probability that Bal Bharati Public School will be represented at NITK if the policy of NITK is to select one candidate from any one school?

Solution: Let A be the event of representation of Bal Bharati Public School at NITK, and let A_1, A_2, A_3 be the events of selection of Swati, Suraj and Srikar. Then

$$P(A_1)=0.5,\quad P(A_2)=0.2,\quad P(A_3)=0.3$$

Also,

$$P\left(\frac{A}{A_1}\right)=0.3,\ P\left(\frac{A}{A_2}\right)=0.5,\ P\left(\frac{A}{A_3}\right)=0.8$$

Therefore,

$$P(A)=P(AA_1)+P(AA_2)+P(AA_3)=P(A_1)\cdot P\left(\frac{A}{A_1}\right)+P(A_2)\cdot P\left(\frac{A}{A_2}\right)+P(A_3)\cdot P\left(\frac{A}{A_3}\right)$$

$$=(0.5\times 0.3)+(0.2\times 0.5)+(0.3\times 0.8)=0.49\approx\frac{1}{2}$$

1.8 Random Variables

A random variable is a numerically valued function defined over a sample space. In fact, it is easier to work with numbers such as 1, 2, ..., rather than symbols such as heads and tails. Hence, we associate a real number with each possible outcome of an experiment, such as a '0' for tail and a '1' for head in the flips of a coin experiment. The mapping function that assigns a number to each outcome is called a random variable.

Consider a random experiment with sample space S. Let λ be a sample point of sample space S. A random variable $X(\lambda)$ can be defined as a single-valued function that is assigned a real number called the value of $X(\lambda)$ to each denoted X, sample point λ of S as shown in Fig. 1.4.

The sample space S is the domain of random variable X and the collection of all numbers, that is, values of $X(\lambda)$, is the range of random variable X. It may be noted that two or more sample points can give a single value of $X(\lambda)$, but two different numbers $X(\lambda_1)$ and $X(\lambda_2)$ cannot be associated with the same sample point. If we consider the simple experiment of throwing a die, the sample space S is given by $S=[1, 2, 3, 4, 5, 6]$. We now define a random variable X such that X takes the values that are squares of each of the sample points.

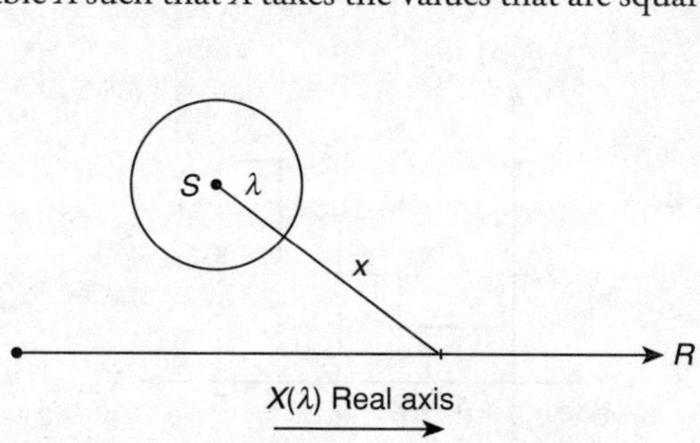

Figure 1.4 | A random variable.

Then the outcomes of the experiment are mapped into ($1^2, 2^2, 3^2, 4^2, 5^2, 6^2$), that is, real numbers 1, 4, 9, 16, 25 and 36 are assigned to each of the sample points 1, 2, 3, 4, 5, 6 of the sample space S:

$$X = [1, 4, 9, 16, 25, 16, 25, 36]$$

Furthermore, if X takes on only a finite number of distinct values (as in the above die experiment), then X is called a *discrete random variable* (*drv*). If X can assume any value within one or more intervals on the real line, then X is called a *continuous random variable* (*crv*). There are many physical systems (experiments) that produce continuous outputs (outcomes). Such systems generate an infinite number of outputs (outcomes) over an observation interval. For example, the noise voltage generated in an electronic amplifier has a continuous amplitude. The exact time of arrival of a telephone call in a telephone exchange is an example of a crv, whereas the number of telephone calls arriving in a finite time is an example of a drv.

Once the random variable is assigned, we can perform many forms of analysis. For example, various outcome probabilities of an experiment can be plotted as a function of the random variable. An extension of this plot is the *distribution function* or *cumulative distribution function* (CDF).

1.8.1 Cumulative Distribution Function

The CDF of X is defined by (Fig. 1.5)

$$F_X(x) = P(X \le x) - \infty < x < \infty \tag{1.29}$$

It may be noted that the set $\{X < x\}$ defines an event or a combination of outcomes. Here, uppercase letters are random variables and lowercase letters are the values they take on. For example, let the die experiment be defined by a random variable as assigning of the number 1 to the outcome of 'one dot' facing up, 2 to the outcome of 'two dots', 3 to 'three dots', etc. In this case, the event $X \le x$ includes the one-dot outcome if x lies between 1 and 2. If x is between 1 and 3, the event includes one-dot and two-dot outcomes. Similarly, if X takes values between 1 and 6, the CDF takes discrete values as shown in Fig. 1.6. This is because $P(X \le x)$ gives six probabilities:

$$P(X \le 1) = \frac{1}{6}, P(X = 2) = \frac{2}{6}, \ldots$$

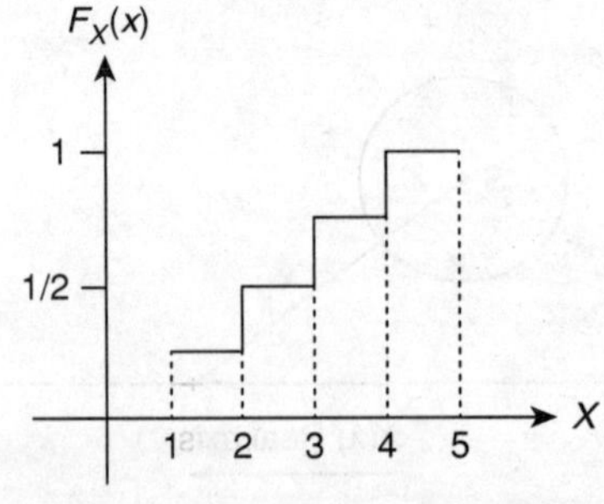

Figure 1.5 | $F_X(x)$ as a staircase function.

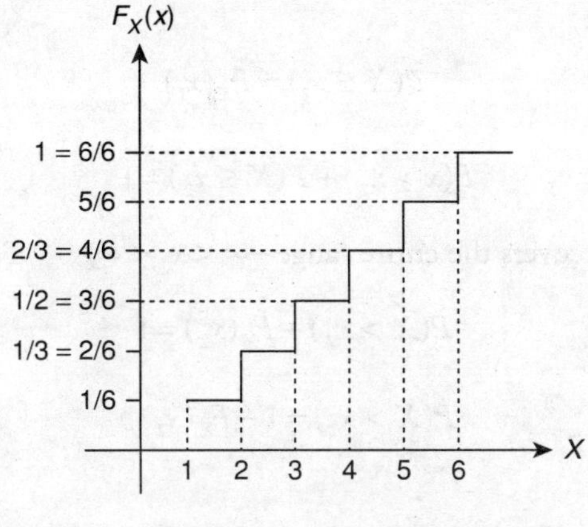

Figure 1.6 | $F_X(x)$ taking discrete values.

It may be noted that a distribution function or CDF can never decrease with an increasing argument because any increase in the argument can only add outcomes to the event and the probabilities of these added outcomes cannot be negative. With these observations, CDF has the following properties:

1. $0 \le F_X(x) \le 1$ (1.30)

that is, the CDF is bounded between 0 and 1 as it is defined as the probability of some event $(X \le x)$.

2. $F_X(-\infty) = 0 \quad \text{and} \quad F_X(\infty) = 1$ (1.31)

that is, $x = -\infty$ means no possible event. Hence, $P(X \le -\infty)$ will always be zero. That is,

$$F_x(-\infty) = 0$$

Also, $x = \infty$ means that $P(X \le \infty)$ includes the probability of all possible events. Therefore, the probability of a certain event is 1. Hence, $F_x(\infty) = 1$.

3. $F_X(x_1) \le F_X(x_2) \quad \text{if } x_1 < x_2$ (1.32)

This property indicates that CDF is a monotonic non-decreasing function of x. Three events $X \le x_1$, $x_1 < X \le x_2$ and $X > x_1$ are shown in Fig. 1.7.
The three events happen to be mutually exclusive, and the sum of their probabilities is given by

$$P(X \le x_1) + P(x_1 < X \le x_2) + P(X > x_2) = P(X \le \infty) = 1$$

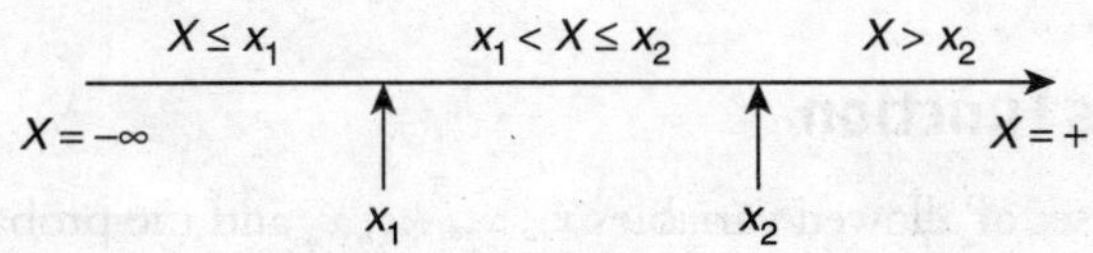

Figure 1.7 | Three events $X \le x_1$, $x_1 < X \le x_2$ and $X > x_1$.

Here,

$$P(X \le x_1) = F_X(x_1)$$

and
$$P(x > x_2) + P(X \le x_2) = 1$$

(since $X > x_2$ and $X \le x_2$ covers the entire range $-\infty < x_2 < \infty$)

$$P(X > x_2) + F_X(x_2) = 1$$

or
$$P(X > x_2) = 1 - F_X(x_2)$$

Therefore,

$$F_X(x_1) + P(x_1 < X \le x_2) + 1 - F_X(x_2) = 1$$

or
$$P(x_1 < X \le x_2) = F_X(x_2) - F_X(x_1) \quad \text{for } x_2 > x_1$$

Since $P(x_1 < X \le x_2)$ is a probability function, we get

$$P(x_1 < X \le x_2) > 0$$

Therefore,

$$F_X(x_2) - F_X(x_l) > 0 \quad \text{for } x_2 > x_1$$

or
$$F_X(x_2) > F_X(x_1) \quad \text{for } x_2 > x_1$$

or
$$F_X(x_1) \le F_X(x_2) \quad \text{for } x_1 \le x_2$$

As $x_2 > x_1$, $F_X(x_2) > F_X(x_1)$. This means that $F_X(x)$ goes on increasing as variable x is increased and hence the name cumulative.

4. $$F_X(a^+) = F_X(a), \quad a^+ = \lim_{0 < \varepsilon \to 0} a + \varepsilon \tag{1.33}$$

As we have seen

$$P(a < X \le b) = F_X(b) - F_X(a)$$

$$P(X > a) = 1 - F_X(a)$$

$$P(X < b) = F_X(b^-), \quad b^- = \lim_{0 < \varepsilon \to 0} b - \varepsilon$$

1.8.2 Probability Mass Function

A drv X is characterized by a set of allowed variables $x_1, x_2, \ldots, x_n$ and the probabilities of the random variable taking on one of these values based on the outcome of the underlying random experiment. The probability that $X = x_i = X(\lambda_i)$ is denoted by $P(X = x_i)$ and is called the *probability mass function* (PMF).

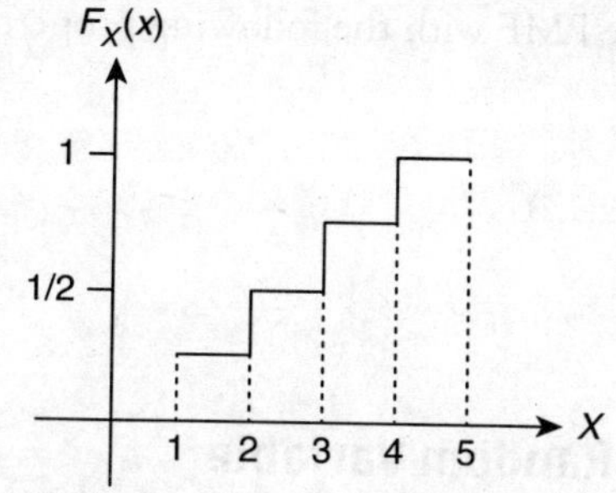

Figure 1.8 | $F_X(x)$ as a staircase function.

When X is a drv with CDF $F_x(x)$ giving rise to a staircase function as shown in Fig. 1.8, we have seen that $F_X(x)$ is constant between jumps. This gives rise to a function called PMF given by

$$P_X(x) = P(X = x)$$

Here, we assume that the jumps in $F_X(x)$ of a drv X occur at the points $x_1, x_2, \ldots, x_n$ as shown in Fig. 1.9 as a mapping of outcomes of discrete events $\{x_1, x_2, \ldots, x_n\}$ along the line.

By definition of CDF, we have

$$F_X(x) = P(X \le x)$$

As there are no events before $X = x_1$, we have $F_X(x) = 0$ for $X < x_1$. Also, as all the events $x_1, x_2, \ldots, x_n$ are mutually exclusive, we have

$$P(x_l \le X \le x_n) = P(X = x_1) + P(X = x_2) + \cdots + P(X = X_n) = \sum_{i=1}^{n} P(X = x_i)$$

Furthermore,

$$F_X(x) = 1 \quad \text{for} \quad X \ge x_n$$

Since $x > x_n$ includes all possible events, we get

$$F_X(x) = \begin{cases} 0 & \text{for } X < x_1 \\ 1 & \text{for } X > x_n \end{cases} = \sum_{i=1}^{n} P(X = x_i) \quad \text{for} \quad x_1 \le X \le x_n \tag{1.34}$$

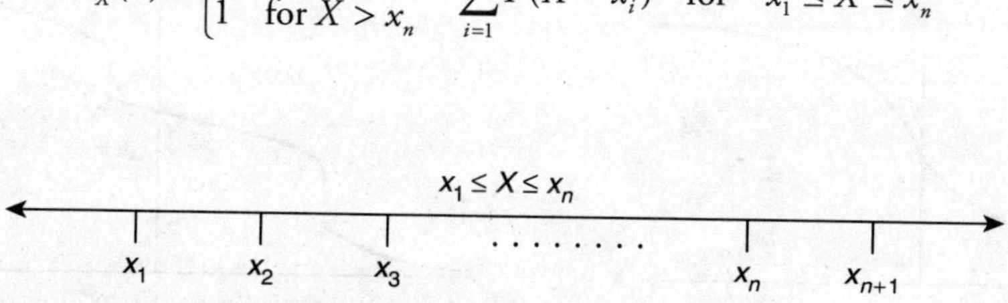

Figure 1.9 | Jumps in $F_X(x)$ of a drv X.

$P(X = x)$ being defined by $P_X(x)$ is the PMF with the following properties:

1. $0 \le P_X(x_i) \le 1, \quad i = 1, 2, \ldots$ (1.35)

2. $P_X(x) = 0 \quad \text{if } x \ne x_i \quad (i = 1, 2, \ldots)$ (1.36)

3. $\sum_i P_X(x_i) = 1$ (1.37)

1.8.3 CDF for a Continuous Random Variable

In some instances, the probability function of a crv may take negative values in which case the CDF starts with a zero value at some negative value of the random variable X and goes on increasing toward positive values of the random variable X as shown in Fig. 1.10. It approaches unity as $X \to \infty$. In fact, a random variable is called continuous if $F_X(x)$ is a continuous function.

1.8.4 CDF for a Mixed Random Variable

A random variable is called mixed if it is continuous in nature but has some discontinuities. The CDF of a mixed random variable is again a non-decreasing function in certain parts of the real line representing the random variable and has jumps at some discrete values of X as shown in Fig. 1.11.

1.8.5 Probability Density Function

If we consider a random variable 'X' with CDF $F_X(x)$, then $FC_X(x)$ is continuous and also has a derivative $dF_X(x)/dx$ that exists everywhere except at possibly a finite number of points and is piecewise continuous. This derivative of the distribution function (CDF) is known as the probability density function (PDF) of the crv X. That is,

$$f_X(x) = \frac{dF_X(x)}{dx} \tag{1.38}$$

1.8.5.1 *Properties of PDF*

1. $f_X(x) \ge 0$ for all values of x. That is, PDF is non-zero for all values of x. As CDF increases monotonically, the derivative of CDF will always be positive.

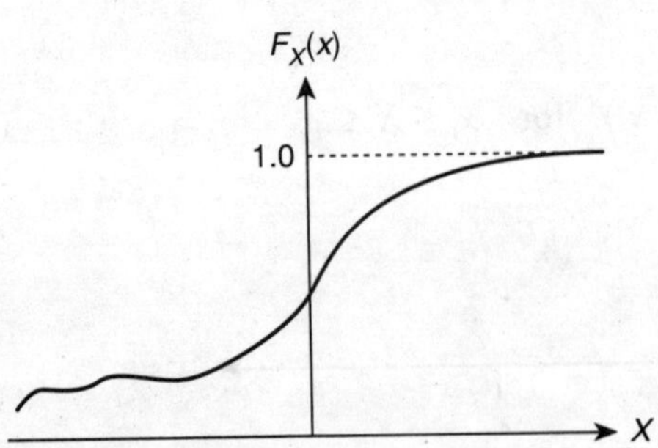

Figure 1.10 | CDF for a crv.

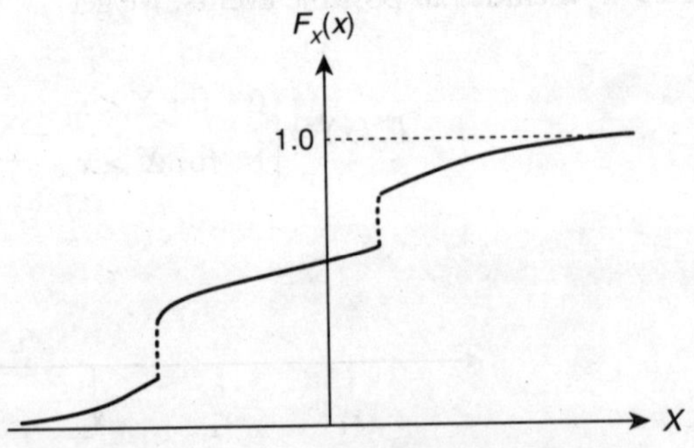

Figure 1.11 | CDF of a mixed random variable.

2. $\int_{-\infty}^{\infty} f_X(x)dx = 1$. That is, the area under the PDF curve is unity. We know that

$$f_X(x) = \frac{dF_X(x)}{dx}$$

Integrating both sides, we get

$$\int_{-\infty}^{\infty} f_X(x)dx = \int_{-\infty}^{\infty} \frac{dF_X(x)}{dx} dx = [F_X(x)]_{-\infty}^{\infty} = [F_X(\infty) - F_X(-\infty)] = 1 - 0 = 1$$

3. $f_X(x) = \int_{-\infty}^{x} F_X(x)dx$. Since $f_X(x)$ is the derivative of $F_X(x)$, $F_X(x)$ is the integral of $f_X(x)$.

4. $P(x_1 < X \leq x_2) = \int_{x_1}^{x_2} f_X(x)dx$ or $P(X \leq a) = F_X(a) = \int_{-\infty}^{a} f_X(x)dx$

That is, the probability of the event $(x_1 < X \leq x_2)$ is simply given by the area under the PDF curve in the range $(x_1 < X \leq x_2)$. Since the events $(X \leq x_1)$ and $\{x_1 < X \leq x_2\}$ are disjoint, the additive principle can be used to prove that

$$P(X \leq x_1) + P(x_1 < X \leq x_2) = P(X \leq x_2)$$

$$P(x_1 < X \leq x_2) = P(X \leq x_2) - P(X \leq x_1) = F_X(x_2) - F_X(x_1)$$

or

$$= \int_{-\infty}^{x_2} F_X(x)dx - \int_{-\infty}^{x_1} F_X(x)dx$$

that is,

$$P(x_1 < X \leq x_2) = \int_{x_1}^{x_2} f_X(x)dx$$

EXAMPLE 1.36

Determine the CDF for an experiment of tossing a coin. Assume head maps to '1' and tail maps to '–1'.

Solution: Tossing a coin has two outcomes, head and tail, and hence the sample space is given by $S = [H, T]$. As head maps to 1 and tail to –1, let rv X be defined as $X = [1, -1]$. Now

$$P(X = 1) = P(X = -1) = \frac{1}{2}$$

and CDF is given by

$$FX(x) = P(X \leq x) = P(X < -1) + P(X = -1) + P(X = 1) + P(X > 1)$$

$$F_X(x_{-1}) = P(X \leq x_{-1}) = P(X < x_{-1}) + P(X = x_{-1})$$

where

$$x_{-1} = -1 = 0 + \frac{1}{2} = \frac{1}{2}$$

Also,

$$F_X(x_{+1}) = P(X \le x_1) = P(X < x_{-1}) + P(X = x_{-1}) + P(X = x_1)$$

where

$$x_1 = +1 = 0 + \frac{1}{2} + \frac{1}{2} = 1$$

Therefore,

$$F_X(x) = F_X(x_{-1}) = ½ \quad \text{for} \quad x = -1$$

$$= F_X(x_{+1}) = 1 \quad \text{for} \quad x = 1$$

The same is shown in Fig. 1.12.

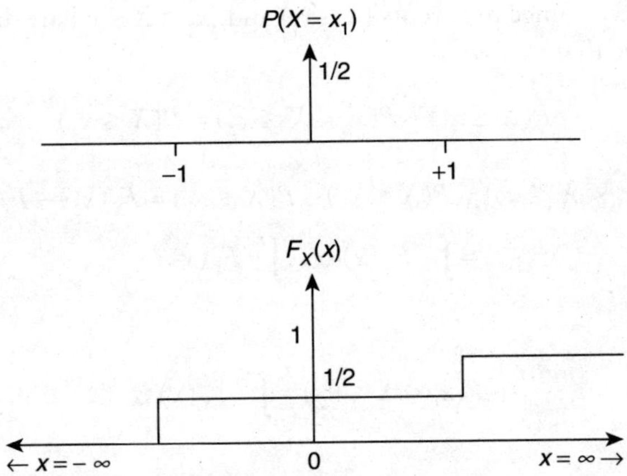

Figure 1.12 | Probability of random variable X and its CDF.

EXAMPLE 1.37

Determine the CDF for the random variable X whose PDF is shown in Fig. 1.13.

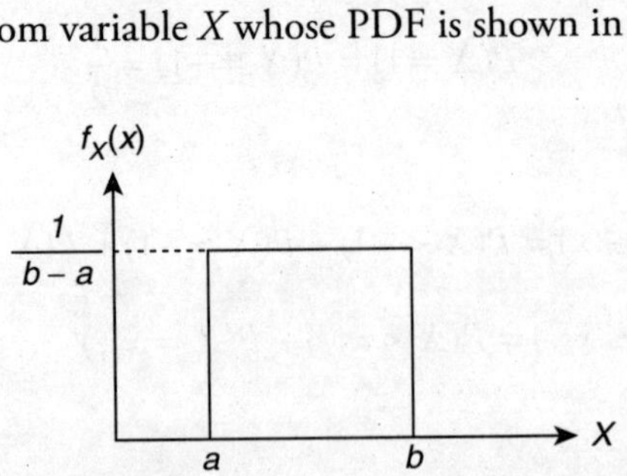

Figure 1.13 | PDF of X.

Solution: The PDF shown in Fig. 1.13 can be mathematically represented as

$$f_X(x) = 0 \qquad \text{for} \quad x < a$$

$$= \frac{1}{b-a} \qquad \text{for} \quad a \le x \le b$$

$$= b \qquad \text{for} \quad a > b$$

Such a PDF is known as a uniform PDF or uniform distribution. CDF can be obtained from the PDF by simple integrating the PDF. That is,

$$f_X(x) = \frac{x-a}{b-a}$$

The same is plotted in Fig. 1.14.

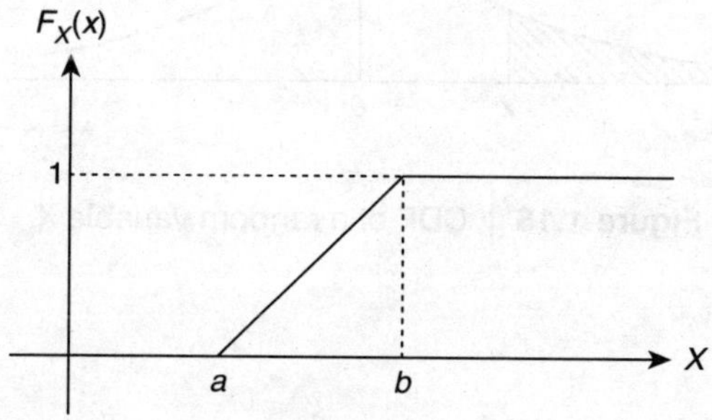

Figure 1.14 | CDF for the random variable X.

EXAMPLE 1.38

The PDF of a random variable X is given by $f_X(x) = a\,e^{-b|x|}$. Determine the relationship between a and b, CDF and probability that the output lies between -1 and 2. Assume $-\infty < x < \infty$ and $a = 3$.

Solution: It is given that $f_X(x) = a\,e^{-b|x|}$.

Relationship between a and b: We know that

$$\int_{-\infty}^{\infty} f_X(x)dx = 1 \Rightarrow \int_{-\infty}^{0} a\,e^{+bx}\,dx + \int_{0}^{\infty} a\,e^{-bx}\,dx = 1$$

$$\Rightarrow \frac{a}{b}[e^{bx}]_{-\infty}^{0} + \frac{a}{b}[e^{-bx}]_{0}^{\infty} = 1 \Rightarrow \frac{a}{b}(1-0)\frac{a}{b}(0-1) = 1$$

$$\Rightarrow \frac{a}{b} + \frac{a}{b} = 1 \Rightarrow \frac{2a}{b} = 1 \Rightarrow b = 2a$$

1. CDF: CDF is defined as (Fig. 1.15)

$$f_X(x) = \int_{-\infty}^{x} f_X(x)dx$$

Here,

$$f_X(x) = a\,e^{-b|x|}$$

or
$$f_X(x) = a\,e^{+bx} \quad \text{for} \quad x < 0 = a\,e^{-bx} \quad \text{for} \quad x > 0$$

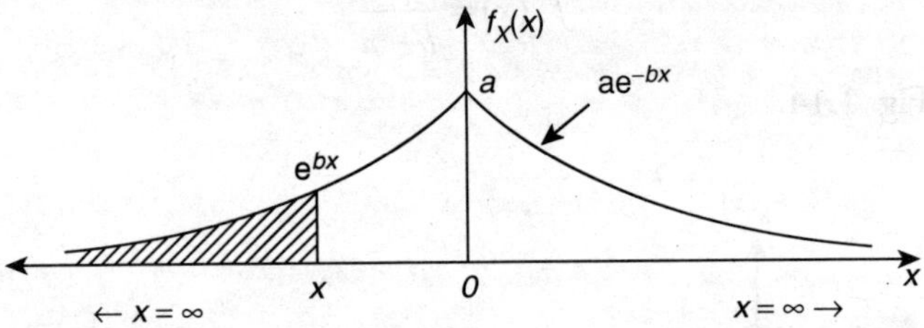

Figure 1.15 | CDF of a random variable *X*.

CDF: For $x < 0$, we have

$$F_X(x) = \int_{-\infty}^{x} a\,e^{+bx}\,dx = \frac{a}{b}[e^{bx}]_{-\infty}^{x} = \frac{a}{b}[e^{+bx} - 0] = \frac{a}{b}e^{bx} \quad \text{for } x < 0$$

or
$$-\infty < x < 0$$

CDF: For $x > 0$ (Fig. 1.16), we have

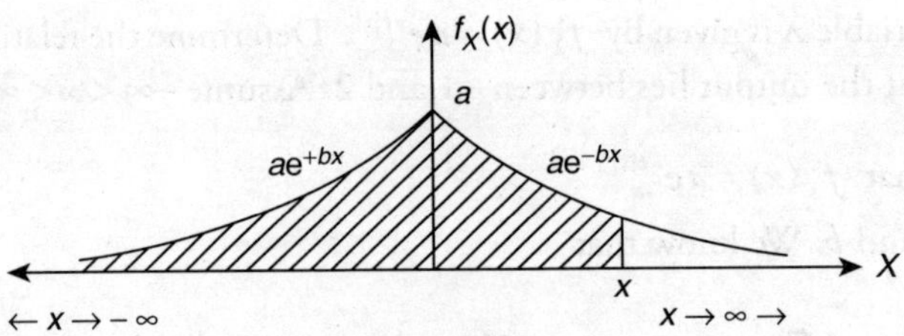

Figure 1.16 | CDF.

$$F_X(x) = \int_{-\infty}^{x} f_X(x)\mathrm{d}x = \int_{-\infty}^{0} a\,e^{+bx}\,dx + \int_{0}^{x} a\,e^{-bx}\,dx = \frac{a}{b}[e^{bx}]_{-\infty}^{0} + \frac{a}{-b}[e^{-bx}]_{0}^{x}$$

$$= \frac{a}{b}(1-0) - \frac{a}{b}(e^{-bx} - 1) = \frac{a}{2a} - \frac{a}{2a}(e^{-bx} - 1) = \frac{1}{2} - \frac{1}{2}(e^{-bx} - 1) - \frac{1}{2}e^{-bx}$$

Therefore,

$$F_X(x) = \begin{cases} \frac{1}{2}e^{bx} & \text{for } x < 0 \\ 1 - \frac{1}{2}e^{-bx} & \text{for } x > 0 \end{cases}$$

2. The probability that the random variable X lies between -1 and 2:
Assuming $a = 3$, we have

$$P(-1 \le X \le +2) = \int_{-1}^{2} f_X(x)dx = \int_{-1}^{0} a\,e^{+bx}\,dx + \int_{0}^{2} a\,e^{-bx}\,dx = \frac{a}{b}[e^{bx}]_{-1}^{0} + \frac{a}{-b}[e^{-bx}]_{0}^{2}$$

$$= \frac{1}{2}[1 - e^{-b}] - \frac{1}{2}[e^{-2b} - 1] \quad (\text{Here } b = 2a = 2 \times 3 = 6)$$

$$= \frac{1}{2}\{[1 - e^{-6}] - [e^{-12} - 1]\} = 1 - \frac{1}{2}e^{-6} - \frac{1}{2}e^{-12} = 1 - \frac{1}{2}e^{-6}(1 + e^{-6})$$

1.8.6 Joint CDF and Joint PDF

It is possible to define two or more random variables on the sample space of a single random experiment. We can define CDF for two random variables $F_{XY}(x, y)$, known as the *joint CDF*, $F_{XY}(x, y)$, given by

$$F_{XY}(x, y) = P(X \le x, Y \le y)$$

The joint CDF has the following important properties:

1. Joint CDF is always non-negative, that is $F_{XY}(x, y) \ge 0$.
2. Joint CDF is always a monotonic non-decreasing function of both x and y.
3. Two random variables X and Y will be called independent if

$$F_{XY}(x, y) = F_X(x) \cdot F_Y(y) \quad \text{for every value of } x \text{ and } y$$

The joint PDF of two (or more) random variables X and Y is given by the partial derivative of the joint CDF as

$$f_{XY}(x, y) = \frac{\partial^2 F_{XY}(x, y)}{\partial x \cdot \partial y}$$

The partial derivative is taken as differentiation with respect to two variables x and y. The joint PDF has the following properties:

1. Joint PDF is always non-negative, that is, $f_{XY}(x, y) \ge 0$.
2. The total volume under the surface of joint PDF is unity (volume because $f_{XY}(x, y)$ is a two-dimensional (2D) function representing a surface in the XY plane), that is,

$$\int_{-\infty}^{\infty}\int_{-\infty}^{\infty} f_{XY}(x, y)dx\,dy = 1$$

3. We have

$$P(x_1 \le X \le x_2, y_1 \le Y \le y_2) = \int_{y_1}^{y_2}\int_{x_1}^{x_2} f_X(x) f_Y(y) dx\, dy$$
$$= \int_{y_1}^{y_2} f_Y(y) dy \int_{x_1}^{x_2} f_X(x) dx$$

where X and Y are statistically independent.

EXAMPLE 1.39

Show that the total volume under the surface of joint PDF is unity.

Solution: We have to prove that

$$\int_{-\infty}^{\infty}\int_{-\infty}^{\infty} f_{XY}(x, y) dx\, dy = 1$$

Now

$$\text{LHS} = \int_{-\infty}^{\infty}\int_{-\infty}^{\infty} f_{XY}(x, y) dx\, dy = [F_{XY}(x, y)]_{x=y=-\infty}^{x=y=\infty}$$

But

$$F_{XY}(x, y) = P(X \le x, Y \le y)$$

Therefore,

$$\text{LHS} = [P(X \le x, Y \le y)]_{x=y=-\infty}^{x=y=\infty} = P(X \le \infty, Y \le \infty) - P(X \le -\infty, Y \le -\infty) = 1 - 0 = 1$$

We have $P(X \le \infty, Y \le \infty) = 1$ as it includes all possible events, whereas $P(X \le -\infty, Y \le -\infty)$ is a null event and hence zero.

EXAMPLE 1.40

Prove that $f_{XY}(x, y) = f_X(x) \cdot f_Y(y)$, where X and Y are statistically independent.

Solution: We know that

$$f_{XY}(x, y) = \frac{\partial^2 F_{XY}(x, y)}{\partial x \cdot \partial y}$$

If X and Y are statistically independent, we get

$$f_{XY}(x, y) = \frac{d}{dx}[F_{XY}(x, y)] \frac{d}{dy}[F_{XY}(x, y)] = f_X(x) \times f_Y(y)$$

Note: When PDFs $f_X(x)$ and $f_Y(y)$ for a single random variable are obtained from the joint PDF $f_{XY}(x, y)$, then $f_X(x)$ and $f_Y(y)$ are known as *marginal PDFs (or marginal densities)*.

That is,

$$f_X(x) = \frac{d}{dx}[F_X(x)] = \frac{d}{dx}[P(X \le x), -\infty \le y \le \infty]$$

$$= \frac{d}{dx}\left[\int_{-\infty}^{\infty}\int_{-\infty}^{\infty} f_{XY}(x, y)dx\,dy\right] = \int_{-\infty}^{\infty} f_{XY}(x, y)dy$$

Similarly,

$$f_Y(y) = \int_{-\infty}^{\infty} f_{XY}(x, y)dx$$

1.8.7 Conditional PDF

It is possible that, out of the two random variables, one may take a fixed value. Let $X = x$ out of two random variables X and Y. Then, conditional PDF of Y given that $X = x$ can be defined as

$$f_Y\left(\frac{y}{x}\right) = \frac{f_{XY}(x, y)}{f_X(x)}$$

where $f_X(x)$ is the marginal PDF of random variable X and $f_{XY}(x, y)$ is the joint PDF of X and Y. Similarly, conditional PDF of X given that $Y = y$ can be defined as

$$f_X\left(\frac{x}{y}\right) = \frac{f_{XY}(x, y)}{f_Y(y)}$$

Conditional PDF has the following important properties provided random variables X and Y are statistically independent:

1. $f_X(x/y) \ge 0$ and $f_Y(y/x) \ge 0$
2. $\int_{-\infty}^{\infty} f_X(x/y)dx = 1$ and $\int_{-\infty}^{\infty} f_Y(y/x)dy = 1$
3. $f_Y(y/x) = f_Y(y)$ and $f_X(x/y) = f_X(x)$

1.9 Statistical Averages

The PDF provides all the information about a random variable. However, there are simpler statistical parameters that provide information about a random variable that basically characterize the PDF. These are called statistical averages, also referred to as ensemble averages (EA) or expected values. Some of these are the mean, variance, standard deviation and moments of a random variable. Let us briefly define these parameters.

1.9.1 First Average/Mean/Expectation of Random Variable 'X'

Let x_i, $i = 1, 2, \ldots, m$, represent the values of the random variable. Let n_i represent the number of times the outcome associated with x_i occurs. The mean or average or expected value or first moment of the random variable X after N performances of the experiment is given by

$$X_{av} = \sum_i \frac{n_i}{N} - x_i$$

As $N \to \infty$, (n_i/N) becomes the probability $P(x_i)$, and hence we get

$$X_{\text{av}} = \overline{X} = m_x = E[X] = \sum_i P(x_i)x_i \quad (X\text{: discrete})$$

where X_{av} represents the dc value of the signal. To find the average value of a crv X, we simply weight x by the density function and integrate the product, that is,

$$E[X] = X_{\text{av}} = m_x = \int_{-\infty}^{\infty} x f_X(x)dx \quad (X\text{: continuous})$$

In general, the average of any function of the random variable, say, $y = g(x)$, the expected value of y is given by

$$y_{\text{av}} = [g(x)]_{\text{av}} = \int_{-\infty}^{\infty} g(x) \cdot f_X(x)dx = \overline{g(x)} = E[g(x)]$$

We also, often, find the expected value of power of the random variable. This is given the name moment. Thus, the expected value of x^n is known as the nth moment of the random variable X. If we first shift the random variable by its mean and then take a moment of the resulting shifted variable, the central moment results. Furthermore, the expectation operation is linear, that is,

$$E[X+Y] = E[X] + E[Y]$$

$$E[cX] = cE[X]$$

where c is a constant.

1.9.2 Second Average or $E(X^2)$ (Mean Square Value)

The second moment is extremely important as it relates to power. It is known as the mean square value (MSV), denoted by σ_X:

$$\sigma_X = \overline{X^2} = E[X^2] = \sum_{i=1}^{\infty} x_1^2 P(x_i), \quad X\text{: discrete}$$

or

$$E[X^2] = \int_{-\infty}^{\infty} x^2 f_X(x)dx, \quad X\text{: continuous}$$

The MSV indicates the total power in the signal.

1.9.3 *n*th Moment

The nth moment of a random variable X is defined by

$$E[X^n] = \begin{cases} \sum x_i^n P_X(x_i), & X\text{: discrete} \\ \int_{-\infty}^{\infty} x^n f_X(x)dx, & X\text{: continuous} \end{cases}$$

1.9.4 Variance

Variance is the second central moment and is given by

$$\sigma_X^2 = E[X - m_x]^2 = \begin{cases} \sum (x_i - m_x)^2 P_X(x_i), & X\text{: discrete} \\ \int_{-\infty}^{\infty} (x - m_x)^2 f_X(x)dx, & X\text{: continuous} \end{cases}$$

The variance gives a measure of how far we can expect the variable to deviate from its mean value dispersion. As the variance gets larger, the density function tends to spread out. The positive square root of the variance, that is, $\sqrt{\sigma^2} = \sigma$, is known as the *standard deviation.* Also,

$$\sigma_X^2 = E[X^2] - m_x^2 = E[X^2] - \{E[X]\}^2$$

since

$$\sigma_X^2 = E[(X - m_x)^2] = E[X^2 - 2m_x X + m_x^2] = E[X]^2 - 2m_x E[X] + m_x^2$$

$$= E[X]^2 - 2m_x \cdot m_x + m_x^2$$

$$\sigma_X^2 = E[X]^2 - m_x^2$$

1.9.5 Standard Deviation

The square root of variance is known as the standard deviation of random variable *X*. It provides a measure of spread observed over the values of *X* relative to mean:

$$\text{Standard deviation} = \sqrt{\text{Variance}}$$

that is,

$$\text{Standard deviation} = \sqrt{\sigma_X^2} = \sigma_X$$

or

$$\sigma_X = \sqrt{E[X - m_x]^2}$$

Also,

$$\sigma_X = \sqrt{\sigma_X^2} = \sqrt{E[X - m_x]^2} = \left[\int_{-\infty}^{\infty} (X - m_x)^2 f_X(x)dx\right]^{1/2}$$

The product $(X - m_x)^2 \cdot f_X(x)dx$ indicates the effective widths of the PDF $f_X(x)$ of *X* shifted by mean value m_x. If there is a positive real number ε, such that $|X - m_x| \geq \varepsilon$, then Chebyshev inequality states that for any positive number ε, we have

$$P[|\, x - m_x \,|] \geq p\,|\varepsilon| \leq \frac{\sigma x^2}{\varepsilon^2}$$

or

$$p(\varepsilon) \leq \frac{\sigma x^2}{\varepsilon^2}$$

1.9.6 Joint Moment of a Random Variable (*X*, *Y*)

The (*k*, *n*)th moment of a 2D random variable (*X*, *Y*) is defined as

$$M_{kn} = [X^k Y^n] = \begin{cases} \sum_{y_j z} \sum_{x_i} x_i^k \cdot y_j^n P_{XY}(x_i, y_j), & X\text{: discrete} \\ \int_{-\infty}^{\infty} \int_{-\infty}^{\infty} x^k y^n f_{XY}(x, y) dx dy, & X\text{: continuous} \end{cases}$$

The (1, 1)th joint moment of a random variable (*X*, *Y*) is known as the correlation of *X* and *Y* and is given by

$$M_{11} = E[XY]$$

If the correlation between *X* and *Y* is zero, that is, $E[XY] = 0$, then *X* and *Y* are called orthogonal.

1.9.7 Covariance and Correlation Coefficient

The covariance of *X* and *Y* is defined as

$$\text{Cov}(X, Y) = \sigma_{XY} = E[(X - m_x) \cdot (Y - m_j)] = E[XY] - E[X] \cdot E[Y]$$

If $\text{Cov}(X, Y) = 0$, then *X* and *Y* are uncorrelated. That is, if $E[XY] = E[X] \cdot E[Y]$, then *X* and *Y* are uncorrelated. However, it does not imply that they are independent. But if *X* and *Y* are independent, then they are definitely uncorrelated. The correlation coefficient is defined as

$$\rho(X, Y) = \rho_{XY} = \frac{\sigma_{XY}}{\sigma_X \sigma_Y}; -1 \le \rho_{XY} \le 1$$

1.10 Frequently Encountered Density Functions

In Example 1.37, we have seen a uniformly distributed PDF. Although uniform PDF is encountered in some communication experiments, a majority of the random variables follow densities other than uniform. The most frequently encountered PDFs other than uniform are exponential, Gaussian, binomial, Rayleigh and Poisson.

Generally, binomial and Poisson are used with drv, whereas uniform, Gaussian and Rayleigh PDFs are used with crv. We briefly describe these PDFs in this section.

1.10.1 Uniform Distribution

This distribution has been discussed in Example 1.37, but the same is reiterated here for completeness. The uniform PDF is described by the equation shown in Fig. 1.17:

$$f_X(x) = \begin{cases} 0 & \text{for } x \le a \\ \dfrac{1}{b-a} & \text{for } a < x \le b \\ 0 & \text{for } x > b \end{cases}$$

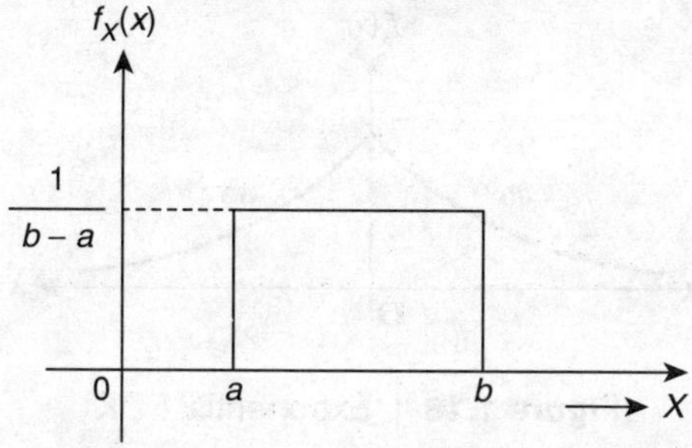

Figure 1.17 | PDF of *X*.

The uniform PDF is generally employed for crv. We now determine the mean and variance of uniform PDF. Mean for a crv is defined by

$$m_X = \int_{-\infty}^{\infty} x \cdot f_X(x)dx = \frac{1}{b \quad a}\left[\frac{x^2}{2}\right]_a^b = \left(\frac{1}{b-a}\right)\frac{1}{2}\cdot(b^2 - a^2)$$

$$= \left(\frac{1}{b-a}\right)\frac{1}{2}\cdot(b+a)(b-a) = \frac{a+b}{2}$$

Variance is given by

$$\sigma_X^2 = \int_{-\infty}^{\infty}(x-m_x)^2 \cdot f_X(x)dx = \int_a^b (x-m_x)^2 \cdot \left(\frac{1}{b-a}\right)dx$$

Let $x - m_x = y$, then $dx = dy$. When $x = a$, we get

$$y = x - m_x = a - m_x$$

When $x = b$, we get

$$y = b - m_x$$

So

$$\sigma_X^2 = \int_{a-mx}^{b-mx} y^2 . \frac{1}{b-a}dy = \frac{1}{b-a}\left[\frac{y^3}{3}\right]_{a-mx}^{b-mx}$$

$$= \frac{1}{3(b-a)}[y^3]_{a-[(a+b)/2]}^{b-[(a+b)/2]} = \frac{1}{3(b-a)}[y^3]_{(a-b)/2}^{-[(b-a)/2]}$$

$$= \frac{1}{3(b-a)}\left[\left(\frac{b-a}{2}\right)^3 - \left(\frac{a-b}{2}\right)^3\right] = \frac{(a-b)^2}{12}$$

1.10.2 Exponential Distribution

The exponential PDF is defined by the following relation:

$$f_X(x) = e^{-b|x|} \quad \text{for all values of } x$$

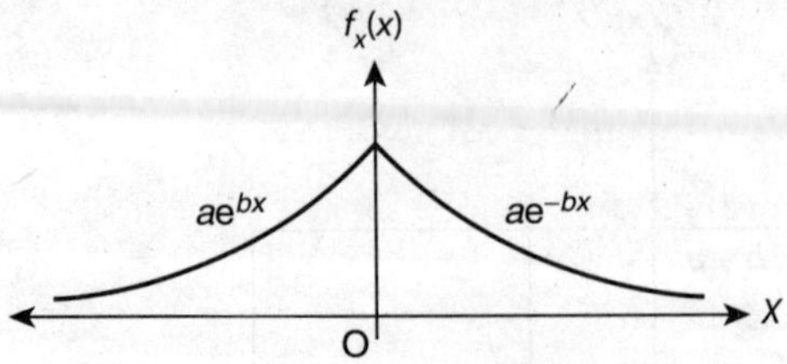

Figure 1.18 | Exponential PDF.

This is shown in Fig. 1.18.

1.10.3 Rayleigh Distribution

Rayleigh distribution is used for crv that can be obtained from two Gaussian random variables X and Y expressed in polar form with $R = \sqrt{X^2 + Y^2}$ and $\phi = \tan^{-1} Y / X$. X and Y have zero mean values and variance of μ^2. Such a distribution is given by

$$f_X(x) = \begin{cases} \dfrac{x}{\mu^2} \exp\left(-\dfrac{x^2}{2\mu^2}\right), & x > 0 \\ 0 & , \quad x < 0 \end{cases}$$

It is as shown in Fig. 1.19.

The mean of Rayleigh PDF is given by

$$m = \bar{x} = E(x) = \int_{-\infty}^{\infty} x f x(x) dx = \sqrt{\frac{\pi}{2}} \mu$$

The variance MSV and deviation of Rayleigh PDF can be shown to be

$$\bar{x}^2 = E(x^2) = \int_{-\infty}^{\infty} x^2 f x(x) dx = 2\mu^2$$

$$\sigma^2 = E(x^2) - [E(x)]^2 = \mu^2 \left(2 - \frac{\pi}{2}\right)$$

$$\text{rms value} = \sqrt{\sigma^2} = \mu \sqrt{\frac{4 - \pi}{2}}$$

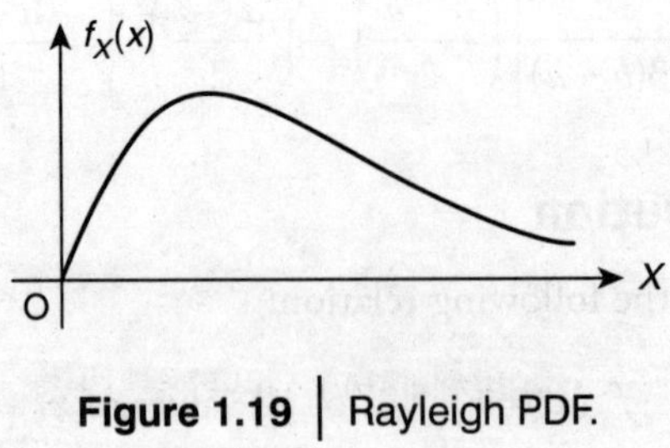

Figure 1.19 | Rayleigh PDF.

1.10.4 Gaussian PDF (Normal Distribution)

The Gaussian PDF is given by

$$f_X(x)=\frac{1}{\sqrt{2\pi\sigma^2}}e^{-(x-m)^2/2\sigma^2} \quad \text{for all values of } x$$

where m is the mean and σ^2 is the variance. If $m = 0$, we get

$$f_X(x)=\frac{1}{\sqrt{2\pi\sigma^2}}e^{-(x^2/2\sigma^2)}$$

which is Gaussian normal, and the PDF with mean m is shown in Fig. 1.20.

1.10.5 Binomial Distribution

The binomial distribution is given by

$$f_X(\text{x})=\sum\nolimits_{x=0}^{n} p(x=k)\delta(x-k)\frac{n!}{(n-k)!k!}$$

that is

$$f_X(x)=\sum\nolimits_{k=0}^{n} {}^nC_k p^k (1-p)^{n-k}\,\delta(x-k)$$

where ${}^nC_k$ is the binomial coefficient $\delta(x - k)$ and represents that PDF is not continuous but weighted by probability at every sample point:

$$F_X(x) = \text{CDF} = P(X \leq x) = \sum\nolimits_{k=0}^{x} {}^nC_{kp}^k (1-p)^{n-k}$$

$$\text{Mean} = m = \text{n}p$$

Variance is given as

$$\sigma_x^2 = np(1-p)$$

where p is the probability of success. Standard deviation is given as

$$\sigma_x = \sqrt{np(1-p)}$$

where $1 - p$ is the probability of failure.

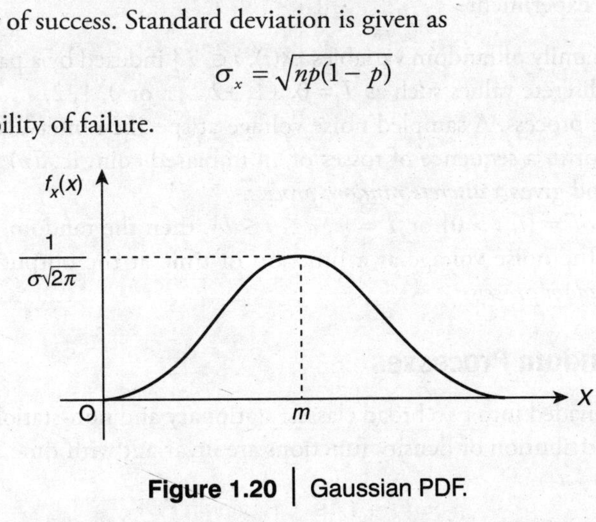

Figure 1.20 | Gaussian PDF.

1.10.6 Poisson Distribution

It is the limiting case of binomial distribution with $n \to \infty$, $p \to 0$ and np is finite. A random variable X is called a Poisson random variable with parameter α (<0) if

$$P(X = k) = e^{-\alpha} \frac{\alpha^k}{k!} \quad k = 0, 1, 2, \ldots$$

and

$$f_X(x) = e^{-\alpha} \sum_{k=0}^{n} \frac{\alpha k}{k!}, \quad n \le x < n+1$$

The mean $m_x = \alpha$ and variance $\sigma_x^2 = \alpha$. The binomial distribution is very useful in digital communications to 'determine the number of errors (x) in a message of n digits'. The Poisson distribution is useful in problems of data transmission of a large volume of data and when the error rates are low. It may be used to monitor the number of calls arriving at a telephone switching center during various intervals of time.

The Gaussian normal distribution is more useful as most naturally occurring random phenomena are approximately normal. The central limit theorem also states that the sum of a large number of independent random variables under certain conditions can be approximated by a Gaussian distribution.

1.11 Random Processes

Random processes are used to model message waveforms as well as noise waveforms that are encountered in communication systems. In the following sections, we define several classes of random processes and develop the important concepts of correlation and power spectral density (PSD).

Random variables have numerical values in the sense that they are numerically valued functions defined for each outcome (or outcomes) of an experiment. If each outcome (or outcomes) of an experiment is assigned a numerically valued function $X(t)$, where t is a parameter, a parametric family of functions called *random process* or *stochastic process* is obtained. The parameter 't' is normally time, although it can be anything else. Thus, a random process is a function of two parameters:

1. Time
2. The outcome of an experiment

A random process $X(t)$ is a family of random variables $\{X(t), t \in T\}$ indexed by a parameter t belonging to an index set T. If T contains discrete values such as $T = 0, \pm 1, \pm 2, \ldots$, or $0, 1, 2, \ldots$, then the random process is said to be a discrete time process. A sampled noise voltage at specified intervals of time is an example of a discrete random process or in a sequence of tosses of an unbiased coin, if $X(n)$ represents the number of heads in the first n tosses and gives a *discrete random process.*

If $T = [t, \infty \le t \le \infty]$ or $T = [t, t > 0]$ or $T = [t, a \le t \le b]$, then the random process is referred to as a continuous time process. The noise voltage as a function of time at the output of a radio receiver is an example of a *continuous random process.*

1.11.1 Classes of Random Processes

Random processes can be divided into two broad classes: stationary and non-stationary. A stationary process is one in which the joint distribution or density functions are invariant with time, else it is a non-stationary random process.

Furthermore, a stationary process can be strictly stationary or wide sense stationary. A random process is strictly stationary if $X(t)$ and $X(t-\alpha)$ have the same statistical properties [such as mean, PDFs, autocorrelation function (ACF), variance, standard deviation] for all α such that t and $t+\alpha \in T$. That is, for a random process to be stationary in the strict sense, the PDFs and CDFs of all orders must be invariant under any finite time translation. For example, a second-order stationary process has a second-order density function given by

$$f_X(t_1)X(t_2)(x, y, t_1, t_2) = f_X(t_1+\alpha)\, X(t_2+\alpha), (x, y, t_1+\alpha, t_2+\alpha)$$

However, it is difficult to establish that a random process is stationary in the strict sense and hence a wide sense stationary process (WSSP) is defined.

A random process $X(t)$ is said to be stationary in the wide sense if its mean and correlation are stationary. The WSSP involves only the first and second moments and not the PDF.

A simple way to understand the above parameter is to consider a random process consisting of many signals of the same type. (This set of signals is called ensemble.) Let X_1, X_2, X_3, …, be different random variables, as a function of time representing the noise voltage of, say, various resistors (simultaneously being observed) as shown in Fig. 1.21.

Let the values of these random variables be x_1, x_2, x_3, etc., at a given timing instant $t = t_1$. If there are N such values of the N random variables (called N numbers of the ensemble), the average value at $t = t_1$ is

$$\overline{X} = \frac{x_1 + x_2 + \cdots + x_N}{N}$$

This is the EA across the various random variables (across averaging), that is, at $t = t_1$. If the same EA is taken along the time axis at various instants of time, then it is time averaging (along averaging). Also, if we measure $\overline{x^2(t)}$ at $t = t_1$, the amplitude of noise voltages $x(t_1)$, and add up all the voltages and divide by the number of resistor noise voltage (noise sources), we get EA of $\overline{x^2(t)}$.

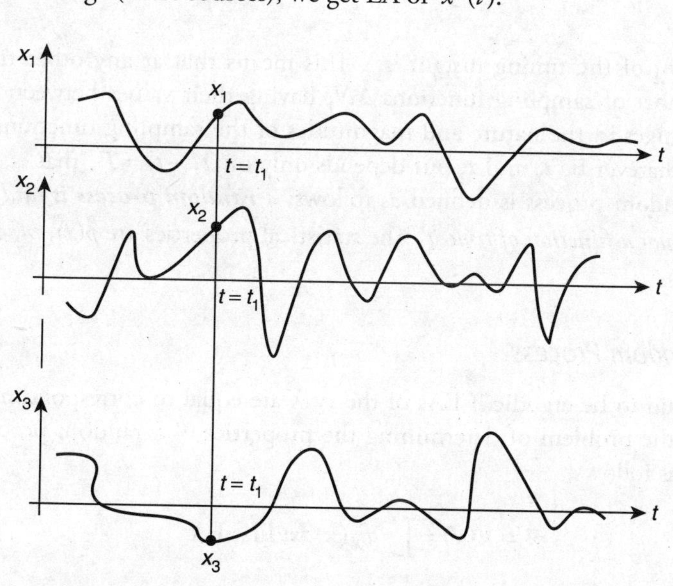

Figure 1.21 | Ensemble average and timing average.

Furthermore, $X(t_1)$ is a random variable and so has an associated PDF. The EAs will be the same as statistical averages. Hence, we can write the ensemble or statistical average of $X_2(t_1)$ as $E[X_2(t_1)] = \overline{X^2(t_1)}$.

The first PDF can be obtained by considering a random process X at an instant of time $t = t_1$ by taking the values $(X_1, X_2, X_3, \ldots, X_n)$ lying between X and $X + \Delta x$. Therefore,

$$\text{First PDF} = P_1(X_1, t_1) = \lim_{\substack{N\to\infty \\ \Delta x\to 0}} \frac{\Delta N / N}{\Delta x}$$

Similarly,

$$\text{Second PDF} = P_2(X_1, t_1, X_2, t_2) = \lim_{\substack{N\to\infty \\ \Delta x_1, \Delta x_2 \to 0}} \frac{\Delta N_2 / N}{\Delta x_1 \cdot \Delta x_2}$$

The value of P_2 depends on t_1 and t_2 and the distance between the two times, that is, $(t_2 - t_1)$. Also, ΔN_2 is the number of member functions having values between X_1 and $X_1 + \Delta X_1$ at t_1 and X_2 and $X_2 + \Delta x_2$ at t_2 and of gN sample functions. Besides

$$P_1(X_1, t_1) = \int_{x_1=-\infty}^{x_2=+\infty} P_2(X_1, t_1; X_2, t_2) dx_2$$

or

$$P_1(x_1, t_1) = \int_{-\infty}^{\infty} P_2 \, dx_2$$

For a stationary random process (statistics not changing over a given time frame), all PDFs are independent of the origin of time, that is,

$$P_1(x_1, t_1) = \lim_{\substack{N\to\infty \\ \Delta x\to 0}} \frac{\Delta N_1 / N}{\Delta x}$$

and will be independent of the timing instant 't_1'. This means that at any other timing instant, say 't_2', we have the same number of sampling functions ΔN_1 having their values between X_1 and $X_1 + \Delta X_1$, that is, there will be no changes in the nature and magnitudes of the sampling functions with time. Similarly, P_2 remains the same whatever be t_1 and t_2 but depends only on $t_2 - t_1 = T$, that is, $P_2(x_1, t_1, X_2, t_1 + T)$. Hence, a stationary random process is defined as follows: *a* ***random process*** *is said to be* ***stationary*** *if its statistical properties are not a function of time 't'.* The statistical properties are $p(x)$, m, $\overline{x}^2$ and σ^2. Therefore, $p(x), m, \overline{x}^2, \sigma^2 \neq f(t)$.

1.11.1.1 Ergodic Random Process

A random process is said to be ergodic if EAs of the rv X are equal to corresponding time averages (TAs). Ergodicity deals with the problem of determining the properties of a random process, such as mean and ACF. EAs are defined as follows:

$$\overline{x} = E(x) = \int_{-\infty}^{\infty} f_X(x) dx\text{: first EA}$$

$$\overline{x}^2 = E(x^2) = \int_{-\infty}^{\infty} x^2 f_X(x) dx\text{: second EA}$$

$$\overline{x}^n = E(x^n) = \int_{-\infty}^{\infty} x^n f_X(x)dx: n\text{th EA}$$

TAs are defined as follows:

$$\langle x(t) \rangle = \lim_{T\to\infty} \frac{1}{T} \int_{-T/2}^{T/2} x(t)dt$$

$$\langle x^2(t) \rangle = \lim_{T\to\infty} \frac{1}{T} \int_{-T/2}^{T/2} x^2 x(t)dt$$

$$\langle x^n(t) \rangle = \lim_{T\to\infty} \frac{1}{T} \int_{-T/2}^{T/2} x^n x(t)dt$$

Therefore, for ergodic random processes

$$\langle x(t) \rangle = E(x); \langle x^2(t) \rangle = E[x^2]; \cdots; \langle x^n(t) \rangle = E[x^2]$$

A process may be mean ergodic or autocorrelation ergodic or both. A process is ergodic normally means that it is both mean ergodic and correlation ergodic. It is quite difficult to prove that a process is ergodic or not. Only the EA and TA equivalence does suggest ergodicity in which case the random process is supposed to consist of a set of signal sources, that is, identical environment and the process is stationary. In practice, it is hard to decide on the basis of data if a random process is ergodic. In order to be ergodic, the random process must be stationary and randomness must be evident in time variation as well as selection of sample function. Ergodicity deals with the problem of determining the properties of a random process, such as mean and ACF.

Summarizing, a random process $X(t)$ is called strict sense stationary [strict sense stationary process (SSSP)] if its statistics are invariant to shift of origin or, in other words, invariant to a shift of origin, that is, if

$$f_X(x_1, \ldots, x_n; t_1, \ldots, t_n) = f_X(x_1, \ldots, x_n; t_1 + \Delta t, \ldots, t_n + \Delta t) \quad \text{for any } \Delta t$$

that is, the first-order density of a stationary random process $x(t)$ will be independent of t, meaning

$$f_X(x_1; t) = f_X(x_1)$$

Similarly,

$$f_X(x_1, x_2; t_1, t_2) = f_X(x_1, x_2; t_1 + \Delta t_1, t_2 + \Delta t_2) \quad \text{for any '}\Delta t\text{'}$$

that is,

$$f_X(x_1, x_2; t_1, t_2) = f_X(x_1, x_2; z = t_2 - t_1)$$

A strictly stationary random process consists of two random variables $x(t)$ and $x(t+\tau)$ that are independent of t and depend only on the timing difference $\tau = t_2 - t_1$.

A random process $x(t)$ is called wide sense stationary (WSSP) if its mean $E[x(t)] = m_x$ is constant and if its ACF depends only on the time difference τ, $E[x(t) \cdot x(t+\tau)] = R_{xx}(\tau)$. If $\tau = 0$, $R_{xx}(0) = E[x_2(f)]$, and hence the average power of a WSSP is independent of t_1.

Note: SSSP is a WSSP, but a WSSP is not necessarily an SSSP.

EXAMPLE 1.41

Determine $E(x)$, $E[x^2]$, $E[\cos x]$ and $E[(x - m_x)^2]$ for a random variable x that is uniformly distributed.

Solution: We have

$$E[x] = \int_{-\infty}^{\infty} xP_x(x)dx = \frac{1}{2\pi}\int_0^{2\pi} x\,dx = \pi$$

$$E[x^2] = \int_{-\infty}^{\infty} x^2 P_x(x)dx = \frac{1}{2\pi}\int_0^{2\pi} x^2\,dx = \frac{4}{3}\pi$$

$$E[\cos x] = \int_{-\infty}^{\infty} \cos x\, P_x(x)dx = \frac{1}{2\pi}\int_0^{2\pi} \cos x\,dx = 0$$

$$E[(x - m_x)^2] = E[(x-\pi)^2] = \int_{-\infty}^{\infty} (x-\pi)^2 P_x(x)dx = \frac{1}{2\pi}\int_0^{2\pi} (x-\pi)^2 = \frac{\pi^2}{3}$$

EXAMPLE 1.42

Why is the Gaussian distribution density function the most encountered density function central in the real world? Give complete details including limit theorem.

Solution: The reasons why the Gaussian distribution is the most commonly encountered density function are attributed to the central limit theorem. The Gaussian or normal density function is defined as

$$f_X(x) = \frac{1}{\sqrt{2\pi\sigma}} e^{-\{[-(x-m)^2]/2\sigma^2\}}$$

where m and σ are given constants known as mean and standard deviation. The center position or symmetry point of the density (mean, m) and deviation (σ) from the mean position indicates the spread of the density. The distribution is shown in Fig. 1.16.

As σ increases, the bell-shaped curve gets wider and the peak decreases. Alternatively, as σ decreases, the density curve sharpens into a narrow pulse with a higher peak.

To find out the probabilities that Gaussian variables lie within a certain range, it is necessary to integrate the density function. Since the Gaussian density function defined above cannot be integrated in closed form, it is computed and tabulated under the name error function (erf). The error function of x is defined by the integral given by

$$\text{erf}(x) = \frac{2}{\sqrt{\pi}}\int_0^x e^{-u^2}\,du$$

It can be shown that $\text{erf}(\infty) = 1$. Therefore,

$$\frac{2}{\sqrt{\pi}}\int_0^x e^{-u^2}\,du = \text{erf}(\infty) - \text{erf}(x) = 1 - \text{erf}(x)$$

For the sake of convenience, 1 – erf(x) is tabulated as a complementary error function, that is,

$$\text{erfc}(x) = 1 - \text{erf}(x)$$

The area under a Gaussian density curve with any values of m and δ can be expressed in terms of error functions. The probability that a random variable x lies between x_1 and x_2 for Gaussian PDF is given by

$$p(x_1 < x < x_2) = \frac{1}{\sqrt{2\pi}\cdot\delta}\int_{x_1}^{x_2} e^{-(x-m)^2/2\sigma^2}\,dx$$

Let $u = (x-m)/\sqrt{2}\sigma$. Then

$$p(x_1 < x < x_2) = \frac{1}{\pi}\int_{(x_1-m)/\sqrt{2}\delta}^{(x_2-m)/\sqrt{2}\delta} e^{-u}\,du = \frac{1}{2}\text{erf}\left(\frac{x_2-m}{\sqrt{2}\sigma}\right) - \frac{1}{2}\text{erf}\left(\frac{x_1-m}{\sqrt{2}\delta}\right)$$

It may be noted that both x_1 and x_2 are greater than m since erf is not defined for negative arguments. The complementary error function (erfc) is sometimes called the Q function or co-error function. Q function is given by

$$Q(x) = \int_x^{\infty}\frac{1}{\sqrt{2\pi}}e^{u^2/2}\,du$$

$$Q(-\infty) = 1 \quad \text{and} \quad Q(-x) = 1 - Q(x)$$

Q function can be related to erf by

$$Q(x) = \frac{1}{2}\text{erfc}\left(\frac{x}{\sqrt{2}}\right)$$

and

$$p(x_1 < x < x_2) = \frac{1}{\sqrt{2\pi\sigma}}\int_{x_1}^{x_2} e^{-(x-m)^2/2\sigma^2}\,dx$$

$$\frac{1}{\sqrt{2\pi}}\int_{x_1=m/\sigma}^{(x_2-m/)\sigma} e^{-u^2/2}\,du = Q\left(\frac{x_1-m}{\sigma}\right) - Q\left(\frac{x_2-m}{\sigma}\right)$$

Now, we come to the question why Gaussian density occurs so frequently in the real world. It is known that all quantities normally dealt within the real world have bounded ranges. The two conditions that should be satisfied for the sum of many random variables to start appearing Gaussian are:

1. Individual variances and their infinite sum must approach infinity (as the number of variables added together approaches infinity).
2. The component densities must become zero outside some range.

The above points are the essence of central limit theorem. For example, let us consider adding together two uniform random variables where each is distributed between –1 and + 1 as shown in Fig. 1.22.

After the first variables are added, the resulting density will be the convolution of the two original densities as shown in Fig. 1.23. This looks like a triangular density (not Gaussian), but we must remember that only two variables have been summed. If a third variable is added, Fig. 1.23 is convolved once more with the uniform density to get a parabolic curve that resembles a bell-shaped Gaussian density as shown in Fig. 1.24. As more and more variables are added, the series converts to a Gaussian density even if the densities at the start were not uniform.

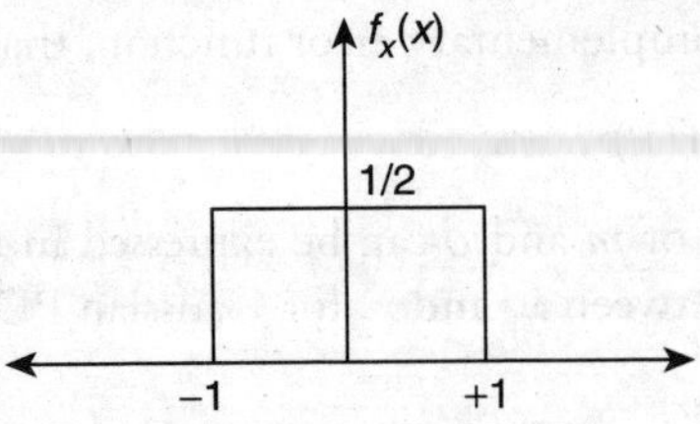

Figure 1.22 | Uniform distribution.

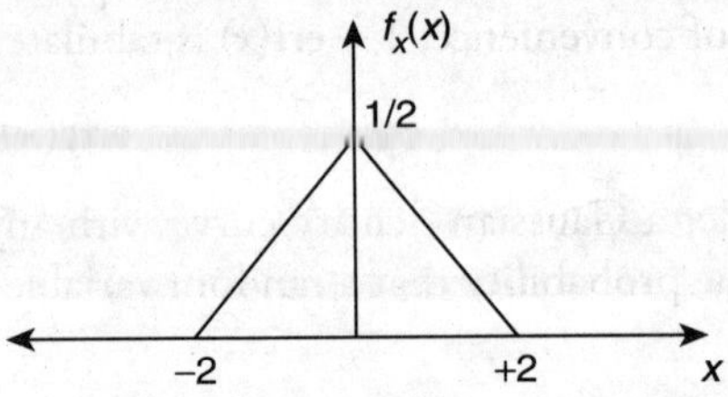

Figure 1.23 | Convolution $f_X(x) * f_X(x)$.

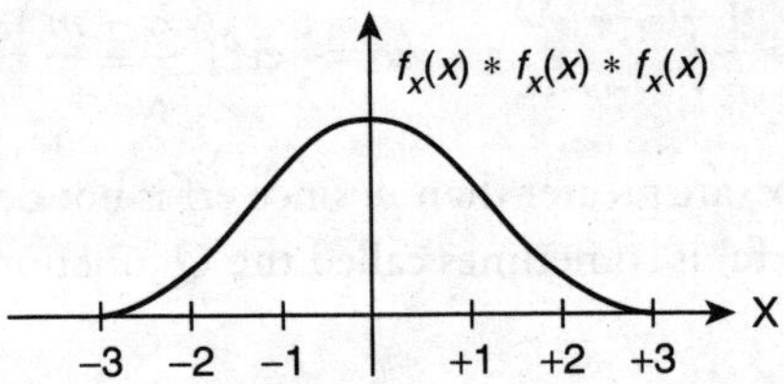

Figure 1.24 | Proof of central limit theorem by convolution of three uniform distributions.

Some advantages of the Gaussian density models are:

1. $P(x \leq \infty, y \leq \infty) = \int_{-\infty}^{x} P(x)dx \int_{-\infty}^{y} P(y)dy$

   If x and y are statistically independent, we get

$$P(x \leq \infty, y \leq \infty) = \int_{-\infty}^{\infty}\int_{-\infty}^{\infty} P(x, y)dx\,dy$$

2. Gaussian PDF provides a good mathematical model for various physically observed random phenomena.
3. Gaussian PDF satisfies superposition theorem, that is, a linear combination of Gaussian random variables leads to a random variable that is also Gaussian.
4. Gaussian PDF is possibly the only PDF by which a complete statistical analysis of both linear and non-linear systems can be carried out.
5. The Fourier transform (FT) of a Gaussian pulse is also Gaussian.

EXAMPLE 1.43

A rv X has a double exponential PDF given by

$$f_X(x) = a\,e^{-b|x|} \quad \text{for all values of } x$$

Determine:

(a) The relation between a and b of $f_X(x)$ (PDF).
(b) The dc voltage contained in a given signal.

(c) Total power contained in a given signal.
(d) rms value contained in a given signal.
(e) ac power contained in a given signal.
(f) CDF for all values of *x*.
(g) Total probability that the random variable *x* lies in between −1 and 2 [i.e., $p(-1 \le x \le +2)$].

Solution: We have

$$P(x) = \begin{cases} a\,e^{bx}, & -\infty < x \le 0 \\ a\,e^{-bx}, & 0 \le x < \infty \end{cases}$$

(a) Relation between *a* and *b* of $p(x)$:

$$\int_{-\infty}^{\infty} p(x)\,dx = 1 \Rightarrow \left[\int_{-\infty}^{0} a\,e^{bx} + \int_{0}^{+\infty} a\,e^{-bx}\right]dx = 1 \Rightarrow \frac{a}{b}[1-0] - \frac{a}{b}[0-1] = 1 \Rightarrow b = 2a$$

(b) Mean, $m = E[x] = \overline{x} = \int_{-\infty}^{\infty} xf(x)dx = \int_{-\infty}^{0} xa\,e^{bx}\,dx + \int_{0}^{\infty} xa\,e^{-bx}\,dx - \int_{-\infty}^{0} xa\,e^{bx}\,dx$

Put $x = -x$. Therefore, $m = 0$.

(c) We have

$$E[x^2] = \overline{x}^2 = \int_{-\infty}^{\infty} x^2 f(x)dx = \int_{-\infty}^{0} x^2 a\,e^{bx}\,dx + \int_{0}^{\infty} x^2 a\,e^{-bx}\,dx$$

After solving the integral, we get

$$E[x^2] = \frac{1}{18}$$

(d) $\sigma^2 = E(x^2) - (E(x))^2 = \dfrac{1}{18}$

(e) rms value $= \sqrt{\sigma^2} = \dfrac{1}{\sqrt{18}} = \dfrac{1}{3\sqrt{2}}$ V

(f) CDF for $x \to -\text{ve}$, $x < 0$ is given as

$$p(X \le x) = \int_{-\infty}^{x} f(x)dx = \int_{-\infty}^{x} a\,e^{bx}\,dx = \frac{a}{b}e^{bx} = \frac{1}{2}e^{bx}$$

since $b = 2a$. CDF for $x \to +\text{ve}$, $x > 0$ is given as

$$p(X \le x) = \text{CDF for } x > 0$$

$$p(X \le x) = \int_{-\infty}^{x} f(x)\,dx = \int_{-\infty}^{a} ae^{bx}\,dx + \int_{0}^{x} ae^{-bx}\,dx$$

$$= \frac{a}{b}[1-0] + \frac{a}{-b}[e^{-bx} - 1] = \frac{a}{b}[1 - e^{-bx} + 1]$$

Since $b = 2a$, we get

$$p(X \leq x) = \frac{1}{2}[1 - e^{-2ax} + 1]$$

that is,

$$p(X \leq x) = \frac{1}{2}[2 - e^{-2ax}] = 1 - \frac{e^{-2ax}}{2}$$

(g) We have

$$(-1 \leq P(x) \leq 2) = \int_{-1}^{2} f_X(x)dx = \int_{-1}^{+2} a\, e^{b|x|}\, dx = \int_{1}^{0} a\, e^{-bx}\, dx + \int_{0}^{+2} a\, e^{bx}\, dx$$

since $m = nP$.

1.12 Joint CDF

CDF of two random variables X and Y is defined as the probability that the random variable X is less than or equal to a specified value X and that the random variable Y is less than or equal to a specified value Y. The joint distribution function is defined as follows:

$$F_{XY}(x, y) = P(X \leq x, Y \leq y); \quad -\infty < x, y < \infty$$

The CDF of X, $F_X(x)$ can be obtained from the joint CDF by the following expression:

$$F_X(x) = P(X \leq x) = P\,|X \leq x,\; y \leq \infty| = F(x, \infty)$$

Similarly,

$$F_Y(y) = P(Y \leq y) = P\,|Y \leq y, x \leq \infty| = F(\infty,\; y)$$

1.13 Joint PDF

The function $f_{XY}(x, y)$ called the joint PDF of X and Y. It is defined as the partial derivative of the joint distribution function $F_{XY}(x, y)$ with respect to dummy variables x and y, that is,

$$f_{XY}(x, y) = \frac{\partial^2 F_{XY}(x, y)}{\partial x \cdot \partial y}$$

Partial derivative is taken since the differentiation is with respect to x and y. The joint PDF volume under the surface of the joint PDF is equal to unity, that is,

$$\int_{-\infty}^{\infty}\int_{-\infty}^{\infty} f_{XY}(x, y)dx\, dy = 1$$

The joint PDF is continuous everywhere since joint CDF is continuous.

1.14 Autocorrelation Function

The ACF gives the measure of similarity, match or coherence between the signal and its replica delayed by a variable period. It is a function of the delay variable. There are three cases that can be considered, and ACF has been defined for each of these cases as $R(\tau)$, where $\tau = t_2 - t_1$ (time difference) is the delay parameter or scanning parameter.

The ACF of any signal represents the regularity of the common properties between the signal $x(t)$ with the same signal when it is displaced by some time interval 'τ'. In general,

$$R(\tau) = \langle x(t_1) \cdot x(t_2) \rangle$$

where

$$t_2 - t_1 = \tau \Rightarrow t_2 = t_1 + \tau$$

or

$$t_1 - t_2 = \tau \Rightarrow t_2 = t_1 - \tau$$

Therefore,

$$R(\tau) = \langle x(t_1) \cdot x(t_1 - \tau) \rangle$$

or

$$\langle x(t) \cdot x(t - \tau) \rangle$$

1. Random signals:

$$R(\tau) = \lim_{T \to \infty} \frac{1}{T} \int_{-T/2}^{T/2} x(t)x(t - \tau)dt$$

2. Periodic signal or power signal:

$$R(\tau) = \frac{1}{T} \int_{-T/2}^{T/2} x(t)x(t - \tau)dt$$

3. Energy signal or pulse type signal:

$$R(\tau) = \int_{-\infty}^{\infty} x(t)x(t - \tau)dt$$

1.14.1 Properties of ACF

1. If the random process is stationary, then $R(\tau)$ depends on the difference between two time instants t_1 and t_2:

$$R(\tau) = R(t_1, t_2) = R(t_1, t + \tau)$$

2. If the random process is ergodic, then

- $R(t_1, t_2) = R(\tau) = \lim_{T \to \infty} \frac{1}{T} \int_{-T/2}^{T/2} x(t)x(t - \tau)dt = \langle x(t) \cdot x(t - \tau) \rangle$

- $R(t)$ is always an even function of time τ. Therefore,

$$R(\tau) = R(-\tau)$$

Proof: Let

$$R(\tau) = \langle x(t) \cdot x(t-\tau) \rangle \tag{1.39}$$

$$R(-\tau) = \langle x(t) \cdot x(t+\tau) \rangle$$

Let $t+\tau = u$ or $t = u-\tau$. Therefore,

$$R(\tau) = \langle x(u-\tau) \cdot x(u) \rangle = \langle x(u) \cdot x(u-\tau) \rangle \tag{1.40}$$

From Eqs. (1.39) and (1.40), we get

$$R(\tau) = R(-\tau)$$

3. $R(0) \geq |R(\tau)|$

Proof: We have

$$\langle [x(t) \pm x(t-\tau)]^2 \rangle \geq 0$$

$$\langle x^2(t) \rangle = R(0)$$

Also,

$$\langle x(t-\tau) \cdot x(t-\tau) \rangle = R(0)$$

$$\langle x^2(t-\tau) \rangle = R(0)$$

From Eq. (1.39), we get

$$R(0) \pm 2R(\tau) + R(0) \geq 0$$

$$2R(0) \pm 2R(\tau) \geq 0$$

$$R(0) \pm R(\tau) \geq 0$$

$$R(0) \geq \pm R(\tau)$$

$$R(0) \geq |R(\tau)|$$

4. The ACF of the input signal of a communication system and the ACF of the noise is equal to the ACF of the output signal if the noise is additive in nature (AWGN; Fig. 1.25):

$$R_y(\tau) = R_x(\tau) + R_n(\tau)$$

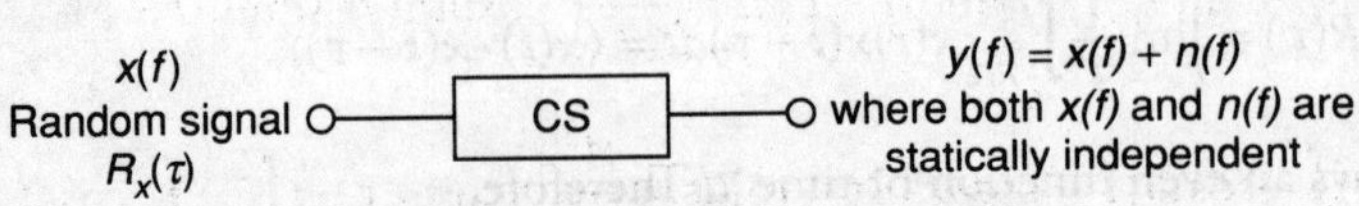

Figure 1.25 | ACF.

5. If $x(t)$ contains periodic component in addition to the noise, then $R(\tau)$ will also contain the periodic components with the same time period. That is, if $x(t)$ is periodic, then $R(\tau)$ is also periodic with the same period.
6. Although a given time function corresponds to a unique value of $R(\tau)$, a given $R(\tau)$ does not correspond to a unique time function:

$$x(t) \rightarrow R_x(\tau)$$

$$R_x(\tau) \rightarrow x(t)$$

Therefore, the phase relationship or the phase of $x(t)$ is not incorporated while finding the original function $x(t)$ from its ACF.
7. The ACF and the spectral density form an FT pair:

$$\text{FT}\,|R(\tau)| = G(\omega)$$

$$\text{FT}^{-1}\,|G(\omega)| = R(\tau)$$

$$R(t) \rightleftarrows G(w)$$

8. Wiener-Khintchine theorem: The ACF for $\tau = 0$ gives power content in the random signal $x(t)$:

$$R(\tau) = \langle x(t)\cdot x(t-\tau)\rangle$$

$$R(0) = \langle x(t)\cdot x(t)\rangle = \langle x^2(t)\rangle = E[X^2]$$

which is the total power content in the signal $x(t)$. Also,

$$P = x^2(t) = \langle x^2(t)\rangle = E[X^2] = R(0)$$

EXAMPLE 1.44

For $x(t) = A\sin w_0 t$, find $R(t)$.

Solution: As $x(t)$ is a periodic function, we get

$$R(\tau) = \frac{1}{T}\int_0^T x(t)\cdot x(t-\tau)dt$$

$$R(\tau) = \frac{1}{T}\int_0^T A\sin\omega_0 t\cdot A\sin\omega_0(t-\tau)dt = \frac{A^2}{2T}\int_0^T 2\sin\omega_0 t\cdot\sin\omega_0(t-\tau)dt$$

$$= \frac{A^2}{2T}\int_0^T [\cos\omega_0\tau - \cos\omega_0(2t-\tau)]dt = \frac{A^2}{2T}\left[(\cos\omega_0\tau)\cdot t\Big|_0^T - \underbrace{\int_0^T \cos\omega_0(2t-\tau)dt}_{=0}\right]$$

$$R(\tau)=\frac{A^2}{2T}[T\cos\omega_0\tau]\Rightarrow R(\tau)=\frac{A^2}{2}\cos\omega_0\tau$$

$$x(t)=A\sin\omega_0 t$$

$R(\tau)$ plot is shown in Fig. 1.26.

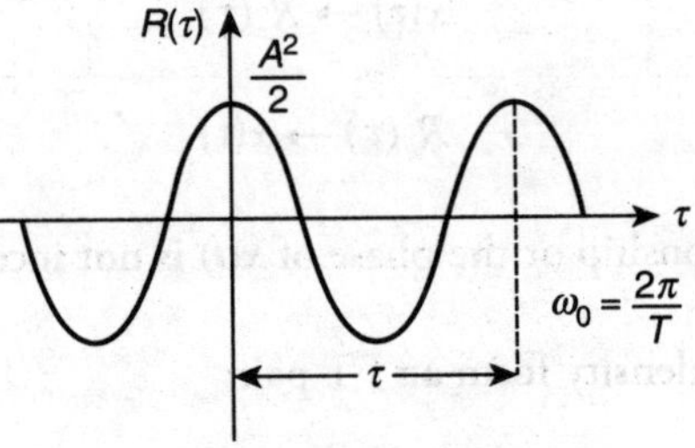

Figure 1.26 | Plot of $R(\tau)$.

Conclusion:

1. $R(\tau)$ is a periodic function having the fundamental frequency same as that of the given function $x(t)$.
2. $R(\tau)$ is an even function of τ.
3. $R(0)$ has a maximum value for all other values of $R(\tau)$.
   Therefore,
   $$R(0)\geq|R(\tau)|$$
4. The power content in the signal is
   $$P=R(0)=\frac{A^2}{2}$$
   $$P=\overline{x^2(t)}=\overline{A\sin(\omega_0 t)^2}=\overline{\frac{A^2}{2}[1-\cos 2\omega_0 t]}=\frac{A^2}{2}-\frac{A^2}{2}\cdot 0=\frac{A^2}{2}$$

EXAMPLE 1.45

$x(t)$ of a periodic pulse train is shown in Fig. 1.27. Find $R(\tau)$.

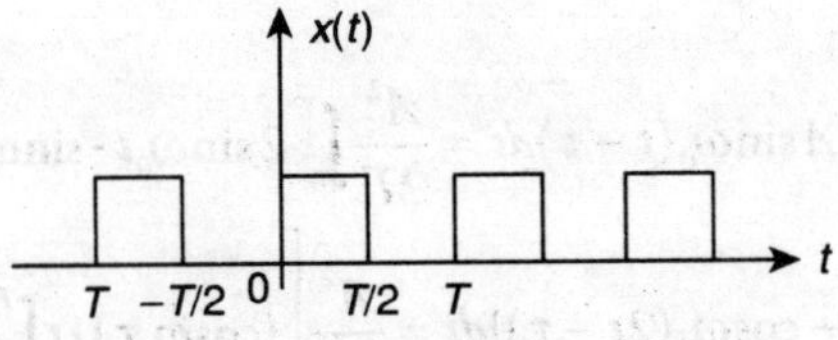

Figure 1.27 | Periodic pulse train.

Solution: We have (Fig. 1.28)

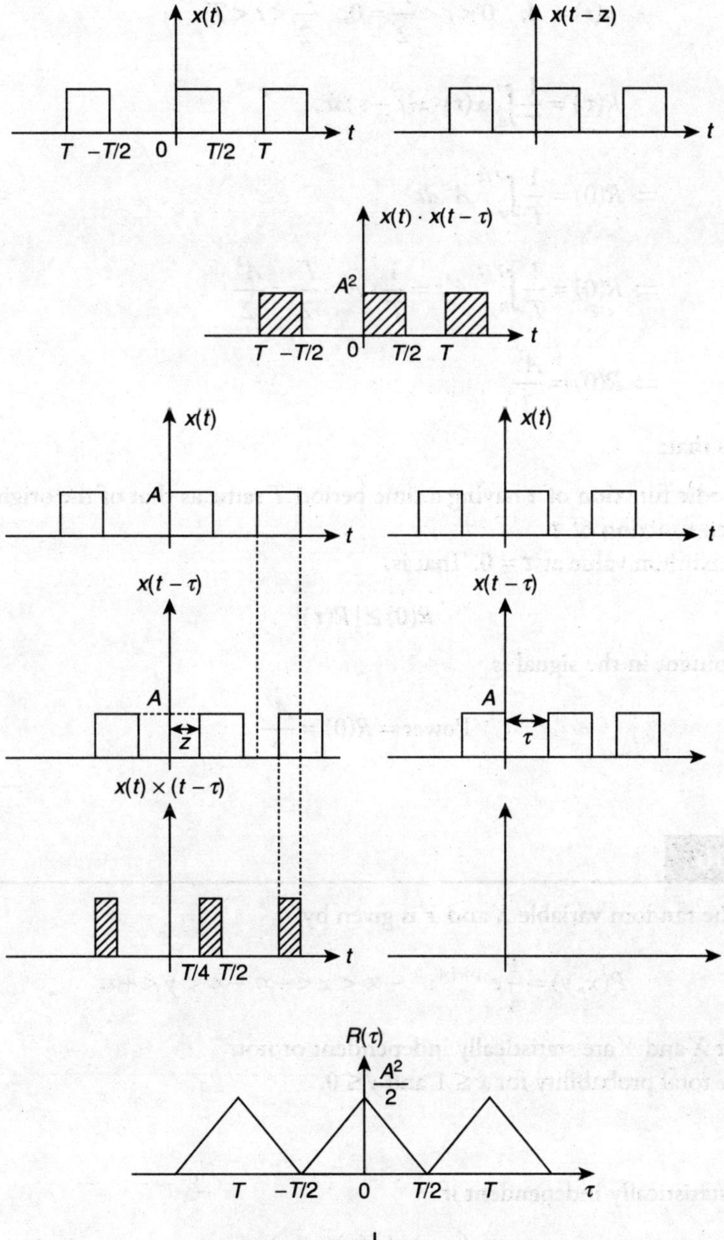

Figure 1.28 | $R(\tau)$ plot.

$$R(\tau) = \frac{1}{T}\int_{-T/2}^{+T/2} x(t)\cdot x(t-\tau)dt = \langle x(t)\cdot x(t-\tau)\rangle$$

$$x(t) = A;\quad 0 < t < \frac{T}{2} = 0;\quad \frac{T}{2} < t < T$$

$$R(\tau) = \frac{1}{T}\int_{0}^{T} x(t)\cdot x(t-\tau)dt$$

$$\Rightarrow R(0) = \frac{1}{T}\int_{0}^{T/2} A^2\, dt$$

$$\Rightarrow R(0) = \frac{1}{T}\int_{0}^{T/2} A^2 t = \frac{1}{T}\cdot A^2\cdot\frac{T}{2} = \frac{A^2}{2}$$

$$\Rightarrow R(0) = \frac{A^2}{2}$$

This example shows that:

1. $R(\tau)$ is a periodic function of τ having a time period T same as that of the original function $x(t)$.
2. $R(\tau)$ is an even function of τ.
3. $R(0)$ has a maximum value at $\tau = 0$. That is,

$$R(0) \geq |R(\tau)|$$

4. The power content in the signal is

$$\text{Power} = R(0) = \frac{A^2}{2}$$

EXAMPLE 1.46

The joint PDF of the random variable X and Y is given by

$$P(x, y) = \frac{1}{4}e^{-|x|-|y|};\quad -\infty < x < +\infty, -\infty < y < +\infty$$

1. Find whether X and Y are statistically independent or not.
2. Calculate the total probability for $x \leq 1$ and $y \leq 0$.

Solution:

1. X and Y are statistically independent if

$$p(x, y) = p(x)\cdot p(y)$$

$$p(x, y) = \underbrace{\frac{1}{2}e^{-|x|}}_{p(x)}\cdot\underbrace{\frac{1}{2}e^{-|y|}}_{p(y)}$$

$$p(x, y) = p(x) \cdot p(y)$$

where

$$p(x) = \frac{1}{2}e^{-|x|}; \quad -\infty < x < +\infty$$

$$p(y) = \frac{1}{2}e^{-|y|}; \quad -\infty < y < +\infty$$

Hence, x and y are statistically independent variables (Fig. 1.29).

2. We have

$$P(x \le 1; y \le 0) = P(-\infty < x \le 1; -\infty < y \le 0)$$

$$= \int_{-\infty}^{y}\int_{-\infty}^{y} p(x, y)dx\,dy = \int_{-\infty}^{y} p(y)dy \cdot \int_{-\infty}^{x} p(x)dx$$

$$= \int_{-\infty}^{0} \frac{1}{2}e^{y}\,dy \cdot \left[\int_{-\infty}^{0} \frac{1}{2}e^{+x}\,dx + \int_{0}^{1} e^{-x}\,dx\right]$$

$$= \frac{1}{2}\int_{-\infty}^{0} e^{y} \cdot \left[\frac{1}{2}\int_{-\infty}^{0} e^{x} + \left(-\frac{1}{2}\right)\int_{0}^{1} e^{-x}\right] = \frac{1}{4}[1-0]\cdot[(1-0)-(e^{-1}-1)]$$

$$= \frac{1}{4}[1-e^{-1}+1] = \frac{1}{4}[2-e^{-1}] = \frac{1}{2} - \frac{1}{4}e^{-1}$$

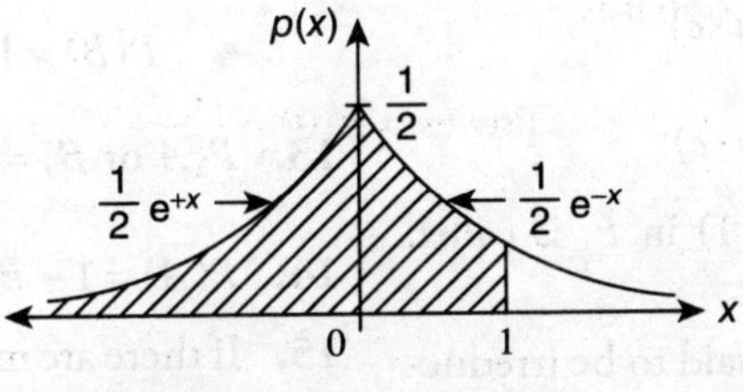

Figure 1.29 | Plot of $p(x)$.

$$P(x \ge 1; y \le 0) = \frac{1}{2} - 0.091969 = 0.408$$

Summary

1. A set G associated with an operator * is said to be a group if:
   - The operator * is associate.
   - For every element $a \in G$, there exists a unique element e in G such that $a * e = a$.
   - For every element $a \in G$, there has to be an inverse element b such that $a * b = e$.
2. Let $\langle G, * \rangle$ be a group and H be a subgroup of G. Then for an element 'a' $\in G - H$, the right and left cosets of H can be constructed as

$H * a$ and $a * H$, respectively. It is obvious that for a commutative group, left and right cosets are the same.

3. A ring R is a set with two operations (addition and multiplication) with the following properties being satisfied:
   - R is an Abelian group under addition.
   - Closure under multiplication:
   $$\forall(a,b) \in R\, a \cdot b = c \in R$$
   - Associative under multiplication:
   $$\forall(a,b,c) \in R (a \cdot b) \cdot c = a \cdot (b \cdot c)$$
   - Multiplication is distributive over addition $a \cdot (b + c) = (a \cdot b) + (a \cdot c)$.
4. A field F is a set of elements associated with two operations + and · satisfying the following properties:
   - F forms a commutative group under addition.
   - $F - \{0\}$ or $F\backslash\{0\}$ forms a commutative group under multiplication.
   - The operations + and · are distributive:
   $$a \cdot (b + c) = (a \cdot b) + (a \cdot c)$$
   $$(a + b) \cdot c = (a \cdot c) + (b \cdot c)$$
5. An element with order $(q - 1)$ in F_q is called the primitive element of F_q.
6. A polynomial $q(x) \in F_q[x]$ is said to be irreducible if its roots are not present in $F_q(x)$.
7. An irreducible polynomial $f(x) \in F_p[x]$ of degree 'm' is said to be primitive if the smallest integer n such that $f(x)|x^n - 1$ is $n = p^m - 1$.
8. A minimal polynomial defined for an element β belongs to F_q^m is the smallest-degree nonzero monic polynomial $p(x) \in F_q[x]$ such that $p(\beta) = 0$.
9. Let R be a ring. A non-empty subset $I \subset R$ is said to be an ideal in R if it satisfies the following conditions:
   - I forms a group under addition operation in R.
   - For every $r \in R$ and $a \in I$, $a \cdot r = b \in I$.
10. The set V can be qualified as a vector space if it satisfies the following conditions:
    - Set V forms a commutative group under vector addition.
    - For any element $f \in F$ and $\underline{v} \in V$, the scalar product $f \times \underline{v} \in V$.

    (a) The operations '+' and '·' have to be distributive.

    That is, $\forall f_1, f_2 \in F$ and $\underline{v}_1, \underline{v}_2 \in V$:
    $$f_1 \cdot (v_1 + v_2) = f_1 \cdot v_1 + f_1 \cdot v_2$$
    $$(f_1 + f_2) \cdot v_1 = f_1 \cdot v_1 + f_2 \cdot v_2$$
    (b) Associativity:
    $$(f_1 \cdot f_2) \cdot v = f_1 \cdot (f_2 \cdot v)$$
    (c) Multiplicative identity 1 in F will also serve as a multiplicative identity for scalar multiplication.
11. $P(A) = \lim_{N\to\infty} \frac{n_A}{N}$.
12. $0 \le P(A) \le 1$:
    - $P(A) = 0$: null probability
    - $P(B) = 1$: certain event probability
13. $P(A \text{ or } B) = \lim_{N\to\infty} \frac{n_A + n_B}{N} = P(A) + P(B)$.
14. $P(\bar{A}) = 1 - P(A)$.
15. If there are mutually exclusive events $A_1, A_2, \ldots, A_m$, then
    $$S = A_1 + A_2 + \cdots + A_m$$
    $$P(A_1) + P(A_2) + \cdots + P(A_m) = P(S) = 1$$
16. If all the events $A_1, A_2, \ldots, A_m$ have the same probability of occurrence or equally likely events, then
    $$P(A_1) = P(A_2) \cdots P(A_m) = \frac{1}{m}$$
17. If events A and B are not mutually exclusive events, then the probability of the union of A and B is given by
    $$P(A + B) = P(A) + P(B) - P(AB)$$

18. If events A and B are mutually exclusive, then $P(AB) = 0$.
19. Let A and B be two events; then the probability of event A given that B has occurred is given by

$$P\left(\frac{A}{B}\right) = \frac{P(AB)}{P(B)}$$

20. Two events A and B are said to be statistically independent if

$$P\left(\frac{A}{B}\right) = P(A)$$

21. If $B_1, B_2, B_3, \ldots, B_n$ are mutually exclusive events and event A occurs only when anyone of $B_1, B_2, B_3, \ldots, B_n$ occurs, then as per Bayes' rule

$$P\left(\frac{B_i}{A}\right) = \frac{P(B_i) \cdot P(A/B_i)}{\sum_{i=1}^{n} P(B_i) \cdot P(A/B_i)}$$

22. The CDF of X is defined by

$$F_X(x) = P(X \le x) \quad -\infty < x < \infty$$

23. $X_{\text{av}} = \sum_i \frac{n_i}{N} - x_i.$

24. $\sigma_X = \overline{X^2} = E[X^2] = \sum_{i=1}^{\infty} x_1^2 P(x_i), \quad X$: discrete.

25. $E[X^2] = \int_{-\infty}^{\infty} x^2 f_X(x)dx, \quad X$: continuous.

26. The nth moment of a random variable X is defined by

$$E[X^n] = \begin{cases} \sum x_i^n P_X(x_i), & X\text{: discrete} \\ \int_{-\infty}^{\infty} x^n f_X(x)dx, & X\text{: continuous} \end{cases}$$

27. $\sigma_X^2 = E[X - m_x]^2$

$$= \begin{cases} \sum (x_i - m_x)^2 P_X(x_i), & X\text{: discrete} \\ \int_{-\infty}^{\infty} (x - m_x)^2 f_X(x)dx, & X\text{: continuous} \end{cases}$$

28. Standard deviation $= \sqrt{\text{variance}}$, that is,

$$\text{Standard deviation} = \sqrt{\sigma_X^2} = \sigma_X$$

$$\text{or } \sigma_X = \sqrt{E[X - m_x]^2}$$

29. The (k, n)th moment of a 2D random variable (X, Y) is defined as

$$M_{kn} = [X^k Y^n]$$

$$= \begin{cases} \sum_{y_j z} \sum_{x_i} x_i^k \cdot y_j^n P_{XY}(x_i, y_j), & X\text{: discrete} \\ \int_{-\infty}^{\infty} \int_{-\infty}^{\infty} x^k y^n f_{XY}(x, y)dx\,dy, & X\text{: continuous} \end{cases}$$

30. Cov (X, Y) $= \sigma_{XY}$

$$= E[(X - m_x) \cdot (Y - m_j)]$$
$$= E[XY] - E[X] \cdot E[Y].$$

REVIEW QUESTIONS

1. Show by counterexample that the integers in the set {0, 1, 2, 3, …, 5} do not form a group under mod 6 multiplication.
2. Find the order of the group $\langle G, \oplus 7 \rangle$.
3. Consider $G = \{0, 1, 2, 3, 4, 5, 6\}$. Test whether G is a group under addition modulo 7 and multiplication modulo 7.
4. Prove that the inverse of an element in group G is unique.
5. Show that all groups with four elements are Abelian.
6. Find the orders of each of the elements in the group of order 8 under mod 8 addition.
7. Consider an integer group $G = \{0, 1, 2, \ldots, 31\}$ under mod 32 addition. Show that $H = \{0, 4, 8, 12, 16, 20, 24, 28\}$ forms a subgroup of G. Decompose into cosets with respect to H.
8. Prove that $\phi(p_1 \cdot p_2) = \phi(p_1) \cdot \phi(p_2) = (p_1 - 1)(p_2 - 1)$.
9. Prove that $(a * b)^{-1} = b^{-1} * a^{-1}$.
10. Determine the primitive elements for F_7 under mod 7.

11. Construct the operation table for GF(5).
12. Construct the operation table for GF(7).
13. Prove that $\phi(p^m) = p^{m-1}(p-1)$ for a prime p.
14. Compute $\phi(210)$ and $\phi(3135)$.
15. Prove that $\phi(p^m \cdot r^n) = p^{m-1}r^{n-1}(p-1)(r-1)$ for distinct primes p and r.
16. Prove that $\sum_{x/n} \phi(x) = n$.
17. Prove that the order of a GF F_q is a power of prime.
18. Examine whether F_5 = {0, 1, 2, 3, 4} mod 5 forms a field.
19. Determine whether $(x^3 + x^2 + 1)$ is an irreducible polynomial over $F_2[x]$.
20. Determine whether $f(x) = x^2 + x + 1$ is primitive over $F_2[x]$.
21. Construct a table for F_2^5 based on the primitive polynomial $p(x) = 1 + x^2 + x^5$. Let α be a primitive element of F_2^5. Find the minimal polynomial of α^3 and α.
22. Construct an extension field of F_2^4 over F_2 with $p(x) = x^4 + x + 1$.
23. List the possible orders taken on by the elements in the field GF(65) and determine the number of elements in the field that display each allowed order.
24. Investigate whether $\mathfrak{Z}$, a set of integers, forms a ring.
25. Prove that the set of units forms a group under multiplication.
26. V_5 is the vector space of binary 5-tuples. The canonical vector space for V_5 is {(10000), (01000), (00100), (00010), (00001)}. Express the vector (11011) as a linear combination of the vectors.
27. S = {(11010, (00111), (10101), (10001), (00010)} also forms a basis for V_5. Express the vector (11011) as a linear combination of the vectors in S.

Further Reading

[1] Richerd E Blahut, *Algebraic Codes for Data Transmission*, Cambridge University Press: Cambridge; 2003.

[2] Willium E Ryan and Shu Lin, *Channel Codes: Classical and Modern*, Cambridge University Press: Cambridge; 2009.

[3] Tood K Moon, *Error Control Coding: Mathematical Methods and Algorithms*, John Wiley & Sons, Inc.: Hoboken, NJ; 2005.

[4] Shu Lin and Daniel J Costello, *Error Control Coding: Fundamentals and Applications*, Prentice Hall Series, Inc.: Englewood Cliffs, NJ; 1983.

[5] Wilbur R Davenport, Jr, and William L Root, *An Introduction to the Theory of Random Signals and Noise*, McGraw Hill: New York; 1958.

[6] Peter Sweeney, *Error Control Coding*, John Wiley & Sons, Inc.: New York; 2002.

[7] Peyton Z Peebles, *Probability, Random Variables and Random Signal Principles*, Second Edition, McGraw Hill: New York; 1987.

[8] Harold Mott, *Appendix B: Probability and Random Processes, in Remote Sensing with Polarimetric Radar*, John Wiley & Sons, Inc.: Hoboken, NJ; 2006.

[9] John A Gubner, *Probability and Random Processes for Electrical and Computer Engineers*, Cambridge University Press: Cambridge; 2006.

[10] Thomas W Judson, *Abstract Algebra: Theory and Applications*, Stephen F. Austin State University: Nacogdoches, TX; 2010.

2 Information Theory

'Measure what is measurable, and make measurable what is not so.'

–Galileo

Learning Objectives

After reading this chapter, you will be able to:

- Define the information content of a message.
- Emphasize the need for measure of information and average information content of a system.
- Develop a mathematical model to measure the information content of a message.
- Detail the properties of entropy.
- Develop a Markov model to measure entropy for a dependent source.

2.1 Introduction

Today we are living in the era of information. Modern communication being one of the key areas of interest, information exchange in an efficient manner is the need of the day. Until 1948, when Claude E Shannon published his premiere work on "Mathematical Theory on Communication" in Bell System Technical journal, information was considered to be an abstract entity that could not be measured. However, he has given a mathematical model for measuring information.

2.2 Measure of Information

An information source generates the information; however, the amount of information conveyed by the source is different for different symbols it emits. A mathematical modeling can be formulated to quantify the amount of information conveyed by a symbol. Consider the following statements:

1. It rained heavily in Cherrapunji yesterday.
2. There was a heavy rainfall in Rajasthan last night.

Although both statements infer the occurrence of heavy rainfall, the amount of information conveyed by them is different. The first statement will not create any surprise as heavy rainfall is a common event in Cherrapunji. However, the second statement will certainly create some degree of surprise as it is less likely to have heavy rainfall in Rajasthan.

From the above example, it can be concluded that the amount of information conveyed by a message is inversely proportional to its probability of occurrence. Therefore, we can write the amount of information conveyed or self-information of a message k, I_k, is inversely proportional to its probability of occurrence p_k, that is,

$$I_k \propto \frac{1}{p_k} \tag{2.1}$$

Also there are some other facts on information:

1. The information conveyed by a message cannot be negative. It has to be at least 0, that is,
$$I_k \geq 0 \tag{2.2}$$
2. If the event is definite, that is, if the probability of the occurrence of the event is 1, then the corresponding information conveyed by the event will be 0. That is
$$\text{If } p_k = 1 \text{ then } I_k = 0 \tag{2.3}$$
3. The information conveyed by composite statement which is independent is simply given by the sum of the individual self-information contents. That is,
$$I(m_1, m_2) = I(m_1) + I(m_2) \tag{2.4}$$

The only mathematical operator that satisfies the relations (2.2)–(2.4) is the logarithm operator. Therefore, the self-information content of a message is given by

$$I_k = \log_r \frac{1}{p_k} \text{ units} \tag{2.5}$$

where p_k is the probability of occurrence of kth message. The unit of the self-information is dependent on the base of the logarithm used.

1. If 'r' = 2, the unit is bits.
2. If 'r' = e, the unit is nats.
3. If 'r' = 10, the unit is Hartley or Decits.

In our entire discussion, unless otherwise specified, the unit of self-information is considered to be bits.

EXAMPLE 2.1

Consider a binary system emitting two symbols {0, 1} with probabilities 0.6 and 0.4, respectively. Find the information conveyed by bit '0' and bit '1'.

Solution: We have the self-information content of a symbol given by

$$I_k = \log_2 \frac{1}{p_k} \text{ bits}$$

Probability of the occurrence of '0' at the source output is $p(0) = 0.6$ and the probability of the occurrence of '1' at the source output is $p(1) = 0.4$. Therefore,

$$I_0 = \log_2 \frac{1}{p_0} = \log_2 \frac{1}{0.6} = 0.7368 \text{ bits}$$

Similarly,

$$I_1 = \log_2 \frac{1}{p_1} = \log_2 \frac{1}{0.4} = 1.3219 \text{ bits}$$

EXAMPLE 2.2

Consider a source emitting two symbols s_0 and s_1 with the corresponding probabilities 3/4 and 1/4, respectively. Find the self-information of the symbols in

(a) Bits.
(b) Decits.
(c) Nats.

Solution:

(a) We have

$$I_k = \log_2 \frac{1}{p_k} \text{bits}$$

$$I_{s0} = \log_2 \frac{1}{p(s_0)} = \log_2 \frac{1}{(3/4)} = 0.415 \text{bits}$$

$$I_{s1} = \log_2 \frac{1}{p(s_1)} = \log_2 \frac{1}{(1/4)} = 2 \text{bits}$$

(b) We have

$$I_k = \log_{10} \frac{1}{p_k} \text{decits}$$

$$I_{s0} = \log_{10} \frac{1}{p(s_0)} = \log_{10} \frac{1}{(3/4)} = 0.124 \text{decits}$$

$$I_{s1} = \log_{10} \frac{1}{p(s_1)} = \log_{10} \frac{1}{(1/4)} = 0.602 \text{decits}$$

(c) We have

$$I_k = \log_e \frac{1}{p_k} \text{ nats}$$

$$I_{s0} = \log_e \frac{1}{p(s_0)} = \log_e \frac{1}{(3/4)} = 0.287 \text{ nats}$$

$$I_{s1} = \log_e \frac{1}{p(s_1)} = \log_e \frac{1}{(1/4)} = 1.386 \text{ nats}$$

EXAMPLE 2.3

A pair of dice is rolled simultaneously. The outcome of the first dice is considered to be '*x*' and that of the second as '*y*'. Three events are defined as

P = {(x, y) such that ($x + y$) is exactly divisible by 3}

Q = {(x, y) such that ($x + y$) is an even number}

R = {(x, y) such that ($x + y$) = 7}

Which event conveys more information? Justify your answer with mathematical calculation.

Solution: To find which event conveys more information, we need to find the probabilities of the events. Less probable the event, more will be the information conveyed. To find the probabilities, find the sets of sample space and events P, Q and R.

S = {(1,1), (1,2), (1,3), (1,4), (1,5), (1,6), (2,1), (2,2), (2,3), (2,4), (2,5), (2,6), (3,1), (3,2), (3,3), (3,4), (3,5), (3,6), (4,1), (4,2), (4,3), (4,4), (4,5), (4,6), (5,1), (5,2), (5,3), (5,4), (5,5), (5,6), (6,1), (6,2), (6,3), (6,4), (6,5), (6,6)}

P = {(1,2), (1,5), (2,1), (2,4), (3,3), (3,6), (4,2), (4,5), (5,1), (5,4), (6,3), (6,6)}

Q = {(1,1), (1,3), (1,5), (2,2), (2,4), (2,6), (3,1), (3,3), (3,5), (4,2), (4,4), (4,6), (5,1), (5,3), (5,5), (6,2), (6,4), (6,6)}

R = {(1,6), (2,5), (3,4), (4,3), (5,2), (6,1)}

Then

$$p(P) = \frac{12}{36} \;;\; p(Q) = \frac{18}{36} \;;\; p(R) = \frac{6}{36}$$

As the probability of occurrence of event R is less, it conveys more information. This statement can be justified by considering the self-information of events P, Q and R.

$$I_k = \log_2 \frac{1}{p_k} \text{ bits}$$

$$I_P = \log_2 \frac{1}{p(P)} = \log_2 \frac{1}{12/36} = 1.584 \text{ bits}$$

Similarly,

$$I_Q = \log_2 \frac{1}{p(Q)} = \log_2 \frac{1}{18/36} = 1 \text{ bits}$$

$$I_R = \log_2 \frac{1}{p(R)} = \log_2 \frac{1}{6/36} = 2.584 \text{ bits}$$

As $I_R > I_P$ and I_Q, event R conveys more information.

2.3 Average Information Content (Entropy) of a Zero Memory Source

A zero memory source or a discrete memoryless source is the one in which the emission of the current symbol is not dependent on the emissions of the previous symbols. Consider a source emitting symbol $S = \{s_1, s_2, s_3, \ldots, s_N\}$ with respective probabilities

$$P = \{p_1, p_2, p_3, \ldots, p_N\}.$$

Now consider a long message of length 'L' emitted by the source. Then it contains

$$p_1 L \text{ number of symbols of } `s_1'$$
$$p_2 L \text{ number of symbols of } `s_2'$$
$$\cdots$$
$$\cdots$$
$$\cdots$$
$$p_N L \text{ number of symbols of } `s_N'$$

The self-information of 's_1' is given by

$$I_{s1} = \log_2 \frac{1}{p_1} \text{ bits}$$

In other words, each symbol of 's_1' conveys information of $\log_2(1/p_1)$ bits and such p_1L number of 's_1' symbols are present on an average in a length of 'L' symbols. Therefore, the total information conveyed by symbols of type 's_1' is

$$p_1 L \log_2 \frac{1}{p_1} \text{ bits}$$

Similarly, total information conveyed by symbols of type 's_2' is

$$p_2 L \log_2 \frac{1}{p_2} \text{ bits}$$

$$\cdots$$
$$\cdots$$

Total information conveyed by symbols of type 's_N' is

$$p_N L \log_2 \frac{1}{p_N} \text{ bits}$$

Therefore, the total information conveyed by the source is simply the sum of all these information contents, that is,

$$I_{\text{TOTAL}} = p_1 L \log_2 \frac{1}{p_1} + p_2 L \log_2 \frac{1}{p_2} + \cdots + p_N L \log_2 \frac{1}{p_N}$$

Thus, the average information conveyed by the source by emitting 'L' symbols is denoted by its entropy $H(S)$, which is given by the expression

$$H(S) = \frac{I_{\text{TOTAL}}}{L}$$

Therefore

$$H(S) = \frac{\left[p_1 L \log_2 \frac{1}{p_1} + p_2 L \log_2 \frac{1}{p_2} + \cdots + p_N L \log_2 \frac{1}{p_N}\right]}{L}$$

$$= \frac{L\left[p_1 \log_2 \frac{1}{p_1} + p_2 \log_2 \frac{1}{p_2} + \cdots + p_N \log_2 \frac{1}{p_N}\right]}{L}$$

$$= p_1 \log_2 \frac{1}{p_1} + p_2 \log_2 \frac{1}{p_2} + \cdots + p_N \log_2 \frac{1}{p_N}$$

We can write

$$H(S) = \sum_{k=1}^{N} p_k \log_2 \frac{1}{p_k} \text{ bits/sym} \tag{2.6}$$

Equation (2.6) gives the expression for the average information content of a source S. The average rate of information can also be defined for an information system if the symbol rate or the baud rate of the system is known. If the baud rate of the system is r_s sym/s, then the average rate of information is given by

$$R_S = H(S) * r_s \text{ bits/s} \tag{2.7}$$

EXAMPLE 2.4

A discrete memoryless source emits five symbols in every 2 ms. The symbol probabilities are {0.5, 0.25, 0.125, 0.0625, 0.0625}. Find the average information rate of the source.

Solution: The entropy or the average information content of the source is given by

$$H(S) = \sum_{k=1}^{5} p_k \log_2 \frac{1}{p_k} \text{ bits/sym}$$

Substituting the probabilities given in the above equation, we will have

$$H(S) = 0.5 \log_2 \frac{1}{0.5} + 0.25 \log_2 \frac{1}{0.25} + 0.125 \log_2 \frac{1}{0.125} + 0.0625 \log_2 \frac{1}{0.0625} + 0.0625 \log_2 \frac{1}{0.0625}$$

$$= 1.875 \text{ bits/sym}$$

Average rate of information is given by

$$R_S = H(S) * r_s \text{ bits/s}$$

where r_s is the symbol rate. In the problem, it is given that a symbol is emitted for every 2 ms. Therefore,

$$r_s = \frac{1}{2} \times 10^{-3} = 500 \text{ sym/s}$$

So average rate of information is

$$R_S = 1.875 * 500 = 937.5 \text{ bits/s}$$

EXAMPLE 2.5

A discrete source emits one of the following five symbols in every 1 s. The symbol probabilities are {1/4, 1/8, 1/8, 3/16, 5/16}. Find the average information content of the source in nats/sym and Hartley/sym.

Solution: The average information content of the source is nothing but the source entropy which is given by

$$H(S) = \sum_{k=1}^{5} p_k \log_e \frac{1}{p_k} \text{ nats/sym}$$

$$= \frac{1}{4}\log_e \frac{1}{(1/4)} + \frac{1}{8}\log_e \frac{1}{(1/8)} + \frac{1}{8}\log_e \frac{1}{(1/8)} + \frac{3}{16}\log_e \frac{1}{(3/16)} + \frac{5}{16}\log_e \frac{1}{(5/16)}$$

$$= 1.543 \text{ nats/sym}$$

Similarly, $H(S)$ in Hartley/sym is given by

$$H(S) = \sum_{k=1}^{5} p_k \log_{10} \frac{1}{p_k} \text{ Hartley/sym}$$

$$= \frac{1}{4}\log_{10} \frac{1}{(1/4)} + \frac{1}{8}\log_{10} \frac{1}{(1/8)} + \frac{1}{8}\log_{10} \frac{1}{(1/8)} + \frac{3}{16}\log_{10} \frac{1}{(3/16)} + \frac{5}{16}\log_{10} \frac{1}{(5/16)}$$

$$= 0.6704 \text{ Hartley/sym}$$

EXAMPLE 2.6

The output of an information source contains 160 symbols, 128 of which occur with a probability of 1/256 and remaining with a probability of 1/64 each. Find the average information rate of the source if the source emits 10000 sym/s.

Solution: The source entropy is given by

$$H(S) = \sum_{k=1}^{160} p_k \log_2 \frac{1}{p_k} = 128 * \frac{1}{256}\log_2 \frac{1}{(1/256)} + 32 * \frac{1}{64}\log_2 \frac{1}{(1/64)} = 7 \text{ bits/sym}$$

Average rate of information is given by

$$R_S = H(S) * r_s \text{ bits/s}$$

where r_s is the symbol rate given as 10000 sym/s in the problem. Therefore,

$$R_S = 7 * 10000 = 70000 \text{ bits/s}$$

EXAMPLE 2.7

The international Morse code uses a sequence of symbols of dots and dashes to transmit letters of English alphabet. The dash is represented by a current pulse of duration 2 ms and dot by a duration of 1 ms. The probability of dash is half as that of dot. Consider 1 ms duration of gap is given in between the symbols. Calculate

(a) Self-information of a dot and a dash.
(b) Average information content of a dot–dash code.
(c) Average rate of information.

Solution:

(a) Let p_{dot} and p_{dash} be the probabilities of dot and dash, respectively. Given

$$p_{\text{dash}} = \frac{1}{2}\, p_{\text{dot}}$$

Also $p_{\text{dot}} + p_{\text{dash}} = 1$. Therefore,

$$\therefore\ p_{\text{dot}} + \frac{1}{2}\, p_{\text{dot}} = 1 \Rightarrow p_{\text{dot}} = \frac{2}{3}$$

So we have

$$p_{\text{dash}} = \frac{1}{2}\, p_{\text{dot}} = \frac{1}{3}$$

Now

$$I_{\text{dot}} = \log_2 \frac{1}{p_{\text{dot}}} = \log_2 \frac{1}{2/3} = 0.5849 \text{ bits}$$

$$I_{\text{dash}} = \log_2 \frac{1}{p_{\text{dash}}} = \log_2 \frac{1}{1/3} = 1.5849 \text{ bits}$$

(b) $H(S) = \sum_{k=1}^{2} p_k \log_2 \frac{1}{p_k} = p_{\text{dot}} \log_2 \frac{1}{p_{\text{dot}}} + p_{\text{dash}} \log_2 \frac{1}{p_{\text{dash}}} = 0.9182$ bits/sym

(c) From the probabilities of dot and dash, it is clear that for every three symbols transmitted, there will be one symbol of type dash and two of type dot. Also the duration of dash is 2 ms and that of dot is 1 ms, and 1 ms gap is left in between the symbols as follows:

. . – . . – . . –

Therefore, a total of (1 ms + 1 ms + 1 ms + 1 ms + 2 ms + 1 ms) = 7 ms time is required to transmit three symbols. So the symbol rate is given by

$$r_s = \frac{3}{7} \text{ sym/ms} = \frac{3000}{7} \text{ sym/s}$$

$$\Rightarrow R_S = H(S) * r_s = 0.9182 * \frac{3000}{7} = 393.51 \text{ bits/s}$$

2.3.1 Properties of Entropy

The following are the properties of entropy:

1. Entropy is a continuous function of probability.
2. Entropy is a symmetric function of its arguments. In other words, the entropy of a system is the same irrespective of the order in which the symbols are arranged in the list.
3. Upper bound on entropy: In order to define the condition for the upper bound on entropy, consider the following scenarios when election results are declared in case of
   - Two equally strong candidates have contested in a constituency.
   - One contestant is very strong and other one is least expected to win.

Among the two scenarios given above, the result in the first case would give maximum information as the winning probabilities of both candidates are same. However, in the second case as one of the candidates is very strong and expected to win, the election result conveys very little information.

In other words, the entropy of a source will be maximum if all its symbol probabilities are equal. Let us derive the expression for the maximum entropy of a source. Consider the term

$$\log_2 N - H(S) = \log_2 N - \sum_{k=1}^{N} p_k \log_2 \frac{1}{p_k} \tag{2.8}$$

We have the sum of all symbol probabilities emitted by a source as unity, that is,

$$\sum_{k=1}^{N} p_k = 1$$

Multiplying this term to the first-term of the RHS of Eq. (2.8) will not alter the equality:

$$\log_2 N - H(S) = \sum_{k=1}^{N} p_k \log_2 N - \sum_{k=1}^{N} p_k \log_2 \frac{1}{p_k} = \sum_{k=1}^{N} p_k \left[\log_2 N - \log_2 \frac{1}{p_k}\right] = \sum_{k=1}^{N} p_k \log_2 (Np_k)$$

$$\Rightarrow \log_2 N - H(S) = \log_2 e \sum_{k=1}^{N} p_k \ln(Np_k) \tag{2.9}$$

From mathematics, we have the following relation for logarithms:

$$\ln \frac{1}{x} \geq 1 - x \tag{2.10}$$

Above relation turns to be an equation if $x = 1$. Let us reproduce the RHS of Eq. (2.9) starting from the relation given in Eq. (2.10). Further comparing the LHS of Eq. (2.9), we can deduce the upper bound for $H(S)$. After substituting $x = (1/Np_k)$, we get

$$\ln Np_k \geq 1 - \frac{1}{Np_k}$$

Multiplying both sides by $\log_2 e \sum_{k=1}^{N} p_k$, we get

$$\log_2 e \sum_{k=1}^{N} p_k \ln Np_k \geq \log_2 e \sum_{k=1}^{N} p_k \left[1 - \frac{1}{Np_k}\right]$$

The LHS of the above relation represents $\log_2 N - H(S)$ from Eq. (2.9). Therefore,

$$\log_2 N - H(S) \geq \log_2 e \sum_{k=1}^{N} p_k \left[1 - \frac{1}{Np_k}\right]$$

$$\Rightarrow \log_2 N - H(S) \geq \log_2 e \left[\sum_{k=1}^{N} p_k - \sum_{k=1}^{N} \frac{1}{N}\right]$$

But

$$\sum_{k=1}^{N} p_k = 1 \quad \text{and} \quad \sum_{k=1}^{N} \frac{1}{N} = \frac{1}{N} + \frac{1}{N} + \frac{1}{N} + \cdots + \frac{1}{N} (N \text{ times}) = 1$$

Therefore

$$\log_2 N - H(S) \geq \log_2 e[1-1] \Rightarrow \log_2 N - H(S) \geq 0 \Rightarrow H(S) \leq \log_2 N$$

Therefore, the upper bound of the entropy is given by

$$H(S)_{\max} = \log_2 N \text{ bits/sym} \tag{2.11}$$

This condition occurs when $x = 1$, that is,

$$\frac{1}{Np_k} = 1 \Rightarrow p_k = \frac{1}{N}$$

2.3.2 Source Efficiency

The efficiency of an information source is defined as the ratio of the average information conveyed by the source to that of the maximum average information:

$$\eta_S = \frac{H(S)}{H(S)_{\max}} \times 100\% \tag{2.12}$$

The redundancy of the source is defined as

$$R_{\eta S} = 1 - \eta_S = \left[1 - \frac{H(S)}{H(S)_{\max}}\right] = \frac{H(S)_{\max} - H(S)}{H(S)_{\max}} \times 100\% \tag{2.13}$$

EXAMPLE 2.8

Consider a system emitting one of the three symbols A, B and C with respective probabilities 0.7, 0.15 and 0.15. Calculate its efficiency and redundancy.

Solution: The efficiency is given by

$$\eta_S = \frac{H(S)}{H(S)_{\max}} \times 100\%$$

Now

$$H(S)=\sum_{k=1}^{3} p_k \log_2 \frac{1}{p_k} \text{ bits/sym}$$

Substituting the probabilities given in the above equation, we have

$$0.7\log_2 \frac{1}{0.7}+0.15\log_2 \frac{1}{0.15}+0.15\log_2 \frac{1}{0.15}=1.1812 \text{ bits/sym}$$

Now

$$H(S)_{\max}=\log_2 N=\log_2 3=1.5849 \text{ bits/sym}$$

Therefore efficiency is given by

$$\eta_S=\frac{1.1812}{1.5849}\times 100\%=74.52\%$$

The redundancy is given by

$$R_{\eta S}=1-\eta_S=25.48\%$$

EXAMPLE 2.9

A certain digital frame consists of 15 fields. The first and the last field of each frame are same. The remaining 13 fields can be filled by any of the 16 symbols with equal probability. Find the average information conveyed by the frame. Also find the average rate of information if 100 frames are transmitted every second.

Solution: Consider the frame with 15 fields as shown below:

1	2	3	4	5	6	7	8	9	10	11	12	13	14	15

The total average information conveyed by the source is simply the sum of the individual entropies of each field in the frame, that is,

$$H(S)_{\text{Total}}=H_1+H_2+H_3+\cdots+H_{15}$$

As the first and last fields are same for all the frames, it conveys no information, that is, $H_1=H_{15}=0$. Remaining fields can be filled with one of the 16 symbols with equal probability. Therefore, the corresponding entropy is the maximum entropy $H(S)_{\max}$. So

$$H_2=H_3=\cdots=H_{14}=H(S)_{\max}=\log_2 N=\log_2 16=4 \text{ bits/field}$$

Therefore,

$$H(S)_{\text{Total}}=H_1+H_2+H_3+\cdots+H_{15}=13{*}4=52 \text{ bits/frame}$$

Now we know that

$$R_s=H(S){*}\,r_s$$

Given $r_s=100$ frames/s. So

$$R_s=H(S){*}\,r_s=52{*}100=52000 \text{ bits/s}$$

EXAMPLE 2.10

In a facsimile transmission of a picture, there are 4×10^6 pixels/frame. For a good reconstruction of the image at least eight brightness levels are necessary. Assuming all these levels are equally likely to occur, find the average information rate if one picture is transmitted every 4 s.

Solution: Given
Total number of pixels = 4×10^6
Total number of brightness levels = 8
Therefore, total number of different frames $N = 8^{(4 \times 10^6)}$
As all brightness levels are equally likely to occur, all these frames are equiprobable. So

$$H(S) = H(S)_{\max} = \log_2 N = \log_2 (8^{4 \times 10^6}) = 12 \times 10^6 \text{ bits/frame}$$

Now

$$R_S = H(S)^* \, r_s$$

It is given that each picture frame is transmitted in 4 s. Therefore,

$$r_s = \frac{1}{4} \text{ frames/s}$$

So

$$R_S = H(S)^* \, r_s = 12 \times 10^6 \times \frac{1}{4} = 3 \times 10^6 \text{ bits/s}$$

2.4 Extension of Zero Memory Source

Consider a zero memory source emitting two symbols 's_1' and 's_2' with probabilities 'p_1' and 'p_2', respectively. Obviously $p_1 + p_2 = 1$. Also the entropy of the source S is given by

$$H(S) = p_1 \log_2 \frac{1}{p_1} + p_2 \log_2 \frac{1}{p_2} \tag{2.14}$$

Now consider the second-order extension of the source S. This source is denoted as S^2. Now the source S^2 will have four combinations viz. s_1s_1, s_1s_2, s_2s_1 and s_2s_2. Corresponding probabilities are given by

$$s_1s_1 = p(s_1)\, p(s_2) = p_1 \times p_1 = p_1^2$$

$$s_1s_2 = p(s_1)\, p(s_2) = p_1 \times p_2 = p_1 \cdot p_2$$

$$s_2s_1 = p(s_2)\, p(s_1) = p_2 \times p_1 = p_2 \cdot p_1$$

$$s_2s_2 = p(s_2)\, p(s_2) = p_2 \times p_2 = p_2^2$$

Therefore, the entropy of the second-order extension of the source is given by

$$H(S^2) = \sum_{k=1}^{4} p_k \log_2 \frac{1}{p_k} = p_1^2 \log_2 \frac{1}{p_1^2} + p_1p_2 \log_2 \frac{1}{p_1p_2} + p_2p_1 \log_2 \frac{1}{p_2p_1} + p_2^2 \log_2 \frac{1}{p_2^2}$$

$$= 2p_1^2 \log_2 \frac{1}{p_1} + 2p_1p_2 \log_2 \frac{1}{p_1p_2} + 2p_2^2 \log_2 \frac{1}{p_2}$$

$$= 2p_1^2 \log_2 \frac{1}{p_1} + 2p_1p_2 \log_2 \frac{1}{p_1} + 2p_1p_2 \log_2 \frac{1}{p_2} + 2p_2^2 \log_2 \frac{1}{p_2}$$

$$= 2p_1(p_1 + p_2)\log_2 \frac{1}{p_1} + 2p_2(p_1 + p_2)\log_2 \frac{1}{p_2}$$

But we have $p_1 + p_2 = 1$. Therefore

$$H(S)^2 = 2p_1 \log_2 \frac{1}{p_1} + 2p_2 \log_2 \frac{1}{p_2} = 2\left[p_1 \log_2 \frac{1}{p_1} + p_2 \log_2 \frac{1}{p_2}\right]$$

$$\Rightarrow H(S)^2 = 2 \cdot H(S)$$

Similarly, we can show that

$$H(S^3) = 3 \cdot H(S)$$
$$H(S^4) = 4 \cdot H(S)$$

and so on. In general, for an nth-order extension of S

$$H(S^n) = n \cdot H(S) \tag{2.15}$$

EXAMPLE 2.11

Consider a zero memory source emitting three symbols X, Y and Z with respective probabilities {0.6, 0.3, 0.1}. Calculate

(a) Entropy of the source.
(b) All symbols and the corresponding probabilities of the second-order extension of the source. Find the entropy of the second-order extension of the source.
(c) Show that $H(S^2) = 2*H(S)$.

Solution:

(a) We know that

$$H(S) = \sum_{k=1}^{3} p_k \log_2 \frac{1}{p_k} \text{ bits/sym}$$

Substituting the probabilities given in the above equation, we will have

$$0.6 \log_2 \frac{1}{0.6} + 0.3 \log_2 \frac{1}{0.3} + 0.1 \log_2 \frac{1}{0.1} = 1.2954 \text{ bits/sym}$$

(b) Consider the second-order extension as shown in Table 2.1.

Table 2.1 Second-order extension of the system *S*

Symbols	*Probability*
XX	$p(X)*p(X)=0.6*0.6=0.36$
XY	$p(X)*p(Y)=0.6*0.3=0.18$
XZ	$p(X)*p(Z)=0.6*0.1=0.06$
YX	$p(Y)*p(X)=0.3*0.6=0.18$
YY	$p(Y)*p(Y)=0.3*0.3=0.09$
YZ	$p(Y)*p(Z)=0.3*0.1=0.03$
ZX	$p(Z)*p(X)=0.1*0.6=0.06$
ZY	$p(Z)*p(Y)=0.1*0.3=0.03$
ZZ	$p(Z)*p(Z)=0.1*0.1=0.01$

$$H(S^2)=\sum_{k=1}^{9} p_k \log_2 \frac{1}{p_k} \text{ bits/sym}$$

Substituting the given probabilities in the above equation, we will have $H(S^2) = 2.5909$ bits/sym

(c) $2 * H(S) = 2 * 1.2954 = 2.5909$ bits/sym $= H(S^2)$

2.5 Entropy of a Source with Memory

In Sections 2.1–2.4, we have assumed the information source to be memoryless for our analysis. In other words, we considered that the emission of the current symbol from the source is independent of the previous emissions. But most of the sources we consider in real time do have memory. For instance, in English, if the first letter of a word is 'Q', it is more likely to occur that the succeeding letter would be 'U' and so on. Thus in real time, most of the sources are dependent. Hence, the model we discussed for a memoryless source would not suffice.

A dependent probabilistic model is thus required to model such sources. One such model is Markov model. A Markov model is used to represent a source with memory. In general, for an *n*th-order Markov source, the emission of symbol '*s*' at the current instant is dependent on its previous '*n*' symbols.

2.5.1 Markov Model

A system with memory can be represented using a state diagram. A state diagram represents all possible states of a system along with the transition probabilities. Also the symbols emitted by the source in each of the transitions are depicted in a state diagram. From the state diagram, one can construct a tree diagram. From the tree diagram, the probabilities of the symbols emitted by the source can be determined. The probabilities of messages of length '*L*' can be determined by constructing a tree diagram of '*L*' stages.

2.5.2 Entropy and Information Rate

Let the entropy of state 'k' be denoted by H_k. It can be obtained by considering all outgoing probabilities of state 'k':

$$H_k = \sum_{l=1}^{M} p_{lk} \log_2 \frac{1}{p_{lk}} \text{ bits/sym} \tag{2.16}$$

where M is the total number of states
The entropy of the source is given by

$$H = \sum_{k=1}^{M} H_k p_k \text{ bits/sym} \tag{2.17}$$

where p_k is the probability of the kth state.
The average information rate of a source is given by

$$R_S = r_s H \text{ bits/s} \tag{2.18}$$

2.5.3 Average Information per Symbol

The average information content per symbol in a message of length L is given by

$$G_L = \frac{1}{L} \sum_{\forall i} p(m_i) \log_2 \frac{1}{p(m_i)} \text{ bits/sym} \tag{2.19}$$

where $p(m_i)$ is the probability of the messages of length L. The average amount of information per symbol in a long message decreases with increase in L and will be at least equal to $H(S)$, that is,

$$G_1 \geq G_2 \geq G_3 \geq \cdots \geq H(S)$$

In other words,

$$\lim_{N \to \infty} G_L = H(S) \tag{2.20}$$

EXAMPLE 2.12

Consider the following Markov source shown in Fig. 2.1. Find

(a) State probabilities.
(b) State entropies.
(c) Source entropy.
(d) G_1, G_2.
(e) Show that $G_1 > G_2 > H$.

Solution:

(a) To find the state probabilities, we have to first write the state equations. State equations can be written by considering all incoming transition probabilities of the states. Consider the equation for state 1

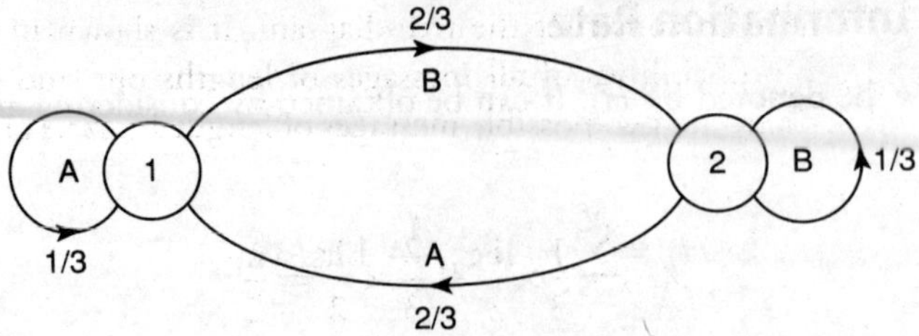

Figure 2.1 | Markov source.

$$p(1) = \frac{1}{3}\, p(1) + \frac{2}{3}\, p(2) \tag{2.21}$$

Similarly for state 2,

$$p(2) = \frac{2}{3}\, p(1) + \frac{1}{3}\, p(2) \tag{2.22}$$

Also the sum of all state probabilities is equal to one. That is,

$$p(1) + p(2) = 1 \tag{2.23}$$

From Eq. (2.21), we get

$$p(1) - \frac{1}{3}\, p(1) = \frac{2}{3}\, p(2) \Rightarrow \frac{2}{3}\, p(1) = \frac{2}{3}\, p(2)$$

Therefore, $p(1) = p(2)$. Substituting this in Eq. (2.23), we get

$$p(1) + p(1) = 1 \Rightarrow p(1) = \frac{1}{2} = p(2)$$

(b) To find the state entropy, we need to consider all outgoing probabilities of the states. We have

$$H_k = \sum_{l=1}^{M} p_{lk} \log_2 \frac{1}{p_{lk}} \text{ bits/sym}$$

For state 1,

$$H_1 = \frac{1}{3}\log_2 \frac{1}{(1/3)} + \frac{2}{3}\log_2 \frac{1}{(2/3)} = 0.918 \text{ bits/sym}$$

Similarly for state 2,

$$H_2 = \frac{1}{3}\log_2 \frac{1}{(1/3)} + \frac{2}{3}\log_2 \frac{1}{(2/3)} = 0.918 \text{ bits/sym}$$

(c) Source entropy is given by

$$H = \sum_{k=1}^{M} H_k p_k \text{ bits/sym} = p\,(1)\, H_1 + p\,(2)\, H_2 = \frac{1}{2} * 0.918 + \frac{1}{2} * 0.918 = 0.918 \text{ bits/sym}$$

(d) To find G_1 and G_2, we need to construct the tree diagram. It is shown in Fig. 2.2. From the tree diagram, we can find the probabilities of all messages of lengths one and two by considering the output of stages 1 and 2. There are two possible messages of length 1, viz. A and B. The corresponding probabilities are

$$p(\mathrm{A}) = \frac{1}{3}\times\frac{1}{2} + \frac{2}{3}\times\frac{1}{2} = \frac{1}{2}$$

$$p(\mathrm{B}) = \frac{2}{3}\times\frac{1}{2} + \frac{1}{3}\times\frac{1}{2} = \frac{1}{2}$$

Corresponding information per symbol G_1 is given by

$$G_L = \frac{1}{L}\sum_i p(mi)\log_2 \frac{1}{p(mi)} \text{ bits/sym}$$

We have $L = 1$. Therefore,

$$G_1 = \frac{1}{1}\sum_i p(mi)\log_2 \frac{1}{p(mi)} = \frac{1}{2}\log_2 \frac{1}{(1/2)} + \frac{1}{2}\log_2 \frac{1}{(1/2)} = 1 \text{ bits/sym}$$

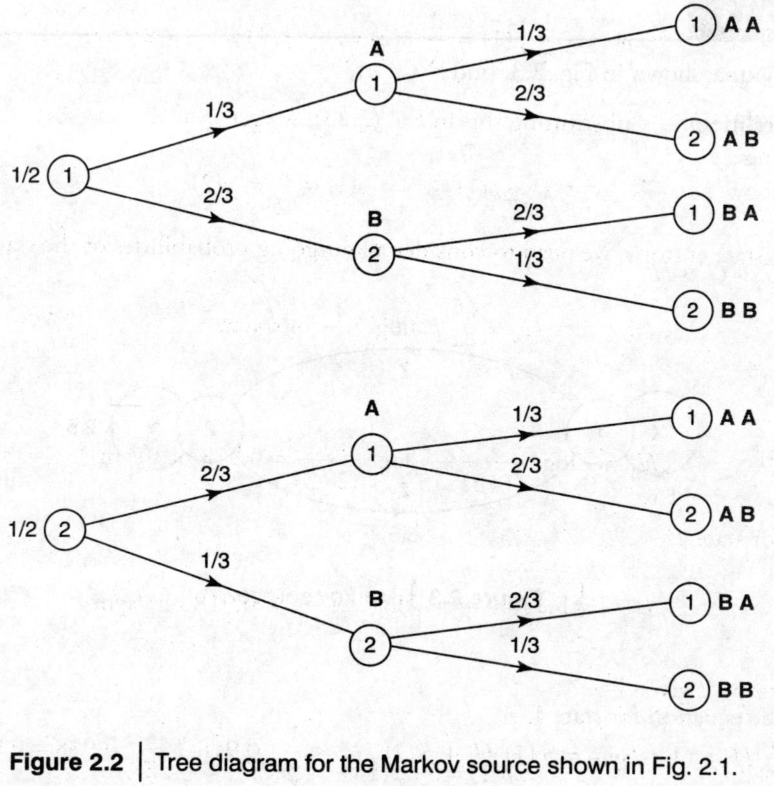

Figure 2.2 | Tree diagram for the Markov source shown in Fig. 2.1.

Similarly from the second stage of the tree, we can get the probabilities of all symbols of length two which are given as follows:

$$P(\text{AA}) = \frac{1}{3}\times\frac{1}{3}\times\frac{1}{2} + \frac{1}{3}\times\frac{2}{3}\times\frac{1}{2} = \frac{1}{6}$$

$$P(\text{AB}) = \frac{2}{3}\times\frac{1}{3}\times\frac{1}{2} + \frac{2}{3}\times\frac{2}{3}\times\frac{1}{2} = \frac{1}{3}$$

$$P(\text{BA}) = \frac{2}{3}\times\frac{2}{3}\times\frac{1}{2} + \frac{2}{3}\times\frac{1}{3}\times\frac{1}{2} = \frac{1}{3}$$

$$P(\text{BB}) = \frac{1}{3}\times\frac{2}{3}\times\frac{1}{2} + \frac{1}{3}\times\frac{1}{3}\times\frac{1}{2} = \frac{1}{6}$$

Therefore,

$$G_2 = \frac{1}{2}\sum_i p(mi)\log_2\frac{1}{p(mi)}$$

$$= \frac{1}{2}\left[\frac{1}{6}\log_2\frac{1}{(1/6)} + \frac{1}{3}\log_2\frac{1}{(1/3)} + \frac{1}{3}\log_2\frac{1}{(1/3)} + \frac{1}{6}\log_2\frac{1}{(1/6)}\right] = 0.959 \text{ bits/sym}$$

(e) From solutions (c) and (d), we can conclude that $G_1 > G_2 > H$.

EXAMPLE 2.13

For the Markov source shown in Fig. 2.3, find

(a) State probabilities.
(b) State entropies.
(c) Source entropy.
(d) G_1, G_2.

Also show that $G_1 > G_2 > H$.

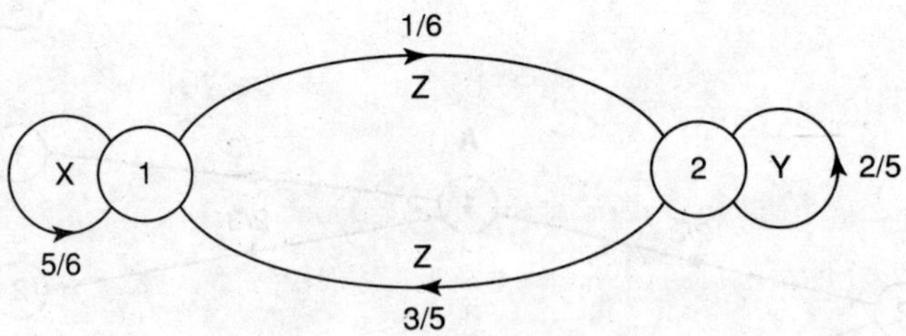

Figure 2.3 | Markov source.

Solution:

(a) Consider the equation for state 1

$$p(1) = \frac{5}{6}p(1) + \frac{3}{5}p(2) \tag{2.24}$$

Similarly for state 2

$$p(2) = \frac{1}{6}\,p(1) + \frac{2}{5}\,p(2) \tag{2.25}$$

Also

$$p(1) + p(2) = 1 \tag{2.26}$$

From Eq. (2.24), we get

$$p(1) = \frac{18}{5}\,p(2)$$

Substituting this in Eq. (2.26), we get

$$\frac{18}{5}\,p(2) + p(2) = 1 \Rightarrow p(2) = \frac{5}{23}$$

Therefore,

$$p(1) = \frac{18}{23}$$

(b) We have

$$H_k = \sum_{l=1}^{M} p_{lk} \log_2 \frac{1}{p_{lk}} \text{ bits/sym}$$

For state 1,

$$H_1 = \frac{1}{6}\log_2 \frac{1}{(1/6)} + \frac{5}{6}\log_2 \frac{1}{(5/6)} = 0.65 \text{ bits/sym}$$

Similarly for state 2

$$H_2 = \frac{3}{5}\log_2 \frac{1}{(3/5)} + \frac{2}{5}\log_2 \frac{1}{(2/5)} = 0.9709 \text{ bits/sym}$$

(c) Source entropy is given by

$$H = \sum_{k=1}^{M} H_k p_k \text{ bits/sym} = p(1)\,H_1 + p(2)\,H_2 = 0.7197 \text{ bits/sym}$$

(d) To find G_1 and G_2, we need to construct the tree diagram. It is as shown in Fig. 2.4.

There are three possible messages of length one and the corresponding probabilities are:

$$p(\text{X}) = \frac{15}{23};\ p(\text{Y}) = \frac{2}{23};\ p(\text{Z}) = \frac{6}{23}$$

Corresponding information per symbol G_1 is given by

$$G_L = \frac{1}{L}\sum_i p(mi)\log_2 \frac{1}{p(mi)} \text{ bits/sym}$$

$$L = 1$$

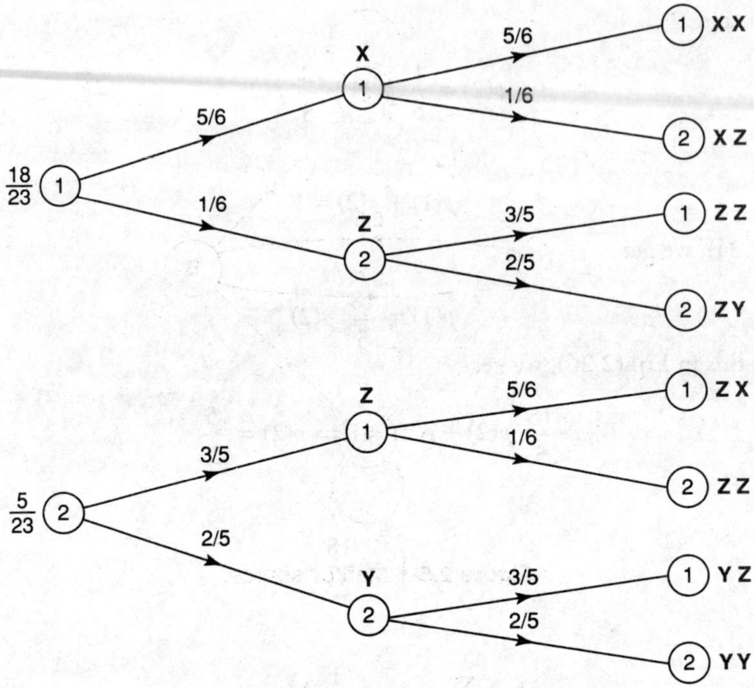

Figure 2.4 | Tree diagram for the Markov source shown in Fig. 2.3.

Therefore,

$$G_1 = \frac{1}{1}\sum_i p(mi)\log_2 \frac{1}{p(mi)} = 1.2142 \text{ bits/sym}$$

Similarly, from the second stage of the tree we can get the probabilities of all symbols of length two which are given as follows:

$$p(\text{XX}) = \frac{25}{46};\ p(\text{XZ}) = \frac{5}{46};\ p(\text{ZZ}) = \frac{1}{10};\ p(\text{ZY}) = \frac{6}{115};\ p(\text{ZX}) = \frac{5}{46};\ p(\text{YZ}) = \frac{6}{115};\ p(\text{YY}) = \frac{4}{115}$$

Therefore,

$$G_2 = \frac{1}{2}\sum_i p(mi)\log_2 \frac{1}{p(mi)} = 1.0597 \text{ bits/sym}$$

From solutions (c) and (d), we can conclude that $G_1 > G_2 > H$.

EXAMPLE 2.14

Consider the Markov source shown in Fig. 2.5. Find

(a) State probabilities.
(b) State entropies.
(c) Source entropy.

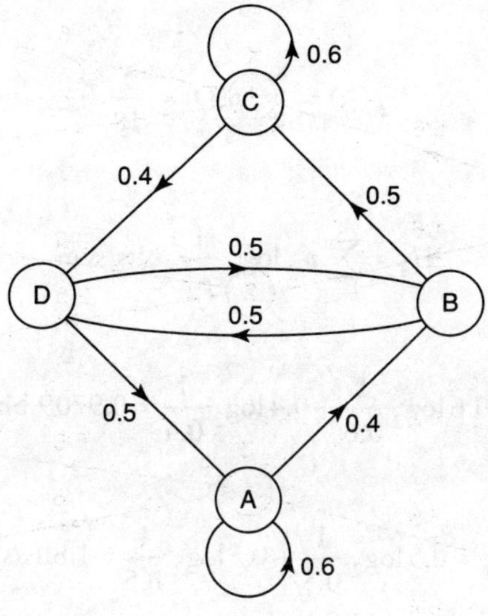

Figure 2.5 | Markov source.

Solution:

(a) We can write the state equations for four states as follows:

$$p(A) = 0.6\,p(A) + 0.5\,p(D) \tag{2.27}$$

$$p(B) = 0.4\,p(A) + 0.5\,p(D) \tag{2.28}$$

$$p(C) = 0.5\,p(B) + 0.6\,p(C) \tag{2.29}$$

$$p(D) = 0.5\,p(B) + 0.4\,p(C) \tag{2.30}$$

Also

$$p(A) + p(B) + p(C) + p(D) = 1 \tag{2.31}$$

From Eq. (2.27)

$$p(\text{A}) = \frac{5}{4}\,p(\text{D})$$

From Eq. (2.28)

$$p(B) = p(D)$$

From Eq. (2.29)

$$p(\text{C}) = \frac{5}{4}\,p(\text{D})$$

Substituting these relations in Eq. (2.31), we get

$$\frac{5}{4}\,p(\text{D}) + p(\text{D}) + \frac{5}{4}\,p(\text{D}) + p(\text{D}) = 1 \Rightarrow p(\text{D}) = \frac{2}{9} = p(\text{B})$$

Therefore,

$$p(\text{A}) = \frac{5}{4};\, p(\text{D}) = \frac{5}{18}$$

(b) We have

$$H_k = \sum_{l=1}^{M} p_{lk} \log_2 \frac{1}{p_{lk}} \text{ bits/sym}$$

For state A,

$$H_A = 0.6\log_2 \frac{1}{0.6} + 0.4\log_2 \frac{1}{0.4} = 0.9709 \text{ bits/sym}$$

For state B,

$$H_B = 0.5\log_2 \frac{1}{0.5} + 0.5\log_2 \frac{1}{0.5} = 1 \text{ bits/sym}$$

For state C,

$$H_C = 0.6\log_2 \frac{1}{0.6} + 0.4\log_2 \frac{1}{0.4} = 0.9709 \text{ bits/sym}$$

Finally for state D,

$$H_D = 0.5\log_2 \frac{1}{0.5} + 0.5\log_2 \frac{1}{0.5} = 1 \text{ bits/sym}$$

(c) Source entropy is given by

$$H = \sum_{k=1}^{M} H_k p_k \text{ bits/sym} = p(\text{A})\, H_\text{A} + p(\text{B})\, H_\text{B} + p(\text{C})\, H_\text{C} + p(\text{D})\, H_\text{D} = 0.9838 \text{ bits/sym}$$

EXAMPLE 2.15

Design a system to report the heading of collection of 400 cars. The heading levels are heading straight (S), turning left (L) and turning right (R). This information is to be transmitted every second. Construct a model on the basis of following test data:

(a) On an average during reporting interval, 200 cars were heading straight, 100 were turning left and remaining were turning right.

(b) Out of 200 cars that reported heading straight, 100 reported going straight during next reporting period, 50 turning left and remaining turning right during the next period.

(c) Out of 100 cars that reported as turning during a signaling period, 50 continued the turn and remaining headed straight during next signaling interval.

(d) The dynamics of the cars did not allow them to change their heading from left to right or right to left during subsequent reporting periods.

Find the entropies of each states, source entropy and rate of information.

Solution: There are three states in the model.

Heading straight (*S*)
Turning left (*L*)
Turning right (*R*)

The Markov model can be constructed on the basis of data given in the problem. It is given that 200 cars were heading straight, 100 were turning left and remaining 100 were turning right in any turning interval on an average. And there are 400 cars in total. Therefore, the probabilities of the states can be determined as follows:

$$p(\mathrm{S}) = \frac{200}{400} = \frac{1}{2}$$

$$p(\mathrm{L}) = \frac{100}{400} = \frac{1}{4}$$

$$p(\mathrm{R}) = \frac{100}{400} = \frac{1}{4}$$

Also from the second and third statements, transition probabilities can be determined. The model constructed on the basis of given data is as shown in Fig. 2.6.

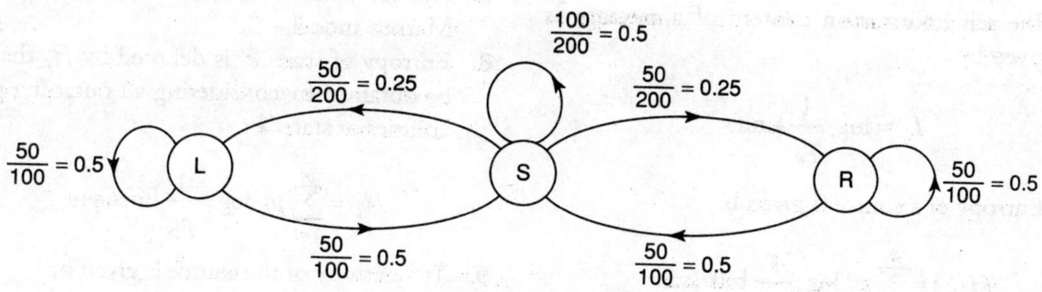

Figure 2.6 | Markov source.

The state entropies can be calculated as follows:

$$H_k = \sum_{l=1}^{M} p_{lk} \log_2 \frac{1}{p_{lk}} \text{ bits/sym}$$

For state *S*,

$$H_S = 0.5\log_2\frac{1}{0.5} + 0.25\log_2\frac{1}{0.25} + 0.25\log_2\frac{1}{0.25} = 1.5 \text{ bits/sym}$$

For state *L*,

$$H_L = 0.5\log_2\frac{1}{0.5} + 0.5\log_2\frac{1}{0.5} = 1 \text{ bits/sym}$$

For state R,

$$H_R = 0.5\log_2 \frac{1}{0.5} + 0.5\log_2 \frac{1}{0.5} = 1 \text{ bits/sym}$$

Source entropy is given by

$$H = \sum_{k=1}^{M} H_k p_k \text{ bits/sym} = p(\text{S})\, H_\text{S} + p(\text{L})\, H_\text{L} + p(\text{R})\, H_\text{R} = 1.25 \text{ bits/sym}$$

The average information rate of a source is given by

$$R_S = r_s\, H \text{ bits/s}$$

Given $r_s = 1$ sym/s. Therefore,

$$R_S = 1 * 1.25 = 1.25 \text{ bits/s}$$

Summary

1. The amount of information conveyed by a message is inversely proportional to its probability of occurrence.
2. The self-information content of a message is given by
$$I_k = \log_r \frac{1}{p_k} \text{ units}$$
3. Entropy of a source is given by
$$H(S) = \sum_{k=1}^{N} p_k \log_2 \frac{1}{p_k} \text{ bits/sym}$$
4. The average rate of information is given by
$$R_S = H(S) * r_s \text{ bits/s}$$
5. The upper bound of the entropy is given by
$$H(S)_{\max} = \log_2 N \text{ bits/sym}$$
6. For an nth-order extended source
$$H(S^n) = n \cdot H(S)$$
7. Sources with memory can be modeled using Markov model.
8. Entropy of state 'k' is denoted by H_k that can be obtained by considering all outgoing probabilities of state 'k':
$$H_k = \sum_{l=1}^{M} p_{lk} \log_2 \frac{1}{p_{lk}} \text{ bits/sym}$$
9. The entropy of the source is given by
$$H = \sum_{k=1}^{M} H_k p_k \text{ bits/sym}$$
10. Average information per symbol is given by
$$G_L = \frac{1}{L} \sum_i p(mi) \log_2 \frac{1}{p(mi)} \text{ bits/sym}$$

Review Questions

1. Define information.
2. Explain how information is measured. Justify the usage of logarithmic function to measure information.
3. Consider a system emitting three symbols $\{X, Y, Z\}$ with probabilities 0.5, 0.3 and 0.2, respectively. Find the information conveyed by each of these symbols.

4. Establish a relationship between Hartley and nats.
5. Establish a relationship between nats and bits.
6. Consider a binary system emitting symbols with probabilities 0.7 and 0.3. Find the self-information of each of the symbols in nats and Hartley.
7. A pair of dice is rolled simultaneously. The outcome of the first dice is considered to be 'x' and that of the second as 'y'. Three events are defined as

   $A = [(x, y)$ such that $(x + y)$ is exactly divisible by 4$]$

   $B = [(x, y)$ such that $3 \le (x + y) \le 8]$

   $C = [(x, y)$ such that $(x + y)$ is a prime number$]$

   which event conveys more information? Justify your answer with mathematical calculation.
8. A source emits one of the six symbols in every 4 ms. The symbol statistics are {0.3, 0.22, 0.20, 0.12, 0.10, 0.06}. Find the average information rate of the source.
9. The output of an information source consists of 100 symbols, 60 of which occur with a probability of 1/120 and remaining with a probability of 1/80 each. Find the average information rate of the source if the source emits 2100 sym/s.
10. A Morse code uses a sequence of symbols of dots and dashes to transmit the information. The dash is represented by a pulse of duration 3 ms and dot of 1 ms. The probability of dash is one-third as that of dot. Consider that 1 ms duration of gap is given in between the symbols. Calculate:
    (a) Self-information of a dot and a dash.
    (b) Average information content of a dot–dash code.
    (c) Average rate of information.
11. Consider a binary source emitting two symbols X and Y. Let the probability of emission of X be 'p'. Plot the function $H(S)$ as a function of 'p'.
12. Consider a system emitting four symbols A, B, C and D with respective probabilities 0.5, 0.3, 0.15 and 0.05, respectively. Calculate its efficiency and redundancy.
13. A data frame consists of ten fields. First field in each frame is the same for some synchronization purpose. However the remaining fields can be filled by any of 32 symbols with equal probability. Find the average rate of information if 500 frames are transmitted in every second.
14. In a facsimile transmission of a picture, there are 2.6×10^6 pixels/frame. For a good reconstruction of the image at least 12 brightness levels are necessary. Assuming all these levels are equally likely to occur, find the average information rate if one picture is transmitted for every four seconds.
15. Consider a zero memory source emitting two symbols A and B with respective probabilities {0.6, 0.4}. Calculate:
    (a) Entropy of the source.
    (b) All symbols and the corresponding probabilities of the third-order extension of the source. Find the entropy of the third-order extension of the source.
    (c) Show that $H(S^3) = 3*H(S)$.
16. For the Markov source shown in Fig. 2.7, find
    (a) State probabilities.
    (b) State entropies.
    (c) Source entropy.
    (d) G_1, G_2.
    Also show that $G_1 > G_2 > H$.

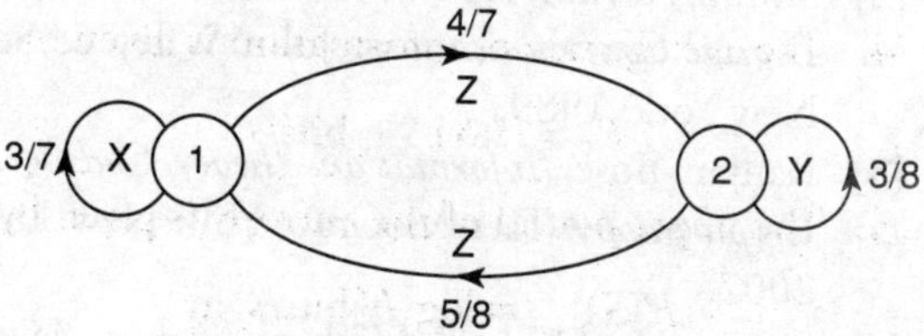

Figure 2.7 | Markov source.

17. For the Markov source shown in Fig. 2.8, find
    (a) State probabilities.
    (b) State entropies.
    (c) Source entropy.
    (d) G_1, G_2
    Also show that $G_1 > G_2 > H$.

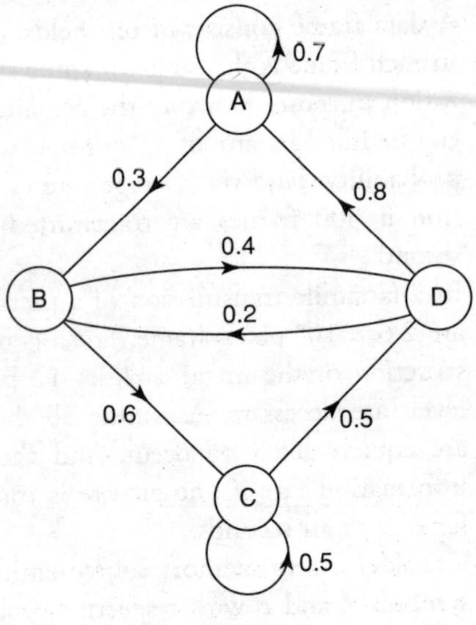

Figure 2.8 | Markov source.

18. Design a system to report the speed of collection of 200 cars on a highway. The speed levels can be high (H), medium (M) and slow (S). This information is to be transmitted every 2 s. Construct a model on the basis of the following test data:

(a) On an average during reporting interval, 100 cars were at medium speed, 50 were at high and remaining were at the slow.

(b) Out of 100 cars that reported to be medium, 50 reported to continue at the same pace during the next reporting period, 25 were reported to go to high and remaining to go to slow during the next period.

(c) Out of 50 cars that were reported as going at high or low pace during a signaling period, 25 continued in the same pace and remaining went to medium pace during next signaling interval.

(d) The rules of the highway authority restrict the change from high to low or low to high pace during subsequent reporting periods.

Find the entropies of each states, source entropy and rate of information.

FURTHER READING

[1] Shanmugam K Sam, *Digital and Analog Communication Systems*, John Wiley & Sons: New York; 1979.

[2] Simon Haykin, *An Introduction to Analog and Digital Communications*, John Wiley & Sons: New York; 1989.

[3] Ranjan Bose, *Information Theory Coding and Cryptography*, Tata McGraw Hill: New Delhi; 2007.

[4] Simon Haykin and Michael Moher, *Modern Wireless Communications*, Pearson Education: Upper Saddle River, NJ; 2007.

[5] Claude Elwood Shannon, *A mathematical theory of communication*, Bell System Technical Journal, Vol. 27, pp. 379–423, 623–656, 1948.

[6] Ian A Glover and Peter M Grant, *Digital Communications*, Pearson Education: Upper Saddle River, NJ; 2004.

[7] Bernard Sklar and Pabitra K Ray, *Digital Communications: Fundamentals and Applications*, Pearson Education: India; 2001.

[8] Andrea Goldsmith, *Wireless Communications*, Cambridge University Press: UK; 2005.

[9] John G Proakis and Masoud Salehi, *Contemporary Communication System using MATLAB*, PWS Publishing Company: Boston, MA, 1998.

[10] John C Mingers, *An evaluation of theories of information with regard to the semantic and pragmatic aspects of information systems*, Systems Practice, Vol. 9, No. 3, pp. 187–209, 1996.

[11] Ghim Hwee Ong, *An algorithm for generating n Huffman codes with a worst case of ($n \log_2 n + n \log_2 \log_2 n$) comparisons,* Proceedings of IEEE Singapore International Conference on Information Engineering '93, Vol. 2, pp. 872–876, 1993.

3 Source Coding

'The main purpose of science is simplicity and as we understand more things, everything is becoming simpler.'

–Edward Teller

Learning Objectives

After reading this chapter, you will be able to:

- Define different types of codes.
- Emphasize the need for source coding in communication systems.
- Design an encoder for different information sources.
- Validate the performance of the coding algorithms in terms of their efficiency.

3.1 Introduction

In a digital communication system, source encoding is the stage that follows the information source, the output of which is given to the source encoder. There is a need to represent each information symbol in terms of a bit sequence, called a codeword, to achieve communication. The codewords take the symbols defined by their code alphabet. For a binary encoder, the codeword takes the symbols (0, 1); for a ternary code, it is (0, 1, 2); for quaternary, it is (0, 1, 2, 3) and so on.

Bandwidth is a very scarce resource in any of the communication systems. Thus, it is always required to represent the data with minimum number of bits. Hence, the source encoding also has to assure a better compression. Source encoding is, therefore, a process of assigning a minimal-length digital sequence to each of the information symbols emitted by the source. The codewords can be of either fixed or variable length. In fixed-length coding, all symbols are assigned the codewords of the same length. However, in variable-length coding, the length of the codewords is different for different symbols. It is advantageous in comparison to fixed-length coding as we can assign a shorter codeword for the symbols that are more likely to occur compared to the rarely occurring symbols. Thus, a better compression can be achieved in such codes.

Compression algorithms are broadly classified as either lossy or lossless depending upon the applications. Some applications such as video conferencing and personal communication can tolerate certain degree of loss in the information, in which case, a higher compression ratio can be achieved, however, at the cost of degradation of the reliability of the system. Lossy compression algorithms are used for such applications. On the contrary, applications such as military or medical information systems demand utmost reliability. Thus, the compression has to be lossless and is bounded by an upper limit given by the average information content of the system (which will be detailed in the upcoming sections).

3.2 Types of Codes

Most of the codes realized in real time are variable-length codes. In this section, we will define the types of codes.

3.2.1 Block Codes

In this type, each symbol will be mapped onto a block of code symbols defined in the code alphabet. The block codes can be of either fixed or variable length. For example:

00	1
01	01
10	110
11	111

3.2.2 Non-Singular Codes

A block code is said to be non-singular if all its codewords are distinct. For example:

00	11
01	10
10	11
11	001
Non-Singular	Singular

3.2.3 Uniquely Decodable Codes

A block code is said to be uniquely decodable if its *n*th extension is also non-singular for all finite values of '*n*'. For example:

00	0
01	10
10	110
11	111

3.2.4 Instantaneous Codes

A uniquely decodable code is said to be an instantaneous code if the end of any codeword can be determined without the interpretation of the succeeding symbol. They are also called prefix codes.

3.2.5 Optimal Codes

Instantaneous codes are called optimal codes if the lengths of the codewords assigned to the symbols are of minimum length.

3.3 Prefix Codes

In Section 3.2.4, we defined instantaneous codes in which one can properly decode the information without any ambiguity or the need for additional information. Let us now define the necessary and sufficient condition for a code to be an instantaneous code.

Table 3.1 | Codewords for four symbols of a source

Symbol	*Codeword*
A	0
B	01
C	11
D	10

To make the things clearer, consider the following scenario: Consider a source emitting four symbols viz. A, B, C and D. Let the codewords assigned to them by a source encoder be as shown in Table 3.1.

Let the transmitted information be 'ABCAD' and, hence, the corresponding codeword transmitted is '00111010'. The receiver keeps decoding the information after receiving the bitstream. As soon as the first bit '0' is received, the receiver decodes it as 'A' because '0' is a valid codeword for 'A'. The next bit received is also '0'. Although the transmitted codeword was '01' corresponding to symbol 'B', the receiver incorrectly decodes it as 'A' because '0' itself is a valid codeword. Next bit that it receives is '1' that is not a valid codeword and, hence, it accepts the next bit getting '11' which is a valid codeword and, hence, it decodes it as 'C'. Similarly, the decoding process is done for the remaining bits also. Thus, the information decoded by the receiver will be 'AACDD', which is not the same as that of the transmitted information. Thus, the codewords assigned for the symbols in Table 3.1 are not instantaneous.

The problem with the decoding in the previous scenario is that the codeword for B has started with symbol '0' that itself is a valid codeword. Thus, the receiver has incorrectly decoded the information as soon as the first symbol of the second codeword is received. From the above scenario, we can conclude that the decoding would be unsuccessful if any of the codewords start with any of the valid codewords of the system. In other words, the necessary and sufficient condition for an instantaneous code is that *no codeword should be a prefix of any other codeword*. Thus, they are also called *prefix codes*.

All prefix codes satisfy the following property:

$$\sum_{k=1}^{N} r^{-lk} \leq 1 \tag{3.1}$$

where 'r' is nothing but the number of symbols in code alphabet, that is $r = 2$ for binary, 3 for ternary, 4 for quaternary and so on.

The inequality represented in Eq. (3.1) is called *Kraft–McMillan inequality*. If the Kraft–McMillan inequality is not satisfied, we cannot construct a prefix code for the given set of codeword lengths. However, the satisfaction of the inequality does not imply that the corresponding codewords are prefix. In other words, *all prefix codes satisfy Kraft–McMillan inequality, but all codes satisfying Kraft–McMillan inequality need not be prefix.*

EXAMPLE 3.1

Table 3.2 gives different codes for a set of five symbols. Determine which of the following codes are prefix codes. Also draw the decision diagram for the prefix codes.

Table 3.2 | Set of codes

Code A	*Code B*	*Code C*	*Code D*
0	1	00	10
10	01	110	111
110	111	1110	110
1110	10	001	01
111	00	011	00

Solution:

Code A: It is not a prefix code as the codeword '111' is a prefix of the codeword '1110'.
Code B: It is not a prefix code as the codeword '1' is a prefix of the codewords '111' and '10'.
Code C: It is not a prefix code as the codeword '00' is a prefix of the codeword '001'.
Code D: It is a prefix code as no codeword is a prefix of other codewords.

Decision tree for the prefix code is shown in Fig. 3.1.

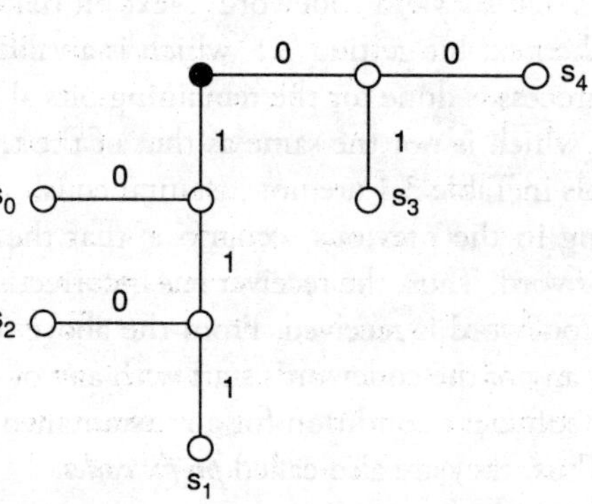

Figure 3.1 | Decision tree for the code D.

EXAMPLE 3.2

Which of the sets of length requirements shown in Table 3.3 can be considered for the construction of the binary prefix codes?

Table 3.3 | Requirement for a code construction

Code P	*Code Q*	*Code R*	*Word Length*
1	2	1	1
1	1	1	2
2	2	1	3
2	1	2	4

Solution: Any set of lengths of the codewords that satisfies the Kraft–McMillan inequality can be considered for the construction of the prefix codes.

Code P: Here, we require to construct one codeword of length 1, one codeword of length of 2, two codewords of length 3 and two codewords of length 4.

We can now check whether the *Kraft–McMillan inequality* is satisfied for the given requirement. Thus, applying these required lengths in Eq. (3.1).

$$\sum_{k=1}^{N} r^{-lk} \leq 1$$

As the required codes are binary, we have

$$\sum_{k=1}^{N} 2^{-lk} \leq 1$$

Substituting the given set of l_k in the above relation, we have

$$\sum_{k=1}^{N} 2^{-lk} = (1\times 2^{-1}) + (1\times 2^{-2}) + (2\times 2^{-3}) + (2\times 2^{-4}) = \frac{9}{8} > 1$$

Therefore, the condition is not satisfied. Thus, we cannot construct a binary prefix code for the given requirement for code P.

Code Q: Similarly, considering the given requirement for the codeword lengths of code Q in Eq. 3.1,

$$\sum_{k=1}^{N} 2^{-lk} = (2\times 2^{-1}) + (1\times 2^{-2}) + (2\times 2^{-3}) + (1\times 2^{-4}) = \frac{25}{16} > 1$$

Therefore, the condition is not satisfied. Thus, we cannot construct a binary prefix code for the given requirement for code Q.

Code R: Also for code R, checking for the Kraft–McMillan inequality, we will have:

$$\sum_{k=1}^{N} 2^{-lk} = (1\times 2^{-1}) + (1\times 2^{-2}) + (1\times 2^{-3}) + (2\times 2^{-4}) = 1 = 1$$

Therefore, the condition is satisfied. Thus, we can construct a binary prefix code for the given requirement for code R. Two such sets of codewords are as follows:

1	0
01	10
001	110
0000	1110

EXAMPLE 3.3

Find the smallest value of '*r*' such that prefix codes can be constructed for the following code-length requirements: $W = (1, 4, 4, 4, 5)$ for the corresponding $L = (1, 2, 3, 4, 5)$.

Solution: From the problem, we require the following code lengths:

'1' codeword of length '1'
'4' codewords of length '2'
'4' codewords of length '3'
'4' codewords of length '4'
'5' codewords of length '5'

We need to now find the minimum value of '*r*' in order to have the fulfillment for Kraft–McMillan inequality given by

$$\sum_{k=1}^{N} r^{-lk} \leq 1$$

$$\Rightarrow \sum_{k=1}^{N} r^{-lk} = (1\times r^{-1}) + (4\times r^{-2}) + (4\times r^{-3}) + (4\times r^{-4}) + (5\times r^{-5}) \leq 1$$

Now to find the minimum value of '*r*' in order to satisfy the above relation, we need to go for trial-and-error method, which is as follows:

Let $r = 2$. Then

$$\sum_{k=1}^{N} r^{-lk} = (1\times 2^{-1}) + (4\times 2^{-2}) + (4\times 2^{-3}) + (4\times 2^{-4}) + (5\times 2^{-5}) = 2.4 > 1$$

Therefore, r cannot be 2.

Consider $r = 3$. We get

$$\sum_{k=1}^{N} r^{-lk} = (1\times 3^{-1}) + (4\times 3^{-2}) + (4\times 3^{-3}) + (4\times 3^{-4}) + (5\times 3^{-5}) = 0.095 < 1$$

Therefore, $r = 3$ can be acceptable for the construction of the prefix code for the given requirements. The code alphabet, therefore, consists of (0, 1, 2).

One possible prefix code for the required lengths considering $r = 3$ is as follows:

0
10
11
12
20
210
211
212
220
2210
2211
2212
2220
22210

22211
22212
22220
22221

3.4 Source Coding Theorem

Consider an information source as shown in Fig. 3.2. Let s_i be the symbols emitted from the source. The output of the source is given to the source encoder whose output is the coded information b_i.

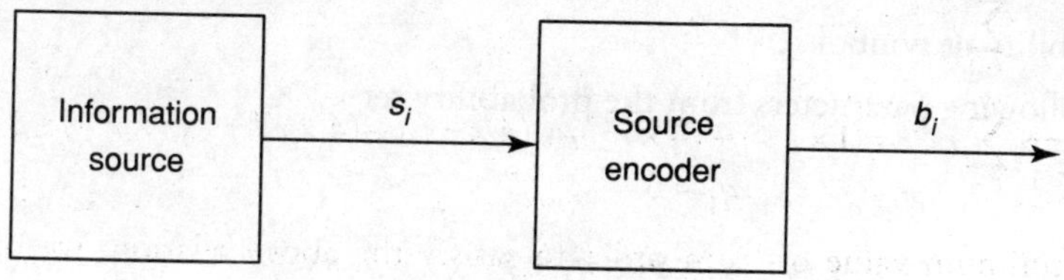

Figure 3.2 | Information system.

Let l_i be the length of the codeword for the ith symbol s_i emitted by the source. The average codeword length L is given by

$$L = \sum_{i=1}^{N} p_i l_i \tag{3.2}$$

The efficiency of the source encoder is given by the ratio of minimum average length to that of average codeword length:

$$\eta_S = \frac{L_{\min}}{L} \times 100\% \tag{3.3}$$

As entropy gives the average information conveyed by the source; no symbol emitted from the source can be represented with lesser bits than that of its entropy. Thus, we have

$$L \geq H(S) \tag{3.4}$$

$$\Rightarrow L_{\min} = H(S)$$

Thus, we require at least $H(S)$ number of bits to represent any of the symbols emitted by the source in order to have lossless communication. Therefore,

Substituting $L_{\min}$ in Eq. (3.3), we get

$$\eta_S = \frac{H(S)}{L} \times 100\% \tag{3.5}$$

The redundancy of the source is given by

$$R_{\eta S} = 1 - \eta_S \tag{3.6}$$

3.5 Shannon's First Encoding Theorem

Shannon has proposed one of the first algorithms on source encoding. The encoding procedure is as follows:

Step 1: Given the source alphabet S and the corresponding probabilities P for a given information source.

Step 2: Arrange the probabilities in the non-increasing order.

Step 3: Compute the length l_i for the codeword corresponding to each symbol s_i given by

$$l_i \geq \log_2 \frac{1}{p_i}$$

where p_i is the probability of symbol s_i.

Step 4: Define the following parameters from the probability set

$$q_1 = 0$$

$$q_2 = p_1 = q_1 + p_1$$

$$q_3 = p_1 + p_2 = q_2 + p_2$$

$$q_4 = p_1 + p_2 + p_3 = q_3 + p_3$$

$$\ldots$$

$$\ldots$$

$$\ldots$$

$$q_{N+1} = 1$$

where N is the total number of symbols in the source alphabet.

Step 5: Expand q_i in binary till l_i number of places after decimal point.

Step 6: The numbers after decimal places in the binary representation of q_i are the codewords for the corresponding symbol s_i.

EXAMPLE 3.4

Consider a source with source alphabet S = (A, B, C, D) with the corresponding probabilities P = (0.1, 0.2, 0.3, 0.4). Find the codewords for symbols using Shannon's algorithm. Also find the source efficiency and redundancy.

Solution:

Step 1: Arrange the probabilities in the non-increasing order and the corresponding symbols we get

$$P = (0.4, 0.3, 0.2, 0.1) \quad S = (\text{D, C, B, A})$$

Step 2: Find the minimum value of l_i such that

$$l_i \geq \log_2 \frac{1}{p_i}$$

$$l_1 \geq \log_2 \frac{1}{p_1} = \log_2 \frac{1}{0.4} \Rightarrow l_1 = 2$$

$$l_2 \geq \log_2 \frac{1}{p_2} = \log_2 \frac{1}{0.3} \Rightarrow l_2 = 2$$

$$l_3 \geq \log_2 \frac{1}{p_3} = \log_2 \frac{1}{0.2} \Rightarrow l_3 = 3$$

$$l_4 \geq \log_2 \frac{1}{p_4} = \log_2 \frac{1}{0.1} \Rightarrow l_4 = 4$$

Step 3: Calculate the parameters q_i.

$$q_1 = 0$$

$$q_2 = p_1 = 0.4$$

$$q_3 = p_1 + p_2 = 0.7$$

$$q_4 = p_1 + p_2 + p_3 = 0.9$$

$$q_5 = p_1 + p_2 + p_3 + p_4 = 1$$

Step 4: Represent q_1, q_2, q_3 and q_4 in binary up to l_i places after decimal points

$$q_1 = (0.0)_{10} = (0.00)_2$$

$$q_2 = (0.4)_{10} = (0.01)_2$$

$$q_3 = (0.7)_{10} = (0.101)_2$$

$$q_4 = (0.9)_{10} = (0.1110)_2$$

The codewords for the symbols using Shannon's algorithm are presented in Table 3.4.

Table 3.4 | Codewords using Shannon's algorithm

Symbol	*Probability (p_i)*	*Codeword*	*Length (l_i)*
D	0.4	00	2
C	0.3	01	2
B	0.2	101	3
A	0.1	1110	4

Step 5: To find the efficiency, we have

$$\eta_S = \frac{H(S)}{L} \times 100\%$$

where $$H(S) = \sum_{k=1}^{N} p_k \log_2 \frac{1}{p_k} = 1.8464 \text{ bits/sym}$$

and $$L = \sum_{i=1}^{N} p_i l_i = (0.4 \times 2) + (0.3 \times 2) + (0.2 \times 3) + (0.1 \times 4) = 2.4 \text{ bits/sym}$$

Therefore,

$$\eta_c = \frac{1.8464}{2.4} \times 100\% = 76.93\%$$
$$R_{\eta S} = 1 - \eta_S = 23.07\%$$

EXAMPLE 3.5

Consider a discrete memoryless source with S = (X, Y, Z) with the corresponding probabilities P = (0.5, 0.3, 0.2).

(a) Find the codewords for the symbols using Shannon's algorithm. Also find the source efficiency and redundancy.

(b) Consider the second-order extension of the source. Recompute the codewords and the efficiency.

Solution:

(a) Consider the following steps.

Step 1: Arrange the probabilities in the non-increasing order and the corresponding symbols;

$$P = (0.5, 0.3, 0.2) \quad S = (\text{X, Y, Z})$$

Step 2: Find the minimum value of l_i such that,

$$l_i \geq \log_2 \frac{1}{p_i}$$
$$l_1 \geq \log_2 \frac{1}{p_1} = \log_2 \frac{1}{0.5} \Rightarrow l_1 = 1$$
$$l_2 \geq \log_2 \frac{1}{p_2} = \log_2 \frac{1}{0.3} \Rightarrow l_2 = 2$$
$$l_3 \geq \log_2 \frac{1}{p_3} = \log_2 \frac{1}{0.2} \Rightarrow l_3 = 3$$

Step 3: Calculate the parameters q_i.

$$q_1 = 0$$
$$q_2 = p_1 = 0.5$$
$$q_3 = p_1 + p_2 = 0.8$$
$$q_4 = p_1 + p_2 + p_3 = 1$$

Step 4: Represent q_1, q_2 and q_3 in binary up to l_i places after decimal points:

$$q_1 = (0.0)_{10} = (0.0)_2$$
$$q_2 = (0.5)_{10} = (0.10)_2$$
$$q_3 = (0.8)_{10} = (0.110)_2$$

Step 5: The codewords are shown in Table 3.5.

Table 3.5 | Codewords using Shannon's algorithm

Symbol	*Probability* (p_i)	*Codeword*	*Length* (l_i)
X	0.5	0	1
Y	0.3	10	2
Z	0.2	110	3

To find the efficiency, we have

$$\eta_S = \frac{H(S)}{L} \times 100\%$$

where
$$H(S) = \sum_{k=1}^{N} p_k \log_2 \frac{1}{p_k} = 1.4854 \text{ bits/sym}$$

and
$$L = \sum_{i=1}^{N} p_i l_i = (0.5 \times 1) + (0.3 \times 2) + (0.2 \times 3) = 1.7 \text{ bits/sym}$$

Therefore,

$$\eta_S = \frac{1.4854}{1.7} \times 100\% = 87.37\%$$

$$R_{\eta S} = 1 - \eta_S = 12.63\%$$

(b) For the second-order extension, we need to find all symbols emitted by the second-order extension of the source and the corresponding probabilities. It is detailed in Table 3.6.

Table 3.6 | Symbols and probabilities for the second-order extension

Symbol	*Probability*
XX	0.25
XY	0.15
XZ	0.10
YX	0.15
YY	0.09
YZ	0.06
ZX	0.10
ZY	0.06
ZZ	0.04

Step 1: Arrange the probabilities in the non-increasing order and the corresponding symbols

$P = (0.25, 0.15, 0.15, 0.10, 0.10, 0.09, 0.06, 0.06, 0.04)$
$S = (XX, XY, YX, XZ, ZX, YY, YZ, ZY, ZZ)$

Step 2: Find the minimum value of l_i such that

$$l_i \geq \log_2 \frac{1}{p_i}$$

$$l_1 \geq \log_2 \frac{1}{p_1} = \log_2 \frac{1}{0.25} \Rightarrow l_1 = 2$$

$$l_2 \geq \log_2 \frac{1}{p_2} = \log_2 \frac{1}{0.15} \Rightarrow l_2 = 3$$

$$l_3 \geq \log_2 \frac{1}{p_3} = \log_2 \frac{1}{0.15} \Rightarrow l_3 = 3$$

$$l_4 \geq \log_2 \frac{1}{p_4} = \log_2 \frac{1}{0.10} \Rightarrow l_4 = 4$$

$$l_5 \geq \log_2 \frac{1}{p_5} = \log_2 \frac{1}{0.10} \Rightarrow l_5 = 4$$

$$l_6 \geq \log_2 \frac{1}{p_6} = \log_2 \frac{1}{0.09} \Rightarrow l_6 = 4$$

$$l_7 \geq \log_2 \frac{1}{p_7} = \log_2 \frac{1}{0.06} \Rightarrow l_7 = 5$$

$$l_8 \geq \log_2 \frac{1}{p_8} = \log_2 \frac{1}{0.06} \Rightarrow l_8 = 5$$

$$l_9 \geq \log_2 \frac{1}{p_9} = \log_2 \frac{1}{0.04} \Rightarrow l_9 = 5$$

Step 3: Finding the parameters q_i.

$$q_1 = 0$$
$$q_2 = 0.25$$
$$q_3 = 0.40$$
$$q_4 = 0.55$$
$$q_5 = 0.65$$
$$q_6 = 0.75$$
$$q_7 = 0.84$$
$$q_8 = 0.90$$
$$q_9 = 0.96$$
$$q_{10} = 1$$

Step 4: Represent q_i in binary up to l_i places after decimal points:

$$q_1 = (0.0)_{10} = (0.00)_2$$
$$q_2 = (0.25)_{10} = (0.010)_2$$
$$q_3 = (0.40)_{10} = (0.011)_2$$
$$q_4 = (0.55)_{10} = (0.1000)_2$$
$$q_5 = (0.65)_{10} = (0.1010)_2$$
$$q_6 = (0.75)_{10} = (0.1100)_2$$
$$q_7 = (0.84)_{10} = (0.11010)_2$$
$$q_8 = (0.90)_{10} = (0.11100)_2$$
$$q_9 = (0.96)_{10} = (0.11110)_2$$

Step 5: The codewords for the second-order extension of the source are shown in Table 3.7.

Table 3.7 | Codewords using Shannon's algorithm

Symbol	*Probability (p_i)*	*Codeword*	*Length (l_i)*
XX	0.25	00	2
XY	0.15	010	3
YX	0.15	011	3
XZ	0.10	1000	4
ZX	0.10	1010	4
YY	0.09	1100	4
YZ	0.06	11010	5
ZY	0.06	11100	5
ZZ	0.04	11110	5

To find the efficiency, we have

$$\eta_S = \frac{H(S)}{L} \times 100\%$$

where $$H(S^2) = \sum_{k=1}^{N} p_k \log_2 \frac{1}{p_k} = 2.9709 \text{ bits/sym} = 2 \times H(S)$$

and $$L = \sum_{i=1}^{N} p_i l_i = 3.36 \text{ bits/sym}$$

Therefore,

$$\eta_S = \frac{2.9709}{3.36} \times 100\% = 88.41\%$$

$$R_{\eta S} = 1 - \eta_S = 11.59\%$$

EXAMPLE 3.6

Consider the following source

$$S = (A, B, C, D, E)$$

$$P = (0.5, 0.25, 0.125, 0.0625, 0.0625).$$

Find the codewords for the symbols using Shannon's algorithm. Also find the source efficiency and redundancy.

Solution:

Step 1: Arrange the probabilities in the non-increasing order and the corresponding symbols

$$P = (0.5, 0.25, 0.125, 0.0625, 0.0625)$$

$$S = (A, B, C, D, E)$$

Step 2: Find the minimum value of l_i such that

$$l_i \geq \log_2 \frac{1}{p_i}$$

$$l_1 \geq \log_2 \frac{1}{p_1} = \log_2 \frac{1}{0.5} \Rightarrow l_1 = 1$$

$$l_2 \geq \log_2 \frac{1}{p_2} = \log_2 \frac{1}{0.25} \Rightarrow l_2 = 2$$

$$l_3 \geq \log_2 \frac{1}{p_3} = \log_2 \frac{1}{0.125} \Rightarrow l_3 = 3$$

$$l_4 \geq \log_2 \frac{1}{p_4} = \log_2 \frac{1}{0.0625} \Rightarrow l_4 = 4$$

$$l_5 \geq \log_2 \frac{1}{p_5} = \log_2 \frac{1}{0.0625} \Rightarrow l_5 = 4$$

Step 3: Finding the parameters q_i as follows:

$$q_1 = 0$$

$$q_2 = 0.5$$

$$q_3 = 0.75$$

$$q_4 = 0.875$$

$$q_5 = 0.9375$$

$$q_6 = 1$$

Step 4: Represent q_i in binary up to l_i places after decimal points

$$q_1 = (0.0)_{10} = (0.0)_2$$

$$q_2 = (0.5)_{10} = (0.10)_2$$

$$q_3 = (0.75)_{10} = (0.110)_2$$
$$q_4 = (0.875)_{10} = (0.1110)_2$$
$$q_5 = (0.9375)_{10} = (0.1111)_2$$

Step 5: The list of codewords is shown in Table 3.8.

Table 3.8 Codewords using Shannon's algorithm

Symbol	*Probability* (p_i)	*Codeword*	*Length* (l_i)
A	0.5	0	1
B	0.25	10	2
C	0.125	110	3
D	0.0625	1110	4
E	0.0625	1111	4

To find the efficiency, we have

$$\eta_S = \frac{H(S)}{L} \times 100\%$$

where

$$H(S) = \sum_{k=1}^{N} p_k \log_2 \frac{1}{p_k} = 1.875 \text{ bits/sym}$$

and

$$L = \sum_{i=1}^{N} p_i l_i = 1.875 \text{ bits/sym}$$

Therefore,

$$\eta_S = \frac{1.875}{1.875} \times 100\% = 100\%$$
$$R_{\eta S} = 1 - \eta_S = 0\%$$

An efficiency of 100% is achieved in this system as the probabilities are of negative powers of 2.

3.6 Shannon–Fano Encoding Algorithm

This is an improvement over Shannon's first algorithm on source coding in the sense that it offers better coding efficiency compared to Shannon's algorithm.

The algorithm is as follows:

Step 1: Arrange the probabilities in the non-increasing order.

Step 2: Group the probabilities into exactly two sets such that the sum of probabilities in both the groups is almost equal. Assign bit '0' to all elements of the first group and bit '1' to all elements of group 2.

Step 3: Repeat step 2 by dividing each group in two subgroups till no further division is possible.

EXAMPLE 3.7

Consider the following source:

$$S = (A, B, C, D, E, F)$$

$$P = (0.10, 0.15, 0.25, 0.35, 0.08, 0.07).$$

Find the codewords for the source using Shannon–Fano algorithm. Also find the source efficiency and redundancy.

Solution:

Step 1: Arrange the given probabilities in the non-increasing order. Let us divide the probabilities into two almost equiprobable groups. The best way of doing so is to group probabilities 0.35 and 0.25 as one group whose sum is 0.6 and the rest of the probabilities as another group with the sum being 0.4. Assign bit '0' to all the elements of the first group and '1' to those of the second group.

Now divide the groups of the first stage into exactly two almost equiprobable subgroups each and assign '0' to the first subgroup and '1' for the second subgroup of each group. Repeat this process till no further division is possible.

0.35	0	0.35	0				
0.25	0	0.25	1				
0.15	1	0.15	0				
0.10	1	0.10	1	0.10	0		
0.08	1	0.08	1	0.08	1	0.08	0
0.07	1	0.07	1	0.07	1	0.07	1

Step 2: The codewords obtained using Shannon–Fano algorithm are presented in Table 3.9.

Table 3.9 | Codewords using Shannon–Fano algorithm

Symbol	*Probability* (p_i)	*Codeword*	*Length* (l_i)
A	0.35	00	2
B	0.25	01	2
C	0.15	10	2
D	0.10	110	3
E	0.08	1110	4
F	0.07	1111	4

To find the efficiency, we have

$$\eta_S = \frac{H(S)}{L} \times 100\%$$

$$\text{where} \quad H(S) = \sum_{k=1}^{N} p_k \log_2 \frac{1}{p_k} = 2.33 \text{ bits/sym}$$

$$L = \sum_{i=1}^{N} p_i l_i = (0.35 \times 2) + (0.25 \times 2) + (0.15 \times 2) + (0.10 \times 3) + (0.08 \times 4) + (0.07 \times 4)$$

$$= 2.4 \text{ bites/sym}$$

Therefore,

$$\eta_S = \frac{2.33}{2.4} \times 100\% = 97.08\%$$

$$R_{\eta S} = 1 - \eta_S = 2.92\%$$

EXAMPLE 3.8

Consider the following source:

$$S = (\text{A, B, C, D, E, F})$$

$$P = (0.4, 0.2, 0.2, 0.1, 0.08, 0.02)$$

Find the codewords by using Shannon–Fano algorithm. Also find the source efficiency and redundancy.

Solution:

Step 1: The probabilities have to be first arranged in the non-increasing order. Then the grouping of the set into two almost equal probabilities is done till no further division is possible. Numbers '0' and '1' are assigned to the first and second groups, respectively, in each stage. The process is detailed as follows:

0.40	0	0.40	0				
0.20	0	0.20	1				
0.20	1	0.20	0				
0.10	1	0.10	1	0.10	0		
0.08	1	0.08	1	0.08	1	0.08	0
0.02	1	0.02	1	0.02	1	0.02	1

Step 2: The codewords thus obtained are presented in Table 3.10.

Table 3.10 | Codewords using Shannon–Fano algorithm

Symbol	*Probability (p_i)*	*Codeword*	*Length (l_i)*
A	0.40	00	2
B	0.20	01	2
C	0.20	10	2
D	0.10	110	3
E	0.08	1110	4
F	0.02	1111	4

To find the efficiency, we have

$$\eta_S = \frac{H(S)}{L} \times 100\%$$

where

$$H(S) = \sum_{k=1}^{N} p_k \log_2 \frac{1}{p_k} = 2.194 \text{ bits/sym}$$

and

$$L = (0.4 \times 2) + (0.2 \times 2) + (0.2 \times 2) + (0.1 \times 3) + (0.08 \times 4) + (0.02 \times 4) = 2.3 \text{ bits/sym}$$

Therefore,

$$\eta_S = \frac{2.194}{2.3} \times 100\% = 95.39\%$$

$$R_{\eta_S} = 1 - \eta_S = 4.61\%$$

3.7 Huffman Code (Compact Codes)

Huffman codes achieve the minimum codeword lengths amongst all other coding algorithms. Hence, they are also called compact codes. Huffman codes are computationally simpler and are widely used in the modern communication system.

The algorithm for encoding the information into an '*r*-ary' codeword is detailed as follows:

Step 1: Compute the number of stages required for the encoding operation, which is given by

$$n = \frac{N - r}{r - 1}$$

where N is the total number of symbols in the source alphabet.

Step 2: The value of '*n*' has to be an integer. If not, append minimum number of dummy symbols with zero probability so as to get '*n*' as an integer value. However, '*n*' will always take an integer value for binary encoding as the denominator in the expression of '*n*' is always 1 ($r - 1 = 2 - 1 = 1$ for binary).

Step 3: Arrange the probabilities in the descending order.

Step 4: Combine the last '*r*' probabilities in the set by summing up as a single probability and place, the sum at the appropriate position in the set by reordering it. Now the set contains '*r* – 1' elements less than the previous stage.

Step 5: Continue step 4 till we reach the position where we have only '*r*' elements. Assign the symbols '0', '1', …, '*r* – 1' to those elements.

Step 6: Traverse back by one stage. Find the '*r*' probabilities in the stage whose sum is placed in the succeeding stage. Assign the codeword assigned to the sum as the prefix for all probabilities. To differentiate, again assign '0','1', …, '*r* – 1' to those probabilities in front of their prefix.

Step 7: Repeat step 6 till first stage is reached.

EXAMPLE 3.9

An information source produces a sequence of independent symbols having the following probabilities:

A	B	C	D	E	F	G
1/3	1/27	1/3	1/9	1/9	1/27	1/27

Construct binary and ternary code using Huffman encoding procedure and find its efficiency.

Solution:

(a) Binary coding

Step 1: Firstly, find the value of n.

$$n = \frac{N-r}{r-1} = \frac{7-2}{2-1} = 5$$

As n is an integer, there is no need of adding any dummy symbols.

Step 2: The complete encoding procedure is presented in Table 3.11.

Table 3.11 | Encoding procedure using Huffman coding

Symbol	*Probability*		*Stage 1*		*Stage 2*		*Stage 3*		*Stage 4*		*Stage 5*	
A	1/3	1	1/3	1	1/3	1	1/3	1	1/3	1	**2/3**	0
B	1/3	00	1/3	00	1/3	00	1/3	00	1/3	00	1/3	1
C	1/9	011	1/9	011	1/9	011	**2/9**	010	**1/3**	01		
D	1/9	0100	1/9	0100	1/9	0100	1/9	011				
E	1/27	01011	**2/27**	01010	**1/9**	0101						
F	1/27	010100	1/27	01011								
G	1/27	010101										

The bold numbers indicate the position of the sum in the respective stages.

Step 3: The final codewords of the symbols using Huffman coding are shown in Table 3.12.

Table 3.12 | Codewords using Huffman algorithm

Symbol	*Probability (p_i)*	*Code*	*Length (l_i)*
A	1/3	1	1
B	1/3	00	2
C	1/9	011	3
D	1/9	0100	4
E	1/27	01011	5
F	1/27	010100	6
G	1/27	010101	6

Step 4: To find the efficiency, we have

$$\eta_S = \frac{H(S)}{L} \times 100\%$$

where
$$H(S) = \sum_{k=1}^{N} p_k \log_2 \frac{1}{p_k} = 1.9371 \text{ bits/sym}$$

and
$$L = \sum_{i=1}^{N} p_i l_i = 2.4074 \text{ bits/sym}$$

Therefore,

$$\eta_S = \frac{1.9371}{2.4074} \times 100\% = 80.46\%$$

$$R_{\eta S} = 1 - \eta_S = 19.54\%$$

(b) Ternary coding

Step 1:

$$n = \frac{N-r}{r-1} = \frac{7-3}{3-1} = 2$$

which is an integer. Hence, no need to add any dummy symbols.

Step 2: The complete process of encoding is given in Table 3.13.

Table 3.13 | Encoding procedure using Huffman coding

Symbol	*Probability*		*Stage 1*		*Stage 2*	
A	1/3	0	1/3	0	1/3	0
B	1/3	1	1/3	1	1/3	1
C	1/9	20	1/9	20	**1/3**	2
D	1/9	21	1/9	21		
E	1/27	220	**1/9**	22		
F	1/27	221				
G	1/27	222				

The bold numbers indicate the position of the sum in the respective stages.

Step 3: The codewords of the symbols are given in Table 3.14.

Table 3.14 | Codewords using Huffman algorithm

Symbol	*Probability* (p_i)	*Code*	*Length* (l_i)
A	1/3	0	1
B	1/3	1	1
C	1/9	20	2
D	1/9	21	2
E	1/27	220	3
F	1/27	221	3
G	1/27	222	3

Step 4: To find the efficiency, we have

$$\eta_S = \frac{H(S)}{L} \times 100\%$$

where
$$H(S) = \sum_{k=1}^{N} p_k \log_3 \frac{1}{p_k} = 1.444 \text{ trinits/sym}$$

and
$$L = \sum_{i=1}^{N} p_i l_i = 1.444 \text{ trinits/sym}$$

Therefore,

$$\eta_S = \frac{1.444}{1.444} \times 100\% = 100\%$$

$$R_{\eta S} = 1 - \eta_S = 0\%$$

EXAMPLE 3.10

Construct a quaternary Huffman code for the following set of message symbols with the respective probabilities

A	B	C	D	E	F	G	H
0.22	0.20	0.18	0.15	0.10	0.08	0.05	0.02

Solution:

Step 1:

$$n = \frac{N-r}{r-1} = \frac{8-4}{4-1} = \frac{4}{3}$$

which is not an integer. The next minimum value for 'N' to have an integer value for 'n' is $N = 10$. Therefore, add two dummy symbols with 0 probabilities for which n becomes

$$n = \frac{N-r}{r-1} = \frac{10-4}{4-1} = 2$$

Step 2: The encoding process is shown in Table 3.15.

Table 3.15 | Encoding using Huffman algorithm

Symbol	*Probability*		*Stage 1*		*Stage 2*	
A	0.22	1	0.22	1	**0.40**	0
B	0.20	2	0.20	2	0.22	1
C	0.18	3	0.18	3	0.20	2
D	0.15	00	0.15	00	0.18	3
E	0.10	01	0.10	01		
F	0.08	02	0.08	02		
G	0.05	030	**0.07**	03		
H	0.02	031				
D_1	0	032				
D_2	0	033				

The bold numbers indicate the position of the sum in the respective stages.

Step 3: The codewords are given in Table 3.16.

Table 3.16 | Codewords using Huffman algorithm

Symbol	*Probability (p_i)*	*Code*	*Length (l_i)*
A	0.22	1	1
B	0.20	2	1
C	0.18	3	1
D	0.15	00	2
E	0.10	01	2
F	0.08	02	2
G	0.05	030	3
H	0.02	031	3

Step 4: To find the efficiency, we have

$$\eta_S = \frac{H(S)}{L} \times 100\%$$

where

$$H(S) = \sum_{k=1}^{N} p_k \log_4 \frac{1}{p_k} = 1.37675 \text{ quaternary digits/sym}$$

and

$$L = \sum_{i=1}^{N} p_i l_i = 1.47 \text{ quaternary digits/sym}$$

Therefore,

$$\eta_S = \frac{1.37675}{1.47} \times 100\% = 93.66\%$$

$$R_{\eta S} = 1 - \eta_S = 6.34\%$$

3.8 Extended Huffman Coding

The Huffman coding that is presented in the previous section offers a better coding efficiency compared to other coding techniques. However, it fails to achieve a good efficiency under certain circumstances. In order to make this point clearer, consider the following scenario.

Consider a source with three symbols S = (A, B, C) with respective probabilities P = (0.8, 0.15, 0.05). Using normal Huffman coding, the codewords can be constructed as shown in Table 3.17.

Table 3.17 | Codewords using Huffman algorithm

Symbol	*Probability* (p_i)	*Code*	*Length* (l_i)
A	0.8	0	1
B	0.15	10	2
C	0.05	11	2

The average codeword length is given by

$$L = 1.2 \text{ bits/sym}$$

But the entropy of the source is $H(S)$ = 0.88 bits/sym and the efficiency is given by 73.33%. Although, this efficiency is good as compared to other coding techniques, it could still be improved if we consider coding the symbols considering 'm' symbols at a time. More is the value of 'm', better will be the efficiency. This can be showed by considering the second extension of the source as considered above. There will be nine combinations and the corresponding probabilities are as follows:

AA	0.64	BC	0.0075
AB	0.12	CA	0.04
AC	0.04	CB	0.0075
BA	0.12	CC	0.0025
BB	0.0225		

The corresponding codewords after applying Huffman algorithm are as shown in Table 3.18.

The average codeword length for this case is L = 1.8675 bits/2-symbols. Thus, number of bits required for encoding each symbol is L = 0.93375 bits/sym. The entropy is $H(S^2)$ = 1.76 bits/ sym. Thus, the efficiency is improved to 94.24%, which is an improvement over the earlier case. Thus, the symbols can be represented

Table 3.18 | Codewords using Huffman algorithm

Symbol	*Probability* (p_i)	*Code*	*Length* (l_i)
AA	0.64	0	1
AB	0.12	100	3
BA	0.12	101	3
AC	0.04	1100	4
CA	0.04	1101	4
BB	0.0225	1110	4
BC	0.0075	11111	5
CB	0.0075	111100	6
CC	0.0025	111101	6

using lesser number of bits using Huffman coding if we consider a group of symbols at a time for encoding. This process of encoding '*m*' symbols at a time is known as *extended Huffman coding.*

EXAMPLE 3.11

Consider a discrete memoryless source with $S = (X, Y, Z)$ with the state probabilities $P = (0.7, 0.15, 0.15)$ for its output.

(a) Apply Huffman encoding algorithm to find the codewords in binary. Find the source efficiency and redundancy.

(b) Consider the second-order extension of the source. Compute the codewords for this extended source and also find its efficiency.

Solution:

(a) Step 1:

$$n = \frac{N-r}{r-1} = \frac{3-2}{2-1} = 1$$

Step 2: The process of encoding is presented in Table 3.19.

Table 3.19 | Encoding procedure using Huffman coding

Symbol	*Probability*		*Stage 1*	
s_0	0.7	0	0.7	0
s_1	0.15	10	**0.3**	1
s_2	0.15	11		

The bold numbers indicate the position of the sum in the respective stages.

Step 3: The final codewords using Huffman algorithm are shown in Table 3.20.

Table 3.20 | Codewords using Huffman algorithm

Symbol	*Probability* (p_i)	*Code*	*Length* (l_i)
s_0	0.7	0	1
s_1	0.15	10	2
s_2	0.15	11	2

Step 4: To find the efficiency, we have

$$\eta_S = \frac{H(S)}{L} \times 100\%$$

where
$$H(S) = \sum_{k=1}^{N} p_k \log_2 \frac{1}{p_k} = 1.18128 \text{ bits/sym}$$

and
$$L = \sum_{i=1}^{N} p_i l_i = 1.3 \text{ bits/sym}$$

Therefore,

$$\eta_S = \frac{1.18128}{1.3} \times 100\% = 90.86\%$$

$$R_{\eta S} = 1 - \eta_S = 9.14\%$$

(b) Now consider the second-order extension of the source. The extension will have nine combinations and the corresponding probabilities are as follows:

s_0s_0	0.49
s_0s_1	0.105
s_0s_2	0.105
s_1s_0	0.105
s_1s_1	0.0225
s_1s_2	0.0225
s_2s_0	0.105
s_2s_1	0.0225
s_2s_2	0.0225

Step 1:

$$n = \frac{N - r}{r - 1} = \frac{9 - 2}{2 - 1} = 7$$

Step 2: The encoding procedure is detailed in Table 3.21.

Table 3.21 | Huffman encoding procedure

Symbol	Probability		Stage 1		Stage 2		Stage 3		Stage 4		Stage 5		Stage 6		Stage 7	
s_0s_0	0.49	1	0.49	1	0.49	1	0.49	1	0.49	1	0.49	1	0.49	1	**0.51**	0
s_0s_1	0.105	001	0.105	001	0.105	001	0.105	001	**0.195**	000	**0.21**	01	**0.30**	00	0.49	1
s_0s_2	0.105	010	0.105	010	0.105	010	0.105	010	0.105	001	0.195	000	0.21	01		
s_1s_0	0.105	011	0.105	011	0.105	011	0.105	011	0.105	010	0.105	001				
s_1s_1	0.105	0000	0.105	0000	0.105	0000	0.105	0000	0.105	011						
s_1s_2	0.0225	000110	**0.045**	00010	0.045	00010	**0.09**	0001								
s_2s_0	0.0225	000111	0.0225	000110	**0.045**	00011										
s_2s_1	0.0225	000100	0.0225	000111												
s_2s_2	0.0225	000101														

The bold numbers indicate the position of the sum in the respective stages.

Step 3: The final codewords using Huffman algorithm are shown in Table 3.22.

Table 3.22 Codewords using Huffman algorithm

Symbol	*Probability* (p_i)	*Code*	*Length* (l_i)
s_0s_0	0.49	1	1
s_0s_1	0.105	001	3
s_0s_2	0.105	010	3
s_1s_0	0.105	011	3
s_1s_1	0.105	0000	4
s_1s_2	0.0225	000110	6
s_2s_0	0.0225	000111	6
s_2s_1	0.0225	000100	6
s_2s_2	0.0225	000101	6

Step 4: To find the efficiency, we have

$$\eta_S = \frac{H(S)}{L} \times 100\%$$

where $H(S^2) = 2 \times H(S) = 2.3624$ bits/sym

and $L = \sum_{i=1}^{N} p_i l_i = 2.395$ bits/sym

Therefore,

$$\eta_S = \frac{2.3624}{2.395} \times 100\% = 98.63\%$$

$$R_{\eta S} = 1 - \eta_S = 1.37\%$$

3.9 Arithmetic Coding

From Section 3.4, we have understood that the average codeword length is lower bounded by the entropy of the source. In other words, entropy is the lowest rate to encode the information. Less is the deviation of average codeword length from entropy, better is its efficiency. Many researches have showed that the maximum deviation of the average codeword length from entropy using Huffman coding is given by the relation (p_{max} + 0.086), where p_{max} is the maximum probability in the source alphabet. Thus, it is evident that for larger source alphabet consisting of many symbols, Huffman codes offer good efficiency because of generally small individual probabilities. However, they fail if the alphabet is small. Although extended Huffman codes discussed in Section 3.8 solve this issue to some extent, it would not be an optimal solution as we require to consider the computation of codewords for all combinations of length '*m*' for every *m*th extension, which is impractical for larger values of '*m*'. Thus, it would be better if we could code a sequence of '*m*' symbols together without actually considering all possible sequences of the same length (unlike we do in extended Huffman coding). Arithmetic coding is one such technique wherein a tag is assigned to each sequence of 'm' symbols. A binary code is then generated for the obtained tag.

In order to assure proper decoding, tag assigned to each set of symbols has to be unique. Generally, a range of [0 1) is considered. Note that '0' is included in the range but not '1'. As there are infinite samples between this range, different tags can be assigned to different set of symbols. The algorithm is detailed in Example 3.12.

EXAMPLE 3.12

Consider a discrete memoryless source with $S = (X, Y, Z)$ with respective probabilities $P = (0.6, 0.2, 0.2)$. Find the codeword for the message 'YXZXY' using arithmetic coding.

Solution:

Step 1: First, divide the range [0 1) in accordance with the probabilities of the symbols. First symbol is 'Y'. Thus, consider the corresponding range of Y, that is, [0.6 0.8).

Step 2: Now again divide this range as per the probabilities of the symbols. As the second symbol to be coded is 'X', consider the corresponding range, that is, [0.6 0.72) and again divide this range in accordance with the probability of occurrence of the symbols.

Step 3: Next symbol to be transmitted is 'Z'. Thus, consider the corresponding range and re-divide the range.

Step 4: As the next symbol is 'X', consider the range [0.696 0.7104) and further divide the range.

Step 5: Finally the last symbol is 'Y' and thus the corresponding range is [0.70464 0.70752). So the tag is in the interval [0.70464 0.70752). One possible choice of the tag is its lower limit and thus the tag for the message 'YXZXY' is 0.70464. Some literatures also suggest the midpoint of the interval being the tag.

A detailed procedure for the generation of the tag is as shown in Fig. 3.3.

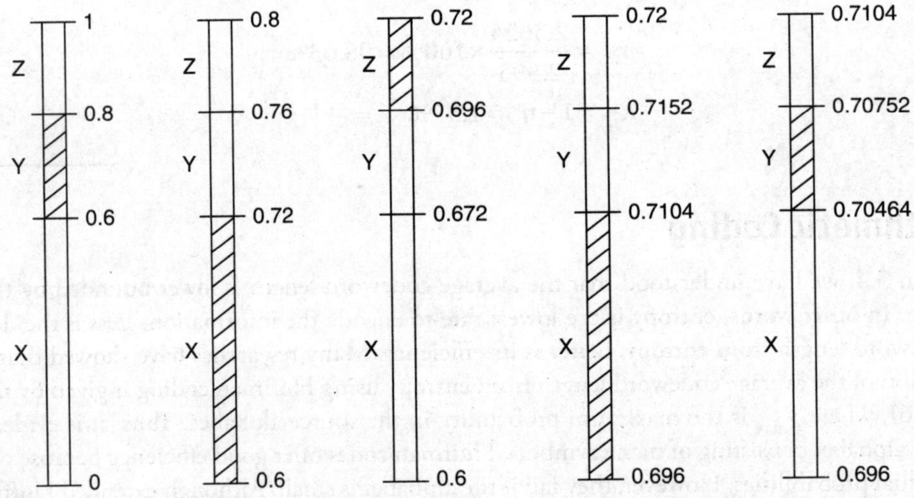

Figure 3.3 | Tag generation in arithmetic coding.

3.10 Lempel–Ziv Algorithm

The source coding algorithms discussed in the previous sections require the statistics of the symbols a priori. However, in real-time situations, the symbol probabilities would be unknown. Also most of the information sources used in the real-time applications do possess memory. That is, the symbol emitted in the present instant depends on the previous symbols emitted. However, Huffman codes do not consider such dependencies for coding. Thus, although Huffman codes work fine for memoryless sources, they fail to achieve optimal efficiency for sources with memory.

For the sources with memory, better coding efficiency can be achieved by considering correlations amongst symbols in source coding. One such source coding algorithm was developed by Lempel and Ziv resulting in Lempel–Ziv algorithm that is popularly known as LZ algorithm.

LZ algorithm is a dictionary-based approach in which a common dictionary is built at both sender and receiver end depending upon the string to be sent. The codeword will be of the form <index, code> where 'index' is the index of the dictionary where the longest match for the input sequence is found, 'code' is the codeword for the symbol succeeding the longest match.

Index '0' is used if the symbol is encountered for the first time and not found in the dictionary. The dictionary is updated in accordance with the input string. Longer the string to be encoded, better will be the compression achieved. Exactly the same process is done at the receiver end for decoding. A detailed explanation of the working of the algorithm is given in Example 3.13.

EXAMPLE 3.13

Encode the following information using LZ algorithm.
"THIS_IS_HIS_HIT"

Solution:

Step 1: Dictionary will be initially empty. The first letter in the input string is 'T' which is appearing for the first time. Thus, an index of '0' followed by the code of 'T' is transmitted. Dictionary is updated with the first entry 'T' at index '1'.

Step 2: Similarly, since the succeeding symbols 'H', 'I', 'S' and '_' appear for the first time, index '0' is used for encoding and the corresponding entries are made in the dictionary.

Step 3: The next symbol in the input string is 'I' is already present in the dictionary. Hence, the algorithm checks for the next symbol in the string, that is, 'S' for a better match. But the string 'IS' is not present in the updated dictionary. Thus, it is encoded as <index(I), code(S)> and the string 'IS' is updated in the dictionary.

Step 4: The next symbol in the input string is '_' that is present at location 5. However, the next symbol succeeding in the string is 'H' resulting in '_H' that is not yet updated in the dictionary. Thus, the string '_H' is coded as <index(_), code (H)> and 'H_' is updated in the next location of the dictionary.

Step 5: The next symbol in the string is 'I' that is present in the dictionary. The succeeding symbol is 'S' resulting in 'IS' that is also present in the dictionary. Thus, the algorithm takes the next symbol '_' for a better match resulting in 'IS_' that is not present. Thus, the coded sequence would be <index (IS), code(_)> and the string 'IS_' is updated in the dictionary.

The above steps are repeated for all further symbols in the string and corresponding codewords are generated. Table 3.23 details the dictionary updating procedure for the given input string. The complete encoding procedure is presented in Table 3.24.

Table 3.23 | Dictionary in LZ algorithm

Index	*Symbol*
1	T
2	H
3	I
4	S
5	_
6	IS
7	_H
8	IS_
9	HI
10	T_

Table 3.24 | Encoded string

Symbol	*Encoded Output*
T	<0, code(T)>
H	<0, code(H)>
I	<0, code(I)>
S	<0, code(S)>
_	<0, code(_)>
IS	<3, code(S)>
_H	<5, code(H)>
IS_	<6, code(_)>
HI	<2, code(I)>
T_	<1, code(_)>

3.11 Run Length Encoding

Run length encoding (RLE) is the simplest form among all compression techniques. In some data transfer applications, it is more likely to have some symbols occurring consecutively. The idea is to represent a longer length of identical symbols with a shorter notation. Although the algorithm seems to be very simple, it could achieve a very good compression ratio when there are longer runs of identical symbols.

To make the algorithm clearer, consider the following scenario. Consider a file to be transmitted consisting of black colored characters on a white background. Thus, there will be only two possible brightness levels say '0' representing black and '1' representing white. Consider the following data to be transmitted.

0000011111000000000000000110000000000011111111000000000001110000000011111000000000

Using RLE, the above information can be represented as follows:

5 0 5 1 15 0 2 1 11 0 8 1 11 0 3 1 8 0 5 1 9 0

It has to be read as: 5 consecutive 0's followed by 5 consecutive 1's followed by 15 consecutive 0's and so on. Thus, a message of 82-symbol long can be represented using only 22 symbols. However, this number would not be exactly 22, as we require some special characters to indicate the beginning and end of RLE and an escape character in between the symbols.

Sometimes, a threshold is considered and only a run longer than the threshold is coded, else it is transmitted uncoded. RLE finds many applications in lossless data compression. Even in joint photographic experts group (JPEG), it is used to represent the quantized data.

3.12 An Overview on Image Compression

As most of the applications involve transmission of images, image compression has become one of the very important classes of the compression techniques. As discussed in Section 3.1, there are two types of compression algorithms, namely,

a. Lossless compression
b. Lossy compression

JPEG is one of the most popular lossy image compression algorithms used in most of the Internet applications. Being a lossy algorithm, the degree of image quality and the corresponding compression ratio achieved can be traded off depending on the user requirement. It was accepted as an international standard in 1992. The source coding techniques discussed in Sections 3.7, 3.9 and 3.11 (i.e. Huffman coding, arithmetic coding and run length coding) are used in the JPEG standard for image compression.

JPEG basically uses transform coding for compression. The general block diagram of a JPEG scheme is as shown in Fig. 3.4.

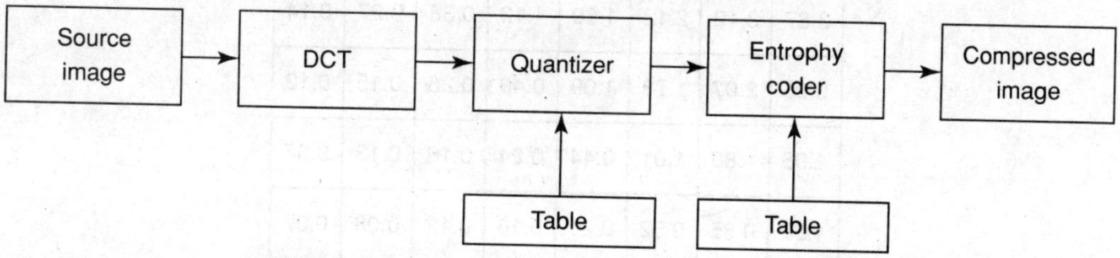

Figure 3.4 | JPEG standard for image compression.

The encoding procedure is detailed as follows:

Step 1: Here, the source image is divided into subimages of size 8 × 8. A typical block of size 8 × 8 is shown in Fig. 3.5.

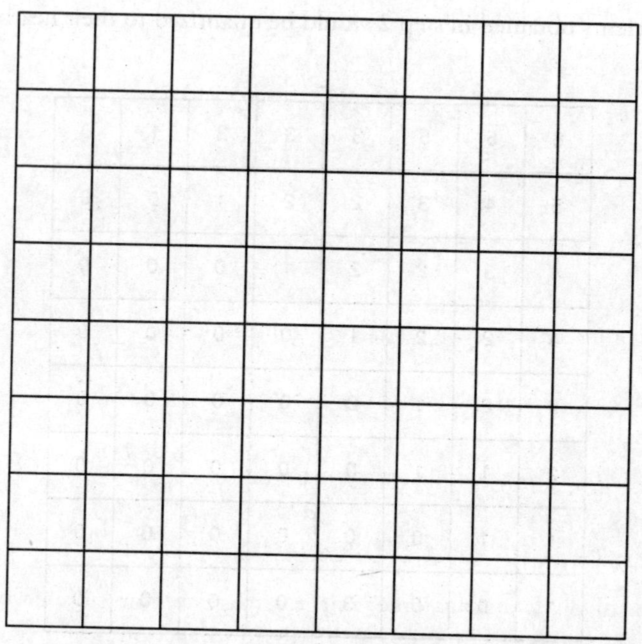

Figure 3.5 | An 8 × 8 block of image.

Step 2: These blocks can then be applied to the discrete cosine transformers (DCT) where the 64 DCT coefficients corresponding to 64 pixel are obtained. The pixel (1, 1) corresponds to the DC component of the signal which carries the maximum information and thus has the maximum value. As we traverse from top to bottom, left to right, the values of the pixels decrease. An example of DCT coefficient for an 8×8 block is as shown in Fig. 3.6.

5.73	5.01	4.97	2.89	2.78	1.52	1.34	0.32
4.98	3.98	3.09	2.32	1.58	1.28	0.35	0.29
3.87	3.12	2.12	1.69	1.12	0.38	0.27	0.14
3.65	2.07	1.73	1.09	0.40	0.26	0.15	0.13
1.95	1.80	1.01	0.44	0.24	0.16	0.13	0.07
1.82	0.85	0.52	0.21	0.16	0.12	0.08	0.07
0.78	0.58	0.21	0.17	0.11	0.09	0.06	0.04
0.63	0.20	0.19	0.10	0.09	0.06	0.05	0.01

Figure 3.6 | DCT coefficients for an 8×8 block of image.

Step 3: The DCT coefficients obtained in step 2 would be quantized to their nearby quantization levels. It is shown in Fig. 3.7.

6	5	5	3	3	2	1	0
5	4	3	2	2	1	0	0
4	3	2	2	1	0	0	0
4	2	2	1	0	0	0	0
2	2	1	0	0	0	0	0
2	1	1	0	0	0	0	0
1	1	0	0	0	0	0	0
1	0	0	0	0	0	0	0

Figure 3.7 | DCT coefficients after quantization.

Step 4: The coefficients are read using a zigzag coding as shown in Fig. 3.8.

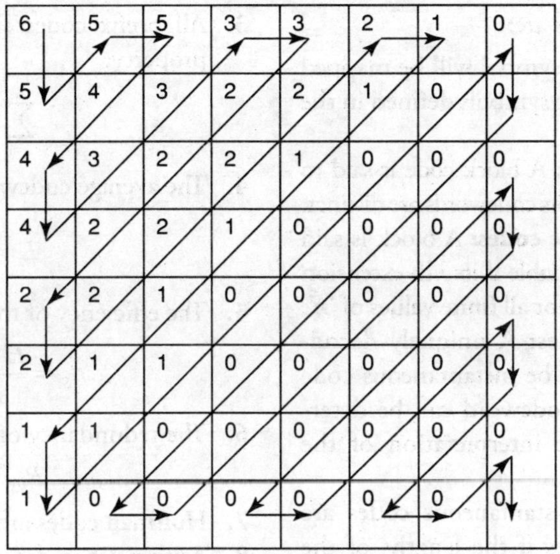

Figure 3.8 | Zigzag coding.

The obtained coefficient string for the above example is given by

6 5 5 5 4 4 4 3 3 3 3 2 2 2 2 2 2 2 2 2 2 1 1 1 1 1 1 1 1 1 1 0 0 0 0 0 0 0 0 0 0 0 0 0 0 0 0 0 0 0 0 0 0 0 0
0 0 0 0 0 0 0 0 0

As there is a long run of 0's, RLE can be used for encoding them. Huffman or arithmetic coding discussed in the previous sections can be used for further compression of the values.

3.13 Introduction to Speech Compression

In the Sections 3.5–3.12, we have seen different algorithms of source coding for text and image data. This section presents an overview on the speech compression techniques. There are many compression techniques proposed for speech compression. Some of them are listed as follows:

1. Linear predictive coder
2. Channel vocoder
3. Code-excited linear prediction
4. Sinusoidal coders
5. Transform coding

Speech compression can also be either lossy or lossless depending on the applications. An ample number of audio compression algorithms have been proposed and developed. Also several audio compression standards have resulted from these. Moving picture experts group (MPEG) is one of the most powerful and popular standards of audio coding. MPEG is a lossy standard for video and audio coding. MPEG-1 or MPEG-2 Layer III is a standard for coding digital audio. It is a lossy compression scheme which is popularly known as MP3.

SUMMARY

1. Different types of codes are:
   - **Block codes:** Each symbol will be mapped onto a block of code symbols defined in the code alphabet.
   - **Non-singular codes:** A block code is said to be non-singular if all its codewords are distinct.
   - **Uniquely decodable codes:** A block is said to be uniquely decodable if its *n*th extension is also non-singular for all finite values of '*n*'.
   - **Instantaneous codes:** A uniquely decodable code is said to be instantaneous code if the end of any codeword can be determined without the interpretation of the succeeding symbol.
   - **Optimal codes:** Instantaneous codes are called optimal codes if the lengths of the codewords assigned to the symbols are of minimum length.
2. The necessary and sufficient condition for an instantaneous code is 'No codeword should be a prefix of any other codeword'. Thus, they are also called prefix codes.
3. All prefix codes should satisfy the following property:
$$\sum_{k=1}^{N} r^{-lk} \le 1$$
4. The average codeword length L is given by
$$L = \sum_{i=1}^{N} p_i l_i$$
5. The efficiency of the source encoder is given by
$$\eta_S = \frac{H(S)}{L} \times 100\%$$
6. The redundancy of the source is given by
$$R_{\eta S} = 1 - \eta_S$$
7. Huffman codes are also called compact codes.
8. Arithmetic codes consider coding a sequence of length '*m*' without considering the coding for all sequences of length '*m*'.
9. LZ algorithm is a dictionary-based approach where the source statistics are not known a priori.
10. JPEG is a lossy image compression algorithm, which uses transform coding.

REVIEW QUESTIONS

1. Explain the need for source coding in communication system.
2. Determine which of the following codes shown in Table 3.25 are prefix codes. Also draw the decision diagram for the prefix codes.

Table 3.25 | Set of codes

Code A	*Code B*	*Code C*	*Code D*
00	11	01	101
10	101	001	1101
110	011	000	1010
0110	110	100	1100
010	1110	110	1111

3. Find the smallest value of '*r*' such that prefix codes can be constructed for the following code length requirements. $W = (1, 2, 3, 4, 5)$ for the corresponding $L = (1, 2, 3, 4, 5)$.
4. The following coding scheme depicted in Table 3.26 has been used to encode the sequence. Draw the decision tree.

Table 3.26 | Coding scheme for problem 4

Source Symbols	*Code B*
A	1
H	01
I	001
S	0001
T	00001
_	00000

If the receiver receives the following bitstream:
000010100100010000000010001000000100
100010000000110000100000000010100100
0100000001100001000000001000100000010
010001

Decode the information.

5. Consider a source with
$S = (A, B, C, D, E, F, G, H, I)$
$P = (0.25, 0.15, 0.15, 0.12, 0.10, 0.08, 0.06, 0.05, 0.04)$.
Find the codewords for the symbols using Shannon's algorithm. Also find the source efficiency and redundancy.

6. Consider a discrete memoryless source with three symbols $S = (A, B, C)$ with $P = (0.6, 0.2, 0.2)$.
   - **(a)** Use Shannon's algorithm and find the codewords for the symbols. Also find the source efficiency and redundancy.
   - **(b)** Consider the second-order extension of the source. Recompute the codewords and the efficiency.

7. Consider the following source emitting nine symbols with the respective probabilities:
$P = (0.22, 0.18, 0.15, 0.12, 0.10, 0.08, 0.07, 0.05, 0.03)$
Find the codewords for the symbols using Shannon–Fano algorithm. Also find the source efficiency and redundancy.

8. Consider the following source

$$S = (A, B, C, D, E, F, G, H)$$

$$P = \left\{\frac{7}{39}, \frac{8}{39}, \frac{6}{39}, \frac{10}{39}, \frac{3}{39}, \frac{1}{39}, \frac{2}{39}, \frac{2}{39}\right\}$$

   - **(a)** Find the binary Huffman codewords for the given source.
   - **(b)** Calculate the codewords considering $r = 3$.
   - **(c)** Find the new set codewords considering quaternary codes.
   - **(d)** Compare the efficiencies in all three cases.

9. A source emits one of the following eight symbols with the following probabilities
$P = (0.40, 0.25, 0.12, 0.08, 0.05, 0.05, 0.03, 0.02)$.
Find the binary, ternary and quaternary codewords using Huffman algorithm.

10. Consider an 8 × 8 binary image shown in Fig. 3.9. Assume that the black color is represented using bit '0' and that of white by bit '1'.
    - **(a)** How many bits are required to transmit this image if the encoding is not used?
    - **(b)** Calculate number of bits required for transmission if binary Huffman coding is used considering two pixels at a time.

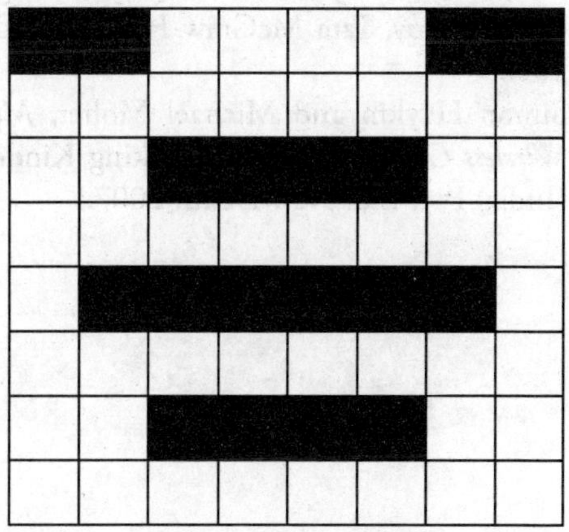

Figure 3.9 | A binary image.

(Hint: Consider all possible two pixel combinations and obtain the probability from the image given and then perform normal binary Huffman coding).

11. Consider a discrete memoryless source with symbols $S = (A, B, C)$ and state probabilities $P = (0.75, 0.15, 0.10)$ for its output.
    - **(a)** Apply Huffman encoding algorithm to find the codewords in binary. Find the source efficiency and redundancy.
    - **(b)** Consider the second-order extension of the source. Compute the codewords for this extended source and find its efficiency.

12. Consider a discrete memoryless source with $S = (X, Y, Z)$ with respective probabilities $P = (0.5, 0.3, 0.2)$. Find the codeword for the message 'YYZXZY' using arithmetic coding.

13. Encode the following input string using LZ algorithm:
'W_PNW_NW_WPN_P'

14. Write a note on run length coding.

15. With the help of a neat block diagram, explain JPEG compression technique.

Further Reading

[1] Shanmugam K Sam, *Digital and Analog Communication Systems*, John Wiley & Sons: New York; 1996.

[2] Simon Haykin, *Digital Communication*, John Wiley & Sons: New York; 2003.

[3] Ranjan Bose, *Information Theory Coding and Cryptography*, Tata McGraw Hill: New Delhi; 2008.

[4] Simon Haykin and Michael Moher, *Modern Wireless Communications*, Dorking Kindersley (India) Pvt. Ltd: New Delhi; 2007.

[5] Claude E Shannon, A Mathematical Theory of Communication, *Bell System Technical Journal*, 27, 379–423, 623–656, 1948.

[6] Khalid Sayood, *Introduction to Data Compression*, 4th Ed., Morgan Kaufmann Publishers: Burlington, MA; 2012.

[7] David Salomon, *Data Compression: The Complete Reference*, 3rd Ed., Springer: New York; 2004.

[8] Raymond W Yeung, *Information Theory and Network Coding*, Springer: New York; 2008.

4 Information Channels

'To talk about communication theory without communicating its real mathematical content would be like endlessly telling a man about a wonderful composer, yet never letting him hear an example of the composer's music.'

–John Robinson Pierce

Learning Objectives

After reading this chapter, you will be able to:

- Define channel models used for communication.
- Detail various entropies for a communication channel.
- Determine the maximum input rate for a channel for error-free transmission.
- Measure the capacity of a channel.
- Discuss and develop the relations for the continuous channels.

4.1 Introduction

Information channels are basically the physical transmission medium over which information is transmitted from the transmitter to the receiver. An information channel can be a continuous channel or a discrete channel depending on whether the inputs and outputs of the channel are analog electrical waveforms or a sequence of symbols. A continuous channel is sometimes referred to as a modulation channel as in the case of a telephone system or high-frequency radio systems. A discrete channel is sometimes referred to as a data communication channel when binary data is transmitted over it, for example, computer to computer link. Generally, channels are noisy in the sense that they affect the signal being transmitted through them by way of disturbances (in terms of amplitude/phase/frequency response variations both in pass-band and out-of-band areas of the signal). The channel basically acts as a filter to the incoming signal due to a change in the characteristics of the channel in various ways, that is, the channel corrupts the signal due to its non-linear behavior and acts as if it is adding or multiplying the signal with random noise (additive or multiplicative noise). These disturbances of the channel introduce errors in the received data by the time the data traverses through the channel. These are called channel errors, which may occur randomly (random errors) or in bursts (burst errors). Ultimately, the channel errors will limit the maximum data rate at which the data can be transmitted over the channel.

For an acceptable bit error rate (or an acceptable probability of error), there is a maximum rate at which the data can be reliably transmitted over the channel. This is known as *channel capacity*.

4.2 Channel Models

We have already seen discrete communication channels These discrete communication channels can be modeled by representing them by a set of input alphabets $X = \{x_1, x_2, \ldots, x_i\}$ consisting of 'i' symbols, a set of output alphabets $Y = \{y_1, y_2, \ldots, y_j\}$ consisting of 'j' symbols and a set of conditional probabilities $P(y_j/x_i)$. In other words, a discrete memoryless channel (DMC) is completely described by the set of transition probabilities $P(y_j/x_i)$, where x_i denotes input symbol, y_j denotes output symbol and $P(y_j/x_i)$ denotes the probabilities of receiving symbol y_j given that symbol x_i was sent (Fig. 4.1).

4.2.1 Channel Matrix (Probability Transition Matrix)

The conditional probabilities $P(y_j/x_i)$ are due to channel impairments or channel noise that modifies the input symbols x_i into y_j, resulting in error at the output of the channel e. This discrete-input, discrete-output channel is characterized by the set $X = \{x_1, x_2, \ldots, x_i\}$ of the possible inputs, the set $Y = \{y_1, y_2, \ldots, y_j\}$ of the possible outputs and a set of conditional probabilities that relate the possible outputs to the possible inputs. The conditional probability $P(y_j/x_i)$ is defined as the channel transition probability denoted by P_{ji}. These conditional probabilities can be represented in the form of a matrix with all input symbols represented row-wise and output symbols column-wise; such a matrix is known as *probability transition matrix* (*PTM*) or simply *channel matrix* (or *noise matrix*), that is,

$$\left[P\left(\frac{y_j}{x_i}\right)\right] = \begin{array}{c} \\ x_1 \\ x_2 \\ \vdots \\ x_n \end{array} \begin{array}{c} \begin{array}{cccc} y_1 & y_2 & \cdots & y_m \end{array} \\ \begin{bmatrix} P\left(\frac{y_1}{x_1}\right) & P\left(\frac{y_2}{x_1}\right) & \cdots & P\left(\frac{y_m}{x_1}\right) \\ P\left(\frac{y_1}{x_2}\right) & P\left(\frac{y_2}{x_2}\right) & \cdots & P\left(\frac{y_m}{x_2}\right) \\ \vdots & & & \\ P\left(\frac{y_1}{x_n}\right) & P\left(\frac{y_2}{x_n}\right) & \cdots & P\left(\frac{y_m}{x_n}\right) \end{bmatrix} \end{array}$$

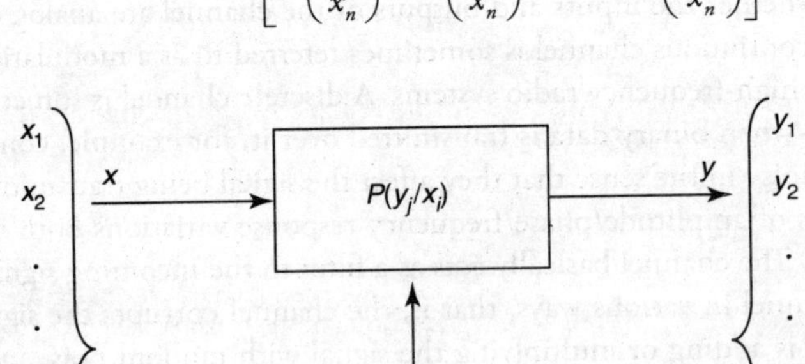

Figure 4.1 | A discrete communication channel.

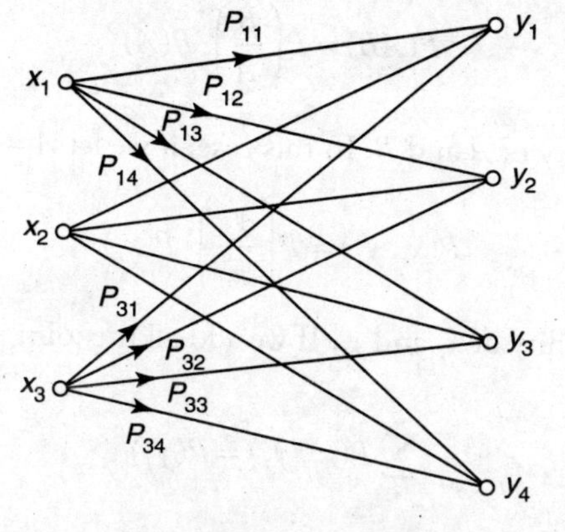

Figure 4.2 | Channel diagram.

Let us consider a discrete memoryless source (DMS) having an input alphabet $X = \{x_1, x_2, x_3\}$ and an output alphabet $Y = \{y_1, y_2, y_3, y_4\}$. The various transition probabilities are marked on a channel diagram as shown in Fig. 4.2.

In Fig. 4.2, P_{11} is the probability that y_1 will be received when x_1 was transmitted (because of channel noise), that is,

$$P_{11} = P\left(\frac{y_1}{x_1}\right); \; P_{12} = P\left(\frac{y_2}{x_1}\right); \; P_{34} = P\left(\frac{y_4}{x_3}\right)$$

Therefore,

$$\left[P\left(\frac{Y}{X}\right)\right] = \begin{array}{c} \\ x_1 \\ x_2 \\ x_3 \end{array} \begin{array}{c} \begin{array}{cccc} y_1 & y_2 & y_3 & y_4 \end{array} \\ \begin{bmatrix} P_{11} & P_{12} & P_{13} & P_{14} \\ P_{21} & P_{22} & P_{23} & P_{24} \\ P_{31} & P_{32} & P_{33} & P_{34} \end{bmatrix} \end{array}$$

Since each input to the channel results in some output, each row of the channel matrix must be unity, that is,

$$\sum_{j=1}^{n} P\left(\frac{y_j}{x_i}\right) = 1 \quad \forall i \tag{4.1}$$

Further, the input probabilities $[P(x)]$ are represented by the row matrix

$$[P(x_i)] = [P(x_1),\ P(x_2), \ldots,\ P(x_n)], \quad i = 1, 2, 3, \ldots,\ n$$

and the output probabilities $[P(y)]$ are represented by the row matrix

$$[P(y_j)] = [P(y_1), P(y_2), \ldots,\ P(y_m)], \quad j = 1, 2, 3, \ldots,\ m$$

From probability theory, we know that

$$P(AB) = P\left(\frac{B}{A}\right) \cdot P(A)$$

Here, $P(AB)$ is the joint probability of A and B. In this case, if we let $A = x_i$ and $B = y_j$, then

$$P(x_i, y_j) = P\left(\frac{y_j}{x_i}\right) \cdot P(x_i) \tag{4.2}$$

Here, $P(x_i, y_j)$ is the joint probability of x_i and y_j. If we add all the joint probabilities for a fixed y_j, then we get $P(y_j)$, that is,

$$\sum_{i=1}^{n} P(x_i, y_j) = P(y_j)$$

This gives the probability of getting the symbol y_j, as follows:

$$P(y_j) = \sum_{i=1}^{n} P\left(\frac{y_j}{x_i}\right) \cdot P(x_i), \quad j = 1,2,\ldots,m \tag{4.3}$$

Suppose that jth symbol is received when ith symbol is transmitted; an error will result in this case. Hence, the probability of error (or error probability) P_e can be written as

$$P_e = \sum_{j=1, j\neq i}^{m} P(y_j) \tag{4.4}$$

that is, all the probabilities will contribute to error except $i = j$ (as in this case correct symbol is received):

$$P_e = \sum_{i=1}^{n} \sum_{j=1, j\neq i}^{m} P\left(\frac{y_j}{x_i}\right) \cdot P(x_i)$$

4.2.2 Joint Probability Matrix

We already know that if x_i are the inputs and y_j are the outputs, then the joint probability is given by

$$P(x_i, y_j) = P\left(\frac{y_j}{x_i}\right) \cdot P(x_i) = P\left(\frac{x_i}{y_j}\right) \cdot P(y_j) \tag{4.5}$$

and also we defined the PTM as

$$\left[P\left(\frac{y_j}{x_i}\right)\right] = \begin{bmatrix} P\left(\frac{y_1}{x_1}\right) & P\left(\frac{y_2}{x_1}\right) & \cdots & P\left(\frac{y_m}{x_1}\right) \\ P\left(\frac{y_1}{x_2}\right) & P\left(\frac{y_2}{x_2}\right) & \cdots & P\left(\frac{y_m}{x_2}\right) \\ \vdots & & & \\ P\left(\frac{y_1}{x_n}\right) & P\left(\frac{y_2}{x_n}\right) & \cdots & P\left(\frac{y_m}{x_n}\right) \end{bmatrix}$$

Multiplying first row of $P(y_j/x_i)$ by $P(x_1)$, second row by $P(x_2)$ and so on, we get

$$\left[P\left(\frac{y_j}{x_i}\right)\right]\cdot P(x_i)=\begin{bmatrix} P\left(\frac{y_1}{x_1}\right)\cdot P(x_1) & P\left(\frac{y_2}{x_1}\right)\cdot P(x_1) & \cdots & P\left(\frac{y_m}{x_1}\right)\cdot P(x_1) \\ P\left(\frac{y_1}{x_2}\right)\cdot P(x_2) & P\left(\frac{y_2}{x_2}\right)\cdot P(x_2) & \cdots & P\left(\frac{y_m}{x_2}\right)\cdot P(x_2) \\ \vdots & & & \\ P\left(\frac{y_1}{x_n}\right)\cdot P(x_n) & P\left(\frac{y_2}{x_n}\right)\cdot P(x_n) & \cdots & P\left(\frac{y_m}{x_n}\right)\cdot P(x_n) \end{bmatrix}$$

But we know that $P(y_j/x_i)\cdot P(x_i)=P(x_i, y_j)$. Thus, we get

$$[P(x_i,y_j)]=\begin{matrix} \\ i=1 \\ i=2 \\ \vdots \\ i=n \end{matrix}\begin{matrix} j=1 & j=2 & \cdots & j=m \\ \left[\begin{matrix} P(x_1,y_1) \\ P(x_2,y_1) \\ \vdots \\ P(x_n,y_1) \end{matrix}\right. & \begin{matrix} P(x_1,y_2) \\ P(x_2,y_2) \\ \\ P(x_n,y_2) \end{matrix} & \begin{matrix} \cdots \\ \cdots \\ \\ \cdots \end{matrix} & \left.\begin{matrix} P(x_1,y_m) \\ P(x_2,y_m) \\ \\ P(x_n,y_m) \end{matrix}\right] \end{matrix} \tag{4.6}$$

This is the joint probability matrix (JPM), which has the following properties:

1. $\sum_{i=1}^{n} P(x_i, y_j) = P(y_j)$, that is, the sum of all the elements of the jth column of JPM gives the probability of the jth output—probability of all output symbols.

2. $P(x_i)=\sum_{j=1}^{m} P\left(\frac{x_i}{y_j}\right)\cdot P(y_j)$, $i=1, 2, 3,\ldots, n$, that is,

$$P(x_i)=\sum_{j=1}^{m} P(x_i, y_j),\quad i=1, 2, 3,\ldots, n$$

since $P(x_i/y_j)\cdot P(y_j)=P(x_i, y_j)$ (i.e. probability of the ith input can be obtained by adding all the elements in the ith row of JPM—probability of input symbols).

3. $\sum_{i=1}^{n} P(x_i)=1.$

Hence,

$$\sum_{i=1}^{n}\sum_{j=1}^{m} P(x_i, y_j)=1$$

that is, the sum of all the elements of JPM is equal to unity.

4.2.3 Binary Symmetric Channel

Let us consider a binary information channel, meaning a discrete channel where there are two input symbols x_0 and x_1 and two output symbols y_0 and y_1 as shown in Fig. 4.3 along with associated probabilities.

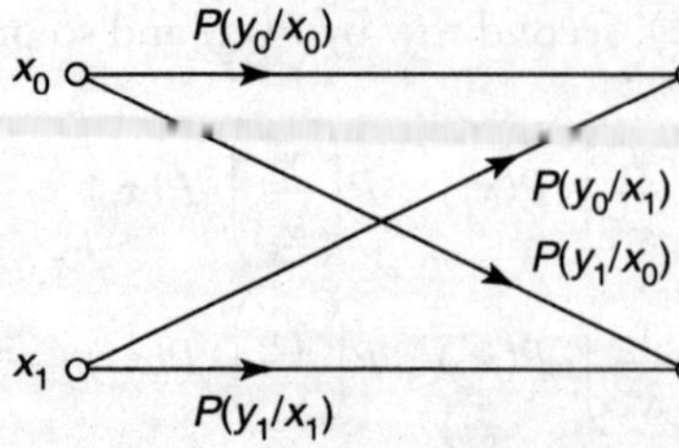

Figure 4.3 | Binary information channel.

The output symbol probabilities are given by

$$P(y_0) = P\left(\frac{y_0}{x_0}\right) \cdot P(x_0) + P\left(\frac{y_0}{x_1}\right) \cdot P(x_1)$$

$$P(y_1) = P\left(\frac{y_1}{x_1}\right) \cdot P(x_1) + P\left(\frac{y_1}{x_0}\right) \cdot P(x_0) \tag{4.7}$$

In matrix form, these give the PTM for a binary symmetric channel (BSC):

$$\begin{bmatrix} P(y_0) \\ P(y_1) \end{bmatrix} = [P(x_0) \quad P(x_1)] \begin{bmatrix} P\left(\frac{y_0}{x_0}\right) & P\left(\frac{y_1}{x_0}\right) \\ P\left(\frac{y_0}{x_1}\right) & P\left(\frac{y_1}{x_1}\right) \end{bmatrix}$$

The binary information channel, shown in Fig. 4.3, is said to be symmetric if

$$P\left(\frac{y_0}{x_0}\right) = P\left(\frac{y_1}{x_1}\right) = P$$

and

$$P\left(\frac{y_0}{x_1}\right) = P\left(\frac{y_1}{x_0}\right) = 1 - P$$

Then the channel diagram for a BSC can be shown as in Fig. 4.4.

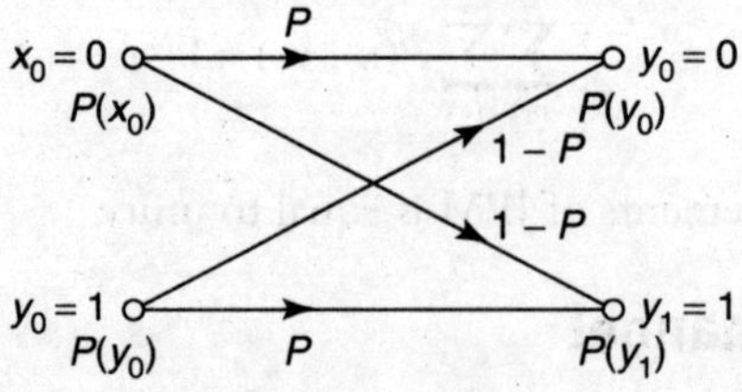

Figure 4.4 | Binary symmetric channel.

We get

$$\begin{bmatrix} P(y_0) \\ P(y_1) \end{bmatrix} = [P(x_0) \quad P(x_1)] \begin{bmatrix} P & 1-P \\ 1-P & P \end{bmatrix}$$

The BSC has two inputs ($x_0 = 0$, $x_1 = 1$) and two outputs ($y_0 = 0$, $y_1 = 1$). This is a symmetric channel as the probability of receiving a '0' when a '0' is sent is the same as the probability of receiving a '1' if a '1' is sent, that is, P, which is the common transition probability.

Now $(1 - P)$ is naturally the error probability because a '1' is received when a '0' is transmitted and similarly a '0' is received when a '1' is transmitted. If $P = 1/2$, BSC channel diagram will be as shown in Fig. 4.5.

We calculate the output probabilities, joint probabilities and conditional probabilities for the BSC.

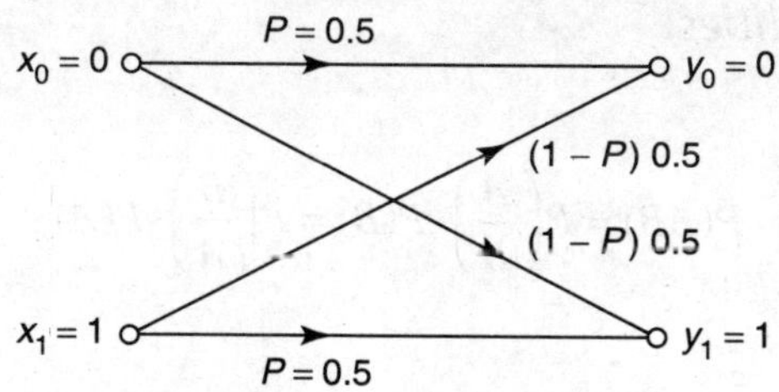

Figure 4.5 | Binary symmetric channel with $P = 0.5$.

4.2.3.1 Output Symbol Probabilities

We have

$$\begin{bmatrix} P(y_0) \\ P(y_1) \end{bmatrix} = [P(x_0) \quad P(x_1)] \begin{bmatrix} P & 1-P \\ 1-P & P \end{bmatrix} = \begin{bmatrix} \frac{1}{2} & \frac{1}{2} \end{bmatrix} \begin{bmatrix} P & 1-P \\ 1-P & P \end{bmatrix} = \begin{bmatrix} \frac{1}{2}P & + \frac{1}{2}(1-P) \\ \frac{1}{2}(1-P) + & \frac{1}{2}P \end{bmatrix}$$

Here, $P = 1/2$. Therefore,

$$\begin{bmatrix} P(y_0) \\ P(y_1) \end{bmatrix} = \begin{bmatrix} \frac{1}{2} \\ \frac{1}{2} \end{bmatrix}$$

that is,

$$P(y_0) = \frac{1}{2} \quad \text{and} \quad P(y_1) = \frac{1}{2}$$

4.2.3.2 Joint Probabilities

We have

$$P(x_0, y_0) = P\left(\frac{y_0}{x_0}\right) \cdot P(x_0) = P \cdot \frac{1}{2} = \frac{1}{2}P$$

$$P(x_1, y_0) = P\left(\frac{y_0}{x_1}\right) \cdot P(x_1) = (1-P) \cdot \frac{1}{2} = \frac{1}{2}(1-P)$$

$$P(x_0, y_1) = P\left(\frac{y_1}{x_0}\right) \cdot P(x_0) = (1-P) \cdot \frac{1}{2} = \frac{1}{2}(1-P)$$

$$P(x_1, y_1) = P\left(\frac{y_1}{x_1}\right) \cdot P(x_1) = P \cdot \frac{1}{2} = \frac{1}{2}P$$

4.2.3.3 Conditional Probabilities

We know that

$$P(AB) = P\left(\frac{A}{B}\right) \cdot P(B) = P\left(\frac{B}{A}\right) \cdot P(A)$$

Therefore,

$$P\left(\frac{x_0}{y_0}\right) \cdot P(y_0) = P\left(\frac{y_0}{x_0}\right) \cdot P(x_0)$$

$$\Rightarrow P\left(\frac{x_0}{y_0}\right) = \frac{P(y_0 / x_0) \cdot P(x_0)}{P(y_0)} = \frac{P \times (1/2)}{1/2} = P$$

Similarly,

$$P\left(\frac{x_1}{y_0}\right) = \frac{P(y_0 / x_1) \cdot P(x_1)}{P(y_0)} = \frac{(1-P) \times (1/2)}{1/2} = 1-P$$

$$P\left(\frac{x_0}{y_1}\right) = \frac{P(y_1 / x_0) \cdot P(x_0)}{P(y_1)} = \frac{(1-P) \times (1/2)}{1/2} = 1-P$$

$$P\left(\frac{x_1}{y_1}\right) = \frac{P(y_1 / x_1) \cdot P(x_1)}{P(y_1)} = \frac{P \times (1/2)}{1/2} = P$$

Summarizing,

$$P(x_0) = P(x_1) = P(y_0) = P(y_1) = \frac{1}{2}$$

$$P\left(\frac{y_1}{x_1}\right) = P\left(\frac{y_0}{x_0}\right) = P$$

$$P\left(\frac{y_1}{x_0}\right) = P\left(\frac{y_0}{x_1}\right) = 1 - P$$

$$P(x_1, y_1) = P(x_0, y_0) = \frac{1}{2}P$$

$$P(x_1, y_0) = P(x_0, y_1) = \frac{1}{2}(1 - P)$$

$$P\left(\frac{x_0}{y_0}\right) = P\left(\frac{x_1}{y_1}\right) = P$$

$$P\left(\frac{x_0}{y_1}\right) = P\left(\frac{x_1}{y_0}\right) = 1 - P$$

EXAMPLE 4.1

For the channel shown in Fig. 4.6, write the channel matrix.

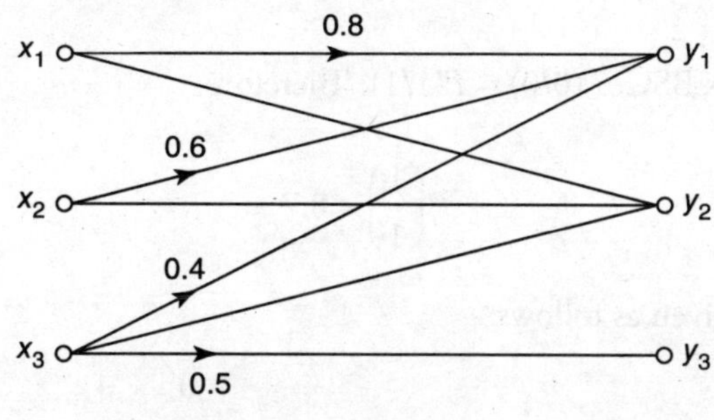

Figure 4.6 | A communication channel.

Solution: For a communication channel, the sum of all outgoing probabilities from any input must be 1. Thus, the missing probabilities can be calculated as follows:

$$P\left(\frac{y_2}{x_1}\right) = 1 - 0.8 = 0.2$$

$$P\left(\frac{y_2}{x_2}\right) = 1 - 0.6 = 0.4$$

$$P\left(\frac{y_2}{x_3}\right) = 1 - (0.4 + 0.5) = 0.1$$

Thus, the channel matrix is given as follows:

$$\text{Channel matrix} = P\left(\frac{y}{x}\right) = \begin{matrix} & y_1 & y_2 & y_3 \\ x_1 & 0.8 & 0.2 & 0 \\ x_2 & 0.6 & 0.4 & 0 \\ x_3 & 0.4 & 0.1 & 0.5 \end{matrix}$$

EXAMPLE 4.2

For the BSC shown in Fig. 4.7, write the channel matrix.

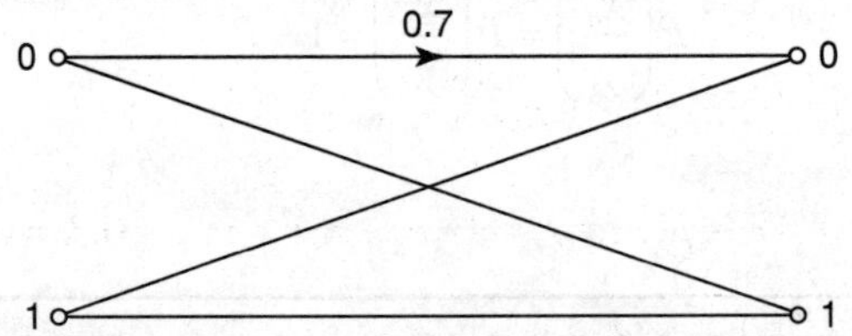

Figure 4.7 | A binary symmetric channel.

Solution: As the channel is BSC, $P(0/0) = P(1/1)$. Therefore,

$$P\left(\frac{1}{1}\right) = 0.7$$

Thus, the channel matrix is given as follows:

$$\text{Channel matrix} = P\left(\frac{y}{x}\right) = \begin{matrix} & 0 & 1 \\ 0 & 0.7 & 0.3 \\ 1 & 0.3 & 0.7 \end{matrix}$$

EXAMPLE 4.3

For the channel matrix given, find the missing entries. Also draw the corresponding channel diagram.

$$\text{Channel matrix} = P\left(\frac{y}{x}\right) = \begin{matrix} & y_1 & y_2 & y_3 \\ x_1 & 0.8 & * & 0.2 \\ x_2 & * & 0.6 & 0.2 \\ x_3 & 0.2 & 0.3 & * \end{matrix}$$

Solution: We know that the sum of all the elements of a row of a channel matrix is equal to unity. Therefore,

$$p\left(\frac{y_1}{x_1}\right)+p\left(\frac{y_2}{x_1}\right)+p\left(\frac{y_3}{x_1}\right)=1$$

$$\Rightarrow p(y_2/x_1) = 1 - p(y_1/x_1) - p(y_3/x_1) = 1 - 0.8 - 0.2 = 0$$

Similarly,

$$p(y_1/x_2) + p(y_2/x_2) + p(y_3/x_2) = 1$$

$$\Rightarrow p(y_1/x_2) = 1 - p(y_2/x_2) - p(y_3/x_2) = 1 - 0.6 - 0.2 = 0.2$$

and

$$p\left(\frac{y_1}{x_3}\right)+p\left(\frac{y_2}{x_3}\right)+p\left(\frac{y_3}{x_3}\right)=1$$

$$\Rightarrow p(y_3/x_3) = 1 - p(y_1/x_3) - p(y_2/x_3) = 1 - 0.2 - 0.3 = 0.5$$

The corresponding channel is as shown in Fig. 4.8.

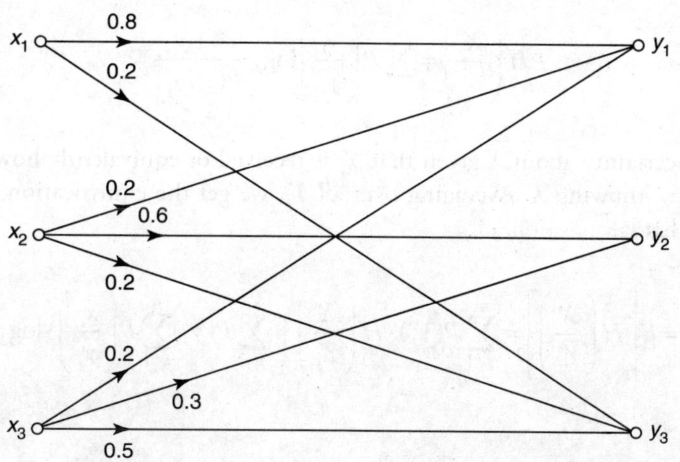

Figure 4.8 | Channel diagram for Example 4.3.

4.3 System Entropies

The input X and output Y of a channel are sources with their own entropies, $H(X)$ and $H(Y)$, as shown in Fig. 4.9.

The input entropy $H(X)$ is given by

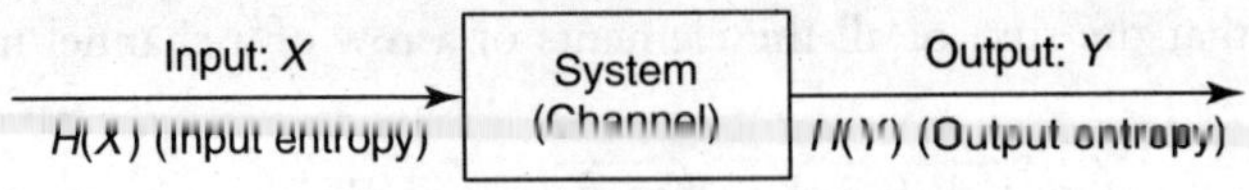

Figure 4.9 | System entropies.

$$H(X) = \sum_{i=1}^{n} P(x_i) \cdot \log_2 \frac{1}{P(x_i)} = -\sum_{i=1}^{n} P(x_i) \cdot \log_2 (P(x_i)) \text{ bits/symbol} \tag{4.8}$$

The output entropy $H(Y)$ is given by

$$H(Y) = -\sum_{j=1}^{m} P(y_j) \cdot \log_2 (P(y_j)) \text{ bits/symbol} \tag{4.9}$$

These source entropies $H(X)$ and $H(Y)$ represent average amounts of information going into and coming out of system (channel) per symbol. Equivalently, these are the average uncertainty about the input and output. The entropy of the input symbols before transmission is generally known as '*priory entropy*'. The entropy of the input symbols after transmission and reception of a particular symbol, say, Y_j, is defined as the *posteriori* or *conditional entropy* denoted by $H(X/Y_j)$, and is given by

$$H\left(\frac{X}{Y_j}\right) = \sum_i P\left(\frac{x_i}{y_j}\right) \log_2 \frac{1}{P(x_i/y_j)} \tag{4.10}$$

This represents the uncertainty about X given that Y_j is received or equivalently how much more information one would gain by knowing X. Averaging over all Y_j, we get the equivocation of X with respect to Y denoted by $H(X/Y)$, that is,

$$H\left(\frac{X}{Y}\right) = E\left[H\left(\frac{X}{Y_j}\right)\right] = \sum_{j=1}^{m} P(y_j) \cdot H\left(\frac{X}{Y_j}\right) = \sum_{j=1}^{m} P(y_j) \sum_{i=1}^{n} P\left(\frac{x_i}{y_j}\right) \cdot \log_2 \frac{1}{P(x_i/y_j)}$$

that is,

$$H\left(\frac{X}{Y}\right) = \sum_j \sum_i P(y_j) \cdot P\left(\frac{x_i}{y_j}\right) \cdot \log_2 \frac{1}{P(x_i/y_j)}$$

$$\Rightarrow H\left(\frac{X}{Y}\right) = \sum_j \sum_i P(x_i, y_j) \cdot \log_2 \frac{1}{P(x_i/y_j)} \text{ bits/symbols} \tag{4.11}$$

$H(X/Y)$, that is, equivocation, specifies the receiver's average uncertainty about X when receiving Y. That is to say, it specifies the average uncertainty about the input of the channel being channel output is known.

It represents the amount of information lost due to noise (inter symbol interference, ISI) with respect to any of the output symbols.

Similarly, if x_i is sent, then the uncertainty about Y is the conditional entropy. In the above equation for $H(X/Y)$, if x and y are interchanged, we get

$$H\left(\frac{Y}{X}\right)=\sum_j\sum_i P(y_j,x_i)\cdot\log_2\frac{1}{P(y_j/x_i)}$$

But

$$P(y_j,x_i)=P(x_i,y_j)$$

Therefore,

$$H\left(\frac{Y}{X}\right)=\sum_j\sum_i P(x_i,y_j)\cdot\log_2\frac{1}{P(y_j/x_i)} \tag{4.12}$$

$H(Y/X)$ is the equivocation of Y with respect to X representing the sender's average uncertainty about Y when X is known or equivalently how much extra information is gained by also knowing Y.

An observer trying to guess both the input of the channel X and its output Y of the channel will have an average uncertainty given by the joint entropy:

$$H\left(\frac{X}{Y}\right)=\sum_i\sum_j P(x_i,y_j)\cdot\log_2\frac{1}{P(x_i,y_j)}=-\sum_i\sum_j P(x_i,y_j)\cdot\log_2 P(x_i,y_j)$$

We know that

$$P(A,B)=P\left(\frac{A}{B}\right)\cdot P(B)$$

Therefore,

$$P(x_i,y_j)=P\left(\frac{x_i}{y_j}\right)\cdot P(y_j)$$

Hence,

$$H(X,Y)=-\sum_i\sum_j P(x_i,y_j)\cdot\log_2\left[P\left(\frac{x_i}{y_j}\right)\cdot P(y_j)\right]$$

Now

$$\log_2\left[P\left(\frac{x_i}{y_j}\right)\cdot P(y_j)\right]=\log_2 P\left(\frac{x_i}{y_j}\right)+\log_2 P(y_j)$$

Therefore,

$$H(X,Y) = -\sum_i \sum_j P(x_i, y_j) \cdot \log_2 \left[P\left(\frac{x_i}{y_j}\right) \right] - \sum_i \sum_j P(x_i, y_j) \cdot \log_2 P(y_j)$$

$$= \sum_i \sum_j P(x_i, y_j) \cdot \frac{1}{\log_2 P(x_i / y_j)} - \sum_j \left\{ \sum_i P(x_i, y_j) \right\} \log_2 P(y_j)$$

$$= H\left(\frac{X}{Y}\right) - \sum_i P(y_j) \cdot \log_2 P(y_j)$$

Since

$$\text{First term} = H\left(\frac{X}{Y}\right) \text{ and } \sum_i P(x_i, y_j) = P(y_j)$$

we get

$$H(X,Y) = H\left(\frac{X}{Y}\right) + H(Y) \tag{4.13}$$

Similarly, it can be shown that

$$H(X,Y) = H\left(\frac{Y}{X}\right) + H(X)$$

We know that

$$P(x_i, y_j) = P\left(\frac{y_j}{x_i}\right) \cdot P(x_i)$$

Therefore,

$$H(X,Y) = -\sum_i \sum_j P(x_i, y_j) \cdot \log_2 \left[P\left(\frac{y_j}{x_i}\right) \cdot P(x_i) \right]$$

$$= -\sum_i \sum_j P(x_i, y_j) \cdot \log_2 \left[P\left(\frac{y_j}{x_i}\right) \right] - \sum_i \sum_j P(x_i, y_j) \cdot \log_2 P(x_i)$$

$$= \sum_i \sum_j P(x_i, y_j) \cdot \frac{1}{\log_2 P(y_j / x_i)} - \sum_i \left\{ \sum_j P(x_i, y_j) \right\} \log_2 P(x_i)$$

$$= H\left(\frac{Y}{X}\right) - \sum_i P(x_i) \cdot \log_2 P(x_i)$$

Since

$$\text{First term} = H\left(\frac{Y}{X}\right) \quad \text{and} \quad \sum_j P(x_i, y_j) = P(x_i)$$

we get

$$H(X,Y) = H\left(\frac{Y}{X}\right) + \sum_i P(x_i) \log_2 \frac{1}{P(x_i)}$$

Therefore,

$$H(X,Y) = H\left(\frac{Y}{X}\right) + H(X) \tag{4.14}$$

If the channel is such that X and Y are statistically independent, then

$$H(X,Y) = H(X) + H(Y)$$

But in real life, one would expect X and Y to be related rather than independent, in which case

$$H(X,Y) = H(X) + H\left(\frac{Y}{X}\right)$$

This relation that we have already proved confirms the interpretation of $H(Y/X)$ as the extra information conveyed by Y when X is already known. It is analogous to the rule $|X \cup Y| = |X| + |Y/X|$ for finite sets X and Y. Similarly,

$$H(X,Y) = H(Y) + H\left(\frac{X}{Y}\right)$$

which corresponds to $|X \cup Y| = |Y| + |X/Y|$. We call $H(X)$, $H(Y)$, $H(X/Y)$, $H(Y/X)$ and $H(X, Y)$ the system entropies. They depend on both the channel characteristics and the input X, which between them will determine Y.

Summarizing, we have

1. Measure of the average uncertainty of the channel input:

$$H(X) = -\sum_i P(x_i) \cdot \log_2 P(x_i)$$

2. Measure of the average uncertainty at the output of the channel:

$$H(Y) = -\sum_j P(y_j) \cdot \log_2 P(y_j)$$

3. Measure of the average uncertainty about the input of the channel being the output of the channel is known—equivocation of Y with respect to X:

$$H\left(\frac{X}{Y}\right) = -\sum_i \sum_j P(x_i, y_j) \cdot \log_2 P\left(\frac{x_i}{y_j}\right)$$

4. Measure of the average uncertainty at the output of the channel given that X was transmitted:

$$H\left(\frac{Y}{X}\right) = -\sum_i \sum_j P(x_i, y_j) \cdot \log_2 P\left(\frac{y_j}{x_i}\right)$$

5. Measure of the average amount of uncertainty of the communication channel as a whole:

$$H(X,Y) = H(X) + H\left(\frac{Y}{X}\right) = H(Y) + H\left(\frac{X}{Y}\right)$$

EXAMPLE 4.4

For the JPM matrix given, find

(a) $H(X)$
(b) $H(Y)$
(c) $H(X,Y)$
(d) $H\left(\frac{Y}{X}\right)$
(e) $H\left(\frac{X}{Y}\right)$

$$\text{JPM} = P(X,Y) = \begin{array}{c} \\ x_1 \\ x_2 \\ x_3 \\ x_4 \end{array}\begin{array}{c} \begin{array}{cccc} y_1 & y_2 & y_3 & y_4 \end{array} \\ \begin{bmatrix} 0.05 & 0 & 0.20 & 0.05 \\ 0 & 0.10 & 0.10 & 0 \\ 0 & 0 & 0.20 & 0.10 \\ 0.05 & 0.05 & 0 & 0.10 \end{bmatrix} \end{array}$$

Solution: We know that the sum of all the elements of a row of JPM gives the corresponding input probability and that of a column gives the corresponding output probability. Therefore,

$$P(X) = [0.30, 0.20, 0.30, 0.20]$$

and

$$P(Y) = [0.10, 0.15, 0.50, 0.25]$$

(a) We have

$$H(X) = -\sum_i P(x_i) \cdot \log_2 P(x_i)$$

Substituting the values of $P(x_i)$ in the above equation, we get

$$= -(0.3 \log_2 0.3 + 0.2 \log_2 0.2 + 0.3 \log_2 0.3 + 0.2 \log_2 0.2)$$

$$H(X) = 1.971 \text{ bits/sym}$$

(b) We have

$$H(Y) = -\sum_j P(y_j) \cdot \log_2 P(y_j)$$

Using the values of $P(Y)$ in the above equation, we get

$$= -(0.10 \log_2 0.10 + 0.15 \log_2 0.15 + 0.5 \log_2 0.5 + 0.25 \log_2 0.25)$$

$$H(Y) = 1.743 \text{ bits/sym}$$

(c) We have

$$H(X,Y) = -\sum_i \sum_j P(x_i, y_j) \cdot \log_2 P(x_i, y_j)$$

Substituting the values of $P(x_i, y_j)$ from the JPM, we have

$$= -(0.05 \log_2 0.05 + 0.20 \log_2 0.20 + 0.05 \log_2 0.05 + 0.10 \log_2 0.10 + 0.10 \log_2 0.10 + 0.20 \log_2 0.20 + 0.10 \log_2 0.10 + 0.05 \log_2 0.05 + 0.05 \log_2 0.05 + 0.10 \log_2 0.10)$$

$$H(X,Y) = 3.122 \text{ bits/sym}$$

(d) We have

$$H\left(\frac{Y}{X}\right) = -\sum_i \sum_j P(x_i, y_j) \cdot \log_2 P\left(\frac{y_j}{x_i}\right)$$

Therefore, to find $H(Y/X)$, we require the matrix $P(Y/X)$. We have

$$P\left(\frac{Y}{X}\right) = \frac{P(X,Y)}{P(X)}$$

Divide each row of the JPM by the corresponding input probabilities. That is, divide all the elements of the first row of the JPM by $P(x_1)$, second row by $P(x_2)$ and so on. Therefore, the channel matrix $P(Y/X)$ is given by

$$P\left(\frac{Y}{X}\right) = \begin{bmatrix} \frac{1}{6} & 0 & \frac{2}{3} & \frac{1}{6} \\ 0 & \frac{1}{2} & \frac{1}{2} & 0 \\ 0 & 0 & \frac{2}{3} & \frac{1}{3} \\ \frac{1}{4} & \frac{1}{4} & 0 & \frac{1}{2} \end{bmatrix}$$

Therefore,

$$H(Y/X) = -\begin{pmatrix} 0.05 \log_2 \frac{1}{6} + 0.20 \log_2 \frac{2}{3} + 0.05 \log_2 \frac{1}{6} + 0.10 \log_2 \frac{1}{2} + 0.10 \log_2 \frac{1}{2} + \\ 0.20 \log_2 \frac{2}{3} + 0.10 \log_2 \frac{1}{3} + 0.05 \log_2 \frac{1}{4} + 0.05 \log_2 \frac{1}{4} + 0.10 \log_2 \frac{1}{2} \end{pmatrix}$$

$$H\left(\frac{Y}{X}\right) = 1.151 \text{ bits/sym}$$

$H(Y/X)$ can also be obtained using Eq. (4.14):

$$H\left(\frac{Y}{X}\right) = H(X,Y) - H(X) = 3.122 - 1.971 = 1.151 \text{ bits/sym}$$

(e) We have

$$H\left(\frac{X}{Y}\right) = -\sum_i \sum_j P(x_i, y_j) \log_2 P\left(\frac{x_i}{y_j}\right)$$

Therefore, we require $P(X/Y)$ to find $H(X/Y) \cdot P(X/Y)$ can be found using the following relation:

$$P\left(\frac{X}{Y}\right) = \frac{P(X,Y)}{P(Y)}$$

that is, divide each column of $P(X,Y)$ by the corresponding output probability $P(Y)$:

$$P\left(\frac{X}{Y}\right) = \begin{bmatrix} \frac{1}{2} & 0 & \frac{2}{5} & \frac{1}{5} \\ 0 & \frac{2}{3} & \frac{1}{5} & 0 \\ 0 & 0 & \frac{2}{5} & \frac{2}{5} \\ \frac{1}{2} & \frac{1}{3} & 0 & \frac{2}{5} \end{bmatrix}$$

Therefore,

$$H(Y/X) = -\begin{pmatrix} 0.05\log_2\frac{1}{2} + 0.20\log_2\frac{2}{5} + 0.05\log_2\frac{1}{5} + 0.10\log_2\frac{2}{3} + 0.10\log_2\frac{1}{5} + \\ 0.20\log_2\frac{2}{5} + 0.10\log_2\frac{2}{5} + 0.05\log_2\frac{1}{2} + 0.05\log_2\frac{1}{3} + 0.10\log_2\frac{2}{5} \end{pmatrix}$$

$$H\left(\frac{X}{Y}\right) = 1.379 \text{ bits/sym}$$

Also, from Eq. (4.13), we have

$$H\left(\frac{X}{Y}\right) = H(X,Y) - H(Y) = 3.122 - 1.743 = 1.379 \text{ bits/sym}$$

EXAMPLE 4.5

Channel matrix for a channel is given as follows:

$$P\left(\frac{Y}{X}\right) = \begin{matrix} & \begin{matrix} y_1 & y_2 & y_3 \end{matrix} \\ \begin{matrix} x_1 \\ x_2 \\ x_3 \end{matrix} & \begin{bmatrix} 0.6 & 0.2 & 0.2 \\ 0.2 & 0.6 & 0.2 \\ 0.2 & 0.2 & 0.6 \end{bmatrix} \end{matrix}$$

Also, the input probabilities of the channel are:

$$P[X] = \left[\frac{1}{3}, \frac{1}{3}, \frac{1}{3}\right]$$

Find:

(a) $H(X)$
(b) $H(Y)$
(c) $H(X,Y)$
(d) $H\left(\frac{Y}{X}\right)$
(e) $H\left(\frac{X}{Y}\right)$

Solution: The JPM can be obtained from the channel matrix using the following relation:

$$P(X,Y) = P\left(\frac{Y}{X}\right) * P(X)$$

Thus, the JPM can be obtained by multiplying each row of the channel matrix by the respective input probabilities:

$$P(X,Y) = \begin{matrix} \\ x_1 \\ x_2 \\ x_3 \end{matrix}\begin{matrix} y_1 & y_2 & y_3 \\ \left[\begin{matrix} \frac{2}{10} & \frac{1}{15} & \frac{1}{15} \\ \frac{1}{15} & \frac{1}{15} & \frac{1}{15} \\ \frac{1}{15} & \frac{1}{15} & \frac{1}{15} \end{matrix}\right] \end{matrix}$$

From JPM, we can find the probabilities of the output symbols:

$$P(Y) = \left[\frac{1}{3}, \frac{1}{3}, \frac{1}{3}\right]$$

(a) We have

$$H(X) = -\sum_i P(x_i) \cdot \log_2 P(x_i)$$

$$= -\left(\frac{1}{3}\log_2\frac{1}{3} + \frac{1}{3}\log_2\frac{1}{3} + \log_2\frac{1}{3}\right)$$

$$H(X) = 1.5849 \text{ bits/sym}$$

(b) We have

$$H(Y) = -\sum_j P(y_j) \cdot \log_2 P(y_j)$$

$$= -\left(\frac{1}{3}\log_2\frac{1}{3} + \frac{1}{3}\log_2\frac{1}{3} + \log_2\frac{1}{3}\right)$$

$$H(Y) = 1.5849 \text{ bits/sym}$$

(c) We have

$$H(X,Y) = -\sum_i \sum_j P(x_i, y_j) \cdot \log_2 P(x_i, y_j)$$

Substituting the values of $P(x_i, y_j)$ from the JPM, we get

$$= -\begin{pmatrix} \frac{2}{10}\log_2 \frac{2}{10} + \frac{1}{15}\log_2 \frac{1}{15} + \frac{1}{15}\log_2 \frac{1}{15} + \frac{1}{15}\log_2 \frac{1}{15} + \frac{1}{15}\log_2 \frac{1}{15} + \\ \frac{1}{15}\log_2 \frac{1}{15} + \frac{1}{15}\log_2 \frac{1}{15} + \frac{1}{15}\log_2 \frac{1}{15} + \frac{1}{15}\log_2 \frac{1}{15} \end{pmatrix}$$

$$H(X,Y) = 2.9549 \text{ bits/sym}$$

(d) We have

$$H\left(\frac{Y}{X}\right) = -\sum_i \sum_j P(x_i, y_j) \cdot \log_2 P\left(\frac{y_j}{x_i}\right)$$

Therefore,

$$= -\begin{pmatrix} \frac{2}{10}\log_2 0.6 + \frac{1}{15}\log_2 0.2 + \frac{1}{15}\log_2 0.2 + \frac{1}{15}\log_2 0.2 + \frac{1}{15}\log_2 0.6 + \\ \frac{1}{15}\log_2 0.2 + \frac{1}{15}\log_2 0.2 + \frac{1}{15}\log_2 0.2 + \frac{1}{15}\log_2 0.6 \end{pmatrix}$$

$$H\left(\frac{Y}{X}\right) = 1.37 \text{ bits/sym}$$

$H(Y/X)$ can also be obtained using Eq. (4.14), as follows:

$$H\left(\frac{Y}{X}\right) = H(X,Y) - H(X) = 2.9549 - 1.5849 = 1.37 \text{ bits/sym}$$

(e) We have

$$H\left(\frac{X}{Y}\right) = -\sum_i \sum_j P(x_i, y_j) \cdot \log_2 P\left(\frac{x_i}{y_j}\right)$$

We require $P(X/Y)$ to find $H(X/Y).P(X/Y)$ can be found using the following relation:

$$P\left(\frac{X}{Y}\right) = \frac{P(X,Y)}{P(Y)}$$

that is, divide each column of $P(X,Y)$ by the corresponding output probability $P(Y)$:

$$P\left(\frac{X}{Y}\right) = \begin{matrix} & y_1 & y_2 & y_3 \\ x_1 & 0.6 & 0.2 & 0.2 \\ x_2 & 0.2 & 0.6 & 0.2 \\ x_3 & 0.2 & 0.2 & 0.6 \end{matrix}$$

Therefore,

$$= -\begin{pmatrix} \frac{2}{10}\log_2 0.6 + \frac{1}{15}\log_2 0.2 + \frac{1}{15}\log_2 0.2 + \frac{1}{15}\log_2 0.2 + \frac{1}{15}\log_2 0.6 + \\ \frac{1}{15}\log_2 0.2 + \frac{1}{15}\log_2 0.2 + \frac{1}{15}\log_2 0.2 + \frac{1}{15}\log_2 0.6 \end{pmatrix}$$

$$H\left(\frac{X}{Y}\right) = 1.37 \text{ bits/sym}$$

Also, from Eq. (4.13), we have

$$H\left(\frac{X}{Y}\right) = H(X,Y) - H(Y) = 2.9549 - 1.5849 = 1.37 \text{ bits/sym}$$

4.4 Mutual Information (Transinformation)

We know that

$$H(X) = \sum_i P(x_i)\log\frac{1}{P(x_i)} \text{ bits/symbols}$$

and also

$$H\left(\frac{X}{Y}\right) = \sum_i\sum_j P(x_i, y_j)\cdot\log_2\frac{1}{P(x_i / y_j)} \text{ bits/symbols}$$

From these relations, we can conclude that when the average information of $H(X)$ is transmitted over an information channel, an average amount of information equal to the equivocation $H(X/Y)$ is lost in the channel due to channel noise. The balance of information received at the receiver with respect to the observed output symbol is referred to as mutual information (denoted by $I(X;Y)$) of a channel and is defined by

$$I(X;Y) = H(X) - H\left(\frac{X}{Y}\right) \text{ bits/symbol} \tag{4.15}$$

Since $H(X)$ represents the uncertainty about the channel input before observing the output of the channel and $H(X/Y)$ gives the uncertainty about the input of the channel after observing the output of the channel, the mutual information $I(X;Y)$ represents the uncertainty about the input of the channel that is resolved by observing the output of the channel:

$$I(X;Y) = \sum_i P(x_i)\log\frac{1}{P(x_i)} - \sum_i\sum_j P(x_i,y_j)\cdot\log_2\frac{1}{P(x_i / y_j)}$$

We know that $\sum_j P(y_j / x_i) = 1$ [since the sum of all the elements in any row of the channel matrix (PTM) is equal to unity]. Including this term in the first term of $I(X;Y)$, we have

$$I(X;Y) = \sum_i P(x_i)\cdot\left[\sum_j P\left(\frac{y_j}{x_i}\right)\right]\cdot\log\frac{1}{P(x_i)} - \sum_i\sum_j P(x_i,y_j)\cdot\log_2\frac{1}{P(x_i / y_j)}$$

$$= \sum_i\sum_j P(x_i)\cdot P\left(\frac{y_j}{x_i}\right)\cdot\log_2\frac{1}{P(x_i)} - \sum_i\sum_j P(x_i,y_j)\cdot\log_2\frac{1}{P(x_i / y_j)}$$

Also,

$$P(x_i,y_j) = P(x_i)\cdot P\left(\frac{y_j}{x_i}\right)$$

Therefore,

$$I(X;Y) = \sum_i\sum_j P(x_i,y_j)\cdot\log\frac{1}{P(x_i)} - \sum_i\sum_j P(x_i,y_j)\cdot\log P\left(\frac{x_i}{y_j}\right)$$

$$= \sum_i\sum_j P(x_i,y_j)\left[\log\frac{1}{P(x_i)} + \log P\left(\frac{x_i}{y_j}\right)\right]$$

Since

$$P\left(\frac{x_i}{y_j}\right) = \frac{P(x_i,y_j)}{P(y_j)}$$

we have

$$I(X;Y) = \sum_i\sum_j P(x_i,y_j)\left[\log\frac{1}{P(x_i)} + \log\frac{P(x_i,y_j)}{P(y_j)}\right]$$

Therefore,

$$I(X;Y) = \sum_i\sum_j P(x_i,y_j)\left[\log\frac{P(x_i,y_j)}{P(x_i)P(y_j)}\right] \text{ bits/symbol}$$

Interchanging X and Y in the above equation, we get

$$I(Y;X) = \sum_i\sum_j P(x_i,y_j)\log\frac{P(x_i,y_j)}{P(x_i)P(y_j)}$$

This shows that $I(X; Y) = I(Y; X)$, meaning that the mutual information exhibits symmetric property and hence known as mutual. Since

$$I(X;Y)=H(X)-H\left(\frac{X}{Y}\right)$$

We can interchange X and Y, getting

$$I(Y;X)=H(Y)-H\left(\frac{Y}{X}\right)$$

where $H(X)$ is the entropy at the input and $H(Y)$ represents the entropy of the output symbols.

4.4.1 Graphical Representation of Mutual Information

We know that

$$I(X;Y)=H(X)-H\left(\frac{X}{Y}\right)$$

We can interpret $H(X)$ as the uncertainty about X when Y is unknown or as the information conveyed by X when Y is unknown. Similarly, $H(X/Y)$ can be interpreted as an uncertainty about X when Y is known or as the information conveyed by X when Y is known. Also, $I(X; Y)$ can be interpreted as the amount of uncertainty about X resolved by knowing Y or as the amount of information about X conveyed by Y.

These interpretations show that $I(X; Y)$ basically represents how much information X and Y have in common, that is, $I(X; Y)$ can be thought of as corresponding to the intersection of sets since $|X \cap Y| = |X| - |X/Y|$.

For example, a movie, say, 'X', is produced based on a novel, say, 'Y'. Then $I(X; Y)$ would represent how much the movie will tell about the novel (commonality between the two).

Similarly, $I(Y; X)$ conveys the amount of information about Y conveyed by X analogous to sets $|Y \cap X| = |Y| - |Y/X|$. We know that

$$H(X;Y)=H(X)+H\left(\frac{Y}{X}\right)$$

and

$$H(X,Y)=H(Y)+H\left(\frac{X}{Y}\right)$$

Subtracting, we get

$$H(X)-H(Y)+H\left(\frac{Y}{X}\right)-H\left(\frac{X}{Y}\right)=0$$

or

$$H(X)-H\left(\frac{X}{Y}\right)=H(Y)-H\left(\frac{Y}{X}\right)$$

that is,

$$I(X;Y)=I(Y;X)$$

This means that the output tells exactly as much about the input as the input tells about the output. Furthermore,

$$H(X, Y) = H(Y) + H\left(\frac{X}{Y}\right)$$

or

$$H\left(\frac{X}{Y}\right) = H(X, Y) - H(Y)$$

Substituting for $H(X/Y)$ in $I(X;Y)$, we have, therefore,

$$I(X; Y) = H(X) - H\left(\frac{X}{Y}\right)$$

that is,

$$I(X; Y) = H(X) + H(Y) - H(X, Y)$$

which is analogous to $|X \cap Y| = |X| + |Y| - |X \cup Y|$.

All the above entropy relations can be represented graphically, as shown in Fig. 4.10. The source entropy $H(X)$ and the destination entropy $H(Y)$ have been represented by two overlapping circles shown as in Figure 4.10. The overlap between the two circles shown as $I(X; Y)$ is the mutual information. The hatched portion on the left circle is the equivocation $H(X/Y)$ and that on the right circle is the equivocation $H(Y/X)$. The joint entropy $H(X, Y)$ is the sum of $H(X)$ and $H(Y)$ minus the common area $I(X; Y)$, that is,

$$H(X,Y) = H(X) + H(Y) - I(X;Y)$$

4.4.2 Properties of Mutual Information *I(X;Y)*

1. Mutual information of a channel exhibits symmetric property, that is,

$$I(X;Y) = I(Y;X)$$

2. Mutual information is always non-negative entity, that is,

$$I(X;Y) \geq 0$$

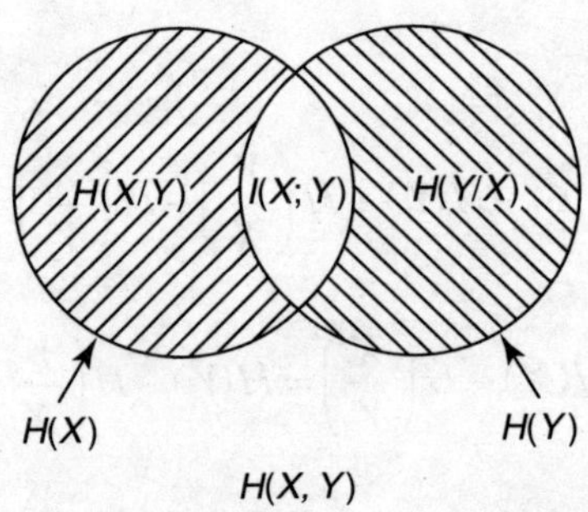

Figure 4.10 | Graphical representation of entropy relations.

Proof: We know that

$$I(X;Y)=\sum_i\sum_j P(x_i,y_j)\log_2\frac{P(x_i,y_j)}{P(x_i)P(y_j)}=\log_2 e\sum_i\sum_j P(x_i,y_j)\ln\frac{P(x_i,y_j)}{P(x_i)P(y_j)}$$

From the inequality, we know that

$$\ln\frac{1}{x}\geq 1-x$$

Putting

$$x=\frac{P(x_i)P(y_j)}{P(x_i,y_j)}$$

we get

$$\ln\frac{P(x_i,y_j)}{P(x_i)P(y_j)}\geq 1-\frac{P(x_i)P(y_j)}{P(x_i,y_j)}$$

Multiplying the equation by $P(x_i, y_j)$ on both sides and taking double summation, we get

$$\sum_i\sum_j P(x_i,y_j)\frac{P(x_i,y_j)}{P(x_i)P(y_j)}\geq\sum_i\sum_j P(x_i,y_j)\left[1-\frac{P(x_i)P(y_j)}{P(x_i,y_j)}\right]$$

Multiplying both sides by $\log_2 e$, we get

$$\log_2 e\sum_i\sum_j P(x_i,y_j)\frac{P(x_i,y_j)}{P(x_i)P(y_j)}\geq\log_2 e\left[\sum_i\sum_j P(x_i,y_j)-P(x_i)P(y_j)\right]$$

that is,

$$I(X;Y)\geq\log_2 e\left[\sum_i\sum_j P(x_i,y_j)-\sum_i\sum_j P(x_i)P(y_j)\right]$$

$$\Rightarrow I(X;Y)\geq\log_2 e\left[\sum_i\sum_j P(x_i,y_j)-\sum_i P(x_i)\cdot\sum_j P(y_j)\right]$$

Here, $\sum_i\sum_j P(x_i,y_j)$ is the sum of all the elements of JPM = 1. Thus,

$$\sum_i P(x_i)=1 \quad\text{and}\quad \sum_j P(y_j)=1$$

Hence,

$$I(X;Y)\geq\log_2 e[1-(1)(1)]$$

that is,

$$I(X;Y)\geq 0$$

3. Mutual information can also be represented in terms of channel entropies. We have already proved that

$$I(X;Y) = H(Y) - H\left(\frac{Y}{X}\right) = H(X) - H\left(\frac{X}{Y}\right)$$

4. Mutual information can be written in terms of joint entropy. We have already proved that

$$I(X;Y) = H(X) + H(Y) - H(X,Y)$$

4.4.3 Average Rate of Information

We know that the rate of transmission from a source X is

$$R = H(X) \cdot r_s \text{ bits/s}$$

where r_s is the symbol rate. Average information rate is decided by how noisy the channel is and how much information can be reconstructed at the receiver. As some amount of information is lost in the noisy channel (because errors are caused in the reconstruction process at the receiver), the net amount of information at the receiver is the mutual information:

$$I(X;Y) = H(X) - H\left(\frac{X}{Y}\right) = H(Y) - H\left(\frac{Y}{X}\right) \text{ bits/sym}$$

Hence, the average rate of information transfer is given as

$$R_{tr} = I(X;Y) \cdot r_s \text{ bits/s}$$

that is,

$$R_{tr} = \left[H(Y) - H\left(\frac{Y}{X}\right) \right] \cdot r_s \text{ bits/s} \tag{4.16}$$

Suppose that the channel is too noisy; it may so happen that the output of the channel (at receiver input) may become statistically independent of the input, that is, if X and Y become independent, then

$$H\left(\frac{Y}{X}\right) = H(Y)$$

in which case

$$I(X;Y) = H(Y) - H(Y) = 0$$

that is, all the information pumped into the channel is lost and no information is transmitted over the channel, hence zero information at the receiver. The channel is said to be useless.

4.4.4 Kullback–Leibler Distance (Relative Entropy)

Consider a discrete distribution that has a probability function p_k and another discrete distribution that has a probability function q_k. Then, we define what is called as the relative entropy of p with respect to q (also called the Kullback–Leibler distance) as is defined by

$$d = \sum p_k \log_2\left(\frac{p_k}{q_k}\right)$$

Since $d(p, q) \neq d(q, p)$ is a convex function of p_k. Also it is always non-negative and equals zero if and only if $p_k = q_k$. Relative entropy is a useful concept which can be applied in quantum information theory.

EXAMPLE 4.6

Find the mutual information for the channel shown in Fig. 4.11. It is given that $P(x_1) = 0.6$ and $P(x_2) = 0.4$.

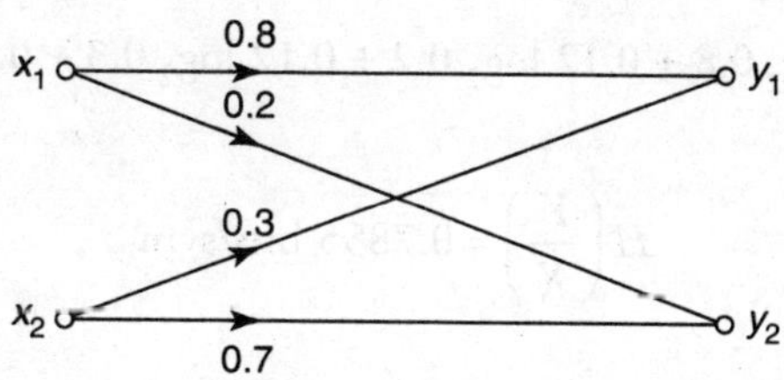

Figure 4.11 | Channel diagram for Example 4.6.

Solution: We have the mutual information given by

$$I(X;Y) = H(X) - H(X/Y) = H(Y) - H(Y/X) \text{ bits/sym}$$

We can consider the following relation:

$$I(X;Y) = H(Y) - H(Y/X) \text{ bits/sym}$$

As $P(Y/X)$ matrix can be directly obtained from the channel diagram, we have

$$P\left(\frac{Y}{X}\right) = \begin{matrix} & y_1 & y_2 \\ x_1 & 0.8 & 0.2 \\ x_2 & 0.3 & 0.7 \end{matrix}$$

Also, the JPM can be obtained from the channel matrix using the following relation:

$$P(X,Y) = P\left(\frac{Y}{X}\right) * P(X)$$

$$P(X,Y) = \begin{matrix} & y_1 & y_2 \\ x_1 & 0.48 & 0.12 \\ x_2 & 0.12 & 0.28 \end{matrix}$$

From JPM, we can find the probabilities of the output symbols as follows:

$$P(Y) = [0.6,\ 0.4]$$

Now

$$H(Y) = -\sum_j P(y_j)\cdot \log_2 P(y_j)$$

$$= -(0.6 \log_2 0.6 + 0.4 \log_2 0.4)$$

Therefore,

$$H(Y) = 0.9709 \text{ bits/sym}$$

Also,

$$H\left(\frac{Y}{X}\right) = -\sum_i \sum_j P(x_i, y_j)\cdot \log_2 P\left(\frac{y_j}{x_i}\right)$$

$$= -(0.48 \log_2 0.8 + 0.12 \log_2 0.2 + 0.12 \log_2 0.3 + 0.28 \log_2 0.7)$$

Therefore,

$$H\left(\frac{Y}{X}\right) = 0.7855 \text{ bits/sym}$$

So

$$I(X;Y) = H(Y) - H(Y/X) = 0.9709 - 0.7855 = 0.1853 \text{ bits/sym}$$

EXAMPLE 4.7

Find the rate of information transmission for the channel shown in Fig. 4.12. It is given that $P(x_1) = 0.5$ and $P(x_2) = 0.5$. Assume $r_s = 10000$ sym/s.

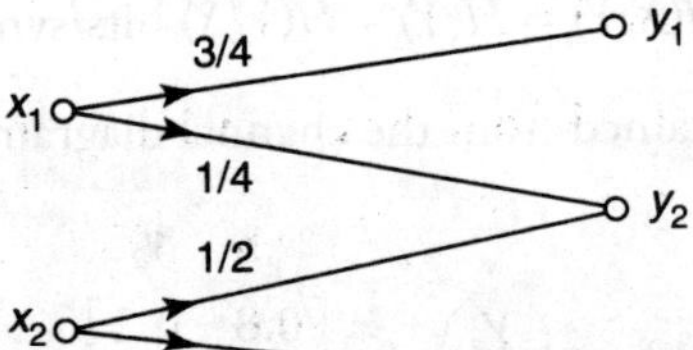

Figure 4.12 | Channel diagram for Example 4.7.

Solution: We have the mutual information given by

$$I(X;Y) = H(Y) - H(Y/X) \text{ bits/sym}$$

As $P(Y/X)$ matrix can be directly obtained from the channel diagram, we have

$$P\left(\frac{Y}{X}\right) = \begin{array}{c} \\ x_1 \\ x_2 \end{array}\begin{array}{c} \begin{array}{ccc} y_1 & y_2 & y_3 \end{array} \\ \begin{bmatrix} \frac{3}{4} & \frac{1}{4} & 0 \\ 0 & \frac{1}{2} & \frac{1}{2} \end{bmatrix} \end{array}$$

Also, the JPM can be obtained from the channel matrix using the following relation:

$$P(X,Y) = P\left(\frac{Y}{X}\right) * P(X)$$

$$P(X,Y) = \begin{matrix} & \begin{matrix} y_1 & y_2 & y_3 \end{matrix} \\ \begin{matrix} x_1 \\ x_2 \end{matrix} & \begin{bmatrix} \frac{3}{8} & \frac{1}{8} & 0 \\ 0 & \frac{1}{4} & \frac{1}{4} \end{bmatrix} \end{matrix}$$

From JPM, we can find the probabilities of the output symbols:

$$P(Y) = \left[\frac{3}{8}, \frac{3}{8}, \frac{1}{4}\right]$$

Now

$$H(Y) = -\sum_j P(y_j) \cdot \log_2 P(y_j)$$

Therefore,

$$H(Y) = -\left(\frac{3}{8}\log_2\frac{3}{8} + \frac{3}{8}\log_2\frac{3}{8} + \frac{1}{4}\log_2\frac{1}{4}\right)$$

$$H(Y) = 1.56128 \text{ bits/sym}$$

Also,

$$H\left(\frac{Y}{X}\right) = -\sum_i \sum_j P(x_i, y_j) \cdot \log_2 P\left(\frac{y_j}{x_i}\right)$$

Therefore,

$$H\left(\frac{Y}{X}\right) = -\left(\frac{3}{8}\log_2\frac{3}{4} + \frac{1}{8}\log_2\frac{1}{4} + \frac{1}{4}\log_2\frac{1}{2} + \frac{1}{4}\log_2\frac{1}{2}\right)$$

$$H\left(\frac{Y}{X}\right) = 0.90568 \text{ bits/sym}$$

So we have

$$I(X;Y) = H(Y) - H(Y/X) = 1.56128 - 0.90568 = 0.65564 \text{ bits/sym}$$

The rate of information transmission is given by

$$R = I(X;Y)\ r_s = 0.65564 \times 1000 = 6556.4 \text{ bits/s}$$

4.5 Channel Capacity

Suppose an information source sends r_s messages per second, and the entropy H bits/message. We then have an information rate given by $R = r_s H$ bits/s. Intuitively, for any given communication system, the number of errors per second will increase when the information rate is increased. It is surprising to note that this does not happen.

Shannon in his famous theorem, known as the Shannon's capacity theorem, has defined that "there exists a maximum rate of information known as Channel Capacity (C). If the information rate, R, is less than channel capacity, C, then one can approach arbitrarily small error probabilities by use of suitable coding techniques." The only hitch is that the encoder has to have longer blocks of signal data to obtain lower error probabilities which will result in longer delays and higher computational requirements.

Thus, Shannon's channel coding theorem can be stated as follows: For a channel with capacity C and an information source with rate R where $R \leq C$, there always exists a coding scheme such that the output of the information source can be transmitted over the channel with an arbitrarily small probability of error. That is for $R \leq C$, error free transmission is possible even in the presence of noise which sets an upper limit on the information rate that can guarantee error free communication. Conversely, if $R \geq C$, then it is not possible to transmit the information without errors.

4.5.1 Shannon–Hartley Theorem (Shannon's Information Capacity Theorem)

Consider a band-limited Gaussian channel operating in the presence of AWGN. The same is shown in Fig. 4.13.

The Shannon–Hartley theorem for channel coding states that the capacity of a white, band-limited Gaussian channel is given by

$$C = B \log_2 \left(1 + \frac{S}{N}\right) \text{ bits/s} \tag{4.17}$$

where C is the capacity (bits per second), B denotes the bandwidth of the channel (Hertz) and S/N is the signal-to-noise ratio. Suppose that a noise with an RMS voltage of α is introduced in the signal during transmission. Assume that the quantization levels of the signal be separated by $\alpha = \lambda\sigma$. If λ is chosen to have a large value, a smaller error probability could be achieved. Further, if each message is represented with a voltage level, we will have M distinct levels for M possible messages. Then the average signal power can be written as

$$S = \frac{M^2 - 1}{12} (\lambda\sigma)^2 \tag{4.18}$$

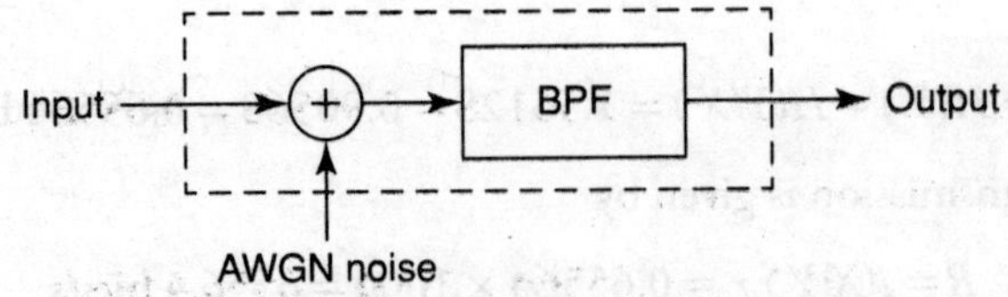

Figure 4.13 | Gaussian channel.

The number of levels for M given average signal power is therefore

$$M = \left(1 + \frac{12}{\lambda^2}\frac{S}{N}\right)^{1/2} \tag{4.19}$$

where $N = \sigma^2$ is the noise power. Assuming that all messages are equally likely, they would carry equal amount of information with an entropy H given by

$$H = \log_2 M = \frac{1}{2}\log_2\left(1 + \frac{12}{\lambda^2}\frac{S}{N}\right) \text{ bits/message} \tag{4.20}$$

We now approximate $T = 0.5/B$ so that rate of information can be written as

$$R = \frac{1}{T} = 2B \text{ messages/s}$$

The rate of information R and substituting for H as per Eq. (4.20), we get

$$R = rH = B\log_2\left(1 + \frac{12}{\lambda^2}\frac{S}{N}\right) \tag{4.21}$$

For $\lambda = 3.5$, this relation gives the maximum information rate as per Shannon–Hartley theorem.

4.5.2 Channel Capacity for Channels of Infinite Bandwidth

The Shannon–Hartley theorem suggests that a channel with infinite bandwidth will have infinite capacity.

However, as $B \to \infty$, the channel capacity does not tend to infinite as increase in bandwidth also tends to increase the noise power. Considering the noise power spectral density as $\eta/2$, the total noise power becomes $N = \eta B$, substituting this in Eq. (4.17), we get

$$C = B\log_2\left(1 + \frac{S}{\eta B}\right) = \frac{S}{\eta}\left(\frac{\eta B}{S}\right)\log_2\left(1 + \frac{S}{\eta B}\right) = \frac{S}{\eta}\log_2\left(1 + \frac{S}{\eta B}\right)^{\eta B/S}$$

We know that

$$\lim_{x\to 0}(1+x)^{1/x} = e$$

Hence, as $x \to S/\eta B$. As $B \to \infty$, the capacity of the channel becomes

$$C_\infty = \lim_{B\to\infty} C = \frac{S}{\eta}\log_2 e = 1.44\frac{S}{\eta} \tag{4.22}$$

Thus for an AWGN channel, the channel capacity C instead of approaching infinity, approaches a limit as we go on increasing the bandwidth. The capacity can be made infinite only by increasing the signal power to infinity. Increasing signal power to infinity is impractical. For finite signal and noise powers, the channel capacity always remains finite.

As the information rate R of a practical bandlimited system is always less than C_∞, we consider the transmission of binary information over a channel at a rate equal to its capacity, that is $R = C$. Consider the average signal power is denoted as S. Then, as the bit duration is $1/C$ s, the average energy per bit is given by $E_h = S/C$.

With $N = \eta B$, we can therefore write

$$\frac{C}{B} = \log_2\left(1 + \frac{E_b}{\eta}\frac{C}{B}\right)$$

Rearranging the above equation, we get

$$\frac{E_b}{\eta} = \frac{B}{C}(2^{C/B} - 1) \tag{4.23}$$

We can plot this relation as shown in Fig. 4.14, which is named as the bandwidth efficiency diagram.

It can be seen that the rock bottom value of the baseband SNR is −1.59 dB ≈ −1.6 dB. It means that below this value it is not possible to have an error free transmission regardless of the information rate. This is called the *Shannon limit*.

4.5.3 Information Redundancy

A redundant source is the one that produces dependent symbols like a Markov source. It generates symbols that are not necessary to convey information. For instance, it is really not necessary to write '*u*' following the letter '*q*' in English language. That is '*u*' is redundant. However, redundancy will be required in communications to facilitate error detection and error correction. If we consider a Markov source, entropy $H(S) < H(\bar{S})$, where $(\bar{S})$ is an adjoint, memoryless source, the source entropy will be reduced. This can hence be used as a measure. In view of this, measurement of the redundancy in a sequence of symbols can be done by knowing the amount of reduction of the system entropy.

When there is no influence of ISI, $H(X)$ would be the entropy at the receiver for any given set of messages $\{X\}$. In the presence of inter symbol influence, the receiver entropy would be $H(Y \mid X)$. The difference between $H(X)$ and $H(Y \mid X)$ gives the reduction in entropy. Usually, that is measured relative to the maximum entropy and termed as relative redundancy:

$$\text{Redundancy} = \frac{\text{Absolute redundancy}}{H(X)}$$

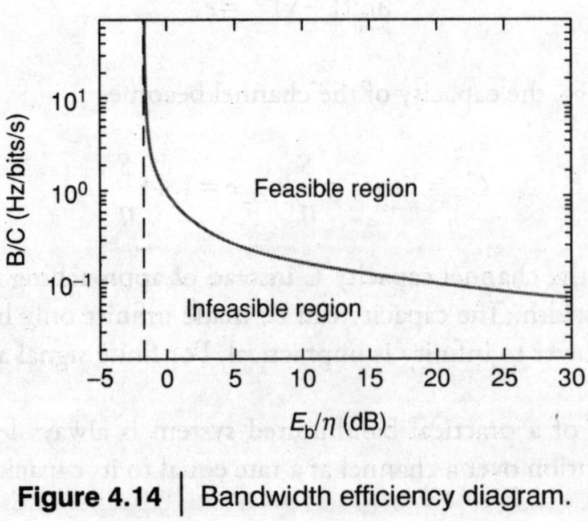

Figure 4.14 | Bandwidth efficiency diagram.

or
$$\text{Redundancy} = 1 - \frac{H(Y|X)}{H(X)}$$

Alternatively,

$$\text{Redundancy} = 1 - \frac{R}{C}$$

where R is the rate of mutual information and C is the capacity of the channel. Hence, efficiency, η, for the channel can be defined as

$$\eta = \frac{\text{Actual rate of mutual information}}{\text{Maximum possible rate}}$$

or
$$\eta = \frac{R}{C}$$

and
$$\eta = 1 - \text{redundancy}$$

EXAMPLE 4.8

For an AWGN channel with 4 kHz bandwidth and noise power spectral density ($N_0/2$) = 10^{-12} W/Hz, the signal power required at the receiver is 0.1 mW. Calculate the capacity of the channel.

Solution: From Eq. (4.17), we have

$$C = B\log_2\left(1 + \frac{S}{N}\right)$$

Given $B = 4\,\text{kHz}$, $S = 0.1\times 10^{-3}$ W, $N = N_0 \times B = 2\times 10^{-12} \times 4000 = 8\times 10^{-9}$ W. Therefore,

$$C = B\log_2\left(1 + \frac{S}{N}\right) = 54444 \text{ bits/s}$$

EXAMPLE 4.9

A CRT terminal is used to enter alphanumeric data into a computer. The CRT is connected through a voice-grade telephone line having usable bandwidth of 3 kHz and an output S/N of 10 dB. Assume that the terminal has 128 characters and data is sent in an independent manner with equal probability.

(a) Find the average information per character.
(b) Find the capacity of the channel.
(c) Find the maximum rate at which data can be sent from the terminal to the computer without error.

Solution:

(a) As all characters are equiprobable, the corresponding entropy would be $H(S)_{\max}$ given by

$$H(S)_{\max} = \log_2 N = \log_2 128 = 7 \text{ bits/character}$$

(b) Given

$$\frac{S}{N} = 10\log_{10}\frac{S}{N} = 10\,\text{dB} = 10\log \Rightarrow \frac{S}{N} = 10 = 10$$

From Eq. (4.17), we have

$$C = B\log_2\left(1+\frac{S}{N}\right)$$

Given $B = 3\,\text{kHz}$. Therefore,

$$C = 10378.295 \text{ bits/s}$$

(c) Average rate of information is given as

$$R_t = r_s H$$

For error-free transmission, we have

$$R_t < C \Rightarrow r_s H < C \Rightarrow r_s < \frac{C}{H}$$

Therefore, $r_s < 1482.614$ characters/s. Hence, the maximum rate at which data can be sent from the terminal to the computer without error is $r_{s,\max} = 1482.614$ characters/s.

4.6 Capacity of Channels

4.6.1 Channel Capacity of a Binary Symmetric Channel

BSC is one of the most commonly used channels. Figure 4.15 shows the channel diagram of a BSC. Here, p is known as the error probability and $q = 1-p$ is the probability of no error.

For a BSC, we have

$$H(Y\,|\,X) = p\log\frac{1}{p} + q\log\frac{1}{q} = H(p)$$

$$H(y) = [p-\alpha(p-q)]\log\frac{1}{[p-\alpha(p-q)]} + [q+\alpha(p-q)]\log\frac{1}{[q+\alpha(p-q)]}$$

$$I(X,Y) = H(Y) - H\left(\frac{Y}{X}\right)$$

The channel capacity is

$$C = 1 + p\log p + q\log q \tag{4.24}$$

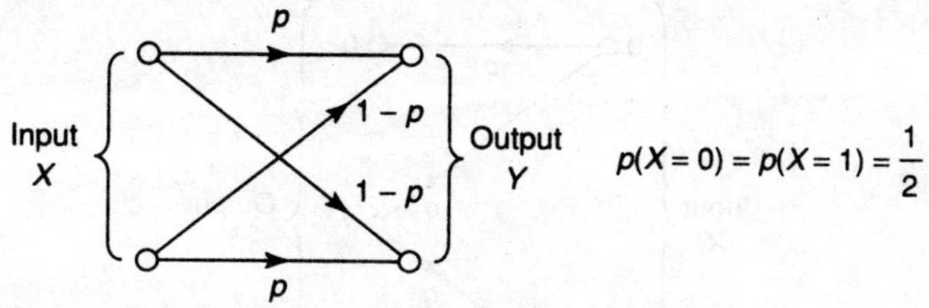

Figure 4.15 | Binary symmetric channel.

This occurs when $\alpha = 0.5$, that is, $P(X = 0) = P(X = 1) = 0.5$. With $P(X = 0) = P(X = 1) = 0.5$, we have

Probability of sending a '1' = Probability of error in the channel

$$\begin{aligned}\text{Probability of error} &= P(Y=1 \mid X=0)\cdot P(X=0) + P(Y=0 \mid X=1)\cdot P(X=1)\\ &= p\times 0.5 + p\times 0.5 = p\end{aligned}$$

Hence, probability of no error = $1 - p = q$. Thus, we have

$$P(Z=1) = p$$

and

$$P(Z=0) = q$$

Additional amount of information supplied therefore is nothing but equivocation and is equal to

$$p\log\frac{1}{p} + q\log\frac{1}{q} = H(X \mid Y) = H(Y \mid X)$$

It may be verified that when the channel is noise free, the channel capacity goes to 1 and for noisy channels, it goes down to 0.

4.6.2 Channel Capacity of a Binary Erasure Channel

A binary erasure channel (BEC) has two inputs (0, 1) and three outputs (0, ?, 1). Figure 4.16 shows the channel diagram of a BEC. The symbol '?' indicates that due to noise, no definite decision can be made as to whether the received symbol is 0 or 1. In this sense, the output is erased and hence the name. In practical cases, whenever the received symbol is '?', the receiver requests the transmitter to retransmit till the decision is taken in favor of either 0 or 1. This ensures 100% correct data recovery. It may be noted that BEC is also a symmetric channel and we have $P(X = 0) = \alpha$ and $P(X = 1) = 1 - \alpha$:

$$H(Y \mid X) = p\log\frac{1}{p} + q\log\frac{1}{q}$$

$$H(X) = \alpha\log\frac{1}{\alpha} + (1-\alpha)\log\frac{1}{(1-\alpha)}$$

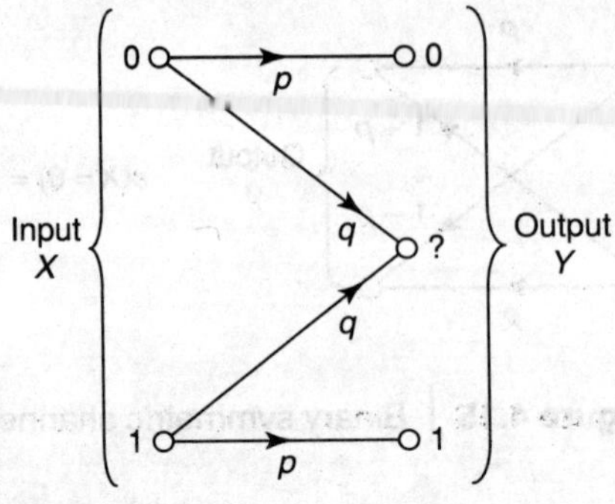

Figure 4.16 | Binary erasure channel.

The JPM is obtained by multiplying the first row of $P(Y|X)$ by α and second row by $(1 - \alpha)$. Hence,

$$P(X,Y) = \begin{bmatrix} q\alpha & p\alpha & 0 \\ 0 & p(1-\alpha) & q(1-\alpha) \end{bmatrix}$$

The probabilities of the output symbols can be obtained by adding elements columnwise, that is

$$P(Y) = [q\alpha, p, q(1-\alpha)]$$

$P(X|Y)$ can be computed as

$$P(X|Y) = \begin{bmatrix} 1 & \alpha & 0 \\ 0 & (1-\alpha) & 1 \end{bmatrix}$$

$$H(X|Y) = \alpha q \log 1 + \alpha p \log\frac{1}{\alpha} + (1-\alpha)p\log\frac{1}{(1-\alpha)} + (1-\alpha)q\log 1 = pH(X)$$

$$I(X,Y) = H(X) - H(X|Y) = (1-p)\,H(X) = qH(X)$$

Hence,

$$C = \max I(X;Y) = q \text{ bits/sym} \tag{4.25}$$

It may be seen that the use of equation $I(X, Y) = H(Y) - H(Y|X)$ is incorrect, as $H(Y)$ involves '?' and the information given by '?' is rejected by the receiver. Also it may be seen that the capacity of a BEC is much better than the BSC, which is obvious due to retransmission strategy. BEC can also be used to increase the channel efficiency further.

4.6.3 Muroga's Theorem

For the channel with noise characteristic, $P(Y|X)$, is square and non-singular, the capacity can be obtained using the following equation:

$$C = \log \sum_{i=1}^{i=n} 2^{-Q_i} \tag{4.26}$$

where Q_i are the solutions of the matrix equation $P(Y|X) \cdot Q = [h]$, where $h = [h_1, h_2, h_3, h_4, \ldots, hn]^t$ are the row entropies of $P(Y|X)$:

$$\begin{bmatrix} p_{11} & p_{12} & p_{13} & \cdots & p_{1n} \\ p_{21} & p_{22} & p_{23} & \cdots & p_{2n} \\ \vdots & \vdots & \vdots & \vdots & \vdots \\ p_{n1} & p_{n2} & p_{n3} & \cdots & p_{nn} \end{bmatrix} \cdot \begin{bmatrix} Q_1 \\ Q_2 \\ \vdots \\ Q_n \end{bmatrix} = \begin{bmatrix} h_1 \\ h_2 \\ \vdots \\ h_n \end{bmatrix}$$

$$C = \log\left\{\sum_{i=1}^{n} 2^{-Q_i}\right\}$$

$$p_i' = 2^{-Q_i - C}$$

where p_i' are obtained from

$$p_i' = p_1 \cdot p_{1i} + p_2 \cdot p_{2i} + p_3 \cdot p_{3i} + \cdots + p_n \cdot p_{ni}$$

$$p_i' = [p_1 \quad p_2 \quad \cdots \quad p_n] \cdot \underbrace{\begin{bmatrix} p_{1i} \\ p_{2i} \\ \vdots \\ p_{ni} \end{bmatrix}}_{i\text{th column of } P[Y|X]}$$

or
$$[p_1', p_2', p_3', \ldots, p_n'] = [p_1, p_2, p_3, \ldots, p_n] P[Y \mid X]$$

From this, we can solve for the source probabilities (i.e. input symbol probabilities):

$$[p_1, p_2, p_3, \ldots, p_n] = [p_1', p_2', p_3', \ldots, p_n'] P^{-1}[Y \mid X]$$

assuming that the inverse exists. Despite the correct value for the channel capacity, this value of C does not lead to physically realizable probability values. Also the values of Q_i cannot be obtained if the inverse of $P[Y|X]$ does not exist. The method however gives a novel method for computing the channel capacity whose noise characteristic, $P(Y|X)$ is square and non-singular.

EXAMPLE 4.10

Show that the channel capacity of a symmetric channel is given by $C = (\log_2 M - h)$, where 'M' is the total number of output symbols.

Solution: A symmetric channel is the one in which the transition probabilities from any of the inputs is the same. In other words, the element set in all rows of a channel matrix is the same. Consider there are N input and M output lines. One possible general channel matrix for a symmetric channel is shown as follows:

$$P\left(\frac{Y}{X}\right)=\begin{bmatrix} p_1 & p_2 & \cdots & p_M \\ p_M & p_1 & & p_3 \\ \vdots & & \ddots & \vdots \\ p_4 & p_2 & \cdots & p_1 \end{bmatrix}$$

From Eq. (4.1), the sum of all the elements in any of the rows of a channel matrix is always 1, that is,

$$\sum_{j=1}^{n} P\left(\frac{Y_j}{X_i}\right)=1 \quad \forall i$$

Therefore,

$$p_1+p_2+p_3+\cdots+P_M=1$$

that is,

$$\sum_{j=1}^{M} P_j=1$$

We have

$$I(X;Y)=H(Y)-H(Y/X) \text{ bits/sym}$$

$$H\left(\frac{Y}{X}\right)=-\sum_i\sum_j P(x_i,y_j)\cdot\log_2 P\left(\frac{y_j}{x_i}\right)=-\sum_i\sum_j P(x_i)P\left(\frac{y_j}{x_i}\right)\cdot\log_2 P\left(\frac{y_j}{x_i}\right)$$

$$=-\sum_i\sum_j P(x_i)P(y_j)\cdot\log_2 P(y_j)=\sum_i x_i\left[-\sum_j P(y_j)\log P(y_j)\right]$$

But $\sum_i P(x_i)=1$. Let

$$h=\left[-\sum_j P(y_j)\log P(y_j)\right]$$

Therefore,

$$H\left(\frac{Y}{X}\right)=h$$

which is a constant for a given channel diagram. The channel capacity is given by

$$C=\max[I(X,Y)]=\max\left[H(Y)-H\left(\frac{Y}{X}\right)\right]=\max[H(Y)]-h$$

$$C = [\log_2 M - h]\,\text{bps} \tag{4.27}$$

hence the proof.

EXAMPLE 4.11

Determine the capacity of the channel as shown in Fig. 4.17.

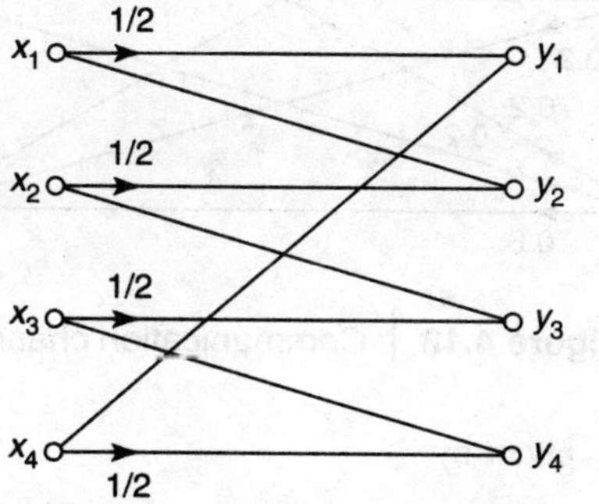

Figure 4.17 | Communication channel.

Solution: The given channel is a symmetric channel, whose channel matrix is given by

$$P\left(\frac{Y}{X}\right) = \begin{bmatrix} \frac{1}{2} & \frac{1}{2} & 0 & 0 \\ 0 & \frac{1}{2} & \frac{1}{2} & 0 \\ 0 & 0 & \frac{1}{2} & \frac{1}{2} \\ \frac{1}{2} & 0 & 0 & \frac{1}{2} \end{bmatrix}$$

The capacity of a symmetric channel is given by

$$C = [\log_2 M - h]\,\text{bps}$$

where

$$h = \left[-\sum_j P(y_j)\log P(y_j)\right] = -\left[\frac{1}{2}\log_2\frac{1}{2} + \frac{1}{2}\log_2\frac{1}{2}\right] = 1\,\text{bit/sym}$$

So

$$C = \log_2 4 - 1 = 1\,\text{bit/sym}$$

EXAMPLE 4.12

The noise characteristics of a channel are as shown in Fig. 4.18. Find the capacity of the channel.

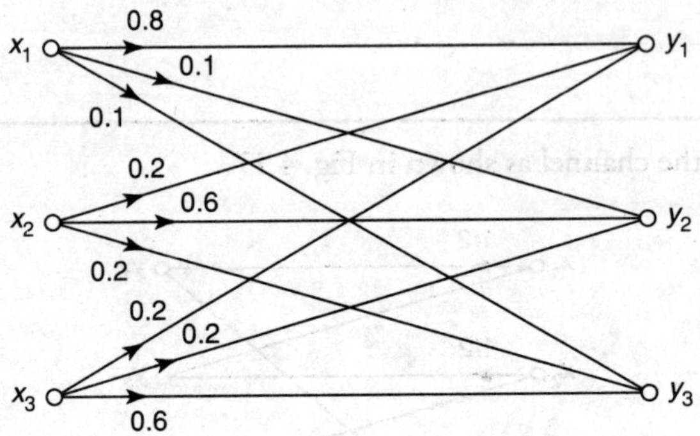

Figure 4.18 | Communication channel.

Solution: The channel matrix is given by

$$P\left(\frac{Y}{X}\right) = \begin{bmatrix} 0.8 & 0.1 & 0.1 \\ 0.2 & 0.6 & 0.2 \\ 0.2 & 0.2 & 0.6 \end{bmatrix}$$

We can go for Muroga's method to solve this problem:

$$\begin{bmatrix} 0.8 & 0.1 & 0.1 \\ 0.2 & 0.6 & 0.2 \\ 0.2 & 0.2 & 0.6 \end{bmatrix}\begin{bmatrix} Q_1 \\ Q_2 \\ Q_3 \end{bmatrix} = \begin{bmatrix} 0.8\log_2 0.8 + 0.1\log_2 0.1 + 0.1\log_2 0.1 \\ 0.2\log_2 0.2 + 0.6\log_2 0.6 + 0.2\log_2 0.2 \\ 0.2\log_2 0.2 + 0.2\log_2 0.2 + 0.6\log_2 0.6 \end{bmatrix} = \begin{bmatrix} -0.922 \\ -1.371 \\ -1.371 \end{bmatrix}$$

The following equations can be formulated using the above relation:

$$0.8Q_1 + 0.1Q_2 + 0.1Q_3 = -0.922$$

$$0.2Q_1 + 0.6Q_2 + 0.2Q_3 = -1.371$$

$$0.2Q_1 + 0.2Q_2 + 0.6Q_3 = -1.371$$

Solving the above equations, we will get

$$Q_1 = -0.7723,\ Q_2 = -1.5207,\ Q_3 = -1.5207$$

So

$$C = \log_2[2^{Q_1} + 2^{Q_2} + 2^{Q_3}] = 0.359 \text{ bit/sym}$$

4.7 Continuous Channels

Generally, the information that is normally transmitted is a continuous speech or picture signal rather than discrete. Hence, information can be thought of in continuous sample space. The sample points in this sample space will form a continuum, in contrast to the discrete case. In view of this, a continuous channel can thus be defined as the one with the input belonging to a continuous sample space and the output is also a sample point belonging to either the same or even a different sample space. Furthermore, we can also define a channel known as the *zero-memory continuous channel.* A zero memory continuous channel is defined as the one in which the channel output statistically depends on the corresponding channels without memory. Here we define information entropy, mutual information and capacity for a continuous source, assuming that there is no time dependence between the messages.

4.7.1 Entropy of Continuous Signals (Differential Entropy)

Various entropies in the discrete case were defined based on the concept of statistical averages of a discrete set. In a similar way, we can define entropies for a continuous channel also in terms of statistical averages of a source probability distribution.

The entropy of a discrete information source is given by

$$H(S)=\sum_{k=1}^{N} p_k \log_2 \frac{1}{p_k} \text{ bits/sym} \tag{4.28}$$

Consider a continuous random variable x_i with a probability density function $f(x)$. Then the summation of the above equation has to be replaced by an integration, and the expression for the entropy of a continuous signal is given by

$$H(X)=\int_{-\infty}^{+\infty} f(x)\log_2 \frac{1}{f(x)}dx \tag{4.29}$$

It is also called a differential entropy.

4.7.2 Mutual Information and Capacity of a Continuous Noisy Channel

Various entropies were defined in Section 4.3. All concepts we discussed for discrete systems hold good for continuous systems also. Thus, we can define equivocation and joint entropies for continuous systems also as follows:

$$H(X,Y)=-\iint_{-\infty}^{+\infty} f(x,y)\log_2 f(x,y)dx\,dy \tag{4.30}$$

$$H\left(\frac{X}{Y}\right)=-\iint_{-\infty}^{+\infty} f(x,y)\log_2 f\left(\frac{x}{y}\right)dx\,dy \tag{4.31}$$

where $f(x, y)$ and $f(x/y)$ are the joint and conditional probability density functions, respectively.

Similarly, the mutual information $I(X;Y)$ is given by

$$I(X;Y) = -\iint_{-\infty}^{+\infty} f(x,y)\log_2 \frac{f(x/y)}{f(x)} dxdy = -\iint_{-\infty}^{+\infty} f(x,y)\log_2 \frac{f(y/x)}{f(y)} dxdy \quad (4.32)$$

and the channel capacity is given by

$$C = \max[I(X;Y)] \quad (4.33)$$

It can be seen that $I(X; Y) \geq 0$, meaning that mutual information of a continuous channel is always positive. Further, if the channel allows transmission of R_s symbols per second, then the channel capacity rate C_s becomes

$$C_s = R_s C \quad (4.34)$$

Summary

1. Measure of the average uncertainty of the channel input:

$$H(X) = -\sum_i P(x_i)\cdot \log_2 P(x_i)$$

2. Measure of the average uncertainty of the channel output:

$$H(Y) = -\sum_j P(y_j)\cdot \log_2 P(y_j)$$

3. Measure of the average uncertainty remaining of the channel at the input after the channel output is known—equivocation of Y with respect to X:

$$H\left(\frac{X}{Y}\right) = -\sum_i\sum_j P(x_i, y_j)\cdot \log_2 P\left(\frac{x_i}{y_j}\right)$$

4. Measure of the average uncertainty of the channel output given that X was transmitted:

$$H\left(\frac{Y}{X}\right) = -\sum_i\sum_j P(x_i, y_j)\cdot \log_2 P\left(\frac{y_j}{x_i}\right)$$

5. Measure of the average uncertainty of the communication channel as a whole:

$$H(X,Y) = H(X) + H\left(\frac{Y}{X}\right) = H(Y) + H\left(\frac{X}{Y}\right)$$

6. The balance of information received at the receiver with respect to the observed output symbol is referred to as mutual information and is defined by

$$I(X;Y) = H(X) - H\left(\frac{X}{Y}\right) \text{ bits/symbol}$$

7. Properties of mutual information:
   - $I(X;Y) = I(Y;X)$
   - $I(X;Y) \geq 0$

8. The joint entropy $H(X,Y)$ is terms of $H(X)$, $H(Y)$ and $I(X;Y)$ is:

$$H(X,Y) = H(X) + H(Y) - I(X;Y)$$

9. The average rate of information transfer:

$$R_{tr} = I(X;Y)\cdot r_s \text{ bits/s}$$

10. The Shannon–Hartley theorem for channel coding gives the channel capacity as

$$C = B\log_2\left(1 + \frac{S}{N}\right)$$

11. The channel capacity of a symmetric channel is given by

$$C = \log_2 M - h$$

where 'M' is the total number of output symbols.

Review Questions

1. For the channel shown in Fig. 4.19, write the channel matrix.

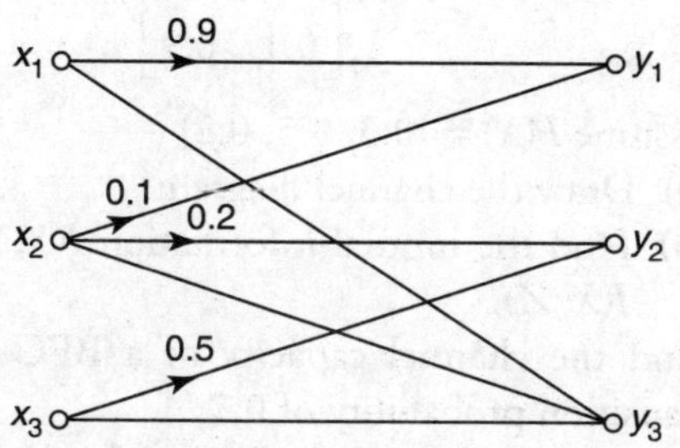

Figure 4.19 | Channel diagram.

2. For the channel matrix given, find the missing entries. Also draw the corresponding channel diagram.

$$\text{Channel matrix} = P\left(\frac{Y}{X}\right) = \begin{array}{c} \\ x_1 \\ x_2 \\ x_3 \\ x_4 \end{array}\begin{array}{c} \begin{array}{cccc} y_1 & y_2 & y_3 & y_4 \end{array} \\ \begin{bmatrix} 0.1 & 0.1 & * & 0.6 \\ 0.3 & 0.4 & 0 & * \\ * & 0.5 & 0.1 & 0.2 \\ 0.1 & * & 0.4 & 0.5 \end{bmatrix} \end{array}$$

3. Show that

$$H(X,Y) = H\left(\frac{X}{Y}\right) + H(Y) = H\left(\frac{Y}{X}\right) + H(X)$$

4. For the JPM matrix given, find

(a) $H(X)$

(b) $H(Y)$

(c) $H(X,Y)$

(d) $H\left(\frac{Y}{X}\right)$

(e) $H\left(\frac{X}{Y}\right)$

$$\text{JPM} = P(X,Y) = \begin{array}{c} \\ x_1 \\ x_2 \\ x_3 \\ x_4 \end{array}\begin{array}{c} \begin{array}{cccc} y_1 & y_2 & y_3 & y_4 \end{array} \\ \begin{bmatrix} 0.15 & 0 & 0 & 0.05 \\ 0 & 0.20 & 0.15 & 0 \\ 0 & 0 & 0.10 & 0.05 \\ 0.10 & 0.10 & 0 & 0.10 \end{bmatrix} \end{array}$$

5. Channel matrix for a channel is given as follows:

$$P\left(\frac{Y}{X}\right) = \begin{array}{c} \\ x_1 \\ x_2 \\ x_3 \end{array}\begin{array}{c} \begin{array}{ccc} y_1 & y_2 & y_3 \end{array} \\ \begin{bmatrix} 0.4 & 0.3 & 0.3 \\ 0.3 & 0.2 & 0.5 \\ 0.1 & 0.4 & 0.5 \end{bmatrix} \end{array}$$

Also, the input probabilities of the channel are

$$P[X] = \left[\frac{1}{2}, \frac{1}{4}, \frac{1}{4}\right]$$

Find

(a) $H(X)$

(b) $H(Y)$

(c) $H(X,Y)$

(d) $H\left(\frac{Y}{X}\right)$

(e) $H\left(\frac{X}{Y}\right)$

6. Consider a BSC with a transition probability of $P(0/0) = P(1/1) = 0.8$. The inputs are equally likely to occur. Draw the channel diagram. Also find:

(a) $H(X)$

(b) $H(Y)$

(c) $H(X,Y)$

(d) $H\left(\frac{Y}{X}\right)$

(e) $H\left(\frac{X}{Y}\right)$

7. Show that $I(X;Y) \geq 0$.
8. Show that $I(X;Y) = I(Y;X)$.
9. Find the rate of information transmission for the JPM given. Assume $r_s = 1000$ sym/s:

$$\text{JPM} = P(X,Y) = \begin{bmatrix} 0.2 & 0.1 & 0.1 \\ 0.1 & 0.3 & 0 \\ 0.1 & 0 & 0.1 \end{bmatrix}$$

10. Consider the cascaded channel with the following channel matrices:

$$P\left(\frac{Y}{X}\right) = \begin{array}{c|ccc} & y_1 & y_2 & y_3 \\ x_1 & 0.7 & 0 & 0.3 \\ x_2 & 0.8 & 0.2 & 0 \\ x_3 & 0 & 0.5 & 0.5 \end{array}$$

$$P\left(\frac{Z}{Y}\right) = \begin{array}{c|cc} & z_1 & z_2 \\ y_1 & 0.7 & 0.3 \\ y_2 & 0.5 & 0.5 \\ y_3 & 0.1 & 0.9 \end{array}$$

Assume $P(X) = [0.3, 0.5, 0.2]$.
   (a) Draw the channel diagram.
   (b) Find the mutual information $I(X; Y)$ and $I(X; Z)$.

11. Find the channel capacity of a BEC with a transition probability of 0.7.
12. Find the capacity of the channel for the following channel matrix:

$$P\left(\frac{Y}{X}\right) = \begin{array}{c|ccc} & y_1 & y_2 & y_3 \\ x_1 & 0.2 & 0.5 & 0.3 \\ x_2 & 0.2 & 0.6 & 0.2 \\ x_3 & 0.1 & 0.1 & 0.8 \end{array}$$

Further Reading

[1] Shanmugam K Sam, *Digital and Analog Communication Systems*, John Wiley & Sons: New York; 1996.

[2] Simon Haykin, *Digital Communication*, John Wiley & Sons: New York; 2003.

[3] Ranjan Bose, *Information Theory Coding and Cryptography*, Tata McGraw Hill: New Delhi; 2008.

[4] Simon Haykin and Michael Moher, *Modern Wireless Communications*, Pearson Education: Upper Saddle River, NJ; 2007.

[5] Jorge Castineira Moreira and Patrick Guy Farrell, *Essentials of Error-Control Coding*, John Wiley & Sons: Chichester; 2006.

5 Error Control Coding

'Everything should be as simple as it is, but not simpler.'

–Albert Einstein

Learning Objectives

After reading this chapter, you will be able to:

- Emphasize the need for error control codes in a communication system.
- Define various error control codes.
- Detail the features of linear block codes.
- Design and analyze the encoding and decoding procedures of linear block codes.
- Discuss some special class of linear block codes involving Hamming and cyclic codes.

5.1 Introduction

In the present world of information systems, digital communication and storage have become ubiquitous parts of our daily lives. The history of modern communication system dates back to 1948 when Shannon proposed a concrete system for the digital communication in his paper '*A Mathematical Theory of Communication*'. He suggested that proper encoding of information in any digital communication or storage systems will lead to substantial increase in the noise immunity of the system without affecting the rate of information transmission and storage. A typical digital communication system is shown in Fig. 5.1.

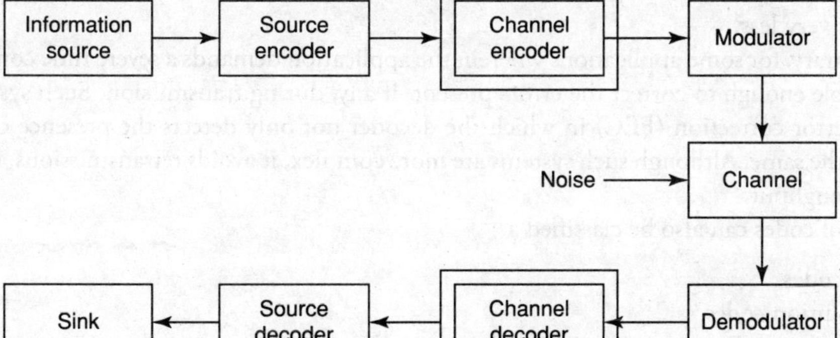

Figure 5.1 | Functional block diagram of a communication system.

The details and working of the information source, source encoder/decoder have been studied in Chapters 2 and 3. The channel encoder transforms a 'k'-bit message sequence to an 'n'-bit codeword by adding $(n - k)$ redundant bits. These redundant bits are added so as to facilitate the receiver for error detection/correction. These bits are also called parity bits and are computed on the basis of some mathematical operations performed over input bits. The ratio $k/n = R$ gives the code rate of the given channel encoder.

5.2 Need for Error Control Coding

Communication channels used for transmission are generally noisy. In other words, data being transmitted through a channel are always prone to interference and noise. If redundancy is not included, the receiver will not have any scope to check the correctness of transmission. For example, consider a binary source emitting symbol k-bits long. Therefore, there will be 2^k possible information symbols. If check bits are not included, then every 'k' bit symbol received will resemble one of the input sequences, despite the presence of errors during transmission, thus restricting the decoder from detecting the presence of errors, if any.

In order to overcome this problem, some sort of redundancy has to be included in the input side so that error patterns do not resemble the valid vectors for a certain number of error bits.

Consider the same example of k-bit message. If $(n - k)$ redundant bits were included so as to make 'n' bit code vector, there will be 2^n possible vectors out of which only 2^k are valid code vectors corresponding to 2^k input sequences. Thus, if any of $2^n - 2^k$ error patterns are received, the receiver can detect them correctly.

Therefore, we can conclude that error control coding is needed for any digital communication or storage system to assure reliability.

5.3 Types of Codes

Error control coding can be categorized into two groups depending on its ability to detect or correct errors. In some systems wherein the probability of errors during transmission is so less that retransmission of the erroneous frames would be a better choice than to devise a complex circuitry at the receiver for error correction. Such type of codes are termed as error detection codes and categorized as automatic repeat request (ARQ). It is a simple system and does not make any attempt to correct errors. Such systems can be used for scenarios where bit error rate (BER) is too small, so that the probability of error being present in the transmission is very less.

On the contrary, for some applications wherein the application demands a severe time constraint, receiver has to be capable enough to correct the errors present, if any, during transmission. Such systems are said to have forward error correction (FEC) in which the decoder not only detects the presence of error but also tries to rectify the same. Although such systems are more complex, it avoids retransmissions, thus, improving the system throughput.

Error control codes can also be classified as:

1. Block codes.
2. Convolution codes.

In block codes, a k tuple binary message block is considered at a time and is encoded to an n-tuple codeword independently. Figure 5.2 gives an overview of a block code. For example, a (7, 4) code is a block code that takes 4 bits of information at a time and converts it into a 7-bit codeword.

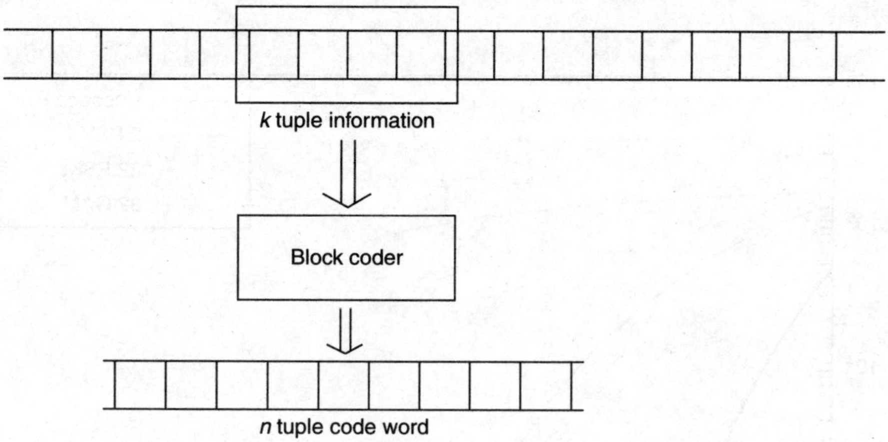

Figure 5.2 | Block code.

Convolution encoders differ from block codes in various ways. One of the major differences is the presence of memory elements in convolution encoder. In other words, the present output of a convolution encoder is also dependent on the past input bits. Also sequences of blocks of inputs and outputs are considered in convolution coding instead of single blocks.

5.4 Coding Gain

Shannon has given a theory in which he specified the importance of (E_b/N_0) and has given a limit for (E_b/N_0) so as to achieve a certain level of BER, where E_b is the energy per bit and N_0 being the noise power spectral density. It has been shown that the amount of (E_b/N_0) required for a coded system to achieve a certain level of BER is less than that of an uncoded system. This gain in (E_b/N_0) due to channel coding is known as *coding gain*.

Figure 5.3 shows the plot of (E_b/N_0) as a function of BER. It is clear from the graph that for a fixed BER, required (E_b/N_0) for a coded system is less compared to a system without coding. The coding gain is also depicted in Fig. 5.3.

5.5 Linear Block Codes

As discussed in Section 5.3, block codes are the type of codes in which a k-tuple information is accepted at a time and an n-tuple codeword is formed. Clearly, $n > k$.

Now we can formally define an (n, k) binary linear block code as a k-dimensional subspace of an n-dimensional vector space V over the field F_2 such that linear combination of any two vectors in the subspace will lead to another vector in the subspace itself. Mathematically, $\forall\ v_1, v_2 \in C,\ v_1 \oplus v_2 \in C$. It is shown in Fig. 5.4.

As k-tuple messages are considered, there are 2^k different input combinations. A unique codeword has to be defined for every set of k-tuple information. In other words, the codeword and information sequence have to satisfy a one-to-one relation. Thus, there will be 2^k valid codewords, that is., the subspace C contains

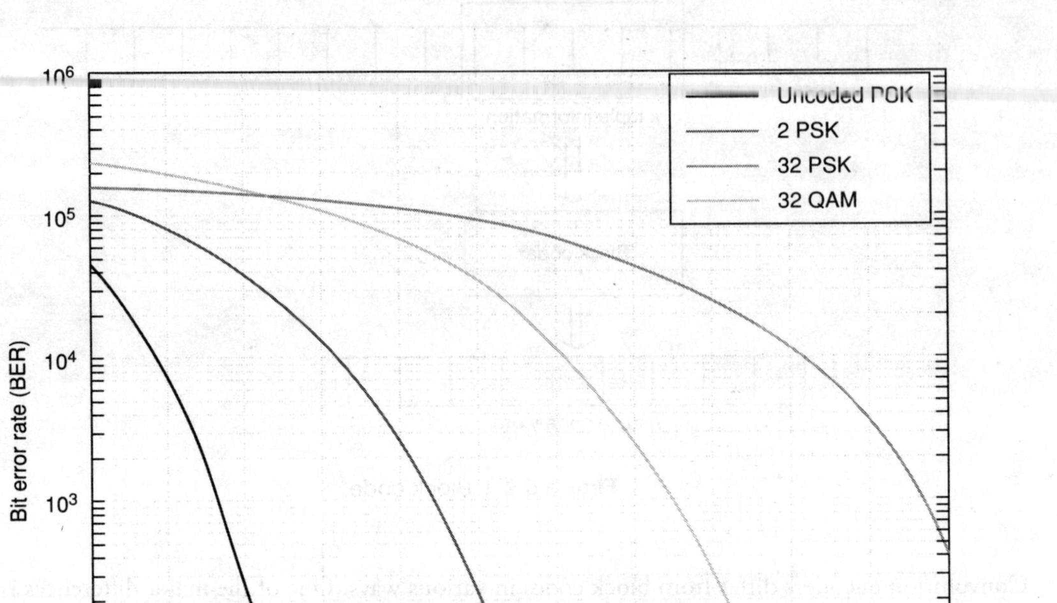

Figure 5.3 | (E_b/N_0) for coded and uncoded systems.

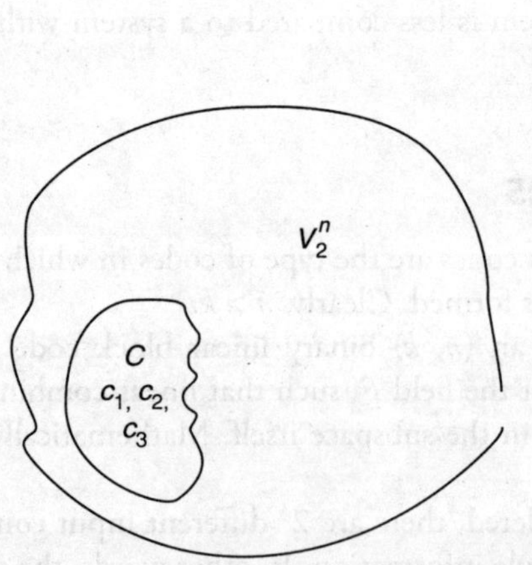

Figure 5.4 | Linear block codes as a vector space.

2^k n-tuple binary vectors. If any vector other than these 2^k valid vectors is received, the receiver can easily make out the presence of error.

From the definition, it is clear that 'C' is a k-dimensional subspace of a vector space V. Thus, we need to identify k n-tuple vectors in the space C which form a basis set for C. Let the basis set be

$$G = \begin{bmatrix} g_1 \\ g_2 \\ . \\ . \\ g_k \end{bmatrix} \begin{matrix} \text{where } g_1 = g_{10} & g_{11} & \cdots & g_{1n-1} \\ g_2 = g_{20} & g_{21} & \cdots & g_{2n-1} \\ \cdots \\ \cdots \\ g_k = g_{k0} & g_{k1} & \cdots & g_{kn-1} \end{matrix} \Bigg\} n\text{-tuple vectors} \tag{5.1}$$

Thus, every codeword in C can be obtained as a linear combination of k n-tuple basis vectors

$$V = u_0 g_1 + u_1 g_2 + \cdots + u_{k-1} g_k = [u_0 \ u_1 \ldots u_{k-1}] \begin{bmatrix} g_1 \\ g_2 \\ . \\ . \\ g_k \end{bmatrix}$$

$$V = [u_0 \ u_1 \ldots u_{k-1}] \begin{bmatrix} g_1 = g_{10} \ g_{11} \cdots g_{1n-1} \\ g_2 = g_{20} \ g_{21} \cdots g_{2n-1} \\ \cdots \\ \cdots \\ g_k = g_{k0} \ g_{k1} \cdots g_{kn-1} \end{bmatrix} = u \cdot G \tag{5.2}$$

Therefore, for any input vector u, the codeword v can be obtained as $v = u \cdot G$. Matrix G is also called generator matrix.

Sometimes the relation can also be represented as $[v] = [u][G]$, where v is the code vector and u is the data vector.

Note: The generator matrix G for given (n, k) values need not be unique.

It is always desirable to represent a codeword in its systematic form as

k-bit information	$(n-k)$ Check bits

Linear block codes (LBC) can be represented in systematic form so that information bits and check bits can be separated from the codeword. For such representation, the generator matrix G has to be of the form either $G = [I_k{:}P]$ in which case the data bits will come at the beginning or $G = [P{:}I_k]$, where data bits come at the end of the codeword. Here I_k is a $k \times k$ identity matrix and P is a $k \times (n-k)$ parity matrix.

EXAMPLE 5.1

Obtain the encoded information for the given message and generator matrix.

$$u=[1\ 0\ 1\ 1] \quad \text{and} \quad G=\begin{bmatrix}1\,1\,1\,1\,0\,0\,0\\1\,0\,1\,0\,1\,0\,0\\1\,1\,0\,0\,0\,1\,0\\0\,1\,1\,0\,0\,0\,1\end{bmatrix}$$

Solution: The code vector for the given data vector can be obtained considering the Eq. 5.2.

$$v=u\cdot G=[1\ 0\ 1\ 1]\begin{bmatrix}1\,1\,1\,1\,0\,0\,0\\1\,0\,1\,0\,1\,0\,0\\1\,1\,0\,0\,0\,1\,0\\0\,1\,1\,0\,0\,0\,1\end{bmatrix}=[0\ 1\ 0\ 1\ 0\ 1\ 1]$$

EXAMPLE 5.2

Obtain all possible code vectors for a (7, 4) LBC in its systematic form for the generator matrix

$$G=\begin{bmatrix}1\,1\,0\,0\,0\,1\,1\\0\,1\,0\,0\,1\,0\,1\\1\,0\,1\,0\,1\,0\,1\\0\,0\,0\,1\,1\,1\,1\end{bmatrix}$$

Solution: First of all, the given generator matrix is not in the systematic form. Thus, first we need to reduce the given G matrix to the form $[I_k{:}P]$ by elementary row operations:

$$r_1\rightarrow r_1+r_2\Rightarrow\begin{bmatrix}1\,0\,0\,0\,1\,1\,0\\0\,1\,0\,0\,1\,0\,1\\1\,0\,1\,0\,1\,0\,1\\0\,0\,0\,1\,1\,1\,1\end{bmatrix}$$

$$r_3\rightarrow r_3+r_1\Rightarrow\begin{bmatrix}1\,0\,0\,0\,1\,1\,0\\0\,1\,0\,0\,1\,0\,1\\0\,0\,1\,0\,0\,1\,1\\0\,0\,0\,1\,1\,1\,1\end{bmatrix}$$

As $k = 4$, there are $2^4 = 16$ different message combinations possible. Codeword corresponding to each of the message sequence can be obtained by just multiplying the respective message vector with the generator matrix.

$$v = u \cdot G = \begin{bmatrix} 0\,0\,0\,0 \\ 0\,0\,0\,1 \\ 0\,0\,1\,0 \\ 0\,0\,1\,1 \\ 0\,1\,0\,0 \\ 0\,1\,0\,1 \\ 0\,1\,1\,0 \\ 0\,1\,1\,1 \\ 1\,0\,0\,0 \\ 1\,0\,0\,1 \\ 1\,0\,1\,0 \\ 1\,0\,1\,1 \\ 1\,1\,0\,0 \\ 1\,1\,0\,1 \\ 1\,1\,1\,0 \\ 1\,1\,1\,1 \end{bmatrix} \begin{bmatrix} 1\,0\,0\,0\,1\,1\,0 \\ 0\,1\,0\,0\,1\,0\,1 \\ 0\,0\,1\,0\,0\,1\,1 \\ 0\,0\,0\,1\,1\,1\,1 \end{bmatrix} = \begin{bmatrix} 0\,0\,0\,0\,0\,0\,0 \\ 0\,0\,0\,1\,1\,1\,1 \\ 0\,0\,1\,0\,0\,1\,1 \\ 0\,0\,1\,1\,1\,0\,0 \\ 0\,1\,0\,0\,1\,0\,1 \\ 0\,1\,0\,1\,0\,1\,0 \\ 0\,1\,1\,0\,1\,1\,0 \\ 0\,1\,1\,1\,0\,0\,1 \\ 1\,0\,0\,0\,1\,1\,0 \\ 1\,0\,0\,1\,0\,0\,1 \\ 1\,0\,1\,0\,1\,0\,1 \\ 1\,0\,1\,1\,0\,1\,0 \\ 1\,1\,0\,0\,0\,1\,1 \\ 1\,1\,0\,1\,1\,0\,0 \\ 1\,1\,1\,0\,0\,0\,0 \\ 1\,1\,1\,1\,1\,1\,1 \end{bmatrix}$$

5.5.1 Parity Check Matrix

As C is a subspace of V, there will always exist a null space or dual space C^1 for C, such that for any vector $v \in C$ and $w \in C^1$, the inner product of v and w, $<v \cdot w> = 0$. Let H denote the basis set for C^1. According to the dimension theorem, H is an $(n-k)$-dimensional subspace of V. Therefore, there exist $(n-k)$ n-tuple vectors in the basis set H of C^1.

$$H = \begin{bmatrix} h_1 \\ h_2 \\ . \\ . \\ h_{n-k} \end{bmatrix} \quad \text{where } \begin{aligned} h_1 &= h_{10}\ h_{11} \ldots h_{1\,n-1} \\ h_2 &= h_{20}\ h_{21} \ldots h_{2\,n-1} \\ &\ldots \\ &\ldots \\ h_{n-k} &= h_{k0}\ h_{k1} \ldots h_{k\,n-1} \end{aligned} \tag{5.3}$$

It is clear from the above discussion that

$$vH^T = 0 \tag{5.4}$$

where v is a code vector in space C, but

$$v = u \cdot G$$

Therefore,

$$u \cdot G \cdot H^T = 0 \Rightarrow G \cdot H^T = 0 \tag{5.5}$$

The basis set of C^1, H is also called parity check matrix. From Eq. (5.4), it is evident that one can make out whether the transmission was successful by just examining the product of the received vector 'r' with the transpose of the parity check matrix H for zero resultant. Non-zero product will depict the presence of error. Parity check matrix H will be either of the form $H = [P^T{:}I_{n-k}]$, if $G = [I_k{:}P]$ or of the form $H = [I_{n-k}{:}P^T]$, when $G = [P{:}I_k]$ where I_{n-k} is an $(n-k) \times (n-k)$ identity matrix and P^T is the transpose of the parity matrix.

EXAMPLE 5.3

Determine H matrix for

$$G = \begin{bmatrix} 1 & 0 & 0 & 1 & 1 & 1 \\ 0 & 1 & 0 & 1 & 0 & 1 \\ 0 & 0 & 1 & 0 & 1 & 1 \end{bmatrix}$$

Solution: G is of the form $[I_3{:}P]$, $n = 6$, $k = 3$. Therefore, H will take the form $[P^T{:}I_{n-k}] = [P^T{:}I_3]$ where

$$P = \begin{bmatrix} 1 & 1 & 1 \\ 1 & 0 & 1 \\ 0 & 1 & 1 \end{bmatrix}$$

Therefore,

$$H = \begin{bmatrix} 1 & 1 & 0 & 1 & 0 & 0 \\ 1 & 0 & 1 & 0 & 1 & 0 \\ 1 & 1 & 1 & 0 & 0 & 1 \end{bmatrix}$$

It can be verified that $GH^T = 0$:

$$\begin{bmatrix} 1 & 0 & 0 & 1 & 1 & 1 \\ 0 & 1 & 0 & 1 & 0 & 1 \\ 0 & 0 & 1 & 0 & 1 & 1 \end{bmatrix} \begin{bmatrix} 1 & 1 & 1 \\ 1 & 0 & 1 \\ 0 & 1 & 1 \\ 1 & 0 & 0 \\ 0 & 1 & 0 \\ 0 & 0 & 1 \end{bmatrix} = \begin{bmatrix} 0 & 0 & 0 \\ 0 & 0 & 0 \\ 0 & 0 & 0 \end{bmatrix}$$

EXAMPLE 5.4

Determine the parity check matrix for a (7, 4) systematic LBC whose parity equations are

$$P_1 = u_0 + u_1 + u_3$$

$$P_2 = u_1 + u_2 + u_3$$

$$P_3 = u_0 + u_2 + u_3$$

Solution: From the parity equations, we can obtain the parity matrix P. We have

$$P_1 = u_0 + u_1 + u_3$$
$$P_2 = u_1 + u_2 + u_3$$
$$P_3 = u_0 + u_2 + u_3$$

$$\Rightarrow [u_0 \quad u_1 \quad u_2 \quad u_3]\begin{bmatrix} 1 & 0 & 1 \\ 1 & 1 & 0 \\ 0 & 1 & 1 \\ 1 & 1 & 1 \end{bmatrix}$$

Therefore,

$$P = \begin{bmatrix} 1 & 0 & 1 \\ 1 & 1 & 0 \\ 0 & 1 & 1 \\ 1 & 1 & 1 \end{bmatrix}$$

Hence,

$$H = [P^T : I_{n-k}] = \begin{bmatrix} 1\,1\,0\,1\,1\,0\,0 \\ 0\,1\,1\,1\,0\,1\,0 \\ 1\,0\,1\,1\,0\,0\,1 \end{bmatrix}$$

EXAMPLE 5.5

Find matrix H for the given generator matrix

$$G = \begin{bmatrix} 1\,1\,0\,1\,0\,0 \\ 1\,1\,1\,0\,1\,0 \\ 0\,1\,1\,0\,0\,1 \end{bmatrix}$$

Solution: In the given problem, G is of the form $[P{:}I_k]$. Therefore, matrix H will take the form

$$H = [I_{n-k}{:}\ P^T]$$

From the dimension of matrix G, we have $n = 6$ and $k = 3$. Also, considering the parity matrix P from the generator matrix, we can write the parity check matrix as

$$H = \begin{bmatrix} 1\;0\;0\;1\;1\;0 \\ 0\;1\;0\;1\;1\;1 \\ 0\;0\;1\;0\;1\;1 \end{bmatrix}$$

5.5.2 Encoding Circuit for an (n, k) LBC

Consider the relation between codeword and information

$$[V] = [u]\,[G]$$

$$[v_0 \;\; v_1 \ldots v_{n-1}] = [u_0 \;\; u_1 \ldots u_{k-1}] \begin{bmatrix} 1\,0 \ldots 0 \; P_{11} & P_{12} \ldots P_{1n-k} \\ 0\,1 \ldots 0 \; P_{21} & P_{22} \ldots P_{2n-k} \\ \ldots & \\ 0\,0 \ldots 1 \; P_{k1} & P_{k2} \ldots P_{kn-k} \end{bmatrix}$$

Expanding the above relation, we get

$$v_0 = u_0$$

$$v_1 = u_1$$

$$\ldots$$

$$\ldots$$

$$\ldots$$

$$v_{k-1} = u_{k-1}$$

$$v_k = u_0 P_{11} + u_1 P_{21} + \cdots + u_{k-1} P_{k-1}$$

$$\ldots$$

$$\ldots$$

$$\ldots$$

$$v_{n-1} = u_0 P_{1n-k} + u_1 P_{2n-k} + \cdots + u_{k-1} P_{kn-k} \tag{5.6}$$

Here, the addition is simply a XOR operation as the system is binary.

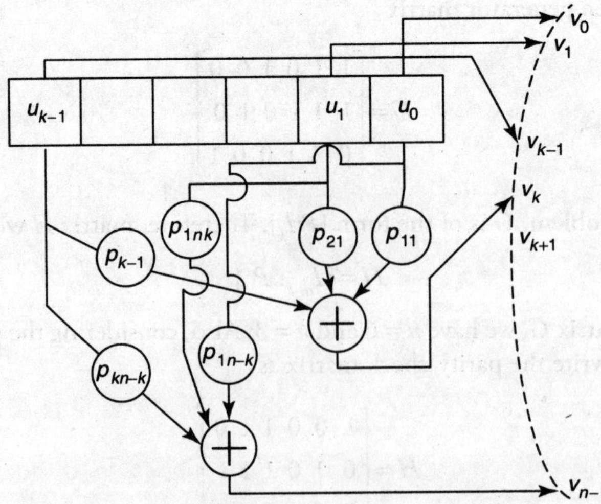

Figure 5.5 | A general (n, k) LBC encoder circuit.

Therefore, the encoder circuit can be realized using a logical circuit satisfying Eq. (5.6). A general encoder circuit for an (n, k) LBC is shown in Fig. 5.5.

EXAMPLE 5.6

Consider a systematic (8, 4) LBC whose parity check equations are

$$v_4 = u_1 + u_2 + u_3$$

$$v_5 = u_0 + u_1 + u_2$$

$$v_6 = u_0 + u_1 + u_3$$

$$v_7 = u_0 + u_2 + u_3$$

(a) Write the generator and parity check matrices.
(b) Draw the encoder diagram.

Solution:

(a) From the given parity equations, we can write the parity matrix as

$$P = \begin{bmatrix} 0 & 1 & 1 & 1 \\ 1 & 1 & 1 & 0 \\ 1 & 1 & 0 & 1 \\ 1 & 0 & 1 & 1 \end{bmatrix}$$

Thus, the generator matrix can be written as

$$G = [I_k : P] = \begin{bmatrix} 1000:0111 \\ 0100:1110 \\ 0010:1101 \\ 0001:1011 \end{bmatrix}$$

Also the parity check matrix H can be obtained as

$$H = [P^T : I_{n-k}] = \begin{bmatrix} 01111000 \\ 11100100 \\ 11010010 \\ 10110001 \end{bmatrix}$$

(b) To write the encoder diagram, we require having the equation for each code bit in the code vector. Consider,

$$[v] = [u]\,[G]$$

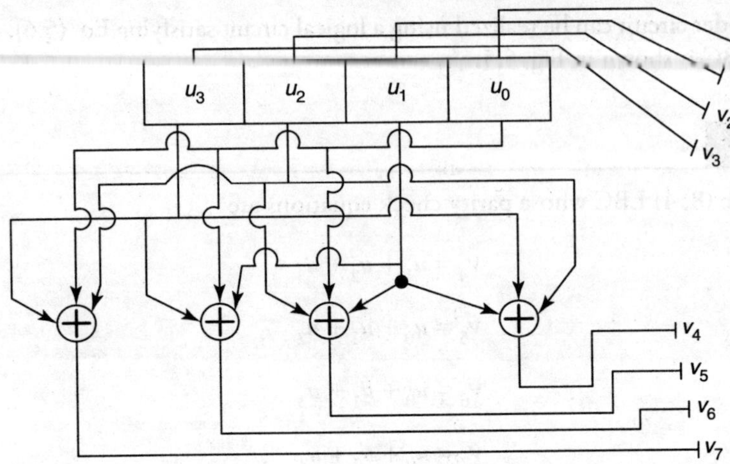

Figure 5.6 | An encoder circuit for the given (8, 4) LBC.

Using the given generator matrix, we can have the following equations:

$$v_0 = u_0$$

$$v_1 = u_1$$

$$v_2 = u_2$$

$$v_3 = u_3$$

$$v_4 = u_1 + u_2 + u_3$$

$$v_5 = u_0 + u_1 + u_3$$

$$v_6 = u_0 + u_1 + u_3$$

$$v_7 = u_0 + u_2 + u_3$$

The encoder circuit can be obtained by realizing the above equations. It is given in Fig. 5.6.

5.5.3 Syndrome Calculation and Error Detection

As discussed in Section 5.5.1, the receiver can detect the presence of errors if the received vector lies outside the subspace C. Let $r = [r_0\ r_1 \ldots r_{n-1}]$ be the received vector for the transmitted codeword $v = [v_0\ v_1 \ldots v_{n-1}]$. Let e be the error introduced during transmission. Therefore

$$r = v + e$$

Consider the parameter, syndrome S, for the received vector r given by

$$S = r\,H^T \tag{5.7}$$

But $r = v + e$; therefore

$$S = (v+e)H^T$$

$$\Rightarrow S = v\,H^T + e\,H^T$$

But $v\,H^T = 0$ from Eq. (5.4); therefore,

$$S = e\,H^T \tag{5.8}$$

Therefore, the syndrome S will be a non-zero entity for a non-zero error pattern. A non-zero syndrome indicates the presence of error during transmission.

Note: 1. As the syndrome is not dependent on the transmitted vector but on the error pattern, syndrome is same for all erroneous vectors with the same error pattern.
2. An error pattern resembling a valid code vector leads to a zero syndrome despite the presence of error. This is because if $e \in C$, $v \oplus e$ will always lie in the subspace C. Therefore, $(v+e)\,H^T = 0$. This is a limitation in LBC.

As $S = e\,H^T$, a single-bit error corresponds to a non-zero syndrome equal to the corresponding row of H^T. Therefore, such single-bit errors can be corrected by just inverting the corresponding bit in the received vector.

EXAMPLE 5.7

For the LBC given in Example 5.2, compute the syndrome for the received vector [0 1 1 0 1 0 0]. Correct the error, if any.

Solution: Given LBC in Example 5.2 is a (7, 4) LBC with

$$G = \begin{bmatrix} 1\,0\,0\,0\,1\,1\,0 \\ 0\,1\,0\,0\,1\,0\,1 \\ 0\,0\,1\,0\,0\,1\,1 \\ 0\,0\,0\,1\,1\,1\,1 \end{bmatrix}$$

Therefore,

$$H = [P^T : I_{n-k}] = \begin{bmatrix} 1101:100 \\ 1011:010 \\ 0111:001 \end{bmatrix}$$

Hence

$$S = rH^T = [0\;1\;1\;0\;1\;0\;\;0]\begin{bmatrix}1&1&0\\1&0&1\\0&1&1\\1&1&1\\1&0&0\\0&1&0\\0&0&1\end{bmatrix} = \begin{bmatrix}0&1&0\end{bmatrix}$$

Syndrome [0 1 0] corresponds to the sixth row in H^T; therefore, the sixth bit in the received vector is erroneous. So the corrected vector is $r' = [0\;\;1\;\;1\;\;0\;\;1\;\;1\;\;0]$. It can be verified that r' is a valid code vector as $r'\,H^T = 0$.

5.5.4 Syndrome Calculation Circuit

Consider the received vector $r = [r_0\; r_1\; \ldots\; r_{n-1}]$ and syndrome $s = [s_0\; s_1\; \ldots\; s_{n-k-1}]$. Then

$$S = rH^T = [r_0\quad r_1 \ldots r_{n-1}]\begin{bmatrix}P_{11} & P_{12} \ldots P_{1n-k}\\ P_{21} & P_{22} \ldots P_{2n-k}\\ \ldots & \\ P_{k1} & P_{k2} \ldots P_{kn-k}\\ 1 & 0\;\ldots\;0\\ 0 & 1\;\ldots\;0\\ \ldots & \\ 0 & 0\;\ldots\;1\end{bmatrix}$$

$$\left.\begin{aligned}s_0 &= r_0P_{11} + r_1P_{21} + \cdots + r_{k-1}P_{k1} + r_k\\ s_1 &= r_0P_{12} + r_1P_{22} + \cdots + r_{k-1}P_{k2} + r_{k+1}\\ \ldots\\ s_{n-k-1} &= r_0P_{k1} + r_1P_{k2} + \cdots + r_{k-1}P_{kn-k} + r_{n-1}\end{aligned}\right\} \quad (5.9)$$

Equation (5.9) can be realized using a logical circuit to obtain the syndrome calculating circuit.

EXAMPLE 5.8

Realize a syndrome calculating circuit for the LBC shown in Example 5.7.

Solution: Given

$$G=\begin{bmatrix}1\ 0\ 0\ 0:1\ 1\ 0\\0\ 1\ 0\ 0:1\ 0\ 1\\0\ 0\ 1\ 0:0\ 1\ 1\\0\ 0\ 0\ 1:1\ 1\ 1\end{bmatrix},\ H=\begin{bmatrix}1101100\\1011010\\0111001\end{bmatrix}$$

Now

$$S = r\,H^T$$

$$[s_0\ \ s_1\ \ s_2]=[r_0\ \ r_1\ \ r_2\ \ r_3\ \ r_4\ \ r_5\ \ r_6]\begin{bmatrix}1&1&0\\1&0&1\\0&1&1\\1&1&1\\1&0&0\\0&1&0\\0&0&1\end{bmatrix}$$

Solving we get

$$s_0 = r_0 + r_1 + r_3 + r_4$$

$$s_1 = r_0 + r_2 + r_3 + r_5$$

$$s_2 = r_1 + r_2 + r_3 + r_6$$

The syndrome calculating circuit is shown in Fig. 5.7.

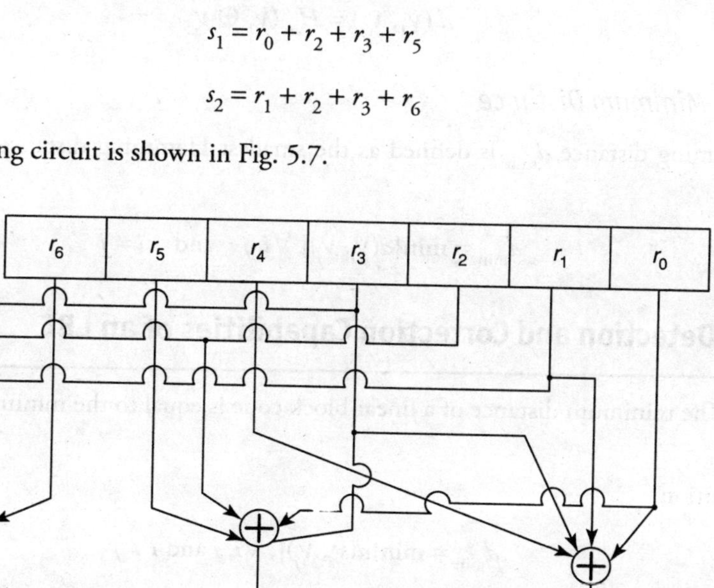

Figure 5.7 | A syndrome calculation circuit for the given (7, 4) LBC.

5.5.5 Distance Properties of a Linear Block Code

In this section we will define some of the distance parameters of an LBC.

Definition 5.1: Hamming Distance

Hamming distance of any two code vectors is defined as the number of bits in which they differ. For example, consider two codewords $v_1 = 1\,1\,0\,1\,0\,1\,0$ and $v_2 = 1\,0\,1\,1\,1\,0\,0$. The Hamming distance between the two codewords is given by $d\,(v_1, v_2) = 4$.

Hamming distance between any two binary codewords can be easily obtained by just counting the number of non-zero elements in the vector $v_1 \oplus v_2$. For the previous example,

$$v_1 \oplus v_2 = 1\,1\,0\,1\,0\,1\,0 \oplus 1\,0\,1\,1\,1\,0\,0 = 0\,1\,1\,0\,1\,1\,0$$

Number of non-zero entries in the resultant is 4. Thus, $d\,(v_1, v_2) = 4$.

Definition 5.2: Hamming Weight

Hamming weight of a codeword is defined as the number of non-zero elements in the vector. For example, Hamming weight of (1 1 0 1 1 0 1) is 5 and that of (1 0 1 1 1 0 0) is 4.

From Definitions (5.1) and (5.2), we can conclude that the Hamming distance of any two codewords v_1 and v_2 is the Hamming weight of the vector formed by performing binary addition of v_1 and v_2. So we have

$$d\,(v_1, v_2) = H_w\,(v_1 \oplus v_2)$$

Definition 5.3: Minimum Distance

Minimum Hamming distance $d_{\min}$ is defined as the smallest Hamming distance between any two codewords in a code:

$$d_{\min} = \min\{d(v_i, v_j)\}\ \forall i, j \quad \text{and} \quad i \neq j$$

5.5.6 Error Detection and Correction Capabilities of an LBC

Theorem 5.1: The minimum distance of a linear block code is equal to the minimum weight of a non-zero code vector.

Proof: By definition,

$$d_{\min} = \min\{d(v_i, v_j)\},\ \forall i, j \text{ and } i \neq j$$

We also have

$$d\,(v_i, v_j) = H_w\,(v_i \oplus v_j)$$

Therefore,

$$d_{\min} = \min\{H_w\,(v_i \oplus v_j)\}$$

Now $v_i \oplus v_j = v_k$ will also be a codeword though not equal to zero vector as $v_i \neq v_j$. Therefore, $d_{\min} = \min\{H_w(v_k)\}\ \forall\ k$ except v_k is an all-zero codeword.

Theorem 5.2: For every code vector of weight 'l' in an LBC, there exist 'l' columns in H matrix whose sum is zero.

Proof: Consider the parity check matrix H as

$$H = [h_0\ h_1\ h_2 \ldots h_{n-1}]$$

where $h_0, h_1, \ldots, h_{n-1}$ are columns in H with respect to $v\,H^T = 0$ for a valid codeword v:

$$v\begin{bmatrix} h_0 \\ h_1 \\ h_2 \\ \cdot \\ \cdot \\ \cdot \\ h_{n-1} \end{bmatrix} = 0 \tag{5.10}$$

Consider the weight of v as 'l', that is, it has 'l' non-zero elements say $v_{i1}, v_{i2}, \ldots, v_{il} = 1$. Therefore, Eq. (5.10) becomes

$$v_{i1}h_{i1} + v_{i2}h_{i2} + \cdots + v_{il}h_{il} = 0$$

$$\Rightarrow h_{i1} + h_{i2} + \cdots h_{il} = 0$$

as $v_{i1} = v_{i2} = \cdots = v_{il} = 1$. There exist '$l$' columns in the H matrix whose sum is zero.
There are a few corollaries for Theorem 5.2.

Corollary 5.2a: An LBC is said to have a $d_{\min}$ of d if there are no fewer than d columns in H matrix whose sum is zero.

Corollary 5.2b: If there are d columns in H matrix whose sum is zero and no fewer than d columns whose sum is zero, then the LBC is said to have a minimum distance of d.

Theorem 5.3: An (n, k) LBC with a minimum distance of $d_{\min}$ is capable of detecting $(d_{\min} - 1)$ bit errors.

Proof: An error can be detected by an LBC if the error pattern does not change the transmitted vector to another valid codeword. A minimum distance of $d_{\min}$ indicates that any two codewords are at least $d_{\min}$ bits apart. Thus, any error pattern of $(d_{\min} - 1)$ or fewer errors will not change the transmitted vector into a code vector. Therefore, code is guaranteed to detect up to $(d_{\min} - 1)$ bit error patterns. Although it can also detect some error patterns of more than $(d_{\min} - 1)$ bits, it is not assured.

To make the theorem clearer, consider an example of an LBC with the code alphabet 111000, 000000, 000111, 111111. The d_{min} for this case is 3, thus it can detect errors up to two bits of errors. In order to verify this, let us consider the vector 111000 for transmission. During transmission, if a single or double bit error occurs, transforming the vector to 111100 or 111110, then the error can be easily detected as the vectors received do not resemble any codeword. Now consider the case of a three-bit error, changing the transmitted vector into 111111. In this case, error cannot be detected as it resembles a valid codeword.

For an (n, k) LBC amongst $2^n - 1$ non-zero error patterns, $(2^k - 1)$ patterns will resemble a codeword. Therefore, total number of detectable error patterns are those which do not resemble a code vector, that is, $2^n - 1 - (2^k - 1) = (2^n - 2^k)$ patterns. Say for a (7, 4) LBC, the code can detect successfully a total of $2^7 - 2^4 = 128 - 16 = (112)$ error patterns out of $2^7 - 1 = 127$ errors.

Theorem 5.4: An (n, k) LBC is capable of correcting up to $\lfloor (d_{min} - 1)/2 \rfloor$ number of error bits for a minimum distance d_{min}.

Proof: Let 't' be the number of error bits the code can correct. Let r be the received vector for the transmitted vector v. Let v^1 be any other code vector. Then the following condition has to be satisfied:

$$d(v, r) + d(v^1, r) \geq d(v, v^1) \tag{5.11}$$

If an error pattern of t-bit error occurs, then

$$d(v, r) = t$$

Also

$$d(v, v^1) \geq d_{min}$$

Therefore,

$$d(v^1, r) \geq d_{min} - t \tag{5.12}$$

The decoder will properly decode the received vector r as v if and only if the received vector r is closer to v than any other vectors v^1 in the code, that is, $d(v, r) < d(v^1, r)\ \forall\ v^1 \neq v$ in code.

Subsituting $d(v, r) = t$ and $d(v^1, r) \geq d_{min} - t$, we get

$$t < d_{min} - t \Rightarrow 2t < d_{min} \Rightarrow t < \frac{d_{min}}{2} \Rightarrow t \leq \frac{d_{min} - 1}{2}$$

Therefore, the LBC can properly correct t-bits of errors where

$$t \leq \frac{d_{min} - 1}{2}$$

Hence

$$t = \left\lfloor \frac{d_{min} - 1}{2} \right\rfloor \tag{5.13}$$

Consider the same example of 111111, 111000, 000111 and 000000. Consider 111000 is transmitted. A received vector 111100, 111010 or 111001 can be properly decoded as 111000 as they are closer to

111000 than any other codewords, whereas if a two-bit error occurs changing the transmitted vector to 111110, the receiver will incorrectly decode it as 111111 as it is closer to that vector than 111000. Therefore, this code is capable of detecting only one-bit errors as

$$d_{\min} = 3 \quad \text{and} \quad t = \frac{3-1}{2} = 1$$

EXAMPLE 5.9

Given the generator matrix for an LBC

$$G = \begin{bmatrix} 1\,1\,1\,0\,1\,0\,0\,0 \\ 1\,0\,0\,1\,1\,1\,0\,0 \\ 1\,1\,1\,0\;0\,0\,1\,0 \\ 0\,1\,1\,0\;0\,0\,1\,1 \end{bmatrix}$$

(a) Find n and k values.
(b) Write G in its systematic form.
(c) Find all codewords.
(d) Find $d_{\min}$.
(e) Find the error detecting and correcting capability of the code.

Solution:
(a) As there are eight columns and four rows in G, $n = 8$ and $k = 4$. It is (8, 4) LBC.
(b) G can be reduced to the form $[P{:}I_k]$ using row operations

$$r_2 \leftarrow r_2 + r_1 \begin{bmatrix} 1\,1\,1\,0\,1\,0\,0\,0 \\ 0\,1\,1\,1\;0\,1\,0\,0 \\ 1\,1\,0\,0\,0\,1\,1\,0 \\ 0\,1\,1\,0\;0\,0\,1\,1 \end{bmatrix}$$

$$r_3 \leftarrow r_3 + r_2 \begin{bmatrix} 1\,1\,1\,0\,1\,0\,0\,0 \\ 0\,1\,1\,1\;0\,1\,0\,0 \\ 1\,0\,1\,1\;0\,0\,1\,0 \\ 0\,1\,1\,0\;0\,0\,1\,1 \end{bmatrix}$$

Finally, $r_4 \leftarrow r_4 + r_3$ gives

$$G = \begin{bmatrix} 1\,1\,1\,0\,1\,0\,0\,0 \\ 0\,1\,1\,1\;0\,1\,0\,0 \\ 1\,0\,1\,1\;0\,0\,1\,0 \\ 1\,1\,0\,1\;0\,0\,0\,1 \end{bmatrix}$$

(c) As $k = 4$ there are $2^k = 16$ combinations, so

$$[v] = [u]\,[G] = \begin{bmatrix} 0\,0\,0\,0 \\ 0\,0\,0\,1 \\ 0\,0\,1\,0 \\ 0\,0\,1\,1 \\ 0\,1\,0\,0 \\ 0\,1\,0\,1 \\ 0\,1\,1\,0 \\ 0\,1\,1\,1 \\ 1\,0\,0\,0 \\ 1\,0\,0\,1 \\ 1\,0\,1\,0 \\ 1\,0\,1\,1 \\ 1\,1\,0\,0 \\ 1\,1\,0\,1 \\ 1\,1\,1\,0 \\ 1\,1\,1\,1 \end{bmatrix} \begin{bmatrix} 1\,1\,1\,0\,1\,0\,0\,0 \\ 0\,1\,1\,1\,0\,1\,0\,0 \\ 1\,0\,1\,1\,0\,0\,1\,0 \\ 1\,1\,0\,1\,0\,0\,0\,1 \end{bmatrix} = \begin{bmatrix} 0\,0\,0\,0\,0\,0\,0\,0 \\ 1\,1\,0\,1\,0\,0\,0\,1 \\ 1\,0\,1\,1\,0\,0\,1\,0 \\ 0\,1\,1\,0\,0\,0\,1\,1 \\ 0\,1\,1\,1\,0\,1\,0\,0 \\ 1\,0\,1\,0\,0\,1\,0\,1 \\ 1\,1\,0\,0\,0\,1\,1\,0 \\ 0\,0\,0\,1\,0\,1\,1\,1 \\ 1\,1\,1\,0\,1\,0\,0\,0 \\ 0\,0\,1\,1\,1\,0\,0\,1 \\ 0\,1\,0\,1\,1\,0\,1\,0 \\ 1\,0\,0\,0\,1\,0\,1\,1 \\ 1\,0\,0\,1\,1\,1\,0\,0 \\ 0\,1\,0\,0\,1\,1\,0\,1 \\ 0\,0\,1\,0\,1\,1\,1\,0 \\ 1\,1\,1\,1\,1\,1\,1\,1 \end{bmatrix}$$

(d) $d_{\min} = 4$

(e) This LBC can detect up to $d_{\min} - 1 = 3$ bit errors and can correct up to $\lfloor (4-1)/2 \rfloor = 1$ bit errors

EXAMPLE 5.10

For the following (6, 3) systematic LBC

$$G = \begin{bmatrix} 1 & 0 & 0 & : & 1 & 0 & 1 \\ 0 & 1 & 0 & : & 0 & 1 & 1 \\ 0 & 0 & 1 & : & 1 & 1 & 0 \end{bmatrix}$$

(a) Find all code vectors.
(b) Draw encoder circuit for the above code.
(c) Find minimum Hamming weight.

Solution:

(a) Code vectors can be obtained considering the following relation:

$$[v] = [u]\,[G]$$

Table 5.1 shows codewords and Hamming weights for (6, 3) LBC.

(b) Now

$$[v] = [u]\,[G]$$

Table 5.1 | Codewords and Hamming weights for the given (6, 3) LBC

[u]	*[v] = [u] [G]*	*Hamming Weight*
0 0 0	0 0 0 0 0 0	…
0 0 1	0 0 1 1 1 0	3
0 1 0	0 1 0 0 1 1	3
0 1 1	0 1 1 1 0 1	4
1 0 0	1 0 0 1 0 1	3
1 0 1	1 0 1 0 1 1	4
1 1 0	1 1 0 1 1 0	4
1 1 1	1 1 1 0 0 0	3

$$(v_0\ v_1\ v_2\ v_3\ v_4\ v_5) = (u_0\ u_1\ u_2)\begin{bmatrix}1 & 0 & 0 & 1 & 0 & 1\\ 0 & 1 & 0 & 0 & 1 & 1\\ 0 & 0 & 1 & 1 & 1 & 0\end{bmatrix}$$

Solving we get

$$v_0 = u_0, \quad v_3 = u_0 + u_2$$

$$v_1 = u_1, \quad v_4 = u_1 + u_2$$

$$v_2 = u_2, \quad v_5 = u_0 + u_1$$

The encoder circuit is shown in Fig. 5.8.

(c) The minimum Hamming weight is $d_{min} = 3$ from Table 5.1.

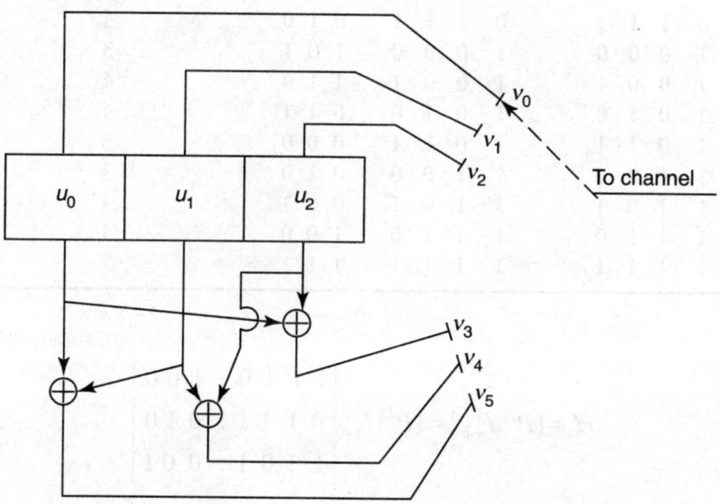

Figure 5.8 | Encoder circuit for the given (6, 3) LBC.

EXAMPLE 5.11

Consider the (7, 4) LBC whose generator matrix is

$$[G]=\begin{bmatrix}1\,0\,0\,0 : 1\,0\,1\\ 0\,1\,0\,0 : 1\,1\,1\\ 0\,0\,1\,0 : 1\,1\,0\\ 0\,0\,0\,1 : 0\,1\,1\end{bmatrix}$$

(a) Find all codewords.
(b) Find the parity check matrix H.
(c) Find the minimum Hamming weight and Hamming distance.

Solution:
(a) The codewords and the corresponding Hamming weights are shown in Table 5.2.

Table 5.2 | Codewords and Hamming weights for the given (7, 4) LBC

[u]	*[v] = [u] [G]*	*Hamming Weight*
0 0 0 0	0 0 0 0 0 0 0	…
0 0 0 1	0 0 0 1 0 1 1	3
0 0 1 0	0 0 1 0 1 1 0	3
0 0 1 1	0 0 1 1 1 0 1	4
0 1 0 0	0 1 0 0 1 1 1	4
0 1 0 1	0 1 0 1 1 0 0	3
0 1 1 0	0 1 1 0 0 0 1	3
0 1 1 1	0 1 1 1 0 1 0	4
1 0 0 0	1 0 0 0 1 0 1	3
1 0 0 1	1 0 0 1 1 1 0	4
1 0 1 0	1 0 1 0 0 1 1	4
1 0 1 1	1 0 1 1 0 0 0	3
1 1 0 0	1 1 0 0 0 1 0	3
1 1 0 1	1 1 0 1 0 0 1	4
1 1 1 0	1 1 1 0 1 0 0	4
1 1 1 1	1 1 1 1 1 1 1	7

(b) We have

$$H=[P^T : I_{n\text{-}k}]=[P^T : I_3]\begin{bmatrix}1\,1\,1\,0 : 1\,0\,0\\ 0\,1\,1\,1 : 0\,1\,0\\ 1\,1\,0\,1 : 0\,0\,1\end{bmatrix}$$

(c) $d_{\min} = 3$ from Table 5.2.

EXAMPLE 5.12

In an LBC, the syndrome is given by

$$S_1 = r_1 + r_2 + r_3 + r_5$$

$$S_2 = r_1 + r_2 + r_4 + r_6$$

$$S_3 = r_1 + r_3 + r_4 + r_7$$

(a) Find the parity check matrix $[H]$.
(b) Draw the encoder circuit.
(c) Find the codeword for all input sequences.
(d) How many errors it can detect and correct?
(e) What is the syndrome for the received data 1 0 1 1 0 1 1?

Solution:

(a) We have

$$s = r\,H^T$$

$$[s_1\ s_2\ s_3] = [r_1\ r_2\ r_3\ r_4\ r_5\ r_6\ r_7]\begin{bmatrix} 1\,1\,1 \\ 1\,1\,0 \\ 1\,0\,1 \\ 0\,1\,1 \\ 1\,0\,0 \\ 0\,1\,0 \\ 0\,0\,1 \end{bmatrix}$$

Therefore

$$H^T = \begin{bmatrix} 1\,1\,1 \\ 1\,1\,0 \\ 1\,0\,1 \\ 0\,1\,1 \\ 1\,0\,0 \\ 0\,1\,0 \\ 0\,0\,1 \end{bmatrix} \Rightarrow H = \begin{bmatrix} 1\,1\,1\,0 : 1\,0\,0 \\ 1\,1\,0\,1 : 0\,1\,0 \\ 1\,0\,1\,1 : 0\,0\,1 \end{bmatrix}$$

(b) We have

$$[G] = [I_k : P] = \begin{bmatrix} 1\,0\,0\,0 : 1\,1\,1 \\ 0\,1\,0\,0 : 1\,1\,0 \\ 0\,0\,1\,0 : 1\,0\,1 \\ 0\,0\,0\,1 : 0\,1\,1 \end{bmatrix}$$

Now

$$[v] = [u]\,[G]$$

$$[v_1\ v_2\ v_3\ v_4\ v_5\ v_6\ v_7] = [u_1\ u_2\ u_3\ u_4]\begin{bmatrix} 1\,0\,0\,0 : 1\,1\,1 \\ 0\,1\,0\,0 : 1\,1\,0 \\ 0\,0\,1\,0 : 1\,0\,1 \\ 0\,0\,0\,1 : 0\,1\,1 \end{bmatrix}$$

Solving we get

$$v_1 = u_1, \quad v_5 = u_1 + u_2 + u_3$$

$$v_2 = u_2, \quad v_6 = u_1 + u_2 + u_4$$

$$v_3 = u_3, \quad v_7 = u_1 + u_3 + u_4$$

$$v_4 = u_4$$

The encoder circuit for the given (7, 4) LBC is shown in Fig. 5.9.

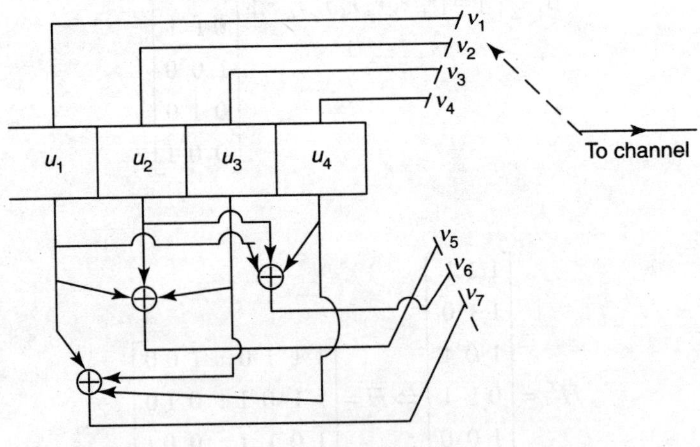

Figure 5.9 | Encoder circuit for the given (7, 4) LBC.

(c) As it is a (7, 4) LBC, there will be 16 combinations of the input sequence. The corresponding codewords and the Hamming weights are given in Table 5.3.

(d) Since $d_{\min} = 3$, it can detect up to $d_{\min - 1} = 3 - 1 = 2$ bit errors.
Error correcting capability

$$t = \frac{d_{\min-1}}{2} = \frac{3-1}{2} = 1 \text{ bit errors}$$

Table 5.3 | Codewords and Hamming weights for the given (7, 4) LBC

[u]	[v] = [u] [G]	Hamming Weight
0 0 0 0	0 0 0 0 0 0 0	–
0 0 0 1	0 0 0 1 0 1 1	3
0 0 1 0	0 0 1 0 1 0 1	3
0 0 1 1	0 0 1 1 1 1 0	4
0 1 0 0	0 1 0 0 1 1 0	3
0 1 0 1	0 1 0 1 1 0 1	4
0 1 1 0	0 1 1 0 0 1 1	4
0 1 1 1	0 1 1 1 0 0 0	3
1 0 0 0	1 0 0 0 1 1 1	4
1 0 0 1	1 0 0 1 1 0 0	3
1 0 1 0	1 0 1 0 0 1 0	3
1 0 1 1	1 0 1 1 0 0 1	4
1 1 0 0	1 1 0 0 0 0 1	3
1 1 0 1	1 1 0 1 0 1 0	4
1 1 1 0	1 1 1 0 1 0 0	4
1 1 1 1	1 1 1 1 1 1 1	7

(e) Syndrome is given as

$$S = rH^T = [1\ 0\ 1\ 1\ 0\ 1\ 1]\begin{bmatrix} 1\ 1\ 1 \\ 1\ 1\ 0 \\ 1\ 0\ 1 \\ 0\ 1\ 1 \\ 1\ 0\ 0 \\ 0\ 1\ 0 \\ 0\ 0\ 1 \end{bmatrix} = [0\ 1\ 0]$$

EXAMPLE 5.13

The parity check bits of a (8, 4) LBC are given by

$$v_5 = u_1 + u_2 + u_4$$

$$v_6 = u_1 + u_2 + u_3$$

$$v_7 = u_1 + u_3 + u_4$$

$$v_8 = u_2 + u_3 + u_4$$

where u_1, u_2, u_3, u_4 are data bits.

(a) Find generator and parity check matrices.

(b) Find all possible code vectors.

(c) Find the minimum Hamming weight.

Solution:

(a) We have

$$[v] = [u]\,[G]$$

From the given equations we can write the parity matrix as

$$P = \begin{bmatrix} 1 & 1 & 1 & 0 \\ 1 & 1 & 0 & 1 \\ 0 & 1 & 1 & 1 \\ 1 & 0 & 1 & 1 \end{bmatrix}$$

Therefore

$$G = [I_k : P] = \begin{bmatrix} 1\,0\,0\,0 & : & 1\,1\,1\,0 \\ 0\,1\,0\,0 & : & 1\,1\,0\,1 \\ 0\,0\,1\,0 & : & 0\,1\,1\,1 \\ 0\,0\,0\,1 & : & 1\,0\,1\,1 \end{bmatrix}$$

$$H = \left[[P^T : I_{n-k}\right] = \begin{bmatrix} 1\,1\,0\,1 : 1\,0\,0\,0 \\ 1\,1\,1\,0 : 0\,1\,0\,0 \\ 1\,0\,1\,1 : 0\,0\,1\,0 \\ 0\,1\,1\,1 : 0\,0\,0\,1 \end{bmatrix}$$

Table 5.4 | Codewords and Hamming weights for the given (8, 4) LBC

[u]	*[v] = [u] [G]*	*Hamming Weight*
0 0 0 0	0 0 0 0 0 0 0 0	...
0 0 0 1	0 0 0 1 1 0 1 1	4
0 0 1 0	0 0 1 0 0 1 1 1	4
0 0 1 1	0 0 1 1 1 1 0 0	4
0 1 0 0	0 1 0 0 1 1 0 1	4
0 1 0 1	0 1 0 1 0 1 1 0	4
0 1 1 0	0 1 1 0 1 0 1 0	4
0 1 1 1	0 1 1 1 0 0 0 1	4
1 0 0 0	1 0 0 0 1 1 1 0	4
1 0 0 1	1 0 0 1 0 1 0 1	4
1 0 1 0	1 0 1 0 1 0 0 1	4
1 0 1 1	1 0 1 1 0 0 1 0	4
1 1 0 0	1 1 0 0 0 0 1 1	4
1 1 0 1	1 1 0 1 1 0 0 0	4
1 1 1 0	1 1 1 0 0 1 0 0	4
1 1 1 1	1 1 1 1 1 1 1 1	8

(b) It is a (8, 4) LBC. Thus, it will have $2^4 = 16$ possible data sequences. The corresponding code vectors can be obtained using the relation:

$$[v] = [u]\,[G]$$

The code vectors are presented in Table 5.4.

(c) Minimum Hamming weight = 4

5.5.7 Standard Array Decoding of an (*n*, *k*) LBC

The most general procedure to decode an LBC is as follows: Let r be the received vector. It will be compared with all valid code vectors in C and it is decoded as a vector v_i if its distance to v_i is lesser than that of any other code vectors. That is, if $d(v_i, r) < d(v_j, r)$, $i \neq j\ \forall\ j$ then the decoded vector is v_i.

As it requires 2^k computations for each received vector, it will be practically infeasible for larger values of k. Thus, another method has been devised in which a set of 2^n received vectors will be grouped into 2^k distinct sets with a valid codeword heading each set. First, the set in which the received vector r resides has to be identified and the decoded vector will simply be the valid codeword heading that set.

The decoding procedure for an (n, k) LBC is as depicted in Fig. 5.10. The decoded vector in this case will be vector v_i as r is residing in the set of v_i. This procedure of decoding is called *standard array decoding*. In this process, a disjoint $2^{n-k} - 1$ cosets will be formed with the valid code vectors C. The procedure of coset decomposition has been discussed in Chapter 1. There will be $(2^{n-k} - 1)$ cosets each of 2^k elements which can be justified using Lagrange's theorem. The construction of the standard array follows the steps given below:

1. First row entries of the array will be the subgroup C constituting the entire code vector space.
2. The first entries of the remaining rows will be a minimum weighted n-tuple vector e_i such that e_i has not appeared in any of the previous rows.
3. The remaining entries of row i will be binary addition of the element e_i with the corresponding entry of the first row.
4. In this way, all $(2^{n-k} - 1)$ cosets will be formulated and the array will be completed.

The first column of the standard array is called the coset leader as it uniquely identifies the corresponding coset. A general standard array for an (n, k) LBC is shown in Table 5.5.

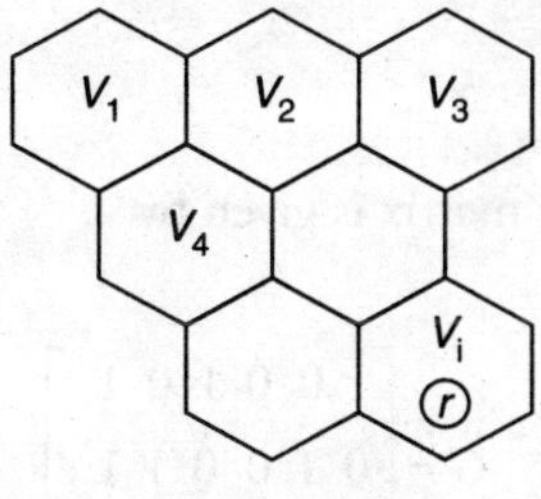

Figure 5.10 | Decoding of an (*n*, *k*) LBC.

Table 5.5 | Standard array for an (n, k) LBC

Coset leader						
v_1	v_2	v_3	.	.	.	v_{2^k}
e_2	$v_2 + e_2$	$v_3 + e_2$	.	.	.	$v_{2^k} + e_2$
e_3	$v_2 + e_3$	$v_3 + e_3$	.	.	.	$v_{2^k} + e_3$
.	.	.				.
.	.	.	.	.	.	.
.	.	.			.	.
$e_{2^{n-k}}$	$v_2 + e_{2^{n-k}}$	$v_3 + e_{2^{n-k}}$	.	.		$v_{2^k} + e_{2^{n-k}}$

As the syndrome is unique for an error pattern e_i, each row of the standard array can be characterized by its corresponding syndrome, which is given by the product of the corresponding coset leader with the matrix H^T. After receiving vector r, syndrome can be computed as $S = rH^T$. Once the syndrome is computed, the corresponding error pattern e can be obtained from the array. Then, the decoded vector can be obtained as

$$v^1 = r + e$$

EXAMPLE 5.14

Construct the standard array for a (6, 3) LBC with the parity matrix

$$\begin{bmatrix} 1 & 0 & 1 \\ 0 & 1 & 1 \\ 1 & 1 & 0 \end{bmatrix}$$

using the same decode as the received vectors.

(a) 1 1 0 0 1 1

(b) 1 0 0 0 0 1

(c) 1 1 0 1 1 1

(d) 0 1 1 0 0 0

Solution: The corresponding generator matrix is given by

$$G = \begin{bmatrix} 1 & 0 & 0 & 1 & 0 & 1 \\ 0 & 1 & 0 & 0 & 1 & 1 \\ 0 & 0 & 1 & 1 & 1 & 1 \end{bmatrix}$$

To construct the standard array, we need to obtain all valid codewords first. The set of valid codewords is given by

$$[v]=[u][G]=\begin{bmatrix}0&0&0\\0&0&1\\0&1&0\\0&1&1\\1&0&0\\1&0&1\\1&1&0\\1&1&1\end{bmatrix}\begin{bmatrix}1&0&0&1&0&1\\0&1&0&0&1&1\\0&0&1&1&1&1\end{bmatrix}=\begin{bmatrix}0&0&0&0&0&0\\0&0&1&1&1&1\\0&1&0&0&1&1\\0&1&1&1&0&0\\1&0&0&1&0&1\\1&0&1&0&1&0\\1&1&0&1&1&0\\1&1&1&0&0&1\end{bmatrix}$$

The first row of the standard array can be filled by the valid code vectors. The number of rows in the standard array will be $2^{n-k} = 2^{6-3} = 2^3 = 8$. Thus, the remaining seven rows have to be filled up considering the minimum weighted error patterns.

The second row can be filled by considering a minimum weighted vector from the set of all n-tuples excluding those which are already present in Table 5.6. A reasonable choice would be 100000. The other entries can be filled up by just performing the binary addition of 100000 with subgroup C (first row of the array). Similarly, the next five row entries can be completed by considering the patterns 010000, 001000, 000100, 000010 and 000001, respectively. By the end of the completion of the seventh row, we have exhausted all one-bit error patterns. Thus, to complete the last row of the array, we have to look for a two-bit vector pattern which has not yet appeared in the table. Vector 110000 could be one such possibility, although it is not the only one. Thus, the last row can be filled up using this vector. The standard array for the given (6, 3) is shown in Table 5.6. Also the syndrome for each of the coset is computed by just multiplying the corresponding coset leader with H^T.

The complete standard array for the given (6, 3) LBC can correct all one-bit error patterns and a single two-bit error pattern (110000 in this case). We can also cross verify this as $d_{min} = 3$ in the given LBC, its error correcting capability $t = (3-1)/2 = 1$.

Table 5.6 | Standard array for a (6, 3) LBC

Syndrome	*Coset leader*						
000	**000000**	**001111**	**010011**	**011100**	**100101**	**101010**	**110110**	**111001**
101	**100000**	101111	110011	111100	000101	001010	010110	011001
011	**010000**	011111	000011	001100	110101	111010	100110	101001
111	**001000**	000111	011011	010100	101101	100010	111110	110001
100	**000100**	001011	010111	011000	100001	101110	110010	111101
010	**000010**	001101	010001	011110	100111	101000	110100	111011
001	**000001**	001110	010010	011101	100100	101011	110111	111000
110	**110000**	111111	100011	101100	010101	011010	000110	001001

Next we can compute the syndrome for the error patterns by performing $S = eH^T$.

$$H^T = \begin{bmatrix} 1 & 0 & 1 \\ 0 & 1 & 1 \\ 1 & 1 & 1 \\ 1 & 0 & 0 \\ 0 & 1 & 0 \\ 0 & 0 & 1 \end{bmatrix}$$

Syndromes for the given problem are (101), (011), (111), (100), (010), (001) and (110), respectively, which are shown as the first column of the standard array.

We can now perform decoding for the given vectors with the help of the constructed standard array.

1. 110011: The syndrome for this received vector can be computed as

$$S = rH^T = 101$$

Compare the obtained syndrome with the syndrome column of the standard array. This corresponds to the coset leader (100000).

Now the corrected vector can be obtained by just performing the binary addition of the received vector with the coset leader, i.e.

$$v^1 = r + e = 110011 \oplus 100000 = 010011.$$

It can also be cross verified as follows:

The given received vector is present in the column with the code vector 010011, thus the decoded vector is 010011. Similar procedure can be followed to decode other given vectors.

2. 100001: Here $v^1 = 100101$.

3. 110111: Here $v^1 = 110110$.

4. 011000: Here $v^1 = 011100$.

EXAMPLE 5.15

Show that all error patterns that differ by a code vector have the same syndrome.

Solution: We have

$$S = rH^T$$

The received vector would be the sum of the transmitted vector and the error pattern,

$$r = v + e$$

So

$$S = (v + e)\, H^T = vH^T + eH^T$$

But $vH^T = 0$ as $GH^T = 0$ and $v = uG$, therefore,

$$S = eH^T$$

It is clear from the above expression that the syndrome depends on the error pattern and not on the code vector. Thus, all erroneous frames with the same error pattern have the same syndrome.

EXAMPLE 5.16

Given a code with parity check matrix H, show that the coset with syndrome S contains a vector of weight w if and only if some linear combination of w columns of H equals S.

Solution: Let us consider a vector with weight 'w', that is, it has 'w' 1's and (n–w) 0's. Let

$$r = [0\ 0\ r_{11},\ r_{12},\ ...,\ r_{1w},\ ...]$$

With respect to $s = rH^T$, let $H = [h_1, h_2, ..., h_n]$, where $h_1, h_2, ..., h_n$ are column vectors. Therefore,

$$s = r\ H^T = [0, \ldots, r_{11}, \ldots, r_{12}, \ldots, r_{1w}, \ldots] \begin{bmatrix} h_1 \\ h_2 \\ \cdot \\ \cdot \\ \cdot \\ h_n \end{bmatrix}$$

As 'r' contains w non-zero elements, the product would be the sum of the 'w' rows of H^T. So, we have

$$S = [h_{i1} + h_{i2} + \cdots + h_{iw}]$$

The linear combination of w columns of H equals S.

5.5.8 General Decoding for an (n, k) LBC

In Section 5.5.7, we have seen that an LBC can be decoded efficiently by making use of standard array but the size of the array will become too large for higher values of n. Thus, only the first two columns (syndrome and coset leader) of the array depicting the syndromes and error patterns could be used for decoding, which is shown in Table 5.7.

It can be easily shown that a general n-tuple error vector $[e'_0\ e'_1 \ldots e'_{n-1}]$ can be represented by the $(n-k)$ tuple syndrome $[s_0\ s_1 \ldots s_{n-k-1}]$ as

$$e'_0 = f(s_0\ s_1 \ldots s_{n-k-1})$$

Table 5.7 | Syndrome and coset leader

Syndrome	*Coset Leader*
0	v_0
s_1	e_1
s_2	e_2
.	.
.	.
.	.
s_{2n-k}	e_{2n-k}

$$e'_1 = f(s_0\, s_1 \ldots s_{n-k-1})$$

$$\ldots$$

$$e'_2 n - k = f(s_0\, s_1 \ldots s_{n-k-1}) \tag{5.14}$$

Thus, the error pattern can be obtained if the syndrome is known. Then the received vector will be added with the computed error pattern to get the decoded vector. The general procedure can be given as follows:

Step 1: Compute the syndrome from the received vector using the relation $S = rH^T$.
Step 2: Obtain the error pattern corresponding to the syndrome.
Step 3: Perform the binary addition of the error pattern and the received vector to get the corrected vector $v^1 = r + e$.

A general decoding circuit for an (*n*, *k*) LBC is shown in Fig. 5.11.

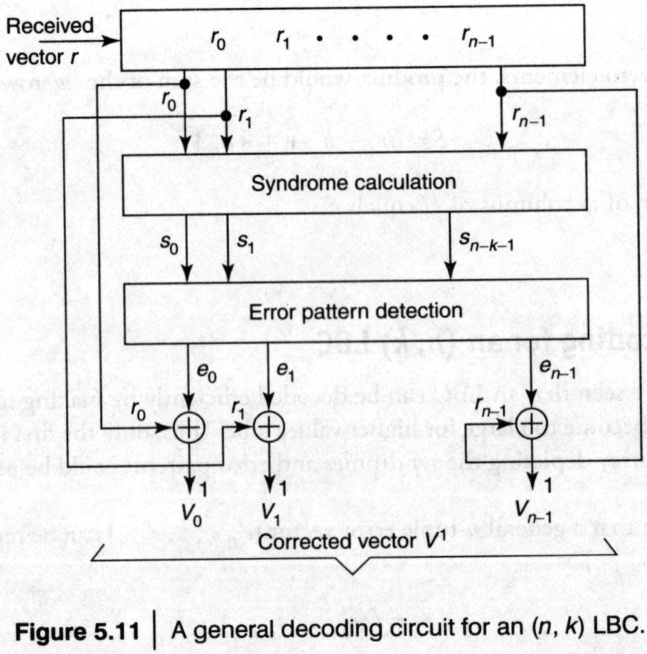

Figure 5.11 | A general decoding circuit for an (*n*, *k*) LBC.

EXAMPLE 5.17

Realize the general decoding circuit for a (6, 3) LBC given in example 5.14.

Solution: Considering only the first two columns of the standard array formed from Table 5.6, we get reduced standard array shown in Table 5.8.

Table 5.8 | Reduced standard array of Table 5.6

$s_0\, s_1\, s_2$	$e_0\, e_1\, e_2\, e_3\, e_4\, e_5$
0 0 0	0 0 0 0 0 0
1 0 1	1 0 0 0 0 0
0 1 1	0 1 0 0 0 0
1 1 1	0 0 1 0 0 0
1 0 0	0 0 0 1 0 0
0 1 0	0 0 0 0 1 0
0 0 1	0 0 0 0 0 1
1 1 0	1 1 0 0 0 0

The expression for syndrome is given by

$$S = rH^T = [r_0\, r_1\, r_2\, r_3\, r_4\, r_5] \begin{bmatrix} 1 & 0 & 1 \\ 0 & 1 & 1 \\ 1 & 1 & 1 \\ 1 & 0 & 0 \\ 0 & 1 & 0 \\ 0 & 0 & 1 \end{bmatrix}$$

Solving we get

$$s_0 = r_0 + r_2 + r_3$$

$$s_1 = r_1 + r_2 + r_4$$

$$s_2 = r_1 + r_2 + r_3 + r_5$$

The error bits e_0, e_1, ..., e_5 can be represented in terms of s_0, s_1, s_2 as follows:

$$e_0 = s_0\, \overline{s_1}\, s_2 + s_0\, s_1\, \overline{s_2} = s_0\, (\overline{s_1}\, s_2 + s_1\, \overline{s_2}) = s_0\, (s_1 \oplus s_2)$$

$$e_1 = \overline{s_0}\, s_1 s_2 + s_0\, s_1\, \overline{s_2} = s_1\, (\overline{s_0}\, s_2 + s_0\, \overline{s_2}) = s_1\, (s_0 \oplus s_2) \qquad (5.15)$$

$$e_2 = s_0\, s_1\, s_2, \qquad e_3 = s_0\, \overline{s_1}\, \overline{s_2}$$

$$e_4 = \overline{s_0}\, s_1\, \overline{s_2}, \qquad e_5 = \overline{s_0}\, \overline{s_1}\, s_2$$

Therefore, the general decoding circuit can be obtained by realizing Eq. (5.15) using a logical circuit shown in Fig. 5.12.

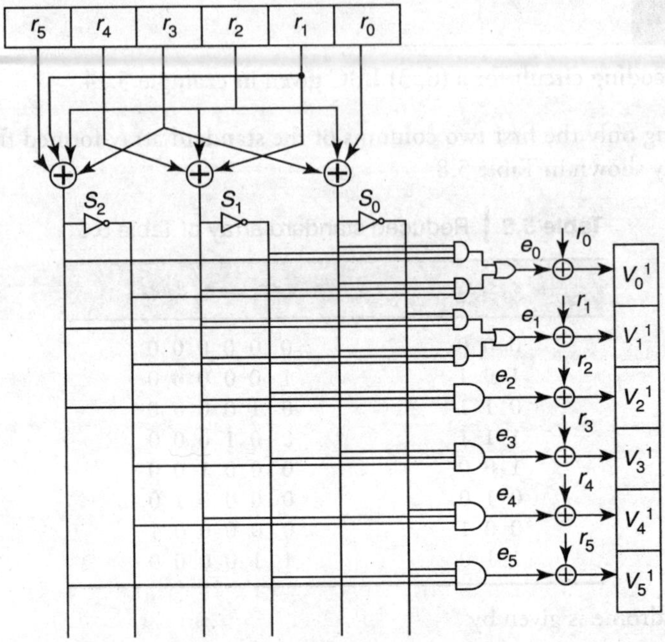

Figure 5.12 | A general decoding circuit for the given (6, 3) LBC.

5.6 The Hamming Codes

Hamming codes are a special set of LBC with d_{min} being 3. In other words, they are capable of correcting up to one-bit error. It is clear from Corollaries 5.2a and b that if the minimum distance of an LBC is 3, then the smallest number of columns of H which are linearly dependent is 3. Thus, no two columns of H matrix should be identical.

The number of rows in H matrix is $(n - k)$, thus there can be $(2^{n-k} - 1)$ distinct non-zero columns possible. Also the number of distinct columns required in matrix H is n. Thus, to have a proper single-bit error correction, we should have the total possible number of distinct combinations of $(n - k)$-tuple, which should be at least equal to n.

In other words,

$$n \leq (2^{n-k} - 1) \quad \text{or} \quad n \leq (2^m - 1), \text{ where } m = n - k$$

Thus, formally, a Hamming code can be characterized as follows:

$$\left.\begin{aligned} n &= 2^m - 1 \\ k &= 2^m - m - 1 \\ n - k &= m \\ d_{min} &= 3 \\ t &= 1 \end{aligned}\right\} \tag{5.16}$$

EXAMPLE 5.18

Design a single-error correcting Hamming code for a message length of 4.

Solution: Given $t = 1$, $k = 4$. Now

$$k = 2^m - m - 1 \Rightarrow 4 = 2^m - m - 1 \Rightarrow 2^m - m = 5 \Rightarrow m = 3$$

Therefore,

$$n = 2^m - 1 = 7$$

So it is a (7, 4) code. To find the parity check matrix, consider its general form

$$H = [P^T : I_{n-K}] = \begin{bmatrix} & 1 & 0 & 0 \\ P : & 0 & 1 & 0 \\ & 0 & 0 & 1 \end{bmatrix}$$

The remaining four columns of H matrix can be obtained from the unused non-zero combinations (0 1 1, 1 0 1, 1 1 0 and 1 1 1). Therefore, one possible parity check matrix would be

$$H = \begin{bmatrix} 0\,1\,1\,1 : 1\,0\,0 \\ 1\,0\,1\,1 : 0\,1\,0 \\ 1\,1\,0\,1 : 0\,0\,1 \end{bmatrix}$$

Therefore, the generator matrix for the designed (7, 4) Hamming code is

$$G = \begin{bmatrix} 1000011 \\ 0100101 \\ 0010110 \\ 0001111 \end{bmatrix}$$

5.6.1 Hamming Bound

If an (n, k) LBC is capable of correcting t-bit errors, then it is necessary to have the number of syndromes to be at least equal to the total number of correctable error patterns, that is,

$$2^{n-k} \geq \sum_{i=0}^{t} {}^nC_i \tag{5.17}$$

The above inequality is called Hamming bound. A code for which the Hamming bound turns out to be an equality is called a perfect code. It is to be noted that all Hamming codes are perfect codes. For example, consider a (7, 4) Hamming code. Here, $n = 7$, $k = 4$ and $t = 1$. Consider the left-hand side of the Hamming bound:

$$2^{n-k} = 2^{7-4} = 8$$

Also the total number of error patterns

$$\sum_{i=0}^{1} {}^{n}C_i = {}^{7}C_0 + {}^{n}C_1 = 1 + 7 = 8$$

Thus, (7, 4) Hamming code is a perfect code. Similarly, it can be shown that (15, 11) (31, 26) (63, 57) Hamming codes are also perfect.

EXAMPLE 5.19

Determine whether the following codes are perfect or not.

(a) (15, 11), $t = 1$

(b) (6, 3), $t = 1$

Solution:

1. We have

$$2^{n-k} = 2^{15-11} = 16$$

$$\sum_{i=0}^{1} {}^{15}C_i = {}^{15}C_0 + {}^{15}C_1 = 16$$

Since $2^{n-k} = \sum_{i=0}^{t} {}^{n}C_i$, therefore, (15, 11) is a perfect code.

2. We have

$$2^{n-k} = 8$$

$$\sum_{i=0}^{t} {}^{n}C_i = \sum_{i=0}^{1} {}^{6}C_i = {}^{6}C_0 + {}^{6}C_1 = 1 + 6 = 7$$

Since $2^{n-k} \neq \sum_{i=0}^{t} {}^{n}C_i$, therefore, (6, 3) is not a perfect code.

5.7 Probability of an Undetected Error Pattern for an LBC over a BSC

In an LBC, the receiver detects the presence of error only if the received vector is not a valid code vector. In other words, if an error pattern changes one valid codeword into another valid codeword, then the receiver is unable to detect the presence of error. Hence, the probability of the receiver not detecting the error is same as the probability that an error pattern is exactly equal to a codeword.

For analysis, consider a BSC with a transition probability of 'p'. The probability of any pattern with 'i' errors is given by $p^i (1-p)^{n-i}$. If there are N_i number of codewords of weight i, then the probability that the error pattern forms a codeword is $N_i \times p^i \times (1-p)^{n-i}$. Thus, the probability of an undetected error pattern is given by

$$P_u = \sum_{i=d......}^{n} N_i \times p^i (1-p)^{n-i} \tag{5.18}$$

Hence the probability of the detection of erroneous codeword is

$$P_d = 1 - P_u \tag{5.19}$$

5.8 Equivalent Codes

Two codes C_1 and C_2 are said to be equivalent $C_1 \sim C_2$ if one code is obtained from the other using the following transformations:

1. Perform arbitrary permutations of the components.
2. Scale non-zero elements independently.

The distance properties of equivalent codes are same. Let G be the generator matrix for the code C_1. Then the generator matrix for the equivalent code C_2 can be obtained by performing elementary row or column operations on matrix G.

5.9 Cyclic Codes

Cyclic codes are an important subclass of linear block codes which satisfy the additional structural requirement so as to have an ease of implementation. Cyclic codes are developed under the strong structure of Galios fields, using efficient encoding and decoding algorithms. These codes can be easily implemented using shift registers and feedback connections.

5.9.1 Algebraic Description of Cyclic Codes

A linear block code is said to be cyclic if and only if $v = (v_0, v_1, v_2, ..., v_{n-1})$ is a code vector then $v' = (v_{n-1}, v_0, v_1, ..., v_{n-2})$ is also a code vector. In other words, if the cyclic shifts of codewords also result in codewords, such linear block codes are said to be cyclic codes. This is a case of automorphism as all permutations of a code map on itself.

As discussed in Chapter 1, i^{th} cyclic shift of a sequence is as good as multiplying the polynomial representation of the sequence with x^i. In other words, if $v = (v_0, v_1, v_2, ..., v_{n-1})$ and $v^i = (v_{n-i}, v_{n-i+1}, ..., v_{n-1}, v_0, v_1, ..., v_{n-i-1})$ be the ith cyclic shift of the sequence, then the polynomial representation of v is given by

$$v(x) = v_0 + v_1x + v_2x^2 + \cdots + v_{n-1}x^{n-1} \tag{5.20}$$

and $v^{(i)}(x)$ can be simply represented as

$$v^{(i)}(x) = x^i v(x) \bmod (x^n+1) \tag{5.21}$$

This can be easily verified as follows: Consider

$$xv(x) = v_0x + v_1x^2 + v_2x^3 + \cdots + v_{n-1}x^n = v_0x + v_1x^2 + v_2x^3 + \cdots + v_{n-1}(x^n+1) + v_{n-1}$$

$$xv(x) \bmod x^n+1 = v_{n-1} + v_0x + v_1x^2 + v_2x^3 + \cdots + v_{n-2}x^{n-1}$$

But $v_{n-1}(x^n + 1) \bmod (x^n + 1) = 0$. Therefore,

$$xv(x) \bmod x^n + 1 = v^{(1)}(x)$$

Similarly, in general,

$$x^i v(x) \bmod x^n + 1 = v^{(i)}(x)$$

Therefore, if $v(x)$ is a subspace of the ring $GF(q)[x]/x^n-1$ then $xv(x), x^2v(x), x^3v(x)$ will all belong to the same subspace C. Also the linear combination of these terms will also belong to the subspace C, that is, $\forall\, a(x) = a_0 + a_1x + a_2x^2 + \ldots + a_{n-1}x^{n-1} \in GF(q)[x]/x^n-1$, then $c(x)\,a(x) \in C$. Therefore, we can conclude that cyclic codes form an ideal (as discussed in Chapter 1) in $GF(q)[x]/x^n-1$.

From the results obtained in Chapter 1, we can have the following inferences on the cyclic codes:

1. As C is an ideal over $GF(q)[x]/x^n-1$, there exists a unique monic polynomial of minimal degree $g(x)$ which is called the generator polynomial and is given by
$$g(x) = g_0 + g_1x + g_2x^2 + \ldots + g_rx^r \text{ where } g_0 = g_r = 1$$
2. Every polynomial in C can be generated by the generator polynomial as
$$v(x) = u(x)\,g(x)$$
where $u(x) = u_0 + u_1x + u_2x^2 + \ldots + u_{k-1}x^{k-1}$ is a message polynomial of k bits.
3. As the code polynomial $v(x)$ will be of degree $(n-1)$, the degree of the generator polynomial $g(x)$ should be $r = (n-k)$.
4. The generator $g(x)$ is a factor of x^n-1. In case of binary codes, as addition and subtraction operations are same, the generator $g(x)$ has to be a factor $x^n + 1$.

For example, consider a cyclic code of length 7. To obtain the generator polynomial, we need to find the factors of x^n-1:

$$x^7 - 1 = x^7 + 1 = (1 + x)\,(1 + x + x^3)\,(1 + x^2 + x^3)$$

To generate a (7, 4) cyclic code we can either use $(1 + x + x^3)$ or $(1 + x^2 + x^3)$ as the generator polynomial as both have degree $n - k = 7 - 4 = 3$.

5.9.2 Non-Systematic Cyclic Codes

As seen in Section 5.9.1 for a message polynomial $u(x) \in GF(q)[x]/x^n - 1$, the corresponding code polynomial $v(x)$ can be generated using the relation

$$v(x) = u(x)\,g(x)$$

EXAMPLE 5.20

Consider a (7, 4) cyclic code with $g(x) = 1 + x + x^3$ and obtain the code polynomial in non-systematic form for the input sequence 1010, 1100.

Solution: Consider the sequence $u = 1\,0\,1\,0$. We have

$$u(x) = 1 + x^2$$

So

$$v(x) = u(x)\,g(x) = (1+ x^2)\,(1 + x + x^3) = 1 + x + x^3 + x^2 + x^3 + x^5 = 1 + x + x^2 + x^5$$

$$v = (1\,1\,1\,0\,0\,1\,0)$$

Similarly, for the sequence $u = 1\ 1\ 0\ 0$,

$$u(x) = 1 + x$$

So

$$v(x) = u(x)\, g(x) = (1 + x)\,(1 + x + x^3) = 1 + x + x^3 + x + x^2 + x^4 = 1 + x^2 + x^3 + x^4$$

$$v = (1\ 0\ 1\ 1\ 1\ 0\ 0)$$

The non-systematic cyclic codes can be implemented using a normal multiplier circuit shown in Fig. 5.13. The figure gives a general circuit for the multiplication of $g(x)$ and $u(x)$.

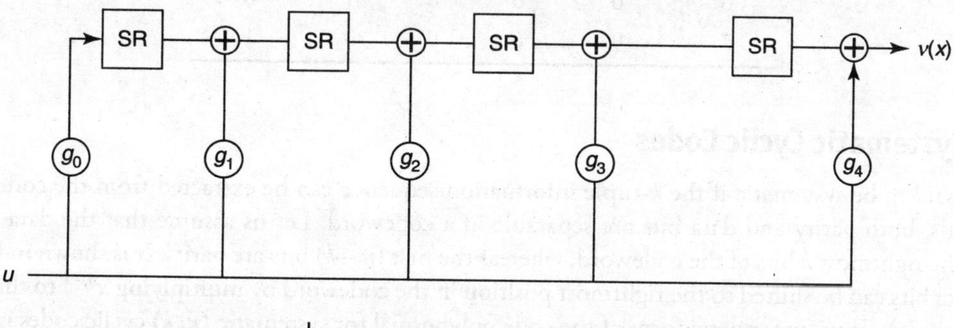

Figure 5.13 | Generation of a non-systematic cyclic code.

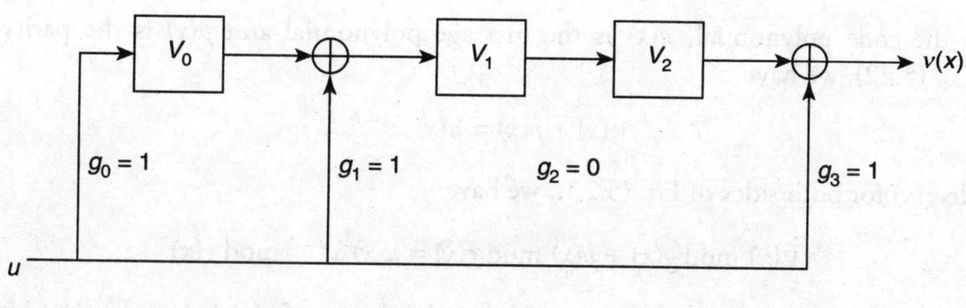

Figure 5.14 | Non-systematic cyclic code for $g(x) = 1 + x + x^3$.

In Example 5.20, we have $g(x) = 1 + x + x^3$. Substituting which in Fig 5.13, results in a simplified circuit shown in Fig. 5.14.

The output obtained from the above encoder circuit can be verified with the normal computation as follows. Let us assume the initial contents of flip-flops to be zeroes, and let the input be 1 1 0 0. The contents of the shift registers after every iteration are detailed in Table 5.9.

After all input bits are loaded to the shift registers, additional zeroes have been inserted so as to flush the contents of the registers. It can be seen from Table 5.9 that the encoded sequence obtained is $v = (1\ 0\ 1\ 1\ 1\ 0\ 0)$, which agrees with our previous calculation.

Table 5.9 | Non-systematic encoding of cyclic codes

Shift	*Input*	*SR contents*			*Output*
		v_0	v_1	v_2	v
0		0	0	0	–
1	0	0	0	0	0
2	0	0	0	0	0
3	1	1	1	0	1
4	1	1	0	1	1
5	0	0	1	0	1
6	0	0	0	1	0
7	0	0	0	0	1

5.9.3 Systematic Cyclic Codes

A code is said to be systematic if the k-tuple information sequence can be extracted from the codeword. In other words, both parity and data bits are separable in a codeword. Let us assume that the data sequence occupies the rightmost k bits of the codeword, whereas the first $(n - k)$ bits are parity. It is shown in Fig. 5.15.

The data bits can be shifted to the rightmost position in the codeword by multiplying x^{n-k} to the message polynomial $u(x)$. Thus, the general form of the code polynomial for systematic (n, k) cyclic codes is given by

$$v(x) = x^{n-k}\, u(x) + p(x) \tag{5.22}$$

where $v(x)$ is the code polynomial, $u(x)$ is the message polynomial and $p(x)$ is the parity polynomial. Rearranging Eq. (5.22), we have

$$v(x) + p(x) = u(x)\, x^{n-k} \tag{5.23}$$

Taking modulo $g(x)$ for both sides of Eq. (5.23), we have

$$v(x) \bmod g(x) + p(x) \bmod g(x) = u(x)\, x^{n-k} \bmod g(x)$$

As $v(x)$ is a multiple of $g(x)$, $v(x) \bmod g(x) = 0$. Also as the degree of $p(x)$ is $(n - k - 1)$ which is less than that of the generator polynomial; so

$$p(x) \bmod g(x) = p(x)$$

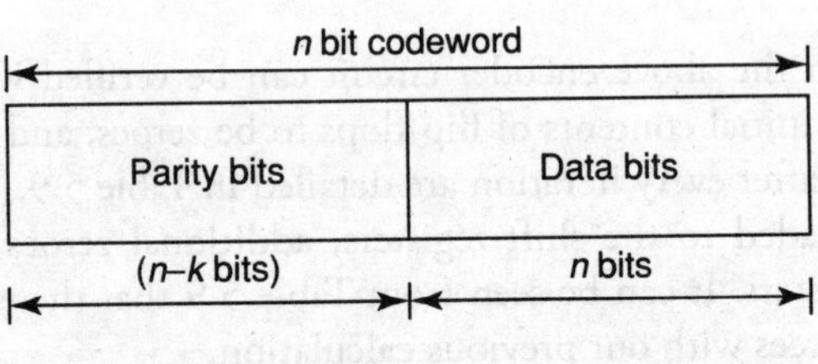

Figure 5.15 | A systematic (n, k) cyclic codes.

Hence,

$$p(x) = u(x)\, x^{n-k} \bmod g(x) \tag{5.24}$$

Thus, from Eq. (5.24) code polynomial in systematic form can be written as

$$v(x) = u(x)\, x^{n-k} + p(x) \tag{5.25}$$

where

$$p(x) = u(x)\, x^{n-k} \bmod g(x)$$

The general procedure to encode an (n, k) cyclic code in systematic form is as follows:

1. Multiply the data polynomial $u(x)$ by x^{n-k} to obtain
$$x^{n-k}\, u(x) = x^{n-k}\, (u_0 + u_1 x + u_2 x^2 + \cdots + u_{k-1}\, x^{-1})$$
$$= u_0 x^{n-k} + u_1\, x^{n-k+1} + u_2 x^{n-k+2} + \cdots + u_{k-1}\, x^{n-1}$$
2. Obtain the remainder polynomial $p(x)$ by dividing $x^{n-k}\, u(x)$ by $g(x)$
$$p(x) = x^{n-k}\, u(x) \bmod g(x)$$
3. Combine $x^{n-k}\, u(x)$ and $p(x)$ to obtain the codeword $v(x)$:
$$v(x) = x^{n-k}\, u(x) + p(k)$$

EXAMPLE 5.21

Consider a (7, 4) cyclic code with generator polynomial $g(x) = 1 + x + x^3$. Obtain the code polynomial in a systematic form for the following information sequences:

(a) 1 0 1 0

(b) 1 1 0 0

Solution:

(a) We have $u = 1\ 0\ 1\ 0$. So $u(x) = 1 + x^2$.

Step 1: Multiply $u(x)$ by $x^{n-k} = x^{7-4} = x^3$. We get

$$x^3 u(x) = x^3(1 + x^2) = x^3 + x^5$$

Step 2: Divide $x^3 u(x)$ by $g(x)$ and obtain the remainder:

$$x^3 + x + 1 \overline{\big)\, x^5 + x^3}$$
$$\underline{x^5 + x^3 + x^2}$$
$$x^2$$

Thus, $p(x) = x^2$.

Step 3: The code polynomial is given by

$$v(x) = x^3u(x) + p(x) = x^3 + x^5 + x^2$$

$$v(x) = x^2 + x^3 + x^5$$

So

$$v = (\underbrace{\overline{0\,0\,1}}_{}\underbrace{1\,0\,1\,0}_{\text{Data}})$$

Parity above the first three bits, Data below the last four bits.

(b) We have $u = 1\,1\,0\,0$. So $u(x) = 1 + x$.

Step 1: $x^3u(x) = x^3 + x^4$

Step 2: Divide $(x^4 + x^3)$ from the generator polynomial, and obtain the remainder as

$$p(x) = x^2 + 1.$$

Step 3: We have

$$v(x) = x^3 + x^4 + x^2 + 1 \Rightarrow v(x) = 1 + x^2 + x^3 + x^4$$

$$v = (\underbrace{1\,0\,1}_{\text{Parity}}\ \underbrace{1\,1\,0\,0}_{\text{Data}})$$

It can be seen from Example 5.21 that the cyclic code in the systematic form will be of the general form given as

$$v = (\underbrace{p_0\ p_1 \ldots p_{n-k-1}}_{(n-k)\text{ Parity bits}}\quad \underbrace{u_0\ u_1\ u_2 \ldots u_{k-1}}_{k\text{-message bits}})$$

5.9.4 Generator and Parity Check Matrices

It has been seen in Section 5.9.1 that an (n, k) cyclic code constitutes a subspace C of a ring of polynomials $GF(q)\,[x]\,/\,x^{n-1}$. Also k, n-tuple vectors $g(x)$, $xg(x)$, $x^2g(x)$, …, $x^kg(x)$ will span the entire C. If these vectors form the row space, we can find the generator matrix for C as

$$G = \begin{bmatrix} g_0 & g_1 & g_2 \cdots g_{n-k} & 0 & 0\ldots0 \\ 0 & g_0 & g_1 \cdots g_{n-k-1} & g_{n-k} & 0\ldots0 \\ \cdots & & & & \\ 0 & 0\ldots0 & g_0 & & g_1 \cdots g_{n-k} \end{bmatrix}_{k\times n}$$

The matrix G is called the generator matrix for the given (n, k) cyclic code. Generally, the matrix G obtained from the above procedure is not in its systematic form $G = [I_k{:}P]$ or $G = [P{:}I_k]$. However, it can be reduced to its standard form by matrix reduction techniques. The generator polynomial $g(x)$ for an (n, k) cyclic code divides $x^n + 1$, that is,

$$x^n + 1 = g(x)\ h(x)$$

where $h(x)$ is a polynomial of degree k. So we get

$$h(x) = h_0 + h_1x + h_2x^2 + \dots + h_{k-1}x^{k-1}\ h_kx^k$$

The parity check matrix H for an (n, k) cyclic code can be obtained by filling the first row of the matrix with an n-tuple vector $(h_k\, h_{k-1} \dots h_1\, h_0\, 0\, 0 \dots 0)$ and cyclically shift it $(n - k - 1)$ times to obtain the remaining rows:

$$H = \begin{bmatrix} h_k & h_{k-1} & \dots & h_1 & h_0 & 0 & \dots & 0 \\ 0 & h_k & \dots & h_2 & h_1 & h_0 & \dots & 0 \\ \dots \\ 0 & 0 & \dots & h_k & h_{k-1} & \dots & h_1 & h_0 \end{bmatrix}_{(n-k)\times n}$$

Again the above matrix is not in the systematic form $H = [P^T{:}I_{n-k}]$ or $[I_{n-k}{:}P^T]$, but it can be made systematic by performing matrix reduction. The matrix $H_{(n-k)\times n}$ will serve as a generator matrix for the dual code $[n, (n-k)]$ of an (n, k) cyclic code.

EXAMPLE 5.22

Obtain the generator and parity check matrices for an (n, k) cyclic code with $g(x) = 1 + x + x^3$.

Solution: The generator matrix will be of the dimension $k \times n = 4 \times 7$. The first row of the matrix can be filled up using the coefficients of $g(x)$ as

$$g(x) = 1 + x + x^3 = (1\,1\,0\,1\,0\,0\,0)$$

The second row can be filled up using the coefficients of $x\,g(x)$ as

$$xg(x) = x + x^2 + x^4 = (0\,1\,1\,0\,1\,0\,0)$$

which is nothing but the cyclic shift of the first row. Similarly, the remaining two rows can be filled up using the coefficients of $x^2g(x)$ and $x^3g(x)$, respectively. Therefore,

$$G = \begin{bmatrix} 110:1000 \\ 011:0100 \\ 001:1010 \\ 000:1101 \end{bmatrix}$$

The above matrix can be reduced to the form $G = [P{:}I_k]$ using the following row reduction technique. Rows 1 and 2 are already in the standard form, whereas for rows 3 and 4, the following reductions can be made:

$$r_3 \leftarrow r_3 + r_1 \quad \text{and} \quad r_4 \leftarrow r_4 + r_1 + r_2$$

$$G = \begin{bmatrix} 110:1000 \\ 011:0100 \\ 111:0010 \\ 101:0001 \end{bmatrix}_{4\times 7}$$

Now the above matrix is of the standard form $G = [P \vdots I_k]$. To obtain the parity check matrix, we should find $h(x)$ such that

$$x^n + 1 = g(x)\ h(x)$$

For the given example, $n = 7$ and $g(x) = 1 + x + x^3$, therefore,

$$x^7 + 1 = (1 + x + x^3)\ h(x)$$

To find $h(x)$, divide $x^7 + 1$ by $1 + x + x^3$ and obtain the quotient

$$\begin{array}{r|l} & x^4 + x^2 + x + 1 \\ \hline x^3 + x + 1 & x^7 + 1 \\ & x^7 + x^5 + x^4 \\ \hline & x^5 + x^4 + 1 \\ & x^5 + x^3 + x^2 \\ \hline & x^4 + x^3 + x^2 + 1 \\ & x^4 + x^2 + x \\ \hline & x^3 + x + 1 \end{array}$$

Therefore,

$$h(x) = 1 + x + x^2 + x^4$$

The first row can be obtained by considering the coefficients of $h(x)$ in the reverse manner, that is, the coefficients of first row could be (1 0 1 1 1 0 0). The remaining two rows can be obtained by cyclically shifting the first row. Thus, the parity check matrix can be obtained as

$$H = \begin{bmatrix} 1 & 0 & 1 & \vdots & 1 & 1 & 0 & 0 \\ 0 & 1 & 0 & \vdots & 1 & 1 & 1 & 0 \\ 0 & 0 & 1 & \vdots & 0 & 1 & 1 & 1 \end{bmatrix}$$

The above matrix is not of the form $H = [I_{n-k} \vdots P^T]$. But it can be reduced to the standard form using the matrix reduction by the following row operation $r_1 \leftarrow r_1 + r_3$:

$$H = \begin{bmatrix} 1 & 0 & 0 & \vdots & 1 & 0 & 1 & 1 \\ 0 & 1 & 0 & \vdots & 1 & 1 & 1 & 0 \\ 0 & 0 & 1 & \vdots & 0 & 1 & 1 & 1 \end{bmatrix}_{3\times 7}$$

$$\qquad I_{n-k} \qquad\qquad P^T$$

It can also be verified that the parity check matrix H could have been obtained from the generator matrix G.

EXAMPLE 5.23

Consider a (7, 4) cyclic code with $g(x) = 1 + x + x^3$. Find the codewords for the message 1 0 1 0 and 1 1 0 0 using the generator matrix.

Solution: The generator matrix for the (7, 4) cyclic code with $g(x) = 1 + x + x^3$ has been obtained from Example 5.22.

$$G = \begin{bmatrix} 110:1000 \\ 011:0100 \\ 111:0010 \\ 101:0001 \end{bmatrix}_{4\times 7}$$

The codeword for the input (1 0 1 0) can be obtained from just getting the product of the input with the generator matrix

$$v = [1\ 0\ 1\ 0] \begin{bmatrix} 110\ 1000 \\ 011\ 0100 \\ 111\ 0010 \\ 101\ 0001 \end{bmatrix} = [0\ \ 0\ \ 1\ \ 1\ \ 0\ \ 1\ \ 0]$$

which agrees with the result we obtained earlier. Similarly, the codeword for the input (1 1 0 0) can be obtained as

$$v = [1\ 1\ 0\ 0] \begin{bmatrix} 110\ 1000 \\ 011\ 0100 \\ 111\ 0010 \\ 101\ 0001 \end{bmatrix} = [1\ \ 0\ \ 1\ \ 1\ \ 1\ \ 0\ \ 0]$$

which again agrees with the result obtained using normal division method.

5.9.5 Encoding of Cyclic Codes Using (*n* – *k*) Shift Registers

As seen from Section 5.9.4, an (*n*, *k*) cyclic code with systematic form can be obtained by performing the following steps:

1. Multiply the message polynomial $u(x)$ by x^{n-k}.
2. Divide $x^{n-k}\,u(x)$ by $g(x)$ and obtain the remainder $p(x)$.
3. The code can be obtained as

$$v(x) = p(x) + x^{n-k}u(x)$$

The above procedure can be accomplished using an $(n - k)$ stage shift register with feedback connection based on the coefficients of the generator polynomial. So, we have

$$g(x) = g_0 + g_1x + g_2x^2 + \cdots + g_{n-k}x^{n-k}$$

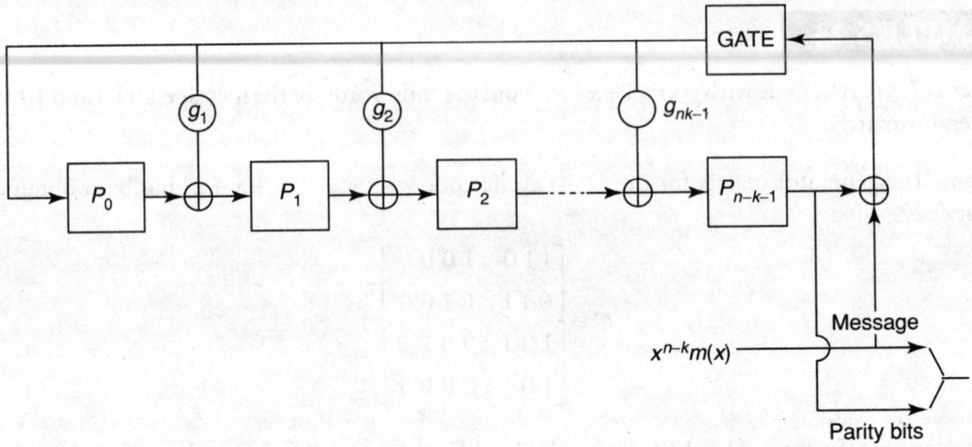

Figure 5.16 | A general encoding circuit for an (n, k) cyclic code.

Now $g_0 = g_{n-k} = 1$ always. Therefore,

$$g(x) = 1 + g_1x + g_2x^2 + \cdots + x^{n-k}$$

A general circuit for encoding an (n, k) cyclic code using an $(n - k)$ stage linear feedback shift register is shown in Fig. 5.16. The encoding procedure using feedback shift register of $(n - k)$ stages involves the following steps:

Step 1: With GATE turned ON, shift the message bits to the shift register.

Step 2: Once all bits are shifted, the remainder will be obtained in the shift registers that can be taken out by turning the GATE OFF.

The pre-multiplication of x^{n-k} to $u(x)$ is performed by shifting the input from the right end.

EXAMPLE 5.24

For a (7, 4) cyclic code with $g(x) = 1 + x + x^3$, obtain the encoded output using shift registers for the input $u(x) = 1 + x^2$.

Solution: The encoder circuit for the given (7, 4) cyclic code with $g(x) = 1 + x + x^3$ is shown in Fig. 5.17. The feedback connection of the above encoder is based on the coefficients of the generator polynomial. The given message $u(x) = 1 + x^2$ corresponds to a sequence of (1 0 1 0). A pre-multiplication of x^{n-k} $u(x)$ can be obtained by performing a cyclic shift of u. In other words, shifting the input from the right end into the shift register performs the task of pre-multiplication. Let us assume the initial contents of registers to be all zeroes. The complete steps of encoding process and the corresponding contents of the shift registers after each shift are shown in Table 5.10.

The content of the shift registers after all input bits being fed, gives the parity bits. Thus, the parity bits for the given input is (0 0 1). Therefore, the resulting code vector will be $v = (0\ 0\ 1\ 1\ 0\ 1\ 0)$. This is same as the previously obtained result.

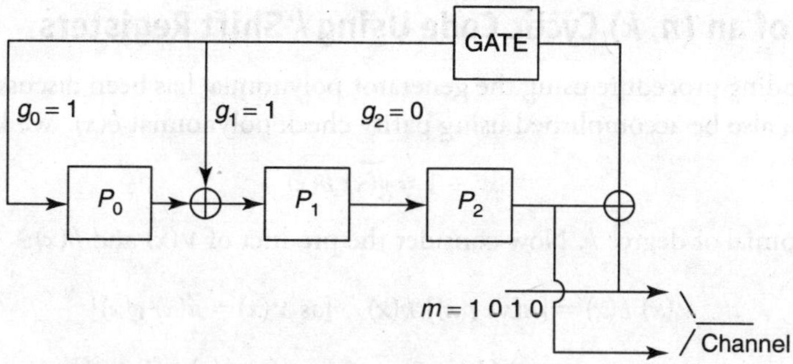

Figure 5.17 | Encoding circuit for a (7, 4) cyclic code with $g(x) = 1 + x + x^3$.

Table 5.10 | Encoding process of a (7, 4) cyclic code

Input	*Shift Register Contents*		
	P_0	P_1	P_2
…	0	0	0
0	0	0	0
1	1	1	0
0	0	1	1
1	0	0	1

EXAMPLE 5.25

Redo Example 5.24 for the input polynomial $u(x) = 1 + x$.

Solution: The same circuit shown in Fig. 5.17 can be used for encoding as the generator polynomial is same. Table 5.11 depicts the complete process of encoding.
Therefore, the encoded sequence is (1 0 1 1 1 0 0).

Table 5.11 | Encoding for $m = 1\,1\,0\,0$

Input	*Shift Register Contents*		
	P_0	P_1	P_2
…	0	0	0
0	0	0	0
0	1	0	0
1	1	1	0
1	0	0	1

5.9.6 Encoding of an (*n*, *k*) Cyclic Code Using *k* Shift Registers

In Section 5.9.5, encoding procedure using the generator polynomial has been discussed. The encoding of a binary cyclic code can also be accomplished using parity check polynomial $h(x)$. We know that

$$x^n + 1 = g(x)\, h(x)$$

where $h(x)$ is a polynomial of degree k. Now consider the product of $v(x)$ and $h(x)$:

$$v(x)\, h(x) = [u(x)\, g(x)]\, h(x) \quad [\text{as } v(x) = u(x)\, g(x)]$$

$$= u(x)\, [1 + x^n] \quad [\text{as } g(x)\, h(x) = 1 + x^n]$$

Therefore,

$$v(x)\, h(x) = u(x) + u(x)\, x^n \tag{5.26}$$

As the degree of $u(x)$ is less than k, the terms $x^k, x^{k+1}, x^{k+2}, \ldots, x^{n-1}$ do not appear in the term $u(x) + u(x)\, x^n$. Therefore, the coefficients of the terms $x^k, x^{k+1}, \ldots, x^{n-1}$ in the product $v(x)\, h(x)$ have to be zero. So we get

$$\sum_{i=0}^{k} h_i v_{l-i} = 0,\ l = k, k+1, k+2, \ldots, n-1 \tag{5.27}$$

But $h_k = 1$. Therefore, we can write Eq. (5.27) as

$$v_{l-k} = \sum_{i=0}^{k-1} h_i v_{l-i},\ l = k, k+1, \ldots, (n-1)$$

This implies

$$v_0 = \sum_{i=0}^{k-1} h_i\, v_{k-i}$$

$$v_1 = \sum_{i=0}^{k-1} h_i v_{k+1-i}$$

$$\cdots\cdots\cdots\cdots\cdots$$

$$v_{n-k-1} = \sum_{i=0}^{k-1} h_i\, v_{n-i-1} \tag{5.28}$$

Whereas the next k bits of the code vector are the message bits

$$v_{n-k} = u_0$$

$$v_{n-k+1} = u_1$$

$$\vdots$$

$$v_{n-1} = u_{k-1} \tag{5.29}$$

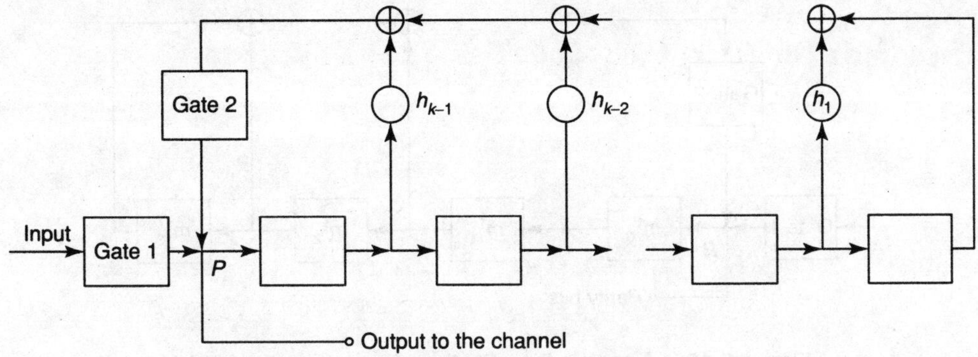

Figure 5.18 | Encoder for an (n, k) cyclic code using $h(x)$.

Equations (5.28) and (5.29) can be incorporated using a feedback shift register of k stages whose connections are based on the coefficients of the parity check polynomial $h(x)$. The encoder for an (n, k) cyclic code based on the parity check polynomial is shown in Fig. 5.18.

The procedure for encoding a message polynomial using a k stage shift register is as follows:

Step 1: With Gate 1 ON and Gate 2 OFF, shift the input bits into the shift register.

Step 2: Once all bits have been shifted into the shift register, turn OFF Gate 1 and turn ON Gate 2.

Step 3: The parity bits will be computed after every shift and will be extracted from the point 'P' in the circuit.

Step 4: Step 3 is repeated for $(n - k)$ times till all parity bits appear at the output.

EXAMPLE 5.26

Obtain the codeword for the message (1 0 1 0) for a (7, 4) cyclic code with $g(x) = 1 + x + x^3$. Use a four-stage shift register for encoding.

Solution: Given $g(x) = 1 + x + x^3$. $h(x)$ can be obtained by dividing $x^7 + 1$ by $g(x)$ as $g(x)\,h(x) = 1 + x^7$.

$$
\begin{array}{r l}
 & 1 + x + x^2 + x^4 \\
x^3 + x + 1 \,\big) & x^7 + 1 \\
 & x^7 + x^5 + x^4 \\
\hline
 & x^5 + x^4 + 1 \\
 & x^5 + x^3 + x^2 \\
\hline
 & x^4 + x^3 + x^2 + 1 \\
 & x^4 + x^2 + x \\
\hline
 & x^3 + x + 1 \\
 & x^3 + x + 1 \\
\hline
 & 0
\end{array}
$$

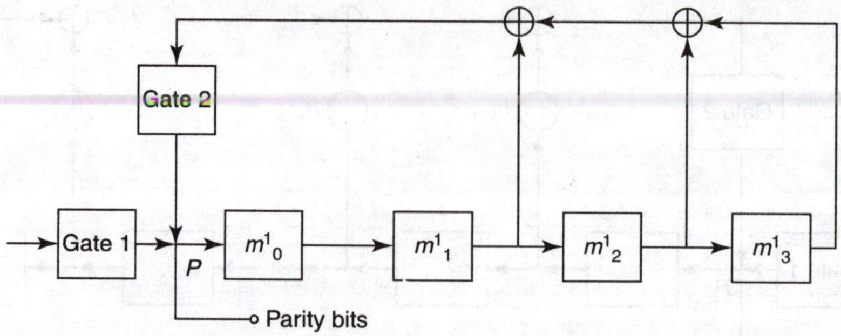

Figure 5.19 | Encoder for a (7, 4) cyclic code using $h(x)$.

Therefore,

$$h(x) = 1 + x + x^2 + x^4$$

The encoder circuit for the given (7, 4) cyclic code using $h(x)$ is shown in Fig. 5.19.
The feedback connections are based on the coefficients of the parity check polynomial $h(x)$. Given data is 1 0 1 0. Initially the shift register contents are zeroes and the first k shifts will shift the input bits to the shift registers. Thus, making the contents of the shift registers to

$$u^1{}_0\, u^1{}_1\, u^1{}_2\, u^1{}_3 = (1\ 0\ 0).$$

The parity check bits can be obtained by next $(n - k)$ shifts as depicted in Table 5.12.
Thus, the parity bits obtained from the circuit are 0 0 1. Therefore, the codeword is (0 0 1 1 0 1 0), which is agreeing with the previous output.

Table 5.12 | Encoding of (7, 4) cyclic code

Shift	*Shift Register Contents*				*Parity*
	$u^1{}_0$	$u^1{}_1$	$u^1{}_2$	$u^1{}_3$	
–	1	0	1	0	–
1	1	1	0	1	1
2	0	1	1	0	0
3	0	0	1	1	0

EXAMPLE 5.27

Redo Example 5.26 for $u(x) = 1 + x$.

Solution: Given $u = (1\ 1\ 0\ 0)$. The output of the encoder circuit shown in Fig. 5.19 for the input (1 1 0 0) is shown in Table 5.13.

Table 5.13 | Encoding for $m = 1\ 1\ 0\ 0$

Shift	*Shift Register Contents*				*Parity*
	$u^1{}_0$	$u^1{}_1$	$u^1{}_2$	$u^1{}_3$	
..	1	1	0	0	..
1	1	1	1	0	1
2	0	1	1	1	0
3	1	0	1	1	1

Therefore, parity bits are (1 0 1) and codeword = (1 0 1 1 1 0 0).

5.9.7 Syndrome Calculation and Error Detection

Consider a received vector $r = (r_0\ r_1\ \dots\ r_{n-1})$. Assuming that the channel is noisy, the received vector may not be the actually transmitted vector. As cyclic codes are a subclass of linear block codes, the same procedure for detection and correction of errors can be used. But a simpler approach would suffice as cyclic codes satisfy additional properties to general LBC.

For cyclic codes, the received vector r can be treated as polynomial of degree $(n - 1)$ or less:

$$r(x) = r_0 + r_1x + r_2x^2 + \cdots + r_{n-1}x^{n-1} \tag{5.30}$$

Now dividing $r(x)$ by $g(x)$, let $a(x)$ be the quotient and $s(x)$ be the remainder. Therefore,

$$r(x) = a(x)\ g(x) + s(x) \tag{5.31}$$

where $s(x)$ is the remainder of degree $(n - k - 1)$ or less which is termed as the syndrome polynomial and the coefficients of the syndrome polynomial constitute the syndrome S.

As the code vector is a multiple of the generator polynomial $g(x)$, the syndrome will be zero if and only if the received polynomial is a valid codeword. The logical circuit to compute the syndrome would be normal $(n - k)$ stage shift register with linear feedback whose connection pattern is dependent on the coefficients of the generator polynomial. A generalized circuit for the syndrome calculation is shown in Fig. 5.20.

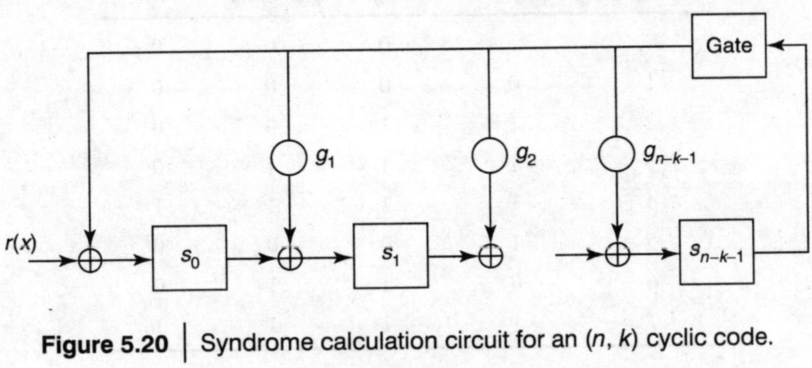

Figure 5.20 | Syndrome calculation circuit for an (n, k) cyclic code.

The circuit operation is as follows:

1. Shift the received vector $r(x)$ from the left end of the circuit considering the initial conditions of all registers to be zero.
2. As soon as all the bits of the received vector are shifted into the registers, the content of the registers will give the syndrome computed.

EXAMPLE 5.28

For a (7, 4) cyclic code with generator polynomial $g(x) = 1 + x + x^3$, construct the syndrome calculation circuit and also obtain the syndrome for the received vector $r(x) = 1 + x^2 + x^3 + x^4 + x^5$.

Solution: Given $r = 1\,0\,1\,1\,1\,1\,0$. The syndrome calculation circuit is shown in Fig. 5.21.

The contents of the registers after each received bit being shifted into the decoder are detailed in Table 5.14.

After all bits of the received vector are fed into the register, we will obtain the syndrome computed for the received vector as the contents of the registers. In the given example, the computed syndrome is 1 1 1. A non-zero syndrome infers the presence of an error in the received vector.

This can be verified by performing a normal division of $r(x)$ by $g(x)$ and obtaining the remainder:

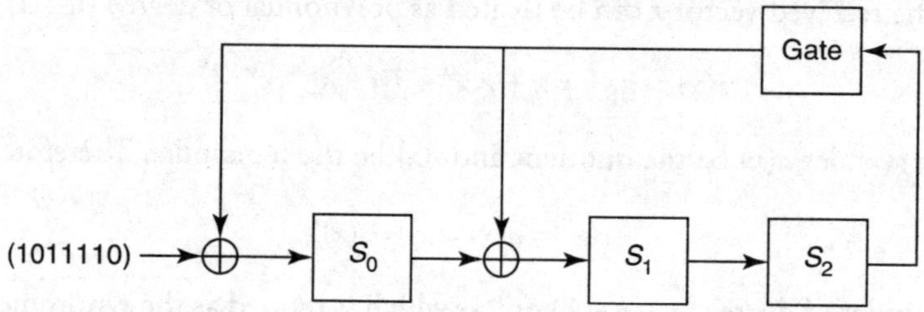

Figure 5.21 | Syndrome calculation circuit for a (7, 4) cyclic code with $g(x) = 1 + x + x^3$.

Table 5.14 | Syndrome calculation

Shift	*Input*	s_0	s_1	s_2
...	...	0	0	0
1	0	0	0	0
2	1	1	0	0
3	1	1	1	0
4	1	1	1	1
5	1	0	0	0
6	0	1	1	0
7	1	1	1	1

$$
\begin{array}{r}
x^2 + x \\
x^3 + x + 1 \overline{\smash{)}\, x^5 + x^4 + x^3 + x^2 + 1} \\
\underline{x^5 + x^3 + x^2} \\
x^4 + 1 \\
\underline{x^4 + x^2 + x} \\
x^2 + x + 1
\end{array}
$$

Therefore,

$$s(x) = 1 + x + x^2 \quad \text{or} \quad s = (1\ 1\ 1)$$

which agrees with the answer obtained by the syndrome calculating circuit.

Note: Syndrome for the shifts of $r(x)$ mod $(x^n + 1)$ is simply the shifts of $s(x)$ mod $(x^n + 1)$.

5.9.8 Decoding of Cyclic Codes

As cyclic codes are a subspace of linear block codes, they can be decoded using the algorithms of linear block codes. The process involves the following three steps:

1. Compute the syndrome.
2. Map the computed syndrome to the error pattern.

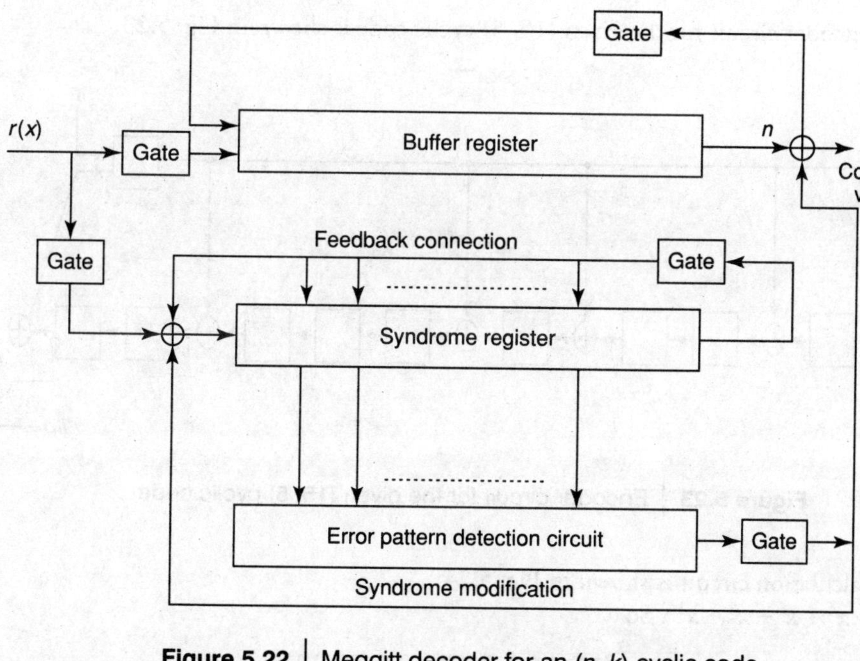

Figure 5.22 | Meggitt decoder for an (n, k) cyclic code.

3. Perform bitwise EXOR operation of the received vector with the error pattern to obtain the corrected vector.

Although, the above procedure is straightforward, it is complex involving complicated circuitry for the increase in the value of n. Also as cyclic codes have better structural properties, simple decoding algorithms have been devised for the decoding of cyclic codes. The procedure to perform the decoding operation is as follows:

1. Decoding is done considering one bit of the received vector at a time.
2. Every time when a syndrome is computed, verify whether the obtained syndrome $s(x)$ corresponds to a correctable error pattern with error being present at the MSB of the received polynomial. If so, the MSB bit is inverted and taken out.
3. Received vector is shifted once and steps 2 and 3 are repeated till all bits of the received vector are taken out.

In general, decoder for the cyclic codes which incorporates the decoding algorithm as specified above is called a Meggitt decoder. Figure 5.22 shows the Meggitt decoder for the cyclic code.

EXAMPLE 5.29

In a (15, 5) cyclic code, the generator polynomial is given by

$$g(x) = 1 + x + x^2 + x^4 + x^5 + x^8 + x^{10}$$

Draw the block diagram of an encoder and syndrome calculator for this code. Find whether $r(x) = 1 + x^4 + x^6 + x^8 + x^{14}$ a valid codeword.

Solution: The encoder circuit for the given (15, 5) cyclic code is shown in Fig. 5.23.

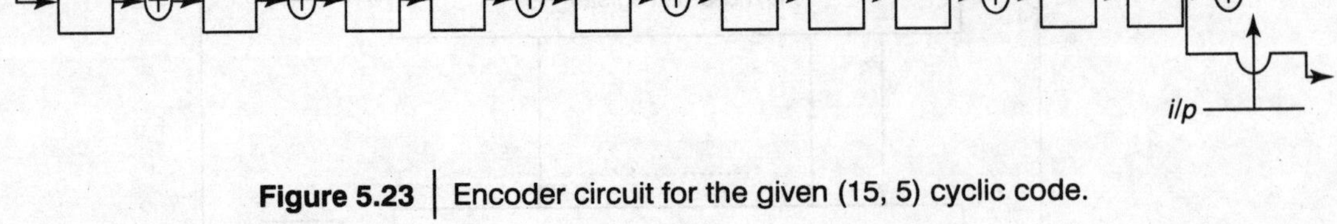

Figure 5.23 | Encoder circuit for the given (15, 5) cyclic code.

The syndrome calculation circuit is shown in Fig. 5.24.
Given $r(x) = 1 + x^4 + x^6 + x^8 + x^{14}$. So

$$r = (1\,0\,0\,0\,1\,0\,1\,0\,1\,0\,0\,0\,0\,0\,1)$$

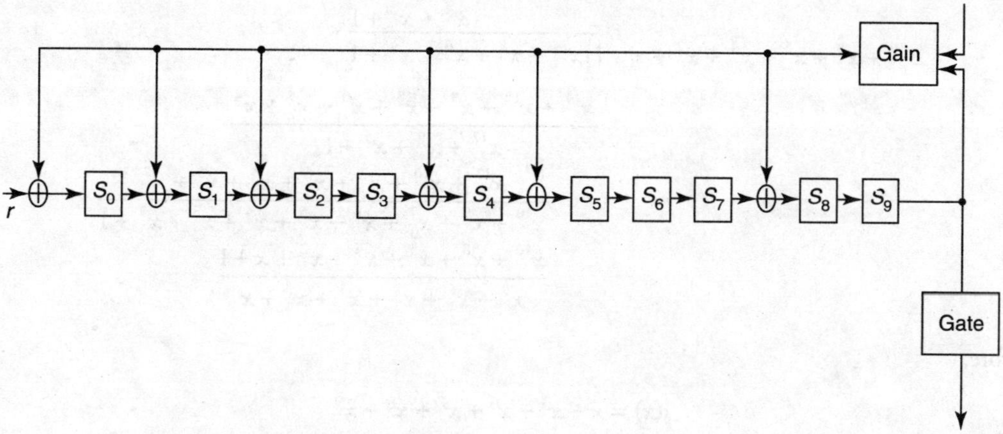

Figure 5.24 | Syndrome calculation circuit for the given (15, 5) cyclic code.

From the syndrome calculating circuit, we can find the syndrome for the given received sequence. The procedure is detailed in Table 5.15.

As the syndrome is non-zero, the given $r(x)$ is not a valid codeword. This can be verified using normal division approach, that is, by dividing $r(x)$ by $g(x)$ and the remainder denotes the syndrome:

$$r(x) = 1 + x^4 + x^6 + x^8 + x^{14}$$

$$g(x) = 1 + x + x^2 + x^4 + x^5 + x^8 + x^{10}$$

Table 5.15 | Syndrome calculation for (15, 5) cyclic code

Input	s_0	s_1	s_2	s_3	s_4	s_5	s_6	s_7	s_8	s_9
...	0	0	0	0	0	0	0	0	0	0
1	1	0	0	0	0	0	0	0	0	0
0	0	1	0	0	0	0	0	0	0	0
0	0	0	1	0	0	0	0	0	0	0
0	0	0	0	1	0	0	0	0	0	0
0	0	0	0	0	1	0	0	0	0	0
0	0	0	0	0	0	1	0	0	0	0
1	1	0	0	0	0	0	1	0	0	0
0	0	1	0	0	0	0	0	1	0	0
1	1	0	1	0	0	0	0	0	1	0
0	0	1	0	1	0	0	0	0	0	1
1	0	1	0	0	0	1	0	0	1	0
0	0	0	1	0	0	0	1	0	0	1
0	1	1	1	1	1	1	0	1	1	0
0	0	1	1	1	1	1	1	0	1	1
1	0	1	0	1	0	0	1	1	1	1

$$\begin{array}{r} x^4+x^2+1 \\ x^{10}+x^8+x^5+x^4+x^2+x+1\overline{)x^{14}+x^8+x^6+x^4+1} \\ \underline{x^{14}+x^{12}+x^9+x^8+x^6+x^5+x^4} \\ x^{12}+x^9+x^5+1 \\ \underline{x^{12}+x^{10}+x^7+x^6+x^4+x^3+x^2} \\ x^{10}+x^9+x^7+x^6+x^5+x^4+x^3+x^2+1 \\ \underline{x^{10}+x^8+x^5+x^4+x^2+x+1} \\ x^9+x^8+x^7+x^6+x^3+x \end{array}$$

Therefore,

$$s(x) = x + x^3 + x^6 + x^7 + x^8 + x^9$$

or

$$s = (0\;1\;0\;1\;0\;0\;1\;1\;1\;1)$$

which is matching with the result obtained from the syndrome circuit.

EXAMPLE 5.30

Given $n \leq 7$, identity (n, k) values of the cyclic code generated by the following generator polynomials.

(a) $g(x) = 1 + x^2 + x^3$

(b) $g(x) = 1 + x + x^2 + x^4$

(c) $g(x) = 1 + x + x^2 + x^3 + x^4$

Solution: The conditions to be fulfilled by the generator polynomials are:

1. Degree of $g(x)$ is $(n - k)$
2. $g(x) \mid x^n + 1$, i.e., $x^n + 1$ is divisible by $g(x)$
   (a) Given $g(x) = 1 + x^2 + x^3$, therefore, $(n - k) = 3$. Let us check for a (7, 4) code $n = 7$. Let us consider $x^n + 1 \mid g(x)$:

$$\begin{array}{r} x^4+x^3+x^2+1 \\ x^3+x^2+1\overline{)x^7+1} \\ \underline{x^7+x^6+x^4} \\ x^6+x^4+1 \\ \underline{x^6+x^5+x^3} \\ x^5+x^4+x^3+1 \\ \underline{x^5+x^4+x^2} \\ x^3+x^2+1 \\ \underline{x^3+x^2+1} \\ 0 \end{array}$$

Therefore, it is a (7, 4) cyclic code.

(b) $g(x) = 1 + x + x^2 + x^4$. Then $n - k = 4$. Let us start with (7, 3) code. We have

$$x^n + 1 = x^7 + 1$$

Now

$$\begin{array}{r}
x^3 + x + 1 \\
x^4 + x^2 + x + 1 \overline{\big) \quad x^7 + 1} \\
\underline{x^7 + x^5 + x^4 + x^3} \\
x^5 + x^4 + x^3 + 1 \\
\underline{x^5 + x^3 + x^2 + x} \\
x^4 + x^2 + x + 1 \\
\underline{x^4 + x^2 + x + 1} \\
0
\end{array}$$

Therefore, (7, 3) is the code.

(c) $g(x) = 1 + x + x^2 + x^3 + x^4$. So $n - k = 4$. Let us consider (7, 3) code. Here

$$x^n + 1 = x^7 + 1$$

Now

$$\begin{array}{r}
x^3 + x^2 \\
x^4 + x^3 + x^2 + x + 1 \overline{\big) \quad x^7 + 1} \\
\underline{x^7 + x^6 + x^5 + x^4 + x^3} \\
x^6 + x^5 + x^4 + x^3 + 1 \\
\underline{x^6 + x^5 + x^4 + x^3 + x^2} \\
1 + x^2
\end{array}$$

Therefore, it is not (7, 3) code. Let us consider (6, 2) code as $n \leq 7$. Hence

$$x^n + 1 = x^6 + 1$$

Now

$$\begin{array}{r}
x^3 + x^2 + x \\
x^3 + x^2 + 1 \overline{\big) \quad x^6 + 1} \\
\underline{x^6 + x^5 + x^3} \\
x^5 + x^3 + 1 \\
\underline{x^5 + x^4 + x^2} \\
x^4 + x^3 + x^2 + 1 \\
\underline{x^4 + x^3 + x} \\
x^2 + x + 1
\end{array}$$

Therefore, it is not (6, 2) code.

Continuing with the next possible combination of $(n, k) = (5, 1)$, we will again get a non-zero remainder after dividing x^5+1 by $g(x)$.

Thus, it will not generate any (n, k) cyclic code for $n \leq 7$.

5.10 Golay Codes

Binary Golay codes are one of the very important classes of linear block codes, since they are one among the very few sets of non-trivial perfect codes. In 1949, Golay discovered a possibility of the combination (23, 12) for the construction for a perfect code. The (23, 12) Golay codes are capable of correcting three errors. As discussed in Section 5.6.1, any code which satisfies the following Hamming bound is called a perfect code:

$$2^{n-k} = \sum_{i=0}^{t} {}^nC_i$$

Substituting $n = 23$ and $k = 12$, we can see that the above equation is satisfied. Thus, Golay codes are a class of perfect codes.

The following are the parameters for a Golay codes.

Number of code bits $n = 23$.

Number of data bits $k = 12$.

Number of parity bits $(n - k) = 11$.

Number of error correcting capability $t = 3$.

Generator polynomial $= g(x) = 1 + x^2 + x^4 + x^5 + x^6 + x^{10} + x^{11}$ or $g(x) = 1 + x + x^5 + x^6 + x^7 + x^9 + x^{11}$. Hence $d_{min} = 7$.

5.11 Shortened Cyclic Codes

As cyclic codes form an ideal, there exists a unique monic polynomial $g(x)$ that can be used for the construction of the cyclic codes. It has been shown in Section 5.9.1 that $g(x)$ has to be a factor of x^n+1. Thus, there will be a limited scope of selecting the generator polynomial for a given length of the codeword n. In order to increase the number of pairs (n, k), shortened cyclic codes were proposed. Here, the last 'l' information bits are assumed to be 0's. And thus, the last 'l' bits of the codeword will be always 0. Hence, the transmission of just $(n - l)$ bits would suffice. After receiving, the receiver appends 'l' zeros at the end of every codeword.

In other words, for all (n, k) cyclic codes, we can construct an $(n - l, k - l)$ shortened cyclic code by considering only $(k - l)$ higher order bits of the information. However, the advantage of algebraic structure of the original (n, k) cyclic code is inherent. Thus, the minimum distance, error detecting and correcting capability of a shortened cyclic code are at least equal to the original code. An $(n-1, k-1)$ shortened cyclic code can be encoded and decoded exactly in the same manner as a normal (n, k) cyclic code.

Summary

1. The ratio $k/n = R$, gives the code rate.
2. Generator matrix for a LBC will be of the form:

$$G = [I_k:P] \text{ or } G = [P:I_k].$$

3. Codewords of a systematic LBC

$$v = u \cdot G$$

4. Parity check matrix H will be of the form. $H = [P^T:I_{n-k}]$.
5. $GH^T = 0$
6. Syndrome $S = r\,H^T$, non-zero syndrome indicates error.
7. $S = e\,H^T$, a single-bit error corresponds to a non-zero syndrome equal to the corresponding row of H^T.
8. Hamming distance of any two code vectors is defined as the number of bits in which they differ.
9. Hamming weight of a codeword is defined as the number of non-zero entries in the vector.
10. The minimum distance of a linear block code is equal to the minimum weight of a non-zero code vector.

$$d\text{min} = \min\{H_W(v_i, v_j)\}\ \forall i, j \text{ and } i \neq j$$

11. An (n, k) LBC with a minimum distance of d_{min} is capable of detecting $(d_{\text{min}} - 1)$ bit errors.
12. An (n, k) LBC is capable of correcting up to $\left\lfloor \frac{d_{\text{min}} - 1}{2} \right\rfloor$ number of error bits for a minimum distance d_{min}.
13. A linear block code is said to be cyclic if $v = (v_0, v_1, v_2, \ldots, v_{n-1})$ is a code vector then $v' = (v_{n-1}, v_0, v_1, \ldots, v_{n-2})$ is also a code vector.
14. Every polynomial in v can be generated by the generator polynomial as

$$v(x) = u(x)\, g(x)$$

15. The generator $g(x)$ is a factor of $x^n - 1$.
16. Systematic (n, k) cyclic codes are given by

$$v(x) = x^{n-k}\, u(x) + p(x)$$

Review Questions

1. Determine H matrix for $G = \begin{bmatrix} 1 & 0 & 0 & 1 & 1 & 1 \\ 0 & 1 & 0 & 1 & 1 & 0 \\ 0 & 0 & 1 & 1 & 0 & 1 \end{bmatrix}$
2. Draw the general encoder diagram for an (n, k) LBC.
3. Determine the parity check matrix for a (7, 4) systematic LBC whose parity equations are

$$P_5 = u_1 + u_2 + u_3$$

$$P_6 = u_0 + u_2 + u_3$$

$$P_7 = u_0 + u_1 + u_2.$$

4. Obtain all possible code vectors for a (6, 3) LBC in its systematic form for the parity matrix

$$P = \begin{bmatrix} 1 & 1 & 1 \\ 1 & 0 & 1 \\ 0 & 1 & 1 \end{bmatrix}$$

5. Determine G and H matrices for the parity matrix given in the previous problem.

6. Consider a systematic (8, 4) LBC whose parity check equations are:

$$v_0 = u_0 + u_2 + u_3$$

$$v_1 = u_1 + u_2 + u_3$$

$$v_2 = u_0 + u_1 + u_2$$

$$v_3 = u_0 + u_1 + u_3.$$

(a) Write the generator and parity check matrices.
(b) Draw the encoder diagram.

7. For the LBC with

$$G = \begin{bmatrix} 1 & 0 & 0 & 1 & 1 & 1 \\ 0 & 1 & 0 & 1 & 1 & 0 \\ 0 & 0 & 1 & 1 & 0 & 1 \end{bmatrix}$$

determine the syndrome and correct the single bit error, if any.
(a) (1 1 1 1 0 1)
(b) (1 0 1 1 1 1)

8. Consider a systematic (7, 4) LBC whose parity check equations are:

$$v_4 = u_1 + u_2 + u_3$$

$$v_5 = u_0 + u_2 + u_3$$

$$v_6 = u_0 + u_1 + u_2$$

(a) Write the generator and parity check matrices.
(b) Draw the encoder diagram.
(c) Compute all possible code vectors.
(d) Find the minimum Hamming distance of the code.
(e) Determine its error detecting and correcting capabilities.
(f) Draw the syndrome calculating circuit for the given code.

9. Consider a (6, 3) LBC with generator matrix

$$G = \begin{bmatrix} 1 & 0 & 0 & 1 & 1 & 1 \\ 0 & 1 & 0 & 1 & 1 & 0 \\ 0 & 0 & 1 & 1 & 0 & 1 \end{bmatrix}$$

Find:
(a) All codewords
(b) All Hamming weights
(c) Minimum weight and minimum distance
(d) Parity check matrix
(e) Draw the encoder circuit

10. Draw the syndrome calculating circuit for the (6, 3) LBC given in the previous problem. Thus, compute the syndrome for the received vector (1 0 0 0 0 1).

11. For a systematic (6, 3) LBC, the parity matrix is

$$P = \begin{bmatrix} 1 & 0 & 1 \\ 0 & 1 & 1 \\ 1 & 1 & 0 \end{bmatrix}$$

(a) Find all possible code vectors.
(b) Find minimum weight of the code.
(c) Find the parity check matrix.
(d) For a received code vector $R = [1\ 1\ 1\ 1\ 0\ 1]$ detect and correct the error.

12. The generator matrix of a (5, 1) repetition code is given as

$$G = [1 : 1\ 1\ 1\ 1]$$

(a) Write the parity check matrix.
(b) Write the standard array.

13. Consider a (15, 5) binary cyclic code with $g(x)= 1 + x + x^2 + x^4 + x^5 + x^8 + x^{10}$. Draw its encoder circuit.

14. Draw the syndrome calculating circuit for a (15, 7) cyclic code with the generator polynomial $g(x) = 1 + x^4 + x^6 + x^7 + x^8$.

15. Consider a (15, 5) binary cyclic code with $g(x)= 1 + x + x^2 + x^4 + x^5 + x^8 + x^{10}$. Find the codeword in systematic form for the input sequence (1 0 1 1 0).

16. For a (7, 4) cyclic code with $g(x) = 1 + x + x^3$, obtain the encoded output using shift registers for the input $u(x) = 1 + x + x^2$.

17. Consider a (7, 4) cyclic code with $g(x) = 1 + x + x^3$. Obtain the syndrome for the received polynomial $r(x) = x^3 + x^5 + x^6$.

18. The generator polynomial of a (15, 7) cyclic code is $g(x) = 1 + x^4 + x^6 + x^7 + x^8$. Find the codeword in systematic form for the message (0 1 0 1 0 1 0), clearly showing the states of registers. Verify your answer by in the computation.

19. Consider a (15, 7) binary cyclic code with $g(x) = 1 + x^4 + x^6 + x^7 + x^8$.
(a) Draw the encoder circuit.
(b) Obtain the codeword for the input (1 0 1 1 1 0 1).
(c) Draw the syndrome calculating circuit.

20. Consider a (15, 5) binary cyclic code with $g(x) = 1 + x + x^2 + x^4 + x^5 + x^8 + x^{10}$.
(a) Draw the encoder circuit.
(b) Find the codeword for the data $u(x) = 1 + x^3 + x^4$.
(c) Draw the syndrome calculating circuit.
(d) Consider the last bit of the codeword computed in part (b) suffer from transmission error, find its syndrome.

Further Reading

[1] Richerd E Blahut, *Algebraic Codes for Data Transmission*, Cambridge University Press: UK; 2003.

[2] Willium E Ryan and Shu Lin, *Channel Codes: Classical and Modern*, Cambridge University Press: UK; 2009.

[3] Tood K Moon, *Error Control Coding: Mathematical Methods and Algorithms*, John Wiley & Sons: New Jersey; 2005.

[4] Shu Lin and Daniel J Costello, *Error Control Coding: Fundamentals and Applications*, Prentice Hall Series, Inc: Englewood Cliffs, New Jersey; 1983.

[5] Peter Sweeney, *Error Control Coding*, John Wiley& Sons: UK; 1991.

[6] Ranjan Bose, *Information Theory, Coding and Cryptography*, Tata McGraw-Hill Education: New Delhi; 2008.

[7] Simon Haykin, *An Introduction to Analog and Digital Communications*, John Wiley & Sons: New York; 1989.

[8] Shanmugam K Sham, *Digital and Analog Communication Systems*, John Wiley & Sons: New York; 1979.

[9] Ian A Glover and Peter M Grant, *Digital Communications*, Pearson Education: UK; 2004.

[10] Bernard Sklar and Pabitra K Ray, *Digital Communications: Fundamentals and Applications*,

Dorking Kindersley (India) Pvt. Ltd: New Delhi; 2001.

[11] Andrea Goldsmith, *Wireless Communications*, Cambridge University Press: UK; 2005.

[12] John G Proakis and Masoud Salehi. *Contemporary Communication System using MATLAB*, PWS Publishing: Boston, MA; 1998.

[13] S K Moschoyiannis, *Group Theory and Error Detecting/Correcting Codes*, Thesis of Master of Science in Information Systems, University of Surrey, 2001.

[14] Dayan Adionel Guimaraes, *Notions of Information Theory and Error-Correcting Codes*, In Digital Transmission, pp. 689–840; Springer: Berlin, Heidelberg, 2009.

[15] Dan C Marinescu, *Classical and Quantum Information*, Academic Press, Elsevier: Oxford, 2011.

[16] Jorge Castineira Moreira and Patrick Guy Farrell, *Essentials of Error-Control Coding*, John Wiley & Sons: Chichester, 2006.

6 Burst Error Correcting Codes

'There can be no such thing, in law or in morality, as actions forbidden to an individual, but permitted to a mob.'

–Ayn Rand

Learning Objectives

After reading this chapter, you will be able to:

- Appreciate the work involved in developing burst error correcting codes.
- Detail various burst error correcting codes.
- Discuss and study the performance of various codes developed in the literature for burst error correction.

6.1 Introduction

Chapter 5 of the book has detailed linear block codes and its variants that have been used for the detection and correction of random errors. They are useful for memoryless binary channels or discrete memoryless channels. Such codes are also termed as random error correcting codes. However, in most of the practical scenarios we come across situations in which the channel is susceptible to the occurrence of errors in bursts. A scratch on a CD will lead to errors in consecutive bits. Also, a lightning may cause an occurrence of error bursts. If random error correcting codes were used for such situations, the decoding process would become inefficient. Thus, novel algorithms were proposed for the detection and correction of such burst errors. This chapter gives an insight into such channel coding schemes.

6.2 Burst Errors

Definition 6.1: A burst length 'l' can be defined as a vector whose non-zero elements are confined to 'l' successive positions in the vector. Consider an example of an error vector: $e = (0\,0\,1\,0\,1\,1\,0\,1\,0\,1\,0\,0\,0)$. This is an example for a burst of length $l = 8$. Similarly, $e = (0\,0\,1\,1\,0\,1\,0\,0\,0\,0)$ is a burst of length 4.

Definition 6.2: A linear code is said to be an l burst correcting code if and only if it is capable of correcting all error bursts of length l or less but not all burst errors of length $l + 1$.

From the above definitions, it is clear that the problem of burst error correcting codes is to design an (n, k) linear code that is capable of correcting burst of length 'l' with the minimum amount of $(n - k)$ parity bits.

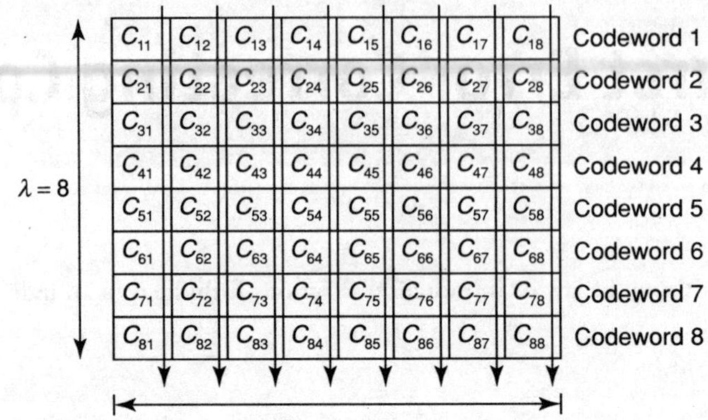

Figure 6.1 | Interleaved code with degree 8.

6.3 Interleaved Codes

Interleaving is one of the techniques used for correcting burst errors. This is a method in which the coded sequences are permuted at the transmitter, thus achieving a spread of errors throughout. Receiver does re-permutation to revert the transmitted information.

For an (n, k) cyclic code, we can always have a $(\lambda n, \lambda k)$ interleaved code by simply arranging λ code vectors along λ rows and transmitting them column-wise. The term λ is referred to as interleaving degree. The process of interleaving is shown in Fig. 6.1.

Figure 6.1 shows an interleaved code for an (8, 4) code with an interleaving degree of 8. Codes are arranged row-wise as shown and will get transmitted column-wise. Thus, the transmitted sequence will be

$(C_{11}, C_{21}, C_{31}, C_{41}, C_{51}, C_{61}, C_{71}, C_{81}), (C_{12}, C_{22}, C_{32}, C_{42}, C_{52}, C_{62}, C_{72}, C_{82}), (C_{13}, C_{23}, C_{33}, C_{43}, C_{53}, C_{63}, C_{73}, C_{83}), (C_{14}, C_{24}, C_{34}, C_{44}, C_{54}, C_{64}, C_{74}, C_{84}), (C_{15}, C_{25}, C_{35}, C_{45}, C_{55}, C_{65}, C_{75}, C_{85}), (C_{16}, C_{26}, C_{36}, C_{46}, C_{56}, C_{66}, C_{76}, C_{86}), (C_{17}, C_{27}, C_{37}, C_{47}, C_{57}, C_{67}, C_{77}, C_{87}), (C_{18}, C_{28}, C_{38}, C_{48}, C_{58}, C_{68}, C_{78}, C_{88})$

Thus, if a burst of errors occurs, the corresponding error locations in the interleaved code will be random. So, random error correcting codes can be used for correcting such bursts. As an example, suppose that bits C_{23}, C_{24}, C_{25} and C_{26} are error prone. Although the error is confined to four consecutive locations in the original order, it will be distributed as four single-bit errors in consecutive blocks after interleaving.

6.4 Product Codes

Let C_1 be an (n_1, k_1) linear block code and C_2 be an (n_2, k_2) linear block code. Then, a product code of $(n_1 n_2, k_1 k_2)$ can be formed as follows: Arrange $(k_1\ k_2)$ information sequence as a matrix of dimension $(k_2 \times k_1)$. Encode each of the k_2 rows using C_1 to obtain n_1 columns. These resulting n_1 columns will then be encoded using C_2 to obtain a complete matrix of dimension $(n_2 \times n_1)$. The procedure explained can be summarized as shown in Fig. 6.2.

The product code, thus, obtained will lead us to code vectors of C_1 on every row and that of C_2 on every column. As codes are linear, we can interchange the order of encoding. The minimum weight of a product code will be equal to the product of the minimum weights of the individual codes. In other words, if code

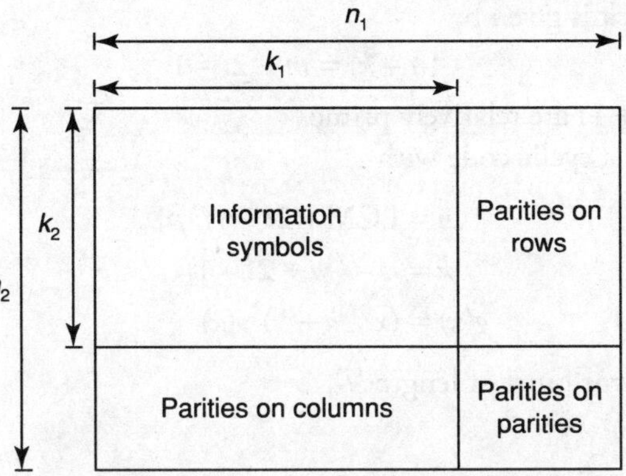

Figure 6.2 | A product code $C_1 \times C_2$.

C_1 has a minimum weight of $d_{\min 1}$ and C_2 has $d_{\min 2}$, then the minimum weight of the product code would be $d_{\min 1} \times d_{\min 2}$. Thus, error correcting capability of a product code is given by

$$t = \left(\frac{d_{\min 1} \cdot d_{\min 2} - 1}{2} \right) \tag{6.1}$$

The burst error correcting capability of a product code can be analyzed as follows: Consider l_1 and l_2 to be the burst error correcting capabilities of codes C_1 and C_2, respectively. If the sequence is transmitted row-wise and a burst of $n_1 l_2$ or less occurs, it will not affect more than $l_2 + 1$ consecutive rows. Thus, each column can be affected at most in l_2 positions, which can be corrected as C_2 is capable of correcting l_2 bursts. Thus, $C_1 \times C_2$ is capable of correcting at least $n_1 l_2$. In the same way, if a burst of $n_2 l_1$ or less occurs when the transmission is done column-wise, each row is affected at most in l_1 positions that can be corrected. Thus, $C_1 \times C_2$ is also capable of correcting an error burst of length at least equal to $n_2 l_1$.

Thus, in general, the burst error correcting capability of a $C_1 \times C_2$ product code is at least equal to $\max(n_1 l_2, n_2 l_1)$.

6.5 Fire Codes

Fire codes were the first class of cyclic codes designed specifically to correct a single burst of errors. The design of a fire code is as follows:

- Let $p(x)$ be an mth degree irreducible polynomial over $GF(2)$.
- Consider ρ be the smallest integer such that

$$p(x) \mid x^{\rho} + 1$$

  where ρ is called as the period of $p(x)$.
- Let 'l' be a positive integer such that $l \leq m$ and $\rho \nmid 2l - 1$.
- The generator polynomial for (n, k) fire code is given by

$$g(x) = (x^{2l-1} + 1)\, p(x)$$

- The length of the code n is given by

$$n = \text{LCM}\,[(2l - 1), \rho]$$

- The number of parity check is given by

$$(n - k) = m + 2l - 1$$

- Note that $p(x)$ and $(x^{2l-1} + 1)$ are relatively prime.
- Thus, an (n, k) fire code is a cyclic code with

$$n = \text{LCM}\ [(2l - 1), \rho]$$
$$k = n - (m + 2l - 1)$$
$$g(x) = (x^{2l-1} + 1)\ p(x)$$

- Fire code can correct an error burst of length 'l'.

EXAMPLE 6.1

Design a fire code considering an irreducible polynomial $p(x) = 1 + x + x^3$.

Solution: The given irreducible polynomial $p(x)$ is primitive. Thus, the period of $p(x)$ is given as

$$\rho = 2^m - 1 = 2^3 - 1 = 7$$

Let $l = 3$. Thus $2l - 1 = 5$. Clearly $7 \nmid 5$

Therefore,

$$g(x) = (x^5+1)\ p(x) = (x^5 + 1)\ (x^3 + x + 1)$$
$$= (x^8 + x^6 + x^5 + x^3 + x + 1)$$
$$n = \text{LCM}\ (5, 7) = 35$$
$$k = 35 - (5 + 3) = 27$$

It is a (35, 27) fire code that is capable of correcting a burst of length 3.

Theorem 6.1 An (n, k) fire code is capable of correcting a burst of length 'l'.

Proof: To prove the above statement, it is sufficient to show that all bursts of length l or less reside in different cosets. Thus, they can be used as coset leaders and form a set of correctable error pattern. Consider monic polynomials $a(x)$ and $b(x)$ of degree $(l_1 - 1)$ and $(l_2 - 1)$, respectively, representing bursts of lengths l_1 and l_2. Let

$$a(x) = 1 + a_1 x + a_2 x^2 + \cdots . + a_{l1-2}\, x^{l1-2} + x^{l1-1}$$
$$b(x) = 1 + b_1 x + b_2 x + \cdots + b_{l2-2}\, x^{l2-2} + x^{l2-1}$$

Consider $l_1 \leq l$ and $l_2 \leq l$. As burst can start at any position in the codeword, it can be represented as $x^i a(x)$ and $x^j b(x)$, where i and j represent the starting position of the burst. Clearly $i, j < n$.

We will prove the above theorem by contradiction. Let us assume $x^i a(x)$ and $x^j b(x)$ reside in the same coset. Thus, the sum of these two polynomials must be a code polynomial.

$$v(x) = x^i a(x) + x^j b(x) \tag{6.2}$$

Assuming $i \leq j$, using division algorithm, we can write

$$j - i = q(2l - 1) + b \tag{6.3}$$

where b is the remainder and q is the quotient obtained after dividing $(j-1)$ by $(2l-1)$. Evidently, $0 \le b \le (2l-1)$.

From Eq. (6.3)

$$j = i + (2l-1)\,q + b \tag{6.4}$$

Substituting Eq. (6.4) in Eq. (6.2), we get

$$v(x) = x^i a(x) + x^{i+(2l-1)\,q+b} b(x)$$

$$= x^i a(x) + x^{i+b}\, b(x)\, [x^{(2l-1)\,q} + 1 + 1]$$

But $1 + 1 = 0$ in binary. So we have

$$v(x) = x^i a(x) + x^{i+b}\, b(x) + x^{i+b}\, b(x)\, [x^{(2l-1)\,q} + 1]$$

$$v(x) = x^i\, [a(x) + x^b\, b(x)] + x^{i+b}\, b(x)\, [x^{(2l-1)q} + 1] \tag{6.5}$$

As per the assumption, $v(x)$ is a codeword. Thus,

$$g(x) \mid v(x)$$

But the factors of $g(x)$ are relatively prime. Therefore, $v(x)$ must be divisible by $x^{(2l-1)} + 1$.

In Eq. (6.5), term $x^{i+b}\, b(x)\, [x^{(2l-1)q} + 1]$ is divisible by $x^{2l-1} + 1$. Therefore, the first term is either divisible by $x^{2l-1} + 1$ or by 0. Therefore, we can have

$$a(x) + x^b\, b(x) = d(x)\,(x^{2l-1} + 1)$$

where $d(x)$ is a quotient polynomial of some degree τ. Therefore,

$$\text{Degree of } d(x)\,(x^{2l-1} + 1) \text{ is } (2l - 1 + \tau) \tag{6.6}$$

We have $\deg\{a(x)\} < 2l - 1$. Therefore,

$$\deg\,[x^b\, b(x)] = 2l - 1 + \tau$$

But

$$\deg\,[b(x)] = l_2 - 1$$

So

$$\deg\,[x^b\, b(x)] = b + l_2 - 1 = 2l - 1 + \tau$$

$$b + l_2 = 2l + \tau \Rightarrow b = 2l - l_2 + \tau$$

As $l_1 \le l$ and $l_2 \le l$, therefore, $b \ge l_2 + \tau$. Also $b \ge l_1 + \tau$. Hence

$$\left.\begin{array}{l} b \ge l_1 \\ b > (l_1 - 1), \text{ also } b > \tau \end{array}\right\} \tag{6.7}$$

Now consider the term

$$a(x) + x^b\, b(x) = 1 + a_1 x + a_2 x^2 + \cdots + a_{l1-2}\, x^{l1-2} + x^{l1-1} + x^b[1 + b_1 x + b_2 x^2 + \cdots + b_{l2-1}\, x^{l2-2} + x^{l2-1}]$$

It is clear from the expansion that the term $a(x) + x^b\, b(x)$ has a term x^b. But considering the term $d(x)\,(x^{2l-1} + 1)$, we have $\deg\,[d(x)] = \tau < b$. Also $b < (2l - 1)$. Therefore,

$$\tau < b < (2l - 1) \tag{6.8}$$

Therefore, $d(x)\,(x^{2l-1} + 1)$ will not have the term x^b, which contradicts our assumption

$$a(x) + x^b\, b(x) = d(x)\,(x^{2l-1} + 1)$$

Therefore, we must have $d(x) = 0$. This gives $b = 0$. Therefore,

$$a(x) + x^0\, b(x) = 0 \Rightarrow a(x) = b(x)$$

Equation (6.3) becomes

$$(j - i) = q(2l - 1) \tag{6.9}$$

Equation (6.2) becomes

$$v(x) = x^i\, b(x) + x^j\, b(x)$$

$$\Rightarrow v(x) = x^i\, b(x)\,(1 + x^{j-i}) \tag{6.10}$$

We have

$$\deg\,[b(x)] = l_2 - 1 < l$$

We have $l \leq m$. Therefore,

$$\deg\,[b(x)] < m = \deg\,[p(x)]$$

But as $p(x)$ is irreducible, no polynomial of degree less than m can factorize $p(x)$. In other words, $b(x)$ and $p(x)$ must be relatively prime. Therefore, as $v(x)$ given Eq. (6.10) is considered to be a code polynomial, we should have $v(x)$ divisible by $p(x)$ or $(x^{2l-1} + 1)$.

But $b(x)$ is not divisible by $x^{2l-1} + 1$ or by $p(x)$ because $\deg\,[b(x)\} < m$ and $\deg\,[b(x)] < l$.

Therefore, $(x^{j-i} + 1)$ must be divisible by $p(x)$ or $x^{2l-1} + 1$.

As $(x^{j-i} + 1)$ is not divisible by $(x^{2l-1} + 1)$, it has to be divisible by $p(x)$, that is, $p(x) \mid (x^{j-i} + 1)$.

Therefore, $(j - i)$ must be a multiple of the period of $p(x)$, ρ.

But from Eq. (6.9), we know $(j - i)$ must also be a multiple of $(2l - 1)$.

Therefore, $(j - i)$ must be multiple of LCM of $(2l - 1)$ and ρ.

So

$$(j - i) = k^1 \text{LCM}\,[(2l - 1), \rho]$$

But

LCM $[(2l - 1), r] = n$. Therefore,

$$(j - i) = k^1 n$$

$(j - i)$ is a multiple of n that contradicts our assumption that $i, j < n$. Thus, $v(x)$ is not a codeword that implies the presence of bursts $x^i\, a(x)$ and $x^j\, b(x)$ in two different cosets. Therefore, they come under correctable error pattern. So, all bursts of lengths l or less lie under different cosets and thus form correctable error patterns. Therefore, a fire code can correct an error burst of length 'l' or less. As fire codes are cyclic codes, they can also correct end around bursts of length l or less.

6.5.1 Decoding of Fire Codes

Several decoding algorithms were proposed for the decoding of fire codes. One such algorithm is error trapping decoder. Error trapping decoder works for all cyclic codes, but it is well suited for fire codes.

Consider $v(x)$ to be the transmitted vector and $r(x)$ to be the received vector:

$$r(x) = v(x) + e(x)$$

where $e(x)$ is the error polynomial. For a cyclic code, syndrome can be obtained by dividing $r(x)$ by $g(x)$, that is,

$$r(x) = q(x)\, g(x) + s(x) \tag{6.11}$$

Now deg $(s(x)) \leq (n - k - 1)$. Therefore,

$$s(x) = s_0 + s_1 x + s_2 x^2 + \cdots + s_{n-k-1}\, x^{n-k-1} \tag{6.12}$$

Consider an error pattern in which the burst error of length l is confined to 'l' digits:

$$e(x) = e_{n-k-l}\, x^{n-k-l} + e_{n-k-l+1}\, x^{n-k-l+1} + \cdots + e_{n-k-1}\, x^{n-k-1} \tag{6.13}$$

It has been seen in Chapter 5 that if $r^{(i)}(x)$ is obtained by cyclically shifting the received vector by 'i' times, then the corresponding syndrome is obtained by dividing $r^{(i)}(x)$ by $g(x)$ that is equal to $x^i s(x)$ divided by $g(x)$.

For the given error pattern of 'l' burst confined to 'l' consecutive positions, the syndrome digits s_{n-k-l}, $s_{n-k-l+1}, \ldots, s_{n-k-1}$ will correspond to error values and syndromes $s_0, s_1, s_2, \ldots s_{n-k-l-1}$ are zeroes. If the errors are confined to some other consecutive locations, then after some i cyclic shifts they can be shifted to the positions $x^{n-k-l}, x^{n-k-l+1}, \ldots, x^{n-k-1}$ of $r^{(i)}(x)$ and corresponding syndrome is $s^{(i)}(x)$. Thus, x^{n-k-l}, $x^{n-k-l+1}, \ldots, x^{n-k-1}$ of $s^{(i)}(x)$ matches the error positions of $r^{(i)}(x)$ and $x^0, x^1, \ldots, x^{n-k-l-1}$ terms of $s^{(i)}(x)$ will be zeroes. This results in the conclusion that the errors were trapped at the register leading to zeroes at the lower syndrome digits.

A typical error trapping decoder for a fire code is as shown in Fig. 6.3. The operation of error trapping decoding is as follows:

1. With Gates 1 and 2 open, $r(x)$ is shifted into the syndrome register and buffer register. Syndrome register will have the syndrome computed $s(x)$ by the time of completion of shifting $r(x)$.

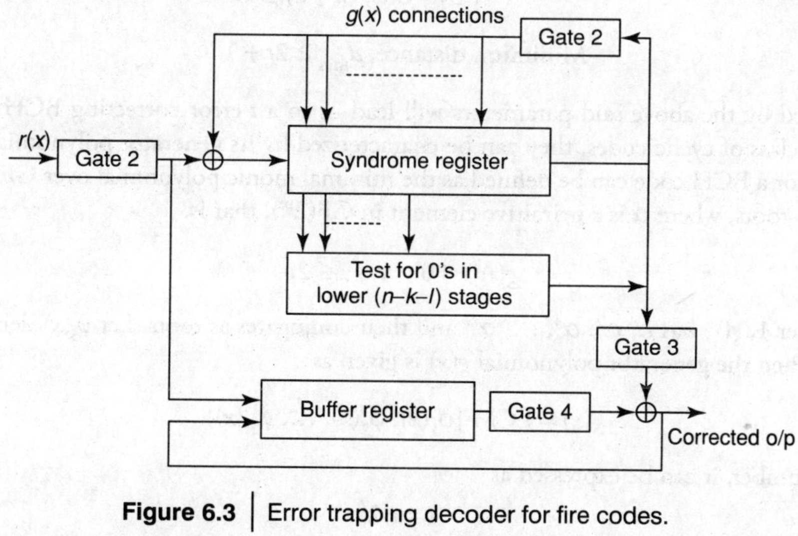

Figure 6.3 | Error trapping decoder for fire codes.

2. Successive shifting of syndrome register is done so as to achieve the condition of all zeroes at the lower $(n - k - 1)$ digits of $s(x)$ and thus trapping errors at right 'l' digits. Three different cases are to be considered under this.
   - If the lower $n - k - l$ digits of syndrome register are zero after shifting i times where $0 \le i \le n - k - l$, then the errors are confined at the parity locations and thus message can be read directly via Gate 4.
   - If the left $(n - k - 1)$ digits of syndrome become zero after shifting $(n - k - l + i)$ times where $1 \le i \le l$, then the error locations are $x^{n-i}, x^{n-1}, x^0, \ldots, x^{l-i-1}$ of $r(x)$. In this case, $(l - i)$ positions of the right side of syndrome register match the errors at $x^0, x^1, \ldots, x^{l-i-1}$ that are parity bits, left i digits of syndrome register matches $x^{n-i}, \ldots, x^{n-1}$ that are message bits which can be corrected by shifting syndrome register content via Gate 3.
   - If the syndrome register contents do not become zero after $(n - k)$ shifts, the buffer register contents will get out via Gate 4 simultaneously with syndrome register contents shifted via Gate 2. If the left $(n - k - l)$ stages of syndrome register become zero, the right l stages of the syndrome register match with the next l message bits that can be corrected by opening Gate 3 and shifting the syndrome bits.
3. If the left $(n - k - l)$ stages of the syndrome register do not become zero after shifting all 'k' information digits, an error burst corresponding to an uncorrectable error pattern has occurred.

6.6 BCH Codes

Bose–Chaudhuri–Hocquenghen (BCH) codes are a set of very powerful random error correcting codes. They form a subset of cyclic codes.

6.6.1 Description of BCH Codes

For any positive integer $m \ge 3$, there exists a BCH code with the following specifications:

$$\text{Block length, } n = 2^m - 1$$

$$\text{Parity bits, } (n - k) \le mt$$

$$\text{Minimum distance, } d_{\min} \ge 2t + 1$$

The code obtained by the above said parameters will lead us to a t error correcting BCH codes. As BCH codes form a subclass of cyclic codes, they can be characterized by its generator polynomial. The generator polynomial $g(x)$ for a BCH code can be defined as the minimal monic polynomial over GF(2) which has α, $\alpha^2, \alpha^3, \ldots, \alpha^{2t}$ as roots, where α is a primitive element in GF(2^m), that is,

$$g(\alpha^i) = 0 \quad 1 \le i \le 2t$$

As seen in Chapter 1, $g(x)$ has $\alpha, \alpha^2, \alpha^3, \ldots, \alpha^{2t}$ and their conjugates as roots. Let $\phi_i(x)$ denote the minimal polynomial α^i. Then the generator polynomial $g(x)$ is given as

$$g(x) = \text{LCM}\,[\phi_1(x), \phi_2(x), \ldots, \phi_{2t}(x)] \tag{6.14}$$

If 'i' is an even number, it can be expressed as

$$i = i_1 2^l$$

where i_1 is an odd number and l is an integer, $l \geq 1$. Then $\alpha^i = \alpha^{i_1 2^l} = (\alpha^{i_1})^{2^l}$ fall under the conjugacy class of α^{i_1}. Therefore, α^i and α^{i_1} fall under the same conjugacy class. So, Eq. (6.14) can be simplified as

$$g(x) = \text{LCM}\ [\phi_1(x), \phi_3(x), \ldots, \phi_{2t-1}(x)] \tag{6.15}$$

As the degree of minimal polynomial is m or less, the generator polynomial degree can be at most equal to mt. Therefore, the parity bits $(n - k)$ can be at most equal to mt.

EXAMPLE 6.2

Design a (15, 7) binary BCH code with $t = 2$.

Solution: Let $m = 4$. Let α be a primitive element in GF(2^4). The minimal polynomials for α^1, α^3 and α^5 are

$$\phi_1(x) = 1 + x + x^4$$
$$\phi_3(x) = 1 + x + x^2 + x^3 + x^4$$
$$= 1 + x + x^2$$

Now

$$g(x) = \text{LCM}\ [\phi_1(x), \phi_3(x), \ldots, \phi_{2t-1}(x)]$$
$$= \text{LCM}\ [\phi_1(x), \phi_3(x)]$$
$$= (1 + x + x^4)(1 + x + x^2 + x^3 + x^4)$$
$$= (1 + x^4 + x^6 + x^7 + x^8)$$

Therefore, the designed BCH code is as follows:

$$d_{\min} \geq 5$$
$$(n - k) \leq 4 \times 2$$
$$\Rightarrow (n - k) \leq 8$$

From the degree of generator polynomial, we have

$$(n - k) = 8$$

Therefore, $k = 7$. This implies that it is a (15, 7) binary BCH code.

6.6.2 Parity Check Matrix

Let $v(x)$ be a code polynomial of a binary BCH code. It is evident that $v(x)$ is a multiple of $g(x)$. In other words, roots of $g(x)$ must also serve as roots of $v(x)$. Therefore, $\alpha, \alpha^2, \alpha^3, \ldots, \alpha^{2t}$ have to be the roots of code polynomial $v(x)$. That is,

$$v(x) = v_0 + v_1 x + v_2 x^2 + \ldots + v_{n-1} x^{n-1}$$

$$v(\alpha^i) = 0 = v_0 + v_1 \alpha^i + v_2 \alpha^{2i} + \ldots + v_{n-1} \alpha^{(n-1)i}$$

In matrix representation, we have

$$(v_0, v_1, \ldots, v_{n-1})\begin{bmatrix}1\\ \alpha^i\\ \alpha^{2i}\\ \cdot\\ \cdot\\ \cdot\\ \alpha^{(n-1)i}\end{bmatrix} = 0, \quad 1 \le i \le 2t \tag{6.16}$$

Expanding the above representation by substituting the values of i, we get the matrix H

$$H^T = \begin{bmatrix}1 & 1 & 1 & 1 \ldots\ldots\ldots\ldots 1\\ \alpha & \alpha^2 & \alpha^3 & \alpha^4 \ldots\ldots & \alpha^{2t}\\ \alpha^2 & (\alpha^2)^2 & (\alpha^3)^2 & (\alpha^4)^2 \ldots\ldots & (\alpha^{2t})^2\\ \ldots & \ldots & \ldots & \ldots & \ldots\\ \ldots & \ldots & \ldots & \ldots & \ldots\\ \alpha^{n-1} & (\alpha^2)^{n-1} & (\alpha^3)^{n-1} & (\alpha^4)^{n-1} \ldots\ldots & (\alpha^{2t})^{n-1}\end{bmatrix} \tag{6.17}$$

and

$$VH^T = 0 \tag{6.18}$$

On the other hand, we can conclude that an n tuple vector $v = (v_0, v_1, \ldots, v_{n-1})$ will be a codeword if and only if $VH^T = 0$. In other words, we can say that the code vector forms a null space of the matrix H. If α^i and α^j form a single conjugacy class, then $v(\alpha^i) = 0$ if and only if $v(\alpha^j) = 0$. This implies that the inner product of $(v_0, v_1, \ldots, v_{n-1})$ with the ith column of H^T equal to zero also guarantees that the inner product of $(v_0, v_1, \ldots, v_{n-1})$ with the jth column of H^T is also zero. Thus, matrix H^T can be reduced by eliminating such redundant columns. The simplified matrix is as follows:

$$H^T = \begin{bmatrix}1 & 1 & 1 & \ldots\ldots & 1\\ \alpha & \alpha^3 & \alpha^5 & \ldots\ldots & \alpha^{2t-1}\\ \alpha^2 & (\alpha^3)^2 & (\alpha^5)^2 & \ldots\ldots & (\alpha^{2t-1})^2\\ \ldots & \ldots & \ldots & \ldots & \ldots\\ \ldots & \ldots & \ldots & \ldots & \ldots\\ \alpha^{n-1} & (\alpha^3)^{n-1} & (\alpha^5)^{n-1} & \ldots\ldots & (\alpha^{2t-1})^{n-1}\end{bmatrix}$$

From this we have

$$H = \begin{bmatrix}1 & \alpha & \alpha^2 & \ldots & \alpha^{n-1}\\ 1 & \alpha^3 & (\alpha^3)^2 & \ldots & (\alpha^3)^{n-1}\\ 1 & \alpha^5 & (\alpha^5)^2 & \ldots & (\alpha^5)^{n-1}\\ \ldots & \ldots & \ldots & \ldots & \ldots\\ \ldots & \ldots & \ldots & \ldots & \ldots\\ 1 & \alpha^{2t-1} & (\alpha^{2t-1})^2 & \ldots & (\alpha^{2t-1})^{n-1}\end{bmatrix} \tag{6.19}$$

EXAMPLE 6.3

Write the parity check matrix for a triple error correcting binary BCH code over GF(2^4).

Solution: $n = 2^m - 1 = 15$

As it is a triple error correcting code, $t = 3$, matrix H can be constructed considering the Eq. 6.19.

$$H = \begin{bmatrix} 1 & \alpha & \alpha^2 & \alpha^3 & \alpha^4 & \alpha^5 & \alpha^6 & \alpha^7 & \alpha^8 & \alpha^9 & \alpha^{10} & \alpha^{11} & \alpha^{12} & \alpha^{13} & \alpha^{14} \\ 1 & \alpha^3 & \alpha^6 & \alpha^9 & \alpha^{12} & \alpha^{15} & \alpha^{18} & \alpha^{21} & \alpha^{24} & \alpha^{27} & \alpha^{30} & \alpha^{35} & \alpha^{36} & \alpha^{39} & \alpha^{42} \\ 1 & \alpha^5 & \alpha^{10} & \alpha^{15} & \alpha^{20} & \alpha^{25} & \alpha^{30} & \alpha^{35} & \alpha^{40} & \alpha^{45} & \alpha^{50} & \alpha^{55} & \alpha^{60} & \alpha^{65} & \alpha^{70} \end{bmatrix}$$

6.6.3 Decoding of BCH Codes

Let $v(x)$ be the transmitted polynomial, $r(x)$ be the received polynomial and $e(x)$ be the error polynomial. Then

$$v(x) = v_0 + v_1x + v_2x^2 + \cdots + v_{n-1}x^{n-1}$$
$$r(x) = r_0 + r_1x + r_2x^2 + \cdots + r_{n-1}x^{n-1}$$
$$r(x) = v(x) + e(x)$$

Syndrome of a t error correcting BCH code will be of $2t$ tuple given by

$$s = (s_1, s_2, \ldots, s_{2t}) = rH^T$$

where H^T is given by Eq. (6.17).

Thus, the ith component of the syndrome vector is given by

$$s_i = r_0 + r_1\alpha^i + r_2\alpha^{2i} + \cdots + r_{n-1}\alpha^{(n-1)i}$$

$$s_i = r(\alpha^i), \quad 0 \le i \le 2t \tag{6.20}$$

Let $\phi_i(x)$ be the minimal polynomial of α^i. Using division theorem we can represent $r(x)$ as

$$r(x) = a_i(x)\ \phi_i(x) + b_i(x)$$

where $a_i(x)$ and $b_i(x)$ are respectively, the quotient and remainder obtained by dividing $r(x)$ by $\phi_i(x)$. Therefore,

$$r(\alpha^i) = a_i(\alpha^i)\ \phi_i(\alpha^i) + b_i(\alpha^i)$$

But $\phi_i(\alpha^i) = 0$ as $\phi_i(\alpha^i)$ is the minimal polynomial of α^i. Therefore,

$$r(\alpha^i) = b_i(\alpha^i)$$

and from Eq. (6.20)

$$s_i = b_i(\alpha^i) \tag{6.21}$$

Also

$$r(x) = v(x) + e(x)$$
$$r(\alpha^i) = v(\alpha^i) + e(\alpha^i)$$

and

$$v(\alpha^i) = 0$$

$$s_i = r(\alpha^i) = e(\alpha^i) \tag{6.22}$$

Suppose an error in t^1 bit position occurs. Then

$$e(x) = x^{j1} + x^{j2} + \cdots + x^{jt1}$$

Let $\gamma_L = \alpha^{jL}$ where $L = 1, 2, \ldots, t_1$. Therefore,

$$e(\alpha^i) = e(\gamma) = \gamma_1 + \gamma_2 + \cdots + \gamma_{t1}$$

From Eq. (6.22) we have

$$s_i = e(\alpha^i)$$

$$s_1 = \alpha^{j1} + \alpha^{j2} + \cdots + \alpha^{jt1}$$

$$s_2 = (\alpha^{j1})^2 + (\alpha^{j2})^2 + \cdots + (\alpha^{jt1})^2$$

$$\cdots$$

$$\cdots$$

$$s_{2t} = (\alpha^{j1})^{2t} + (\alpha^{j2})^{2t} + \cdots + (\alpha^{jt1})^{2t}$$

Substituting $\gamma_L = \alpha^{jL}$ we will have

$$s_1 = \gamma_1 + \gamma_2 + \cdots + \gamma_{t1}$$

$$s_2 = (\gamma_1)^2 + (\gamma_2)^2 + \cdots + (\gamma_{t1})^2$$

$$\cdots$$

$$\cdots$$

$$s_{2t} = (\gamma_1)^{2t} + (\gamma_2)^{2t} + \cdots + (\gamma_{t1})^{2t} \tag{6.23}$$

The positions $1 \le L \le t^1$ will locate errors in the received sequence and are thus called error location pointers. Equation (6.23) denotes a set of $2t$ equations that are also called as power sum symmetric equations. Here, $\gamma_2, \ldots, \gamma_{t1}$ are unknowns. Let us now define a function $\sigma(x)$, called error location polynomial, as

$$\sigma(x) = (1 + \gamma_1 x)(1 + \gamma_2 x) \ldots (1 + \gamma_{t1} x)$$

$$= \sigma_0 + \sigma_1 x + \sigma_2 x^2 + \cdots + \sigma_{t1} x^{t1} \tag{6.24}$$

The roots of the above equation are $\gamma_1^{-1} + \gamma_2^{-1} + \cdots + \gamma_{t1}^{-1}$, which are the inverses of the error locations. The error locations and the coefficients of $\sigma(x)$ are related as

$$\sigma_0 = 1$$

$$\sigma_1 = \gamma_1 + \gamma_2 + \cdots + \gamma_{t1}$$

$$\sigma_2 = \gamma_1 \gamma_2 + \gamma_2 \gamma_3 + \cdots + \gamma_{t1-1} \gamma_{t1} \tag{6.25}$$

$$\cdots$$

$$\sigma_{t1} = \gamma_1 \gamma_2 \cdots \gamma_{t1}$$

From Eq. (6.23) and Eq. (6.25) we can establish the relation between γ_i and s_i as follows:

$$s_1 + \sigma_1 = 0$$
$$s_2 + \sigma_1 s_1 + 2\sigma_2 = 0$$
$$s_3 + \sigma_1 s_2 + \sigma_2 s_1 + 2\sigma_2 = 0$$
$$\cdots$$
$$s_{t1} + \sigma_1 s_{t1} + \cdots + \sigma_{t1-1} s_1 + t^1 \sigma_{t1} = 0 \qquad (6.26)$$

For binary codes, Eq. (6.26) can be reduced by substituting

$$\int i\sigma_i = \begin{cases} \sigma_i, & \text{if } i \text{ is odd} \\ 0, & \text{if } i \text{ is even} \end{cases} \qquad (6.27)$$

Thus, the decoding procedure for a BCH code can be summarized as

1. Compute the syndrome S from the received vector.
2. Determine the polynomial $\sigma(x)$ by calculating its coefficients from the relation of the syndrome S.
3. Solve the error location polynomial $\sigma(x)$ to locate the error positions in the received vector.

6.6.3.1 To Find Error Location Polynomial $\sigma(x)$

Equation (6.26) gives a set of relations called Newton's identity that are used to compute the coefficients of error location polynomial $\sigma(x)$. It is an iterative algorithm proposed by Berlekamp and is thus called *Berlekamp algorithm.*

Initially, a minimum degree polynomial $\sigma^{(1)}(x)$ is obtained such that it satisfies the first relation of Newton's identity. If the same $\sigma^{(1)}(x)$ satisfies the second condition also, then set $\sigma^{(2)}(x) = \sigma^{(1)}(x)$. Else add a correcting term to $\sigma^{(1)}(x)$ to get $\sigma^{(2)}(x)$. Similarly, $\sigma^{(3)}(x)$ is obtained from $\sigma^{(2)}(x)$ in the next round so that first three relations are satisfied. The process continues till we reach $\sigma^{(2t)}(x)$. This gives our required error location polynomial:

$$\sigma(x) = \sigma^{(2t)}(x)$$

The process of obtaining the updation of error location polynomial is as follows: Let $\sigma^{(i)}(x)$ be the minimal degree error location polynomial at ith stage. $\sigma^{(i)}(x)$ is given by

$$\sigma^{(i)}(x) = 1 + \sigma_1{}^{(i)}x + \cdots + \sigma_3{}^{(i)}x^3 + \sigma_{li}{}^{(i)}x^{li} \qquad (6.28)$$

Clearly, $\sigma^{(i)}(x)$ satisfies first 'i' relations of Newton identities given by Eq. (6.26). To get the updated error location polynomial $\sigma^{(i+1)}(x)$ for the next iteration, we need to compute a parameter called *discrepancy* given by

$$d_i = s_{i+1} + \sigma_1{}^{(i)}s_i + \sigma_2{}^{(i)}s_{i-1} + \cdots + \sigma_{li}{}^{(i)}s_{i+1-li} \qquad (6.29)$$

If the function $\sigma^{(i)}(x)$ itself satisfies the $(i+1)^{\text{th}}$ identity also, then $d_i = 0$, in which case $\sigma^{(i+1)}(x)$ will just be the same as $\sigma^{(i)}(x)$. That is,

$$\sigma(i_{t1})(x) = \sigma^{(i)}(x)$$

If $d_i \neq 0$, then the updation $\sigma^{(i+1)}(x)$ can be obtained from $\sigma^{(i)}(x)$. To perform this, get back to j stages to the ith iteration such that $d_j \neq 0$ and $(j - l_j)$ has the maximum value, where l_j is the degree of $\sigma^{(j)}(x)$. Then, the updated error location polynomial will be

$$\sigma^{(i+1)}(x) = \sigma^{(i)}(x) + d_i d_j^{-1} x(i-j)\sigma^{(j)}(x) \tag{6.30}$$

This process is continued till we reach $\sigma^{(2t)}(x)$.

6.6.3.2 To Find Error Locations

As discussed earlier, error locations can be obtained from the error location polynomial. The roots of error location polynomial will give the inverse of the locations of the errors. Consider the error location polynomial

$$\sigma(x) = 1 + \sigma_1 x + \sigma_2 x^2 + \cdots + \sigma_{t1} x^{t1}$$

Obtain the roots of the above equation by substituting 1, α, α^2, α^3, …, α^{n-1} in $\sigma(x)$. Once the roots of $\sigma(x)$ are obtained, the error vector can be obtained by just getting their inverses. This algorithm, called *Peterson's algorithm*, was one of the earliest algorithms for finding the error polynomial.

In the later years, Chien proposed an algorithm that is popularly known as Chien search algorithm. Consider the received vector

$$r(x) = r_0 + r_1 x + r_2 x^2 + \cdots + r_{n-1} x^{n-1}$$

The decoding is done from the higher-order terms, that is, it will start from r_{n-1} term. To check whether r_{n-1} is erroneous, it is as good as checking whether α is a root of $\sigma(x)$. If so, r_{n-1} is erroneous and thus corrects the error. Else, r_{n-1} is error-free. The procedure continues bit by bit till all bits of $r(x)$ are read out.

6.7 Non-Binary BCH Codes and Reed–Solomon Codes

Although binary codes are our main focus of interest, it is always possible to construct a q-ary code over GF(q), where q is a power of a prime number p. The concepts and procedures we discussed for binary codes in the previous sections are also applicable for q-ary codes with a little modification.

A non-binary BCH code can be characterized as follows. For any two positive integers m^1 and t, there exists an (n, k) q-ary BCH code with the following specifications:

$$n = qm^1 - 1$$

$$\text{Parity bits } (n - k) \leq 2m^1 t$$

$$\text{Error correcting capability} = t$$

The generator polynomial of such BCH codes $g(x)$ will have coefficients from GF(q) and the powers of the primitive element α being the roots. In other words, α, α^2, α^3, …, α^{2t} are roots of $g(x)$. Therefore, the generator polynomial can be represented as

$$g(x) = \text{LCM}\ [\phi_1(x), \phi_2(x), \ldots \phi_{2t}(x)] \tag{6.31}$$

where $\phi_i(x)$ is the minimal polynomial for α^i. As the degree of $\phi_i(x)$ is at most equal to m^1 for all i, the degree of $g(x)$ can be at most equal to $m^1 \times 2t$. Therefore, the number of parity bits required would be at most equal to $(2t \times m^1)$.

When $q = 2$, q-ary BCH codes will get reduced to binary BCH codes. There are many special classes in q-ary BCH. One such code set is obtained by letting $m^1 = 1$. This special subclass of BCH codes is called *Reed–Solomon (RS) codes.*

Thus, a 't' error correcting RS code can be characterized as follows:

$$\text{Block length,} \quad n = (q - 1)$$

$$\text{Number of parity check bits, } (n - k) = 2t$$

$$\text{Min. Hamming distance, } d_{\min} = 2t + 1$$

Consider the case when $p = 2$ and thus $q = 2^m$. Let α be a primitive element in GF(2^m). Then, the terms α, α^2, α^3, …, α^{2t} will be the roots of the generator polynomial $g(x)$ and thus the generator polynomial can be expressed as

$$g(x) = (x + \alpha)\,(x + \alpha^2)\,\cdots\,(x + \alpha^{2t})$$

$$= g_0 + g_1x + g_2x^2 + \cdots + g_{2t-1}x^{2t-1} + x^{2t}$$

The resulting code will be a $(n, n - 2t)$ cyclic code. Encoding and decoding of such codes are similar as discussed for binary BCH codes.

Summary

1. A burst length 'l' is defined as a vector whose non-zero elements are confined to 'l' successive positions in the vector.
2. A linear code is said to be an l burst correcting code if and only if it is capable of correcting all bursts of lengths l or less but not all error bursts of length $l + 1$.
3. For an (n, k) cyclic code we can always have an (λ_n, λ_k) interleaved code by simply arranging λ code vectors along λ rows and transmitting them column-wise.
4. Error correcting capability of a product code is given by

$$t = \left(\frac{d_{\min 1} \cdot d_{\min 2} - 1}{2}\right)$$

5. Burst error correcting capability of a $C_1 \times C_2$ product code is at least equal to max $\{n_1l_2, n_2l_1\}$.
6. An (n, k) fire code is a cyclic code with

$$n = \text{LCM}[(2l - 1), \rho]$$

$$k = n - (m + 2l - 1)$$

$$g(x) = (x^{2l-1} + 1)\, p(x)$$

7. Fire code can correct a burst of length 'l'.
8. For any positive integer $m \geq 3$, there exists a BCH code with the following specifications:

$$\text{Block length, } n = 2^m - 1$$

$$\text{Parity bits, } (n - k) \leq mt$$

$$\text{Min. distance, } d_{\min} \geq 2t + 1$$

9. $g(x) = \text{LCM}\ [\phi_1(x), \phi_3(x), \ldots, \phi_{2t-1}(x)]$
10. Decoding procedure for a BCH code can be summarized as:
    - Compute the syndrome S from the received vector.
    - Determine the polynomial $\sigma(x)$ by calculating its coefficients from the relation of the syndrome S.
    - Solve the error location polynomial $\sigma(x)$ to locate the error positions in the received vector.

11. For any two positive integers m^1 and t, there exists an (n, k) q-ary BCH code with the following specifications:

$$n = qm^1 - 1$$

$$\text{Parity bits, } (n - k) \leq 2m^1t$$

$$\text{Error correcting capability} = t$$

12. A 't' error correcting RS code can be characterized as follows:

$$\text{Block length, } n = (q - 1)$$

$$\text{Number of parity check bits, } (n - k) = 2t$$

$$\text{Min. Hamming distance, } d_{\min} = 2t + 1$$

Review Questions

1. What are burst errors? Explain.
2. Determine the burst length for $e = (0\ 0\ 1\ 0\ 1\ 1\ 0\ 1\ 0\ 1\ 0\ 1\ 0\ 0\ 0\ 0\ 0)$.
3. Explain the construction of an interleaved code for a (6, 3) LBC with an interleaving depth of 6.
4. What are product codes? Explain.
5. Design a fire code considering an irreducible polynomial $p(x) = 1 + x + x^4$.
6. Explain the encoding procedure of BCH codes.
7. Design a triple error correcting binary BCH code over GF(2^5).
8. Write the parity check matrix for a (15, 7) binary BCH code with $t = 2$
9. Detail the decoding procedure of a BCH code.
10. What are RS codes? Explain the encoding and decoding algorithms for RS codes.

Further Reading

[1] Richerd E Blahut, *Algebraic Codes for Data Transmission*, Cambridge University Press: UK; 2003.

[2] Willium E Ryan and Shu Lin, *Channel Codes: Classical and Modern*, Cambridge University Press: UK; 2009.

[3] Tood K Moon, *Error Control Coding: Mathematical Methods and Algorithms*, John Wiley & Sons: Hoboken, NJ; 2005.

[4] Shu Lin and Daniel J Costello, *Error Control Coding: Fundamentals and Applications*, Prentice Hall Series, Inc: Englewood Cliffs, NJ; 1983.

[5] Peter Sweeney, *Error Control Coding*, John Wiley & Sons: UK; 1991.

[6] Ranjan Bose, *Information Theory, Coding and Cryptography*, Tata McGraw-Hill Education: New Delhi; 2008.

[7] Simon Haykin, *An Introduction to Analog and Digital Communications*, John Wiley & Sons: New York; 1989.

[8] Shanmugam K Sam, *Digital and Analog Communication Systems*, John Wiley & Sons: New York; 1979.

[9] Ian A Glover and Peter M Grant, *Digital Communications*, Pearson Education: UK; 2004.

[10] Bernard Sklar and Pabitra K Ray, *Digital Communications: Fundamentals and Applications*, Pearson Education: New Delhi; 2001.

[11] Andrea Goldsmith, *Wireless Communications*, Cambridge University Press: UK; 2005.

[12] John G Proakis and Masoud Salehi, *Contemporary Communication System using MATLAB*, PWS Publishing: Boston, MA; 1998.

7 Convolution Codes

'The strength of the team is each individual member ... the strength of each member is the team.'
–Coach Phil Jackson

Learning Objectives

After reading this chapter, you will be able to:

- Understand the basic differences between block codes and convolution codes.
- Define and discuss various distance parameters for the convolution encoder.
- Detail various encoding methods of a convolution encoder.
- Develop and analyze the decoding process of convolution codes.

7.1 Introduction

As discussed in Chapter 5, error control codes have been classified into two categories:

1. Block codes.
2. Convolution codes.

Block codes, as discussed in Chapter 5, are a class of error control codes where a block of *k*-message bits is encoded into an *n*-bit code vector. Convolution codes are linear codes with additional structures in the generator matrix so that the encoder output can be viewed as the convolution of the input with an impulse response. In other words, convolution encoders can be viewed as the digital filters or simply a linear time invariant (LTI) system.

Convolution codes find a large set of applications in modern communication systems. They are preferred to block codes as they provide better performance than block codes for a given encoder/decoder complexity. Also, soft decision decoding algorithms were developed much faster for convolution codes.

Convolution codes differ from block codes in the following perspectives. First, block codes segment a larger data set into blocks and individually encode blocks, whereas in convolution codes, the entire data sequence is mapped onto a codeword. Second, unlike block codes, convolution codes do possess memory. In other words, the output of a convolution encoder not only depends on the present inputs but also on the previous inputs. Thus, convolution codes are not only characterized by their n and k values but also on the number of memory elements used in the encoder. Thus, a typical convolution encoder can be characterized using three tuples (n, k, m) where n is the number of output lines, k is the number of input lines and m is the number of memory elements.

Like block codes, convolution codes can also be categorized into two classes: *systematic* and *non-systematic codes*. In systematic codes, the parity bits and input bits are separable whereas in non-systematic codes there is a one-to-one mapping of the input sequence with the codewords.

7.2 Convolution Encoder

The convolution codes were proposed by Elias in 1955. Let us consider some basic definitions involved in convolution encoding before starting our actual discussion on encoding.

1. **Code rate:** It is defined as the ratio of the number of input lines to that of output lines. In an (n, k, m) convolution encoder, the code rate will be

$$R = k/n$$

If the input message is of length L, the output of a convolution encoder will be of length $n(L+m)$, in which case the code rate will become

$$R = \frac{kL}{n(L+m)}$$

As $L \gg m$

$$R = \frac{kL}{nL}$$

$$\Rightarrow R = \frac{k}{n} \tag{7.1}$$

2. **Constraint length:** It is defined as the maximum number of output bits of the encoder affected by a single input. If there are m memory elements and n output lines in a convolution encoder, the constraint length will be $n(m+1)$.
Consider a (2, 1, 2) convolution encoder as shown in Fig. 7.1.
As seen from Fig. 7.1, a convolution encoder is a combination of shift registers and adders.

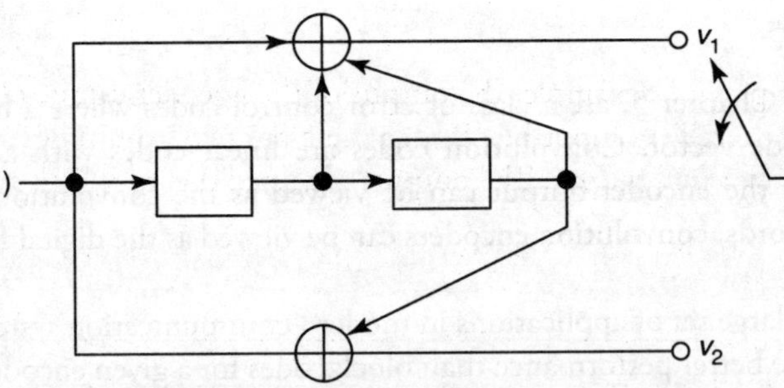

Figure 7.1 | A typical (2, 1, 2) encoder.

EXAMPLE 7.1

Obtain the output of the (2, 1, 2) convolution encoder shown in Fig. 7.1 for the input 11101. Detail the contents of the shift registers after every clock.

Solution: Contents of the shift registers after every clock cycle for the input (11101) are as depicted in Table 7.1.

Table 7.1 | Output of an (2, 1, 2) encoder

Input	*Shift Register Contents*		*Output*	
–	0	0	–	
1	1	0	1	1
1	1	1	0	1
1	1	1	1	0
0	0	1	0	1
1	1	0	0	0
0	0	1	1	0
0	0	0	1	1

The output at every instant/stage is computed as per the connection pattern given in the encoder diagram. Additional zeroes were inserted after the input sequence to acquire the effect of the bits still present in the shift register. In other words, the last bit of the input sequence 1 has its effect for the next two clock cycles also due to the presence of memory elements. Thus, m number of zeroes have to be given as the input so as to get the complete response of the encoder.

Thus, the encoded output for the input (1 1 1 0 1) for the given (2, 1, 2) encoder is (11, 01, 10, 01, 00, 10, 11).

EXAMPLE 7.2

Consider a (3, 2, 2) encoder as shown in Fig. 7.2. Obtain the encoded sequence for the input u_1 = [1 0] and u_2 = [1 1].

Solution: Similar to the previous example, the output of the encoder can be obtained by considering the shift register contents after every input bit. But as there are two input lines, superposition theorem can be applied to obtain the overall output. The outputs obtained due to u_1 and u_2 alone are as shown in Tables 7.2 and 7.3.

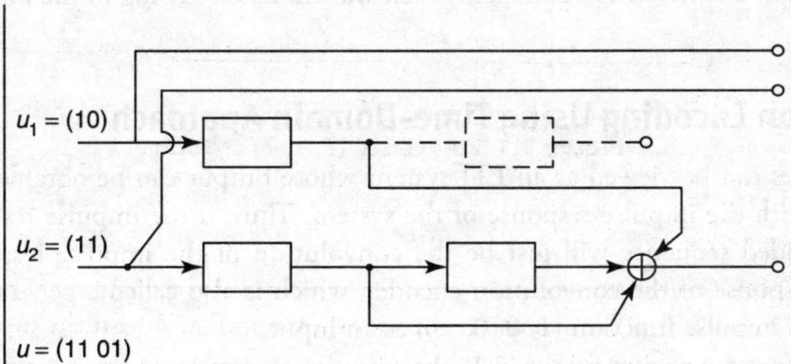

Figure 7.2 | A (3, 2, 2) convolution encoder.

Table 7.2 | Output due to u_1 alone

Input	*SR Contents*		*Output*		
–	0	0	–		
1	1	0	1	0	0
0	0	1	0	0	1
0	0	0	0	0	0
0	0	0	0	0	0

Table 7.3 | Output due to u_2 alone

Input	*SR Contents*		*Output*		
–	0	0	–		
1	1	0	0	1	0
0	0	1	0	1	1
0	0	0	0	0	0
0	0	0	0	0	1

Therefore, the overall output can be obtained as the sum of the individual outputs.

$$v^{(1)} = [1\,0\,0,\,0\,0\,1,\,0\,0\,0,\,0\,0\,0]$$
$$v^{(2)} = [0\,1\,0,\,0\,1\,1,\,0\,0\,0,\,0\,0\,1]$$
$$v = v^{(1)} + v^{(2)} = [1\,1\,0,\,0\,1\,0,\,0\,0\,0,\,0\,0\,1]$$

From the previous examples, it has been shown that the encoded output for a convolution encoder can be obtained by considering the shift register contents after every input bit. Although the method seems to be simple, it is not feasible for large values of *m*, *k* and *n*. Thus, various other methods were proposed to obtain the output of a convolution encoder, which we will be discussing in the following subsections.

7.2.1 Convolution Encoding Using Time-Domain Approach

The convolution codes can be viewed as an LTI system whose output can be obtained by just convolving the input sequence with the impulse response of the system. Thus, if the impulse response of the encoder is obtained, the encoded sequence will just be the convolution of the impulse response with the input sequence. Impulse response of the convolution encoder, which is also called a generator sequence, can be obtained by giving an impulse function (1, 0, 0, ...) as an input.

For the (2, 1, 2) encoder shown in Fig. 7.1, the impulse responses or the generator sequences can be obtained as

$$g_1 = (1\,1\,1),\ g_2 = (1\,0\,1)$$

The generator sequence can be directly obtained from the encoder diagram by just examining the connection patterns at the summers. Then, the outputs v_1 and v_2 can be obtained by convolving the input sequence with the generator sequences. Consider the same input $u = (1\ 1\ 1\ 0\ 1)$. Now

$$v_1 = u_1 * g_1 = (1\ 1\ 1\ 0\ 1) * (1\ 1\ 1) = (1\ 0\ 1\ 0\ 0\ 1\ 1)$$

$$v_2 = u_2 * g_2 = (1\ 1\ 1\ 0\ 1) * (1\ 0\ 1) = (1\ 1\ 0\ 1\ 0\ 0\ 1)$$

Therefore, the output sequence is given by

$$v = [11, 01, 10, 01, 00, 10, 11]$$

which agrees with the previous answer.

Similarly, for a systematic convolution code as shown in Fig. 7.2, the generator sequences are

$$g_1^{(1)} = [1\ 0\ 0],\ g_2^{(1)} = [0\ 0\ 0],\ g_3^{(1)} = [0\ 1\ 0]$$

$$g_1^{(2)} = [0\ 0\ 0],\ g_2^{(2)} = [1\ 0\ 0],\ g_3^{(2)} = [0\ 1\ 1]$$

The corresponding outputs are

$$v_1 = u_1 * g_1^{(1)} + u_2 * g_1^{(2)} = [(10) * (100)] + [(11) * (000)] = (1\ 0\ 0\ 0)$$

$$v_2 = u_1 * g_2^{(1)} + u_2 * g_2^{(2)} = [(10) * (000)] + [(11) * (100)] = (1\ 1\ 0\ 0)$$

$$v_3 = u_1 * g_3^{(1)} + u_2 * g_3^{(2)} = [(10) * (010)] + [(11) * (011)] = (0\ 0\ 0\ 1)$$

Therefore,

$$v = (110, 010, 000, 001)$$

which is again the same as that of the previously obtained sequence.

7.2.2 Encoding Using the Generator Matrix

Like block codes, convolution codes can also be generated by performing multiplication of the generator matrix with the input sequence.

$$v = u \cdot G$$

where G is the generator matrix given by

$$G = \begin{bmatrix} G_0 & G_1 & G_2 & \cdots & & \\ & G_0 & G_1 & G_2 & \cdots & \\ & & G_0 & G_1 & G_2 & \cdots \\ & & & & & \cdots \end{bmatrix}$$

The generator matrix can be obtained from the generator sequences. For the given (2, 1, 2) encoder with generator sequences

$$g_1 = (1\ 1\ 1),\ g_2 = (1\ 0\ 1)$$

the generator matrix is given by

$$G = \begin{bmatrix} g_1^{(1)} g_2^{(1)} & g_1^{(2)} g_2^{(2)} & g_1^{(3)} g_2^{(3)} & \ldots & & \\ & g_1^{(1)} g_2^{(1)} & g_1^{(2)} g_2^{(2)} & g_1^{(3)} g_2^{(3)} & \ldots & \\ & & g_1^{(1)} g_2^{(1)} & g_1^{(2)} g_2^{(2)} & g_1^{(3)} g_2^{(3)} & \ldots \\ & & & & & \ldots\ldots \end{bmatrix}$$

$$G = \begin{bmatrix} 11 & 10 & 11 & \ldots & & \\ & 11 & 10 & 11 & \ldots & \\ & & 11 & 10 & 11 & \ldots \\ & & & & & \ldots\ldots \end{bmatrix}$$

Considering the same input of $u = [1\ 1\ 1\ 0\ 1]$, the encoded sequence can be obtained as

$$v = u \cdot G = [1\,1\,1\,0\,1] \begin{bmatrix} 11 & 10 & 11 & & & & \\ & 11 & 10 & 11 & & & \\ & & 11 & 10 & 11 & & \\ & & & 11 & 10 & 11 & \\ & & & & 11 & 10 & 11 \end{bmatrix} = [11,\, 01,\, 10,\, 01,\, 00,\, 10,\, 11]$$

Similarly, the generator matrix for (3, 2, 2) code is

$$G = \begin{bmatrix} 100 & 001 & 000 & \\ 010 & 001 & 001 & \\ & 100 & 001 & 000 \\ & 010 & 001 & 001 \\ \ldots\ldots & & & \end{bmatrix}$$

The output can be obtained in the same way and can be verified with the previously obtained one.

7.2.3 Encoding Using the Transform-Domain Approach

We know the fact that the convolution in time domain is equivalent to multiplication in the frequency domain. Thus, the output of a convolution encoder can be obtained by multiplying the generator and input sequences in transform domain and then taking the inverse transformation.

The generator sequence can be represented as a generator polynomial as follows:

$$g_i(x) = g_i^{(1)} + g_i^{(2)}x + g_i^{(3)}x^2 + \cdots + g_i^{(m+1)}x^m \tag{7.2}$$

The output of the encoder can be obtained as

$$v_i(x) = u(x)g_i(x)$$

After the code polynomials from all adders are obtained, the final codeword can be computed as follows:

$$v(x) = v_1(x^n) + xv_2(x^n) + x^2v_3(x^n) + \cdots + x^{n-1}v_n(x^n) \tag{7.3}$$

Considering the (2, 1, 2) encoder, the corresponding generator polynomials will become

$$g_1(x) = 1 + x + x^2$$

$$g_2(x) = 1 + x^2$$

The corresponding outputs for $u = [1\ 1\ 1\ 0\ 1]$ are thus

$$v_1(x) = u(x)\ g_1(x)$$

and

$$v_2(x) = u(x)\ g_2(x) = 1 + x + x^3 + x^6$$

where

$$u(x) = 1 + x + x^2 + x^4$$

Therefore,

$$v_1(x) = (1 + x + x^2 + x^4)\ (1 + x + x^2) = (1 + x^2 + x^5 + x^6)$$

The final output would become

$$v(x) = v_1(x^2) + xv_2(x^2) = (1 + x^4 + x^{10} + x^{12}) + x\ (1 + x^2 + x^6 + x^{12})$$

$$= 1 + x^4 + x^{10} + x^{12} + x + x^3 + x^7 + x^{13}$$

$$\Rightarrow v(x) = 1 + x + x^3 + x^4 + x^7 + x^{10} + x^{12} + x^{13}$$

$$\Rightarrow v = (11, 01, 10, 01, 00, 10, 11)$$

The same can be verified for (3, 2, 2) encoder as shown in Fig. 7.2.

$$g_1^{(1)} = 1,\ g_2^{(1)} = 0,\ g_3^{(1)} = x$$

$$g_1^{(2)} = 0,\ g_2^{(2)} = x,\ g_3^{(2)} = x + x^2$$

The corresponding outputs are

$$v_1(x) = u_1(x)\ g_1^{(1)}(x) + u_2(x)g_1^{(2)}(x) = 1$$

$$v_2(x) = u_1(x)\ g_2^{(1)}(x) + u_2(x)g_2^{(2)}(x) = 1 + x$$

$$v_3(x) = u_1(x)\ g_3^{(1)}(x) + u_2(x)g_3^{(2)}(x) = x^3$$

Therefore,

$$v = v_1(x^3) + xv_2(x^3) + x^2v_3(x^3) = 1 + x\ (1 + x^3) + x^2(x^9) = 1 + x + x^4 + x^{11}$$

Hence

$$v = [110, 010, 000, 001]$$

EXAMPLE 7.3

Consider the (3, 1, 2) convolution code with $g^{(1)} = (1\ 1\ 0)$, $g^{(2)} = (1\ 0\ 1)$, $g^{(3)} = (1\ 1\ 1)$.

(a) Find the constraint length.
(b) Find the rate.
(c) Draw the encoder block diagram.
(d) Find the generator matrix.
(e) Find the codeword for the message sequence (1 1 1 0 1) using time-domain and transfer-domain approach.

Solution:

(a) Constraint length = $n(m + 1) = 3(2 + 1) = 9$

(b) Rate = $k/n = 1/3$

(c) $n \to 3 \quad m \to 2 \quad k \to 1$

The encoder diagram can be constructed from the given generator vectors. The elements in the generator sequences give the connection pattern to the respective summers.

The encoder diagram for the given code is shown in Fig. 7.3:

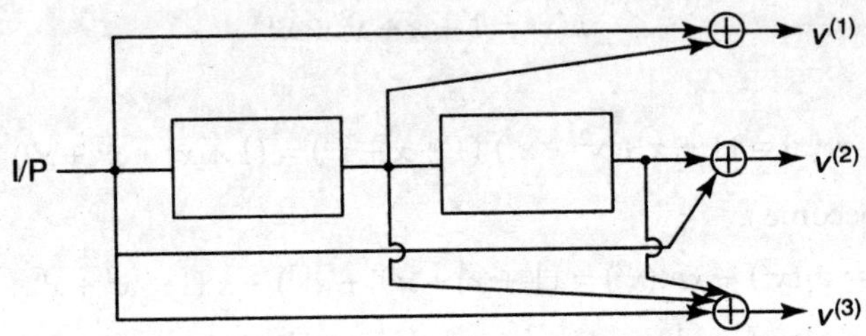

Figure 7.3 | A (3, 1, 2) convolution encoder.

(d) The generator matrix is given by

$$G = \begin{bmatrix} 111 & 101 & 011 & & & & & \\ & 111 & 101 & 011 & & & & \\ & & 111 & 101 & 011 & & & \\ & & & 111 & 101 & 011 & & \\ & & & & 111 & 101 & 011 & \\ & & & & & & \cdots & \end{bmatrix}$$

(e) Using time-domain approach:

The outputs are obtained from the generator sequences as follows:

$$v^{(1)} = u * g^{(1)} = 1\,1\,1\,0\,1 * 1\,1\,0 = 1\,0\,0\,1\,1\,1\,0$$

$$v^{(2)} = u * g^{(2)} = 1\,1\,1\,0\,1 * 1\,0\,1 = 1\,1\,0\,1\,0\,0\,1$$

$$v^{(3)} = u * g^{(3)} = 1\,1\,1\,0\,1 * 1\,1\,1 = 1\,0\,1\,0\,0\,1\,1$$

Thus, the overall output is given by

$$v = (1\,1\,1, 0\,1\,0, 0\,0\,1, 1\,1\,0, 1\,0\,0, 1\,0\,1, 0\,1\,1)$$

Using transform-domain approach:

$$g^{(1)}(x) = 1 + x, \quad g^{(2)}(x) = 1 + x^2, \quad g^{(3)}(x) = 1 + x + x^2$$

The outputs are

$$v^{(1)}(x) = u(x)\, g^{(1)}(x) = (1 + x + x^2 + x^4)(1 + x) = 1 + x + x^2 + x^4 + x + x^2 + x^3 + x^5 = 1 + x^3 + x^4 + x^5$$

$$v^{(2)}(x) = u(x)\, g^{(2)}(x) = (1 + x + x^2 + x^4)(1 + x^2) = 1 + x + x^2 + x^4 + x^2 + x^3 + x^4 + x^6 = 1 + x + x^3 + x^6$$

$$v^{(3)}(x) = u(x)\,g^{(3)}(x) = (1 + x + x^2 + x^4)(1 + x + x^2) = 1 + x + x^2 + x^4 + x + x^2 + x^3 + x^5 + x^2 + x^3 + x^4 + x^6$$
$$= 1 + x^2 + x^5 + x^6$$

The output polynomial is given by

$$v(x) = v^{(1)}(x^n) + xv^{(2)}(x^n) + x^2 v^{(3)}(x^n) = v^{(1)}(x^3) + xv^{(2)}(x^3) + v^{(3)}(x^3)$$
$$= 1 + x^9 + x^{12} + x^{15} + x(1 + x^3 + x^9 + x^{18}) + x^2(1 + x^6 + x^{15} + x^{18})$$
$$= 1 + x^9 + x^{12} + x^{15} + x + x^4 + x^{10} + x^{19} + x^2 + x^8 + x^{17} + x^{20}$$
$$= 1 + x + x^2 + x^4 + x^8 + x^9 + x^{10} + x^{12} + x^{15} + x^{17} + x^{19} + x^{20}$$
$$v = (1\,1\,1, 0\,1\,0, 0\,0\,1, 1\,1\,0, 1\,0\,0, 1\,0\,1, 0\,1\,1)$$

EXAMPLE 7.4

Consider the convolution encoder in Fig. 7.4:

(a) Write the impulse response of the encoder.
(b) Find the output for the message (1 0 0 1 1) using time-domain approach.
(c) Find the output for the message (1 0 0 1 1) using transform-domain approach.

Solution:

(a) The impulse response of the encoder is

$$g^{(1)} = (1\,1\,1)$$
$$g^{(2)} = (1\,0\,1)$$

(b) The output for the message (1 0 0 1 1) using time-domain approach:

$$v^{(1)} = g^{(1)} * u = 1\,0\,0\,1\,1 * (1\,1\,1) = (1\,1\,1\,1\,0\,0\,1)$$
$$v^{(2)} = u * g^{(2)} = 1\,0\,0\,1\,1 * (1\,0\,1) = (1\,0\,1\,1\,1\,1\,1)$$

Thus, the overall output is

$$v = (11, 10, 11, 11, 01, 01, 11)$$

(c) The output for the message (1 0 0 1 1) using transform-domain approach.
The message polynomial for the data given is

$$u(x) = 1 + x^3 + x^4$$

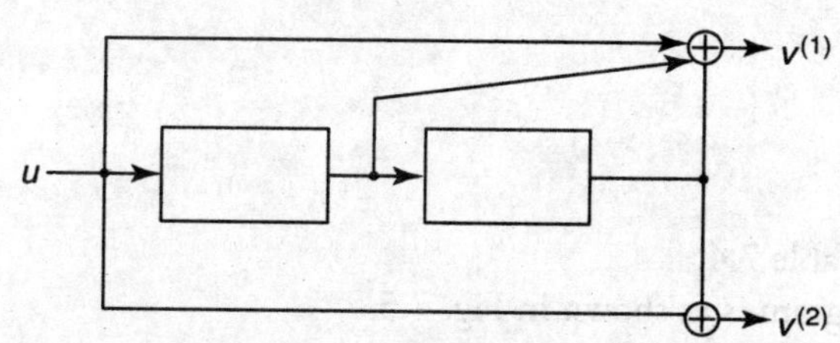

Figure 7.4 | A (2, 1, 2) convolution encoder.

The generator polynomials are

$$g^{(1)}(x) = 1 + x + x^2$$
$$g^{(2)}(x) = 1 + x^2$$

Thus, the output polynomials using transform domain approach are

$$v^{(1)}(x) = u(x) * g^{(1)}(x) = (1 + x^3 + x^4)\,(1 + x + x^2) = 1 + x^3 + x^4 + x + x^4 + x^5 + x^2 + x^5 + x^6$$
$$= 1 + x + x^2 + x^3 + x^6$$
$$v^{(2)}(x) = u(x) * g^{(2)}(x) = (1 + x^3 + x^4)\,(1 + x^2) = 1 + x^3 + x^4 + x^2 + x^5 + x^6 = 1 + x^2 + x^3 + x^4 + x^5 + x^6$$

Thus, the overall code polynomial is

$$v(x) = v^{(1)}\,(x^n) + xv^{(2)}(x^n) = v^{(1)}(x^2) + xv^{(2)}(x^2)$$
$$= 1 + x^2 + x^4 + x^6 + x^{12}] + x(1 + x^4 + x^6 + x^8 + x^{10} + x^{12})$$
$$= 1 + x^2 + x^4 + x^6 + x^{12} + x + x^5 + x^7 + x^9 + x^{11} + x^{13}$$
$$v(x) = 1 + x + x^2 + x^4 + x^5 + x^6 + x^7 + x^9 + x^{11} + x^{12} + x^{13}$$

Code vector can be obtained from the code polynomial, i.e.

$$v = (1\ 1,\ 1\ 0,\ 1\ 1,\ 1\ 1,\ 0\ 1,\ 0\ 1,\ 1\ 1)$$

7.3 Representation of Convolution Code

The methods used for analyzing block codes may not work for convolution codes. Thus, some techniques have been developed for analyzing the structural properties of a convolution code.

Convolution codes can be represented using any of the following three methods:

1. State diagrams.
2. Tree diagrams.
3. Trellis diagram.

7.3.1 State Diagrams

Like any other sequential circuits, a convolution encoder can be characterized by its state diagram. The state table for a (2, 1, 2) convolution encoder can be written as follows: As there are two memory elements, there will be four possible states.

1. s_0 : 0 0
2. s_1 : 0 1
3. s_2 : 1 0
4. s_3 : 1 1

The state table is as shown in Table 7.4.

The corresponding state diagram is as shown in Fig. 7.5.

Although state diagram is one of the easiest ways of representing the encoder, it will not consider the time instant into account. In other words, we cannot decide the present state of the system for a given instant. Thus, tree diagrams can be drawn for a given system.

Table 7.4 | State table for (2, 1, 2) code

Input	*Present State*	*Next State*	*Output*
0	s_0 (0 0)	0 0 (s_0)	0 0
1		1 0 (s_2)	1 1
0	s_1 (0 1)	0 0 (s_0)	1 1
1		1 0 (s_2)	0 0
0	s_2 (1 0)	0 1 (s_1)	1 0
1		1 1 (s_3)	0 1
0	s_3 (1 1)	0 1 (s_1)	0 1
1		1 0 (s_3)	1 0

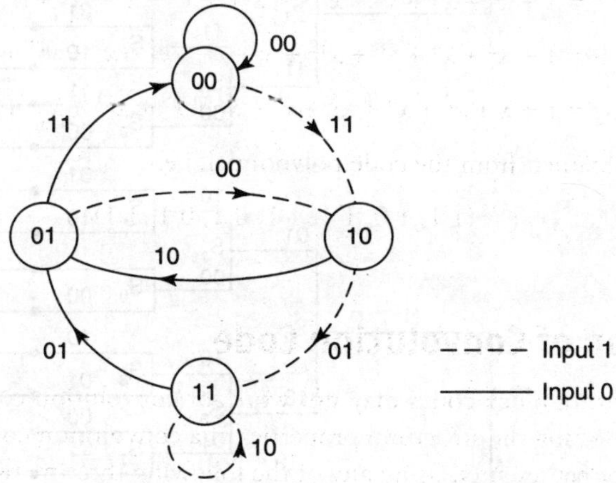

Figure 7.5 | State diagram for a (2, 1, 2) code.

7.3.2 Tree Diagram

The state diagram can be redrawn as a tree considering every codeword represented as a branch in the tree. The tree diagram for a (2, 1, 2) encoder is as shown in Fig. 7.6. The downward branch in each level of the tree corresponds to the output obtained for input '0' and that of upward indicates for the input '1'. In the last three levels, only the outputs and transitions corresponding to input '0' are shown.

The output obtained for the input $u = (1\ 1\ 1\ 0\ 1)$ has been traced from the tree diagram. Thus, the output obtained is (11, 01, 10, 01, 00, 10, 11), which is the same as the previously obtained result.

Although tree diagram is a more efficient way of representing the encoder than the state representation, the main drawback lies in the increased complexity for the higher levels. Thus, an improvement over the tree diagram has been proposed, called the Trellis diagram.

7.3.3 Trellis Diagram

As discussed in the previous subsections, state diagram is not an efficient way of characterizing a convolution encoder as it will not give the precise details about the encoder. Also tree diagram will not serve as an efficient way of representation as it will become bulky for large input size. Thus, the tree representation can

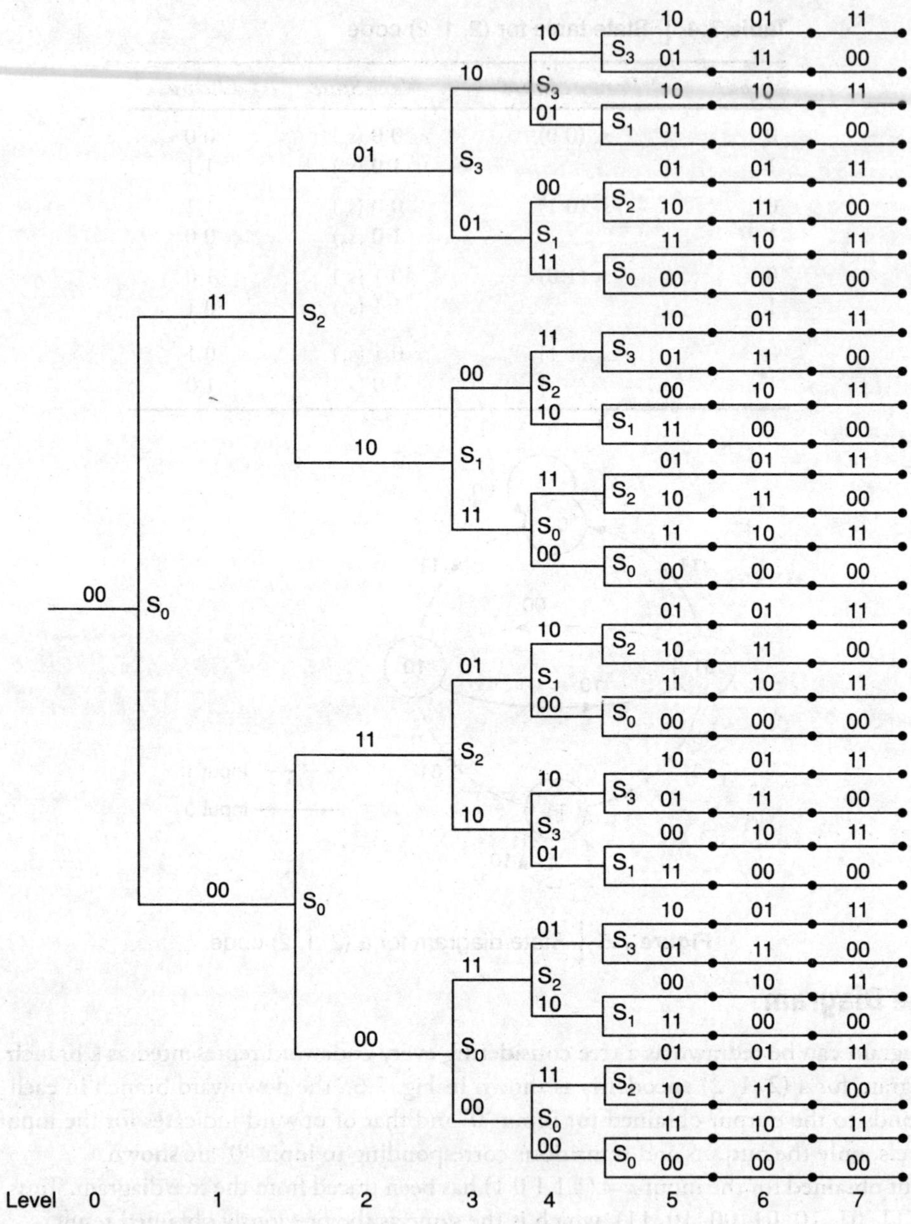

Figure 7.6 | Tree representation of a (2, 1, 2) code.

be improvised by exploiting its redundancy. In Trellis diagram, the very nature of repetition in tree representation is being exploited, thus leading to a compact representation.

The Trellis diagram for the given (2, 1, 2) encoder is shown in Fig. 7.7.

The codeword can be traced for the input (1 1 1 0 1) as shown in Fig. 7.7. The traced output will become (11, 01, 10, 01, 00, 10, 11).

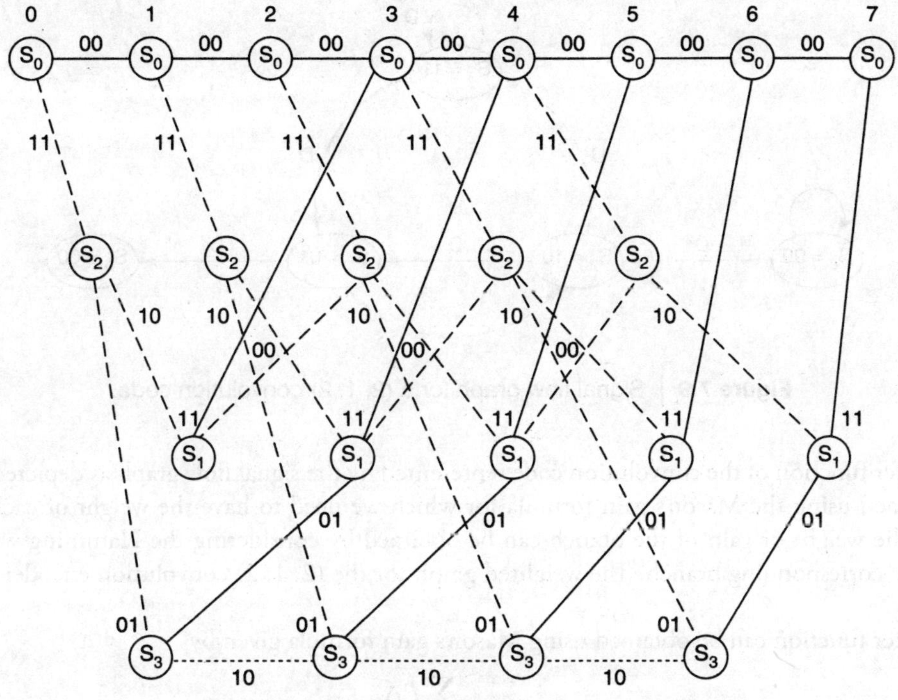

Figure 7.7 | Trellis diagram for a (2, 1, 2) code.

7.4 Transfer Function of a Convolution Code

A convolution encoder can be characterized by its transfer function that can be obtained by considering the gains of the paths diverting and re-merging at all zero states of the encoder.

Consider a (2, 1, 2) convolution encoder as shown in Fig. 7.1. Its corresponding state diagram is as shown in Fig. 7.5. Considering the initial and terminal node to be s_0 and redrawing the state diagram, we get a modified state diagram as shown in Fig. 7.8.

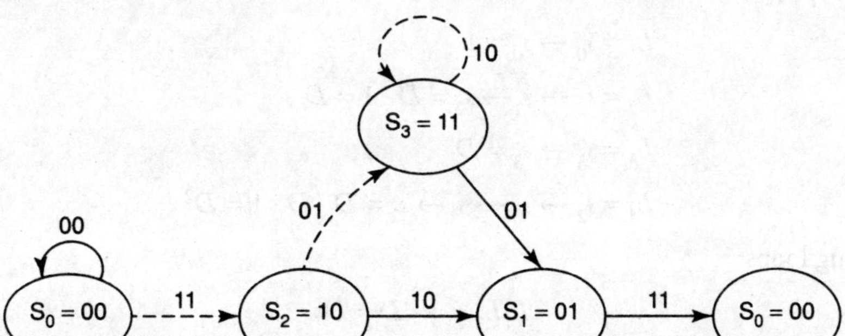

Figure 7.8 | State diagram of a (2, 1, 2) convolution encoder.

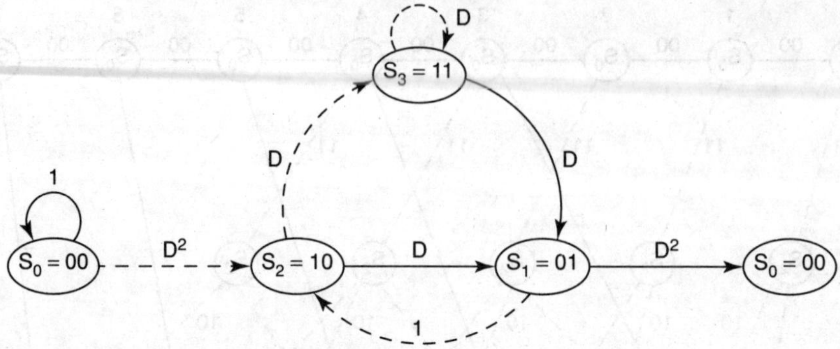

Figure 7.9 | Signal flow graph for a (2, 1, 2) convolution code.

The transfer function of the convolution code represented by the signal flow graph as depicted in Fig. 7.8 can be obtained using the Mason's gain formula for which we need to have the weight of each branch of the graph. The weight or gain of the branch can be obtained by considering the Hamming weight of the output of the corresponding branch. The weighted graph for the (2, 1, 2) convolution encoder is as shown in Fig. 7.9.

The transfer function can be obtained using Mason's gain formula given by

$$T(D) = \frac{\sum_i P_i \Delta_i}{\Delta} \tag{7.4}$$

where P_i is the ith forward path and $\Delta = 1 - \Sigma$ Loop gains + Σ Gains of all two non-touching loop – Σ All 3 non-touching loops + …

Applying this formula to the signal flow graph depicted in Fig. 7.9, we have

Forward paths:

$$P_1 = s_0 \rightarrow s_2 \rightarrow s_1 \rightarrow s_0 = D^2 \cdot D \cdot D^2 = D^5$$

$$P_2 = s_0 \rightarrow s_2 \rightarrow s_3 \rightarrow s_1 \rightarrow s_0 = D^2 \cdot D \cdot D \cdot D^2 = D^6$$

Loops:

$$L_1 = s_0 \rightarrow s_0 = 1$$

$$L_2 = s_2 \rightarrow s_1 \rightarrow s_2 = D \cdot 1 = D$$

$$L_3 = s_3 \rightarrow s_3 = D$$

$$L_4 = s_2 \rightarrow s_3 \rightarrow s_1 \rightarrow s_2 = D \cdot D \cdot 1 = D^2$$

2 – non-touching loops:

$$L_1 L_3 = 1 \cdot D = D$$

$$L_1 L_2 = 1 \cdot D = D$$

$$L_1 L_4 = 1 \cdot D^2 = D^2$$

$$L_3 L_2 = D \cdot D = D^2$$

3 – non-touching loops:

$$L_1L_3L_2 = 1 \cdot D \cdot D = D^2$$

Therefore,

$$\begin{aligned}\Delta &= 1 - (1 + D + D + D^2) + (D + D + D^2 + D^2) - D^2 \\ &= 1 - (1 + 2D + D^2) + (2 + 2D^2) = D^2 \\ &= 1 - 1 - 2D - D^2 + 2 + 2D^2 - D^2 = 2 - 2D\end{aligned}$$

$$\Delta_1 = 1$$

$$\Delta_2 = 1$$

Hence

$$T(D) = \frac{P_1\Delta_1 + P_2\Delta_2}{\Delta} = \frac{D^5 + D^6}{2 - 2D}$$

Thus, the transfer function of the given (2, 1, 2) convolution code is

$$T(D) = \frac{D^5 + D^6}{2 - 2D}$$

7.4.1 Catastrophic Code

A convolution encoder is said to be catastrophic if a finite number of errors at the output sequence generates an infinite number of errors at the decoded sequence. Catastrophic codes are not desirable and thus not used in practice.

Catastrophic codes can be easily identified if there exists a zero output weighted loop corresponding to a non-zero input weight. In other words, if a state diagram is having a self-loop of zero weight other than state zero, then such codes are said to be catastrophic.

The state diagram of a catastrophic convolution encoder is as shown in Fig. 7.10.

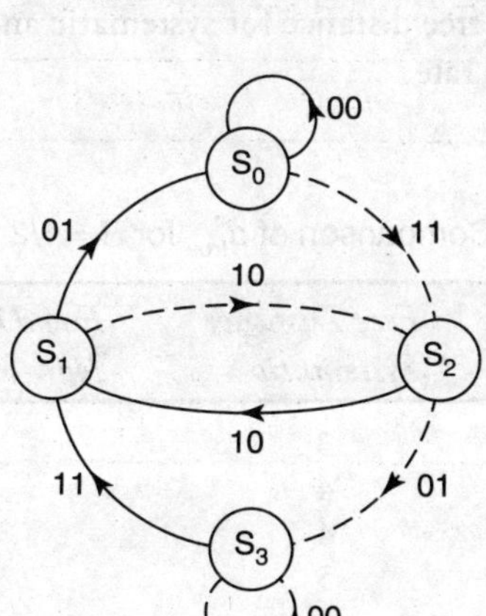

Figure 7.10 | A catastrophic code.

7.5 Distance Properties of Convolution Codes

The performance measure for a convolution encoder depends on the decoding algorithm adopted and the distance properties of the code. In this section we will be defining three distance measures, namely:

1. Minimum free distance.
2. Column distance function.
3. Minimum distance.

7.5.1 Minimum Free Distance (d_{free})

It is defined as the minimum distance among all pairs of codewords in the convolution code alphabet. Mathematically, it is given by

$$d_{\text{free}} \triangleq \min\left\{d(v',v''):u' \neq u''\right\} \tag{7.5}$$

where v' and v'' are codewords corresponding to inputs u' and u''. As there is no restriction to the lengths of the input unlike block codes, it is assumed that zeroes have to be appended to the shorter sequence.

As convolution codes are also linear

$$d(v', v'') = w(v' + v'') = w(v) \tag{7.6}$$

where v is a non-zero code vector. Thus,

$$d_{\text{free}} \triangleq \min\left\{w(v)\right\} u \neq 0 \tag{7.7}$$

Thus, the free distance can be defined as the weight of a non-zero codeword generated by a non-zero input sequence of any length.

Unlike linear block codes, in convolution codes, the block distance properties will not be same if we transform a non-systematic code into a systematic code. In other words, d_{free} will be affected if the convolution codes are made systematic. Free distance in a convolution code will get reduced if the code is made systematic for a given constraint length and rate.

Table 7.5 gives a comparison of the free distance for systematic and non-systematic cases of convolution codes for a given constraint length and rate.

Table 7.5 | Comparison of d_{free} for $R = 1/2$

Constraint Length	*Free Distance Systematic*	*Free Distance Non-Systematic*
2	3	3
3	4	5
4	4	6
5	5	7
6	6	8
7	6	10
8	7	10

7.5.2 Column Distance Function

Column distance function (CDF) for a convolution encoder is defined as the minimum distance between any two codewords in the code alphabet truncated to a length i given that the input sequences are different for first k-bit positions.

$$d_i \triangleq \min\left\{d\left([v']_i,[v'']_i\right):[u']_k \neq [u'']_k\right\} = \min\left\{w[v]_i:[u]_k \neq 0\right\} \tag{7.8}$$

where $[v']_i$ and $[v'']_i$ are the ith truncation of the codewords v' and v'', respectively. In other words, the CDF can be defined as the minimum weight of a non-zero codeword generated by an input sequence whose initial block of k bits are non-zero. As

$$[v] = [u]\ [G]$$

$$[v]_i = [u]_i\ [G]_i$$

therefore,

$$d_i = \min\left\{w[u]_i[G]_i : [u]_0 \neq 0\right\} \tag{7.9}$$

From Eq. (7.9) it is clear that the CDF 'd_i' depends only on the first $n\ (i+1)$ columns of the generator matrix G. Thus, the name column distance function.

7.5.3 Minimum Distance

There are two special cases of CDF, that is, when $i = m$ and when $i \to \infty$. For $i = m$, d_m is called the minimum distance of the convolution encoder. On the other hand, when $i \to \infty$, d_i will become the minimum free distance of the code, that is,

$$\lim_{i\to\infty} d_i = d_{\text{free}} \tag{7.10}$$

Minimum distance is also denoted as $d_{\min}$. Although $d_{\min}$ was considered to be the most prominent distance measure in the earlier years, inventions of new decoding algorithms have replaced $d_{\min}$ by d_{free} and d_i as the important distance parameters.

7.6 Decoding of Convolution Codes

The decoder of a convolution code can take a decision based on one of the following methods: hard decision and soft decision. Consider a rate ½ convolution encoder in which the decoder receives two tuples codewords. In the case of hard decision decoding, these two-tuple codewords will be mapped onto one of the four possible values (0, 0) (0, 1) (1, 0) or (1, 1) directly.

In soft decision decoding, the decoder receives bits from the channel with some degree of reliability consideration. Generally, three bits will serve the purpose. A sequence of 000 represents strongest 0 and sequence 111 represents strongest 1. It is detailed in Fig. 7.11.

Soft decision decoding is generally preferred as it offers a gain of 2 dB over hard decision decoding. In other words, 2 dB less transmitting power can be used for a system using soft decision decoding compared to that of hard decision decoding for a fixed error possibility. Generally, a distance measure involves Hamming distance for a hard decision decoding and Euclidian distance for a soft decision decoding.

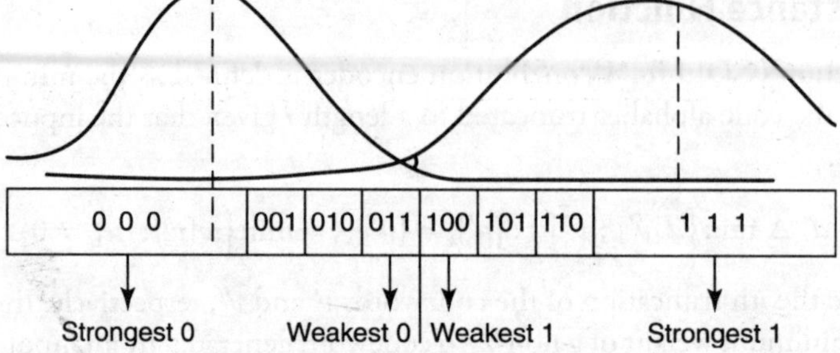

Figure 7.11 | Soft decision decoding.

Viterbi algorithm is one of the optimum decoding algorithms that offers a fixed complexity of decoding. The next section details Viterbi algorithm that can be used for both hard and soft decision decoding.

7.6.1 Decoding of Convolution Codes Using Viterbi Algorithm

Viterbi proposed a method to decode the convolution codes, which has become popularly known as Viterbi decoding. It was also proved to be analogous of finding the shortest path between nodes in a weighted network. Maximum likelihood decoding could be achieved using Viterbi algorithm, which maximizes the log likelihood function. Decoding using Viterbi algorithm can be either hard or soft decision.

7.6.1.1 Definitions

1. **Branch metric $M_n(s_i, s_j)$:** It is defined as the metric obtained during the transition from state i at instant $(n-1)$ to state j at instant n.
2. **State metric $S_M(s_j)$:** It is defined as the cumulative metric of the survivor state s_i at instant $(n-1)$ with the branch metric $M_n(s_i, s_j)$.
$$S_M(s_j) = M_n(s_i, s_j) + S_M(s_i) \tag{7.11}$$
3. **Survivor path:** A state can be reached with more than one path. Each path leads to a different state metric computation. The path which gives the minimum value of the state metric will be considered as the survival path.

As shown in Fig. 7.12, the state metrics computed at j with paths from states i and k are as follows:

$$\begin{aligned} S_M(s_j) \text{ via } i &= S_M(s_i) + M_n(s_i, s_j) \\ S_M(s_j) \text{ via } k &= S_M(s_k) + M_n(s_k, s_j) \end{aligned} \tag{7.12}$$

Among the metrics computed at s_j, the one with minimum value is selected and the corresponding path is called the survivor path.

When a binary symmetric channel is used, the metric is nothing but the Hamming distance, and thus the decoder aims at minimizing the Hamming distance between the received vector and the codeword.

Trellis representation is used for Viterbi algorithm. Consider a data sequence u encoded to form a codeword c. Let the received vector be r. The decoder has to estimate u such that the decoding error probability can be minimized. As the relation between the data and codeword is one to one, the receiver has to estimate

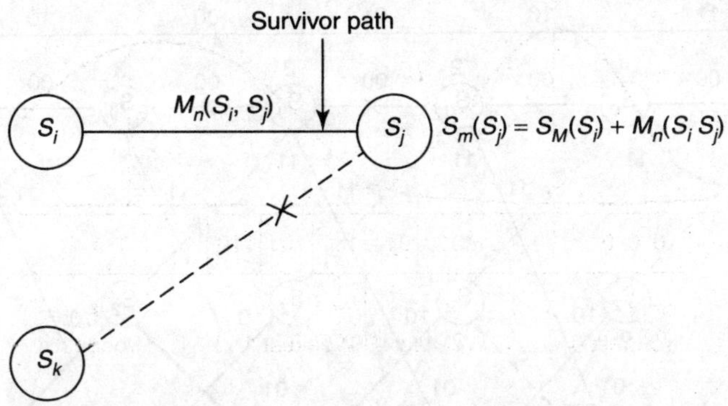

Figure 7.12 | Metric computation.

$\hat{c}$ such that $\hat{u} = u$ if and only if $\hat{c} = c$. Therefore, the criterion to be followed by the Viterbi decoder is to compute the error probability

$$P(r/c) = \prod_{i=1}^{N} P(r_i/c_i) \tag{7.13}$$

where r is the received vector of length N and c is the transmitted codeword of length N.

The log likelihood function can be defined as

$$\log P\left(\frac{r}{c}\right) = \sum_{i=1}^{N} P\left(\frac{r_i}{c_i}\right) \tag{7.14}$$

where

$$P\left(\frac{r_i}{c_i}\right) = \begin{cases} \rho & \text{if } r_i \neq c_i \\ 1-\rho & \text{if } r_i = c_i \end{cases}$$

The estimate $\hat{c}$ at the receiver has to be done so as to minimize the log likelihood function given in the equation.

7.6.2 Add Compare Select Unit

Add compare select unit is the basic building block in the decoding process of convolution codes using Viterbi algorithm. The process is as follows:

1. Compute the state metric of state i from various paths converging at state i.
2. Among the metrics obtained considering all incoming branches to node s_i, select the best path, which will be termed as survivor path. The other incoming paths will be discarded.

7.6.3 Decoding of Convolution Codes for a Binary Symmetric Channel

In this section, we will consider the decoding process of a convolution code applied to a binary symmetric channel (BSC). Thus, the metric can be computed by considering the Hamming distance.

Consider the Trellis diagram for (2, 1, 2) convolution code. Let the received vector be (11, 11, 10, 01, 00, 10, 11). The decoding process is as depicted in Fig. 7.13. The metric at every state is computed

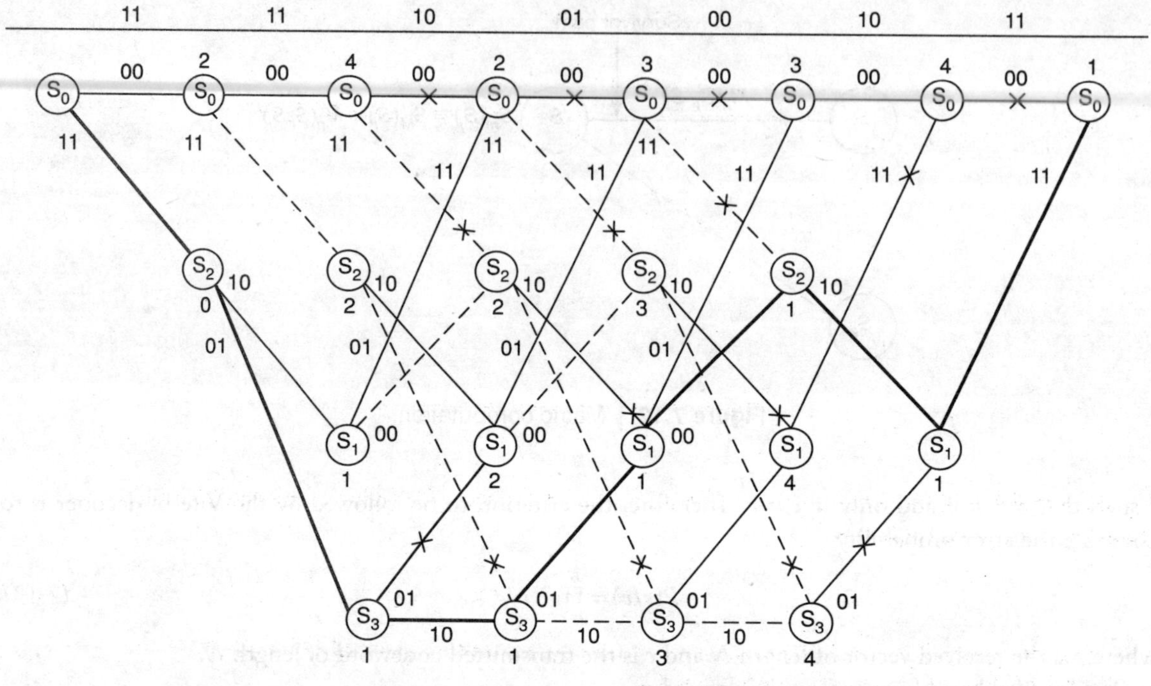

Figure 7.13 | Decoding of a (2, 1, 2) convolution code using Viterbi algorithm.

by considering the sum of the Hamming distance between the received vector and the corresponding branch outputs, with the metric of the predecessor state, the path from which the minimum valued metric is obtained will become the survivor path. If more than one path leads to the same metric with minimum value, one of the paths will be chosen arbitrarily. Once the metrics of all states have been computed, the decoded sequence can be obtained by back-tracing from the end state toward the first state.

In the given problem we consider the received vector to be (11, 11, 10, 01, 00, 10, 11). The metric at every node is computed and is shown with every state in the diagram. Non-survival paths are crossed out so that they are not selected during traceback. One of the paths is arbitrarily selected whenever the minimum metric is obtained from more than one path.

The decoded path is shown in dark line. The decoded sequence from the diagram is

$$\hat{u} = 1\,1\,1\,0\,1\,0\,0$$

The last two bits of the decoded sequence can be neglected as they are padded zeroes at the sender's end. Thus, the decoded sequence will be

$$\hat{u} = 1\,1\,1\,0\,1$$

It can be noted that every single error present in the received vector is been rectified in the decoding process.

The complexity of decoding increases with the increase in the constraint length.

7.6.4 Decoding of a Convolution Code for a Discrete Memoryless Channel

Consider a discrete memoryless channel (DMC) with binary input and quaternary output as shown in Fig. 7.14.

The metric table for the channel is as shown in Table 7.6.

Consider the Trellis diagram for a (2, 1, 2) convolution encoder. Let the received vector be (I_1I_2, I_2I_2, I_2O_1, O_1O_2, I_2O_1, I_2I_2). The decoding procedure is similar to that of a BSC. The metric is computed using the metric table as given in Table 7.6.

If the nodes have multiple entries, metrics corresponding to each entry have to be computed and the one with maximum metric has to be retained unlike BSC. The procedure is continued till the last stage in the Trellis algorithm is reached. The decoded information can be obtained by tracing back the survival paths toward the source.. The complete decoding process is as depicted in Fig. 7.15.

The decoded information is given by

$$\hat{u} = (1\,1\,1\,0\,1\,0\,0)$$

where the last two bits are appended zeroes. Therefore, decoded information will be 1 1 1 0 1.

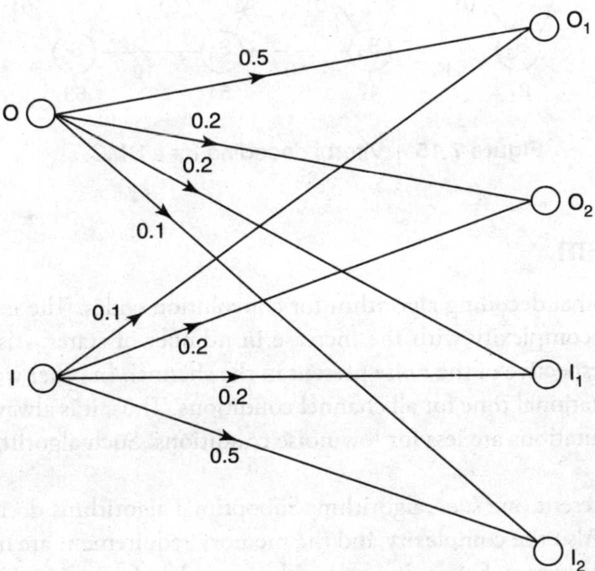

Figure 7.14 | Two input–four output discrete memoryless channel.

Table 7.6 | Metric table for channel given

	0_1	0_2	1_1	1_2
0	10	7	7	0
1	0	7	7	10

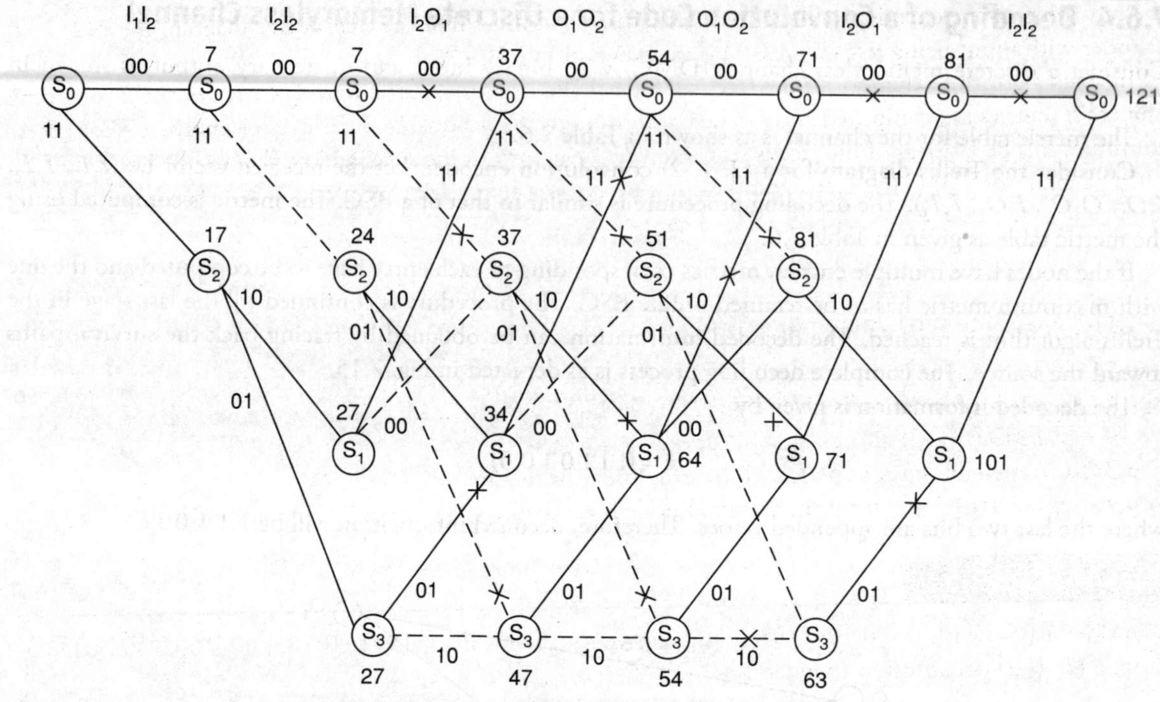

Figure 7.15 | Viterbi decoding for a DMC.

7.7 Stack Algorithm

Viterbi algorithm is an optimal decoding algorithm for convolution codes. The major drawback of Viterbi algorithm is the increasing complexity with the increase in number of states. Also, the Viterbi algorithm offers a fixed complexity irrespective of the noise present in the channel. In other words, the algorithm offers the same amount of computational time for all channel conditions. Thus, it is always better to have an adaptive algorithm whose computations are less for low noise conditions. Such algorithms are called *suboptimal algorithms.*

In this section we will present one such algorithm. Suboptimal algorithms do not always provide maximum likelihood decoding. Also the complexity and the memory requirement are not constant, but they are dependent on the received sequence. Suboptimal algorithms are thus faster than Viterbi algorithm.

Stack algorithm is one such suboptimal algorithm. Stack algorithm is also known as ZJ algorithm named after the scientists Zigangirov and Jelinck who proposed the algorithm.

7.7.1 Algorithm

Like Viterbi algorithms based on Trellis representation, stack algorithms are best dealt with tree representation of the codes. For an (n, k, m) binary convolution code, with an input of length L, the tree will have $(L + m + 1)$ levels. The origin or the root of the tree is the initial state of the encoder. During first L levels, each node will have 2^k outgoing branches. This part of the tree is called the dividing part of the tree. The next $(m + 1)$ levels will have only one outgoing branch corresponding to input zero, which corresponds to the returning of the encoder to all-zero state that is called the tail of the tree. A tree diagram for a (2, 1, 2) encoder with input being $u = (1\ 1\ 1\ 0\ 1)$ is as shown in Fig. 7.6.

In stack algorithm, the root of the tree will be initialized with a metric zero. For each of the 2^k outgoing branches, metrics are computed and stacked according to the decreasing order of their metrics. The process continues till the last leaf of the tree is reached. The first entry in the stack will be the decoded output.

In general, for a BSC the metric can be computed using the relation

$$M(r_i / v_i) = \begin{cases} \log_2 2\rho - R & \text{if } r_i \neq v_i \\ \log_2 2(1-\rho) - R & \text{if } r_i = v_i \end{cases} \tag{7.15}$$

The stack algorithm can be summarized as follows:

Step 1: The root node will be selected as the initial node and the corresponding metric is set to zero.
Step 2: The metrics of the successors of the entry in the top of the stack will be computed and the top entry will be replaced by the 2^k entries of its successor.
Step 3: Rearrange the stack as per the decreasing order of the metric.
Step 4: Repeat steps 3 and 4 till the terminal node is reached.

EXAMPLE 7.5

Consider a BSC with $\rho = 0.10$. Decode the received sequence $r = (11, 11, 10, 01, 00, 10, 11)$ obtained from a (2, 1, 2) convolution encoder.

Solution: Given $R = 1/2$ and $\rho = 0.10$. The metric can be obtained using equation

$$M(r_i/v_i) = \begin{cases} \log_2(2\times 0.1) - 1/2 & \text{if } r_i \neq v_i \\ \log_2 2(1-0.1) - 1/2 & \text{if } r_i = v_i \end{cases}$$

$$\Rightarrow M(r_i / v_i) = \begin{cases} -2.8219 & \text{if } r_i \neq v_i \\ 0.3479 & \text{if } r_i = v_i \end{cases}$$

Therefore, the metric table is given by

	0	1
0	0.3479	−2.8219
1	−2.8219	0.3479

Reducing the table by dividing with 0.3479 and approximating to the nearest integer, we get

	0	1
0	1	−8
1	−8	1

The contents of the stack after every step of the algorithm are shown as follows. The tree diagram of a (2, 1, 2) convolution encoder as shown in Fig. 7.6 is taken for the metric computation.

Step 1:

0 (−16)
1 (2)

The metric is computed for the tree branches corresponding to inputs 0 and 1 by comparing the first 2 type of the vector with the corresponding branch outputs. For the branch corresponding to input 0, the branch output will be (0 0) and the received sequence is (1 1) corresponding to a metric of

$$M(1/0) + M(1/0) = -8 - 8 = -16$$

whereas for that of the other branch, it is

$$M(1/1) + M(1/1) = 1 + 1 = 2$$

Now arranging the stack in decreasing order, we have

1 (2)

0 (−16)

Step 2: Similarly considering the next stage of the tree for the next two tuple of the received sequence 1 1, we obtain the stack after second iteration. But unlike Viterbi decoding, the metric for all possible branches are not computed; instead the top entry of the stack will be fragmented into two parts corresponding to the inputs 0 and 1 of the next stage, respectively. Thus, the second stage of the stack will have the entries for 1 0, 1 1 and 0. The metrics are as follows:

$$1\,0 = \text{Metric of first stage} + M(1/1) + M(1/0) = 2 + 1 - 8 = -5$$

$$1\,1 = 2 + M(1/0) + M(1/1) = 2 + 1 - 8 = -5$$

$$0 = -16$$

Rearranging again in the decreasing order of the metric, we have

1 0 (−5)

1 1 (−5)

0 (−16)

In the same way, the stack contents will get updated after every stage till the terminal node is reached.

Stage 3:

		⇒		
1 0 0	(−12)		1 1	(−5)
1 0 1	(−12)	⇒	1 0 0	(−12)
1 1	(−5)		1 0 1	(−12)
0	(−16)		0	(−16)

Stage 4:

1 1 0	(−21)		1 1 1	(−3)
1 1 1	(−3)		1 0 0	(−12)
1 0 0	(−12)	⇒	1 0 1	(−12)
1 0 1	(−12)		0	(−16)
0	(−16)		1 1 0	(−21)

Stage 5:

1 1 1 0	(−1)		1 1 1 0	(−1)
1 1 1 1	(−19)		1 0 0	(−12)
1 0 0	(−12)	⇒	1 0 1	(−12)
1 0 1	(−12)		0	(−16)

0	(−16)		1 1 1 1	(−19)
1 1 0	(−21)		1 1 0	(−21)

Stage 6:

1 1 1 0 1	(1)		1 1 1 0 1	(1)
1 1 1 0 0	(−17)		1 0 0	(−12)
1 0 0	(−12)		1 0 1	(−12)
1 0 1	(−12)	⇒	0	(−16)
0	(−16)		1 1 1 0 0	(−17)
1 1 1 1	(−19)		1 1 1 1	(−19)
1 1 0	(−21)		1 1 0	(−21)

Stage 7:

1 1 1 1 0	(3)
1 0 0	(−12)
1 0 1	(−12)
0	(−16)
1 1 1 0 0	(−17)
1 1 1 1	(−19)
1 1 0	(−21)

As we have reached the tail end of the tree by the end of stage 6, we need not have to fragment the sequence 1 1 1 0 1 anymore. It can only have input 0 henceforth.

Stage 8:

1 1 1 0 1 0 0	(5)
1 0 0	(−12)
1 0 1	(−12)
0	(−16)
1 1 1 0 0	(−17)
1 1 1 1	(−19)
1 1 0	(−21)

Thus, at the end of stage 8, we will get the decoded sequences given by the top entry of the stack. In this case it is

$$\hat{u}=(1\,1\,1\,0\,1\,0\,0)$$

It is clear from the above example that decoding in sequential algorithm is simpler and much faster compared to Viterbi algorithm. The decoding process for the given received sequence is very simple and is completed in only eight stages as the received vector has only one-bit error. The complexity increases with the increase in the noise present in the channel. It can be clearly understood from the next example.

EXAMPLE 7.6

Consider the received sequence be $r=(11, 11, 11, 11, 00, 10, 11)$. Decode the given received vector using stack algorithm.

Solution: The corresponding stack contents after every stage are as follows.

Stage 1:

Path	Metric		Path	Metric
0	(−16)		1	(2)
		⇒		
1	(2)		0	(−16)

Stage 2:

Path	Metric		Path	Metric
1 0	(−5)		1 0	(−5)
1 1	(−5)	⇒	1 1	(−5)
0	(−16)		0	(−16)

Stage 3:

Path	Metric		Path	Metric
1 0 0	(−3)		1 0 0	(−3)
1 0 1	(−21)	⇒	1 1	(−5)
1 1	(−5)		0	(−16)
0	(−16)		1 0 1	(−21)

Stage 4:

Path	Metric		Path	Metric
1 0 0 0	(−19)		1 0 0 1	(−1)
1 0 0 1	(−1)		1 1	(−5)
1 1	(−5)	⇒	0	(−16)
0	(−16)		1 0 0 0	(−19)
1 0 1	(−21)		1 0 1	(−21)

Stage 5:

Path	Metric		Path	Metric
1 0 0 1 0	(−8)		1 1	(−5)
1 0 0 1 1	(−8)		1 0 0 1 0	(−8)
1 1	(−5)	⇒	1 0 0 1 1	(−8)
0	(−16)		0	(−16)
1 0 0 0	(−19)		1 0 0 0	(−19)
1 0 1	(−21)		1 0 1	(−21)

Stage 6:

Path	Metric		Path	Metric
1 1 0	(−12)		1 0 0 1 0	(−8)
1 1 1	(−12)		1 0 0 1 1	(−8)
1 0 0 1 0	(−8)		1 1 0	(−12)
1 0 0 1 1	(−8)	⇒	1 1 1	(−12)
0	(−16)		0	(−16)
1 0 0 0	(−19)		1 0 0 0	(−19)
1 0 1	(−21)		1 0 1	(−21)

Stage 7:

Path	Metric		Path	Metric
1 0 0 1 0 0	(−15)		1 0 0 1 1	(−8)
1 0 0 1 1	(−8)		1 1 0	(−12)
1 1 0	(−12)		1 1 1	(−12)
1 1 1	(−12)	⇒	1 0 0 1 0 0	(−15)
0	(−16)		0	(−16)
1 0 0 0	(−19)		1 0 0 0	(−19)
1 0 1	(−21)		1 0 1	(−21)

Stage 8:

Path	Metric		Path	Metric
1 0 0 1 1 0	(−24)		1 1 0	(−12)
1 1 0	(−12)		1 1 1	(−12)

Path	Metric		Path	Metric
1 1 1	(−12)		1 0 0 1 0 0	(−15)
1 0 0 1 0 0	(−15)	⇒	0	(−16)
0	(−16)		1 0 0 0	(−19)
1 0 0 0	(−19)		1 0 1	(−21)
1 0 1	(−21)		1 0 0 1 1 0	(−24)

Stage 9:

Path	Metric		Path	Metric
1 1 0 0	(−10)		1 1 0 0	(−10)
1 1 0 1	(−28)		1 1 1	(−12)
1 1 1	(−12)		1 0 0 1 0 0	(−15)
1 0 0 1 0 0	(−15)	⇒	0	(−16)
0	(−16)		1 0 0 0	(−19)
1 0 0 0	(−19)		1 0 1	(−21)
1 0 1	(−21)		1 0 0 1 1 0	(−24)
1 0 0 1 1 0	(−24)		1 1 0 1	(−28)

Stage 10:

Path	Metric		Path	Metric
1 1 0 0 0	(−8)		1 1 0 0 0	(−8)
1 1 0 0 1	(−26)		1 1 1	(−12)
1 1 1	(−12)		1 0 0 1 0 0	(−15)
1 0 0 1 0 0	(−15)		0	(−16)
0	(−16)	⇒	1 0 0 0	(−19)
1 0 0 0	(−19)		1 0 1	(−21)
1 0 1	(−21)		1 0 0 1 1 0	(−24)
1 0 0 1 1 0	(−24)		1 1 0 0 1	(−26)
1 1 0 1	(−28)		1 1 0 1	(−28)

Stage 11:

Path	Metric		Path	Metric
1 1 0 0 0 0	(−15)		1 1 1	(−12)
1 1 1	(−12)		1 1 0 0 0 0	(−15)
1 0 0 1 0 0	(−15)		1 0 0 1 0 0	(−15)
0	(−16)		0	(−16)
1 0 0 0	(−19)	⇒	1 0 0 0	(−19)
1 0 1	(−21)		1 0 1	(−21)
1 0 0 1 1 0	(−24)		1 0 0 1 1 0	(−24)
1 1 0 0 1	(−26)		1 1 0 0 1	(−26)
1 1 0 1	(−28)		1 1 0 1	(−28)

Stage 12:

Path	Metric		Path	Metric
1 1 1 0	(−19)		1 1 0 0 0 0	(−15)
1 1 1 1	(−19)		1 0 0 1 0 0	(−15)
1 1 0 0 0 0	(−15)		0	(−16)
1 0 0 1 0 0	(−15)		1 1 1 0	(−19)
0	(−16)		1 1 1 1	(−19)
1 0 0 0	(−19)	⇒	1 0 0 0	(−19)
1 0 1	(−21)		1 0 1	(−21)
1 0 0 1 1 0	(−24)		1 0 0 1 1 0	(−24)
1 1 0 0 1	(−26)		1 1 0 0 1	(−26)
1 1 0	(−28)		1 1 0	(−28)

Stage 13:

1 1 0 0 0 0 0	(−31)		1 0 0 1 0 0	(−15)
1 0 0 1 0 0	(−15)		0	(−16)
0	(−16)		1 1 1 0	(−19)
1 1 1 0	(−19)		1 1 1 1	(−19)
1 1 1 1	(−19)	⇒	1 0 0 0	(−19)
1 0 0 0	(−19)		1 0 1	(−21)
1 0 1	(−21)		1 0 0 1 1 0	(−24)
1 0 0 1 1 0	(−24)		1 1 0 0 1	(−26)
1 1 0 0 1	(−26)		1 1 0	(−28)
1 1 0	(−28)		1 1 0 0 0 0 0	(−15)

Stage 14:

1 0 0 1 0 0 0	(−31)		0	(−16)
0	(−16)		1 1 1 0	(−19)
1 1 1 0	(−19)		1 1 1 1	(−19)
1 1 1 1	(−19)		1 0 0 0	(−19)
1 0 0 0	(−19)	⇒	1 0 1	(−21)
1 0 1	(−21)		1 0 0 1 1 0	(−24)
1 0 0 1 1 0	(−24)		1 1 0 0 1	(−26)
1 1 0 0 1	(−26)		1 1 0	(−28)
1 1 0	(−28)		1 1 0 0 0 0 0	(−31)
1 1 0 0 0 0 0	(−31)		1 0 0 1 0 0 0	(−31)

Stage 15:

0 0	(−32)		0 1	(−14)
0 1	(−14)		1 1 1 0	(−19)
1 1 1 0	(−19)		1 1 1 1	(−19)
1 1 1 1	(−19)		1 0 0 0	(−19)
1 0 0 0	(−19)		1 0 1	(−21)
1 0 1	(−21)	⇒	1 0 0 1 1 0	(−24)
1 0 0 1 1 0	(−24)		1 1 0 0 1	(−26)
1 1 0 0 1	(−26)		1 1 0	(−28)
1 1 0	(−28)		1 1 0 0 0 0 0	(−31)
1 1 0 0 0 0 0	(−31)		1 0 0 1 0 0 0	(−31)
1 0 0 1 0 0 0	(−31)		0 0	(−32)

Stage 16:

0 1 0	(−21)		1 1 1 0	(−19)
0 1 1	(−21)		1 1 1 1	(−19)
1 1 1 0	(−19)		1 0 0 0	(−19)
1 1 1 1	(−19)		1 0 1	(−21)
1 0 0 0	(−19)		0 1 0	(−21)
1 0 1	(−21)	⇒	0 1 1	(−21)
1 0 0 1 1 0	(−24)		1 0 0 1 1 0	(−24)
1 1 0 0 1	(−26)		1 1 0 0 1	(−26)
1 1 0	(−28)		1 1 0	(−28)
1 1 0 0 0 0 0	(−31)		1 1 0 0 0 0 0	(−31)

1 0 0 1 0 0 0 (–31)	1 0 0 1 0 0 0 (–32)
0 0 (–32)	0 0 (–32)

Stage 17:

1 1 1 0 0 (–21)		1 1 1 0 1 (–17)
1 1 1 0 1 (–17)		1 1 1 1 (–19)
1 1 1 1 (–19)		1 0 0 0 (–19)
1 0 0 0 (–19)		1 0 1 (–21)
1 0 1 (–21)		0 1 0 (–21)
0 1 0 (–21)	⇒	0 1 1 (–21)
0 1 1 (–21)		1 0 0 1 1 0 (–24)
1 0 0 1 1 0 (–24)		1 1 0 0 1 (–26)
1 1 0 0 1 (–26)		1 1 0 (–28)
1 1 0 (–28)		1 1 0 0 0 0 0 (–31)
1 1 0 0 0 0 0 (–31)		1 0 0 1 0 0 0 (–31)
1 0 0 1 0 0 0 (–31)		0 0 (–32)
0 0 (–32)		1 1 1 0 0 (–35)

Stage 18:

1 1 1 0 1 0 (–15)
1 1 1 1 (–19)
1 0 0 0 (–19)
1 0 1 (–21)
0 1 0 (–21)
0 1 1 (–21)
1 0 0 1 1 0 (–24)
1 1 0 0 1 (–26)
1 1 0 (–28)
1 1 0 0 0 0 0 (–31)
1 0 0 1 0 0 0 (–31)
0 0 (–32)
1 1 1 0 0 (–35)

Stage 19:

1 1 1 0 1 0 0 (–13)
1 1 1 1 (–19)
1 0 0 0 (–19)
1 0 1 (–21)
0 1 0 (–21)
0 1 1 (–21)
1 0 0 1 1 0 (–24)
1 1 0 0 1 (–26)
1 1 0 (–28)
1 1 0 0 0 0 0 (–31)
1 0 0 1 0 0 0 (–31)
0 0 (–32)
1 1 1 0 0 (–35)

The decoded sequence is (1 1 1 0 1).

The number of stages required for decoding in Example 7.6 is 18, unlike only 8 stages for Example 7.5. This is because of the increase in the noise present during transmission. Thus, it can be concluded that the number of computations required for sequential decoding will be less for low-noise cases, whereas it is very high for the conditions where a high amount of noise is present during transmission. Sometimes this may be larger compared to the fixed computations involved in Viterbi algorithm. But as the occurrence of high noise is very less likely, the average number of computations required for stack algorithm is lesser compared to that of Viterbi algorithm.

It can also be seen from Examples 7.5 and 7.6 that the decoded path obtained in stack algorithm is the same as that of the Viterbi algorithm even for high-noise condition. Thus, stack algorithm also produces a maximum likelihood decoding in most of the cases. In other words, sequential algorithm also offers the same performance as optimum decoding algorithm for a given error probability.

7.8 Known Good Convolution Codes

Let us now consider some of the most popular convolution codes which are considered to perform better. Some of the rate ½, ⅓ and ¼ convolution codes which offer a larger free distance are presented in Tables 7.7, 7.8 and 7.9, respectively. Here the generator coefficients are represented in octal.

Table 7.7 | Rate ½ good convolution codes

k	*n*	*Generator Coefficients*		d_{free}
3	6	5	7	5
4	8	15	17	6
5	10	23	35	7
6	12	53	75	8
7	14	133	171	10

Table 7.8 | Rate ⅓ good convolution codes

k	*n*	*Generator Coefficients*			d_{free}
3	9	5	7	7	8
4	12	13	17	17	10
5	15	25	37	37	12
6	18	47	75	75	13
7	21	133	175	175	15

Table 7.9 | Rate ¼ good convolution codes

k	*n*	*Generator Coefficients*				d_{free}
3	12	5	7	7	7	10
4	16	13	15	15	17	15
5	20	25	27	33	37	16
6	24	53	67	71	75	18
7	28	135	135	147	163	20

7.9 Turbo Codes

Turbo codes were introduced by Berrou, Thitimajshima and Glavieux. Larger coding gain with respect to an uncoded system can be achieved in turbo codes due to its iterative nature. A parallel concatenated convolution codes (PCCC) is used in turbo encoders, in which data bits are coded using two or more recursive

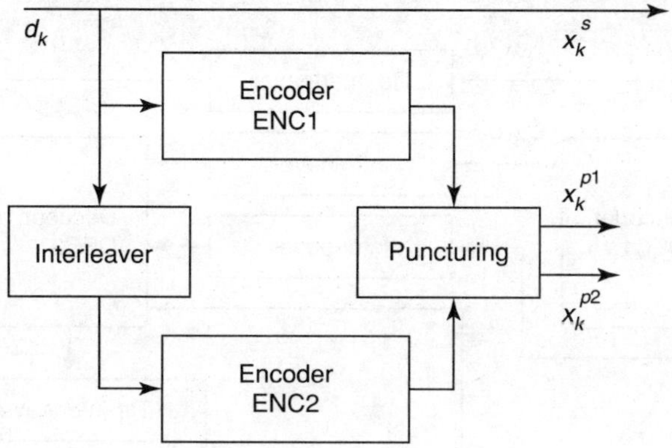

Figure 7.16 | Turbo encoder.

systematic convolution (RSC) coders, each considering the input as interleaved versions of data. Soft decision decoding is used in contrast to hard decision, so as to achieve best results. In a turbo decoding system, two component decoders are used. The decisions obtained from one component decoder are passed onto the input of the other decoder. This process is carried out in an iterative manner so as to achieve reliable decisions. Random interleaving at the encoder and the decoding in an iterative manner assures a high error correction capacity of turbo code.

The turbo encoder of Fig. 7.16 can work as a rate 1/3 encoder when puncturing is not applied. With puncturing, it works as a rate 1/2 encoder. Let $d_k = (d_1, d_2, \ldots, d_N)$ represents the input in binary. The input data sequence is given as the input to the first RSC coder, ENC1 from which a coded bit stream x_k^{p1} is obtained. Random interleaver is used for the interleaving of the data. The interleaved data sequence is given as input to the second RSC encoder ENC2, from which a second coded bit stream x_k^{p2} is obtained. The two encoders are usually the same, but the two parity streams will be sufficiently independent if the interleaving is good. The coded sequence generated by the turbo encoder is a multiplexed and possibly punctured stream that consists of systematic code bits x_k^s along with the parity bits of first and second encoders, x_k^{p1} and x_k^{p2}. For example, let the input d_k be (a_1, d_2, d_3, d_4). Let the corresponding parity bit streams be $x_k^{p1} = (x_1^1, x_2^1, x_3^1, x_4^1)$ and $x_k^{p2} = (x_1^2, x_2^2, x_3^2, x_4^2)$. Then the output of the rate 1/2 turbo encoder will be $(d_1, x_1^1, d_2, x_2^2, d_3, x_3^1, d_4, x_4^2)$. The output of the rate 1/3 turbo encoder will be $(d_1, x_1^1, x_1^2, d_2, x_2^1, x_2^2, d_3, x_3^1, x_3^2, d_4, x_4^1, x_4^2)$.

A typical turbo decoder shown in Fig. 7.17, which consists of two component decoders – Decoder 1, DEC1 which is used to decode sequences from Encoder 1 (ENC1), and decoder 2 (DEC2) for decoding sequences from ENC2. It takes a received code sequences $r_k = \{y_k^s \cdot y_k^p\}$. Both DEC1 and DEC2 are maximum-a-posteriori (MAP) decoders. The systematic values of the received sequence y_k^s and the received sequence parity values belonging to the first encoder, namely y_k^{p1} is given to DEC1. Sequence of soft estimates $L_{e1}(\hat{d}_k)$ at the output of the first decoder, is interleaved and given as a-priori information to DEC2. Encoder and decoder use the same interleavers. There will be three inputs to DEC2, namely: interleaved systematic received values y_k^s received parity sequence from the ENC2, y_k^{p2} and interleaved soft estimates $L_{e1}(\hat{d}_k)$. The a-priori information for DEC1 $L_{e2}(\hat{d}_k)$ is obtained from de-interleaving the soft estimates of DEC2. The above procedure is repeated in an iterative manner. The a-posteriori output of the DEC2 is de-interleaved to obtain the log likelihood representation of the estimate of d_k after required number

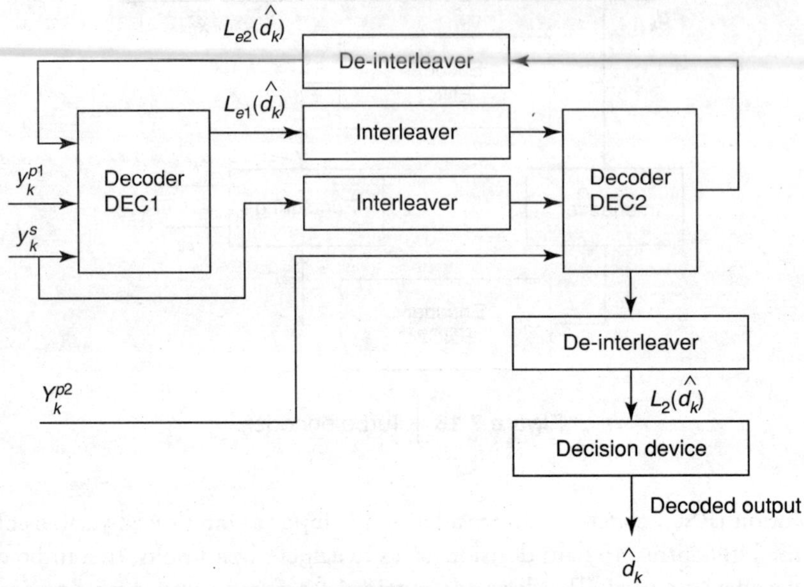

Figure 7.17 | Turbo decoder.

of iterations. Larger negative value of the likelihood ratio $(\wedge \hat{d}_k)$ infers that a bit '0' was more likely to be transmitted. Similarly, bit '1' is more likely to be transmitted if the likelihood ration is a larger positive value. Binary data stream can be then obtained from a hard decision device.

7.9.1 Turbo Decoding Algorithms

Though turbo code exhibits many good features, its computational complexity is very high. A-posteriori probabilities (APPs) for each data bit are required for decoding of turbo codes. Then the data bit value corresponding to the MAP probability for that data bit is taken. Turbo decoding generally uses MAP algorithm. The MAP algorithm divides the paths into two sets, namely, those paths with an information bit one at step k and another that have a zero returning the log-likelihood ratio (LLR) of these two sets. A forward state metric α_k^m, reverse state metric β_k^m and a branch metric $\gamma_k^{j,m}$ at time interval k and state m. The computation of α, β and likelihood ratio are as per the formulae given below:

$$\alpha_k^m = \sum_{j=0} \alpha_{k-1}^{b(j,m)} \gamma_{k-1}^{j,b(j,m)} \tag{7.15}$$

$$\beta_k^m = \sum_{j=0}^{1} \gamma_k^{j,m} \beta_{k+1}^{f(j,m)} \tag{7.16}$$

$$\wedge(\hat{d}_k) = \frac{\sum_m \alpha_k^m \gamma_k^{1,m} \beta_{k+1}^{f(1,m)}}{\sum_m \alpha_k^m \gamma_k^{0,m} \beta_{k+1}^{f(0,m)}}$$

where $\wedge(\hat{d}_k)$ is the likelihood ratio, $b(j, m)$ denotes previous state and $f(j, m)$ denotes next state, given (input, state) as (j, m).

LLR represents a real number corresponding to the soft decision output of a decoder.

$$L(\hat{d}) = L_c(x) + L_a(d) + L_e(\hat{d}) \tag{7.18}$$

where $L_c(x)$, is the channel measurement, $L_a(d)$, is the a-priori knowledge of the data and $L_e(\hat{d})$ is extrinsic LLR, which is the extra knowledge obtained from the decoding process.

To reduce the burden of large computations that are associated with MAP algorithm, some modified versions of the original MAP algorithm are available in literature. Some of them are log-MAP algorithm, soft output Viterbi algorithm (SOVA), max-log-MAP algorithm, and max-log-MAP algorithm with correction factor. Max-log-MAP algorithm reduces computational complexity of log-MAP algorithm, however at the cost of slightly lower BER performance In each step k, it checks for two paths, namely, the best with bit '0' and the best with bit '1', and returns the difference of the log-likelihoods

$$\ln \sum_j e^{a_j} \approx \max_j (a_j) \tag{7.19}$$

In max-log-MAP algorithm with correction factor, Jacobian algorithm is used in the implementation of the log-MAP algorithm which is detailed as follows:

$$\begin{aligned} \ln(e^x + e^y) &= \max(x, y) + \ln(1 + e^{-|x-y|}) \\ &= \max(x, y) + f_c(|x - y|) \end{aligned} \tag{7.20}$$

SOVA decoding works with the same metric as max-log-MAP algorithm, but the reliability information of the decoded bit d_k is computed in a different manner. Here a single competing path is considered per decoding step. For each bit d_k, only the survivor path of the Viterbi algorithm is considered among all the competing paths.

7.10 LDPC Codes

Low density parity check (LDPC) codes were proposed by Gallager in 1961 but these codes were largely ignored until the introduction of turbo codes. LDPC codes were reinvented by Mackay and Neal and by Wiberg in 1996.

Basically, LDPC codes are linear block codes with a very sparse parity check matrix H. For instance, in binary case, a matrix that contains very less number of 1's that are spread among many 0's, hence the name low density parity check. However, the corresponding generator matrix G need not be sparse. The sum–product algorithm can be used for the decoding of LDPC codes. It operates on bipartite graph by the message passing in an iterative manner. Then the parity checks are updated in an iterative manner so as to satisfy all parity equations. The decoder fails if all parity equations cannot be satisfied even after a predefined maximum number of iterations.

LDPC codes differ from turbo codes in terms of the circuit complexities. Unlike turbo codes, LDPC codes offer relatively high encoding complexities with a lesser decoding complexity. In particular, iterative techniques are used in LDPC decoding known as the belief propagation corresponding to those used in

AI applications. Further, the belief propagation decoding can be done in a parallel manner and thus requiring very less complexity for decoding.

LDPC codes are those which approach capacity limits, that is the noise threshold for a memoryless symmetric channel is to be set closer to the theoretical maximum (the Shannon limit). The noise threshold gives an upper bound for the channel noise, up to which the BER can be within a permissible range. LDPC codes can be decoded using iterative belief propagation techniques, in time linear to their block length.

7.10.1 Representation of LDPC Codes

LDPC codes can be represented in two ways: using matrices like any other linear block codes and secondly by a graphical representation.

Matrix Representation

An example for an LDPC matrix is considered first. A parity-check matrix for a (8, 4) code is given in Eq. (7.21).

$$H = \begin{pmatrix} 0 & 1 & 0 & 1 & 1 & 0 & 0 & 1 \\ 1 & 1 & 1 & 0 & 0 & 1 & 0 & 0 \\ 0 & 0 & 1 & 0 & 0 & 1 & 1 & 1 \\ 1 & 0 & 0 & 1 & 1 & 0 & 1 & 0 \end{pmatrix} \tag{7.21}$$

Construction of LDPC Code

There are many algorithms for constructing LDPC codes. Gallager himself has proposed one. MacKay and Neal have introduced one to semi-randomly generate sparse parity check matrices.

A new code can be constructed from a bipartite graph and one or more codes of shorter length, which will be referred to as subcodes. A bipartite graph is shown in Fig 7.18. In bipartite graph, the nodes can be grouped into two disjoint classes. An edge of the graph may connect a node from one set to a node of another. However, no two nodes of the same set can be connected. Digits to which the subcode node is

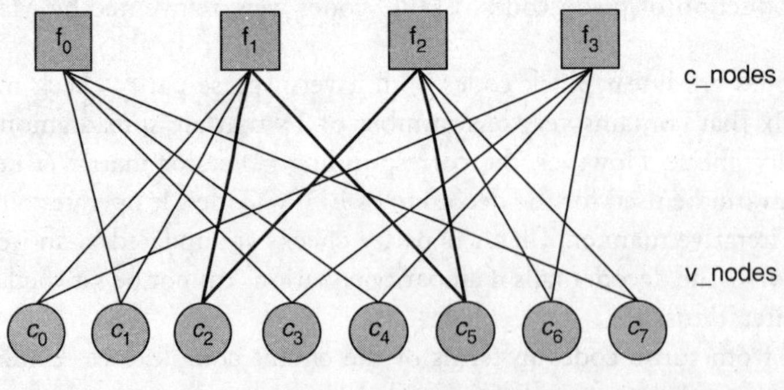

Figure 7.18 | Tanner graph corresponding to the parity-check matrix in Eq. (7.21).

connected forms a word in the corresponding subcode, with the position assigned to each digit corresponds to the label of the connecting edge. Thus, the words in the new code can be defined as a sequence of digits is a codeword if and only if the digits connected to each subcode form a word in the subcode.

Given the matrix H of an arbitrary linear code, the corresponding bipartite graph can be easily constructed by identifying each row with a subcode node, each column with a digit node, and adding an edge in the graph corresponding to each of the nonzero entries in the matrix. The graph so obtained corresponding to a code need not be unique. In other words, more than one graph can be obtained for a same code defined by different matrices. The central idea is to model the equations defining the codes using a graph so as to facilitate encoding and decoding.

Performance and Complexity

LDPC codes can tend to perform near the Shannon limit only if the block lengths are larger. It can be seen that the codes offering such high performances are generally irregular.

Also, larger block lengths imply large G and H matrices. Sparse H matrix has to be reduced to its standard form $[P^T I]$ using elementary matrix reduction operations, thus the resulting matrix need not be sparse. Hence, matrix G of the form $G = [I P]$ is generally not sparse and thus the encoding complexity would be quite high.

As the complexity of the coding is of the order $O(n^2)$ performance of LDPC codes are not good for longer block lengths. Hence, iterative encoding and decoding algorithms are used. These algorithms carry out local calculations and then pass these results via messages in an iterative manner. Local calculations aim at dividing a larger complex problem into simple sub-problems. A sparse H matrix now helps to conquer these algorithms in various ways. Firstly, the local calculations are made simpler and the complexity of combining the sub-problems also has to be reduced. Furthermore, iterative algorithms used at decoders perform closer to the optimum maximum likelihood decoding.

7.11 Introduction to Trellis Coded Modulation

Modulation and coding were considered to be two different independent entities in a digital communication system. Although the goal of both modulation and coding is to achieve error-free transmission over the communication channel, both were considered to be optimized independently of one another. In early 1980's, a novel concept of combining modulation with coding has been proposed resulted in Trellis coded modulation (TCM). Coded modulation further improves the distance properties and thus results in a more efficient data transmission. The idea behind TCM is to code the information symbol-wise instead of coding it as a long bit stream.

7.11.1 Euclidian Distance

It is the distance between any two points on the Euclidian space. The Euclidian distance between any two points (x_1, y_1) and (x_2, y_2) is given by

$$ED = \sqrt{(x_1 - x_2)^2 + (y_1 - y_2)^2} \tag{7.22}$$

In terms of modulation, the Euclidian distance is the distance between any two points in the constellation diagram of a modulation technique. Consider an 8-PSK with 8 points in the constellation diagram shown in Fig. 7.19. Each point in the constellation diagram represents a particular amplitude and phase. The Euclidian distances among the points are shown.

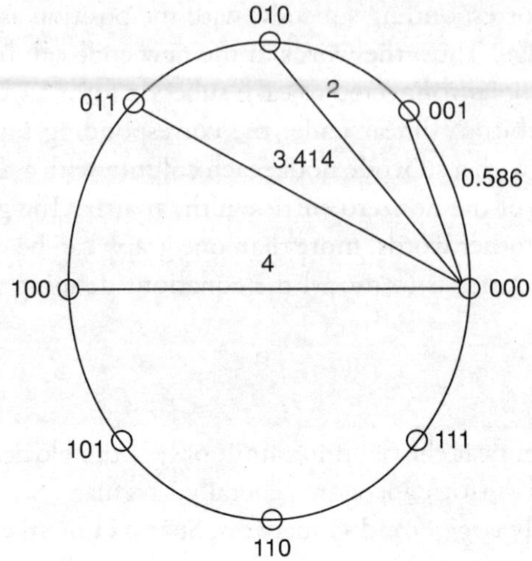

Figure 7.19 | Constellation diagram of an 8-PSK.

The minimum Euclidian distance between any two paths in the Trellis is called the free Euclidian distance, ED_{free}.

7.11.2 Mapping by Set Partitioning

In this method, the partitioning a 2^n-ary signal into subsets such that the minimum Euclidian distance will keep increasing after every partition. Each partition reduces the number of signal points in the constellation, however increases the minimum Euclidian distance.

To make the concept clearer, consider the following example of an 8-ary PSK.

Initially, there will be 8 points in the constellation with a minimum Euclidian distance of d_1 (shown in Fig. 7.20). After the first partition, we will have two partitions of 4 points each with a minimum Euclidian distance of d_2. Obviously, d_2 is greater than d_1 (Fig. 7.21).

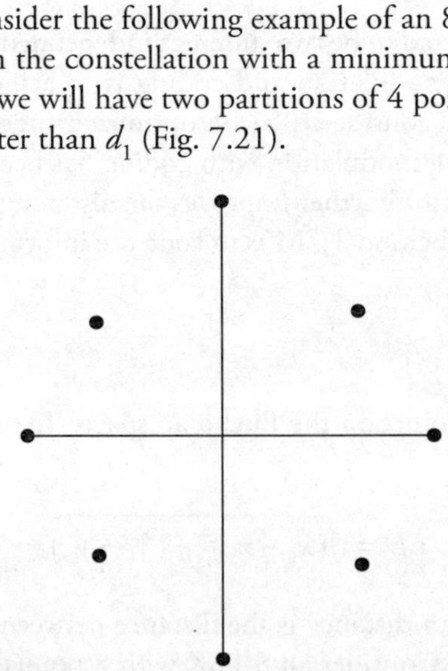

Figure 7.20 | Constellation of an 8-PSK.

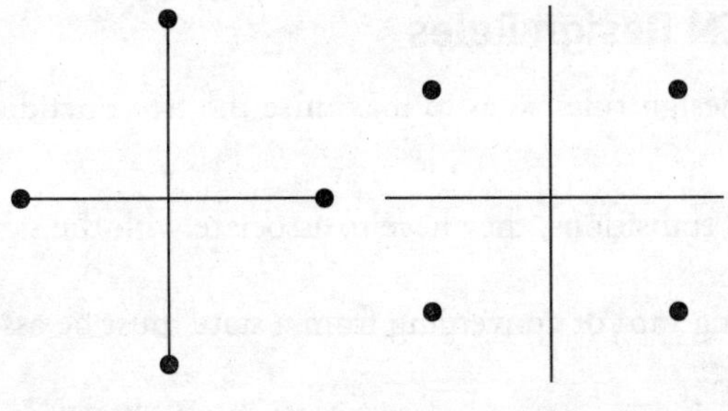

Figure 7.21 | Constellation of an 8-PSK after first partitioning.

After the next level of partition, we have 2 signals each with an increased minimum distance of d_3. It is as shown in Fig. 7.22.

Finally, we will have one signal point in each partition with a minimum Euclidian distance increased to d_4 (Fig. 7.23).

However, it is not required to keep partitioning till we reach partitions with one symbol each. Instead the partitioning is continued till we reach the minimum Euclidian distance larger than the desired minimum Euclidian distance.

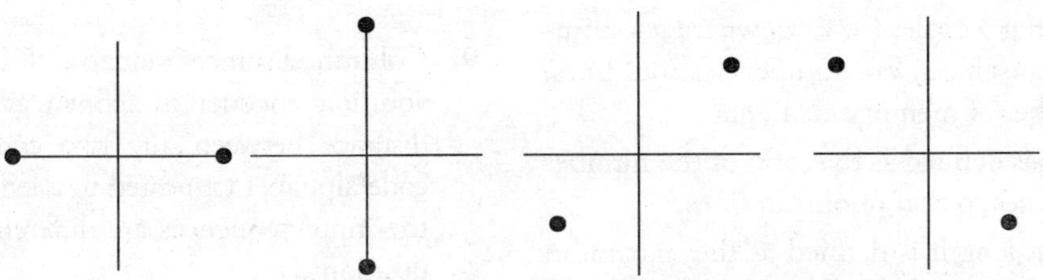

Figure 7.22 | Constellation of an 8-PSK after second partitioning.

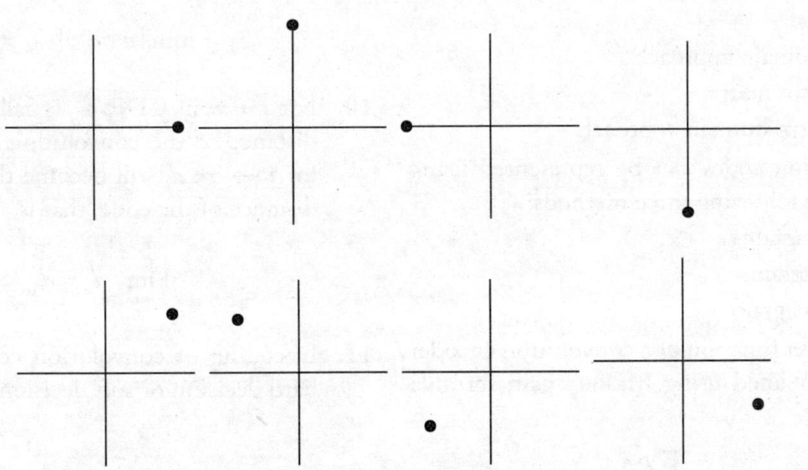

Figure 7.23 | Constellation of an 8-PSK after third partitioning.

7.11.3 Ungerboeck's TCM Design Rules

Ungerboek proposed a set of design rules so as to maximize the free Euclidian distance in TCM. They are as follows:

(a) If there are any parallel transitions, they have to associate with the signals in the lowest layer of the set partitioning tree.

(b) The transitions diverging into or converging from a state must be associated with the signals of the first step of partitioning.

(c) All signals are considered to be of equal frequency in the Trellis diagram.

Summary

1. Error control codes are classified into two categories:
   - Block codes
   - Convolution codes
2. A typical convolution encoder can be characterized using 3 tuples (n, k, m) where n = number of output lines, k = number of input lines, m = number of memory elements
3. Code rate is defined as the ratio of the number of input lines to that of output lines.
4. Constraint length is defined as the maximum number of output bits of the encoder affected by a single input.
5. Encoding of the convolution codes can be done using
   - Time-domain approach
   - Generator matrix
   - Transform-domain approach
6. Convolution codes can be represented using any of the following three methods:
   - State diagrams
   - Tree diagrams
   - Trellis diagram
7. The transfer function of a convolution encoder can be obtained using Mason's gain formula given by

$$T(D) = \frac{\sum_i P_i \Delta_i}{\Delta}$$

8. Minimum free distance (d_{free}) is defined as the minimum distance among all pairs of codewords in the convolution code alphabet.

$$d_{\text{free}} \triangleq \min\left\{d(v', v''): u' \neq u''\right\}$$

9. Column distance function (CDF) for a convolution encoder is defined as the minimum distance between any two codewords in the code alphabet truncated to a length i given that the input sequences are different for first k-bit positions:

$$d_i \triangleq \min\left\{d[v']_i, [v'']_i) : [u']_k \neq [u'']_k\right\}$$

$$= \min\left\{w[v]_i : [u]_k \neq 0\right\}$$

10. For $i = m$ in CDF, d_m is called the minimum distance of the convolution encoder, whereas for $i \to \infty$, d_i will become the minimum free distance of the code, that is,

$$\lim_{i \to \infty} d_i = d_{\text{free}}$$

11. Decoding of convolution code can be either hard decision or soft decision.

Review Questions

1. For the (3, 2, 1) convolution encoder shown in Fig. 7.24, find the codeword for the input sequence $u = [1\ 1\ 0\ 1\ 1\ 0]$ using
   (a) Time-domain approach
   (b) Transform-domain approach
   (c) Matrix method
2. Repeat Problem 1 for $u = [1\ 0\ 1\ 0\ 1\ 1]$.
3. For the convolution encoder shown in Fig. 7.25, find *n, k, m* and code rate. Also find the output sequence for the input message sequence (1 1 0 0 1 1) using time-domain approach.
4. For the convolution encoder shown in Problem 3, compute the encoded sequence for the input $u(x) = 1 + x + x^3 + x^5$. Use transform-domain approach.
5. For the given $r = 1/2$, constraint length $k = 4$ convolution code shown in Fig. 7.26, determine the encoder output produced by the message sequence (1 0 1 1 1) using
   (a) Time-domain approach
   (b) Transform-domain approach
   (c) Matrix method
6. Consider a (2, 1, 2) convolution code with generator polynomials $g_1 = (1\ 0\ 1)$ and $g_2 = (0\ 1\ 1)$. Draw its encoder diagram. Also find the

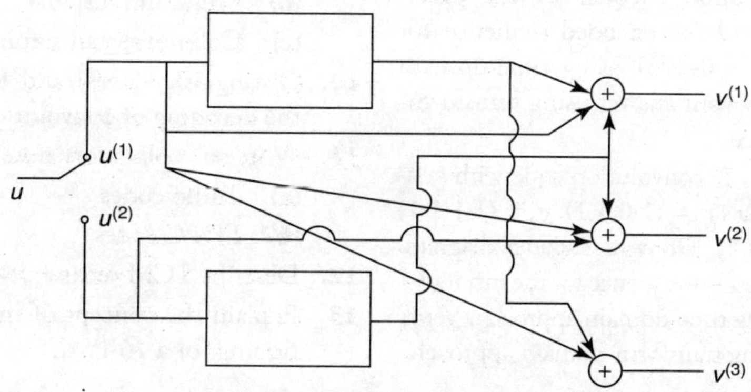

Figure 7.24 | A (3, 2, 1) convolution encoder.

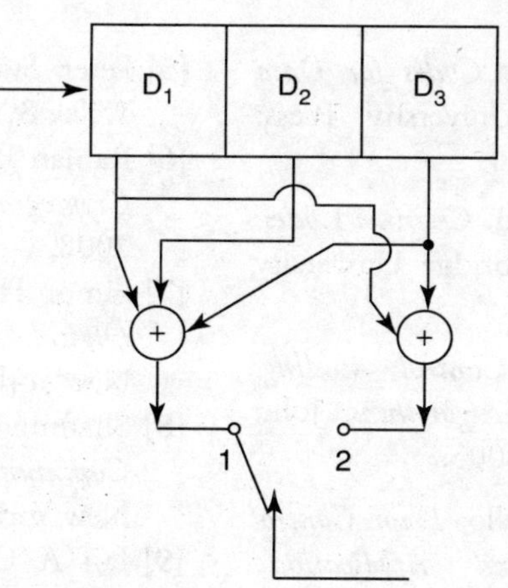

Figure 7.25 | Convolution encoder.

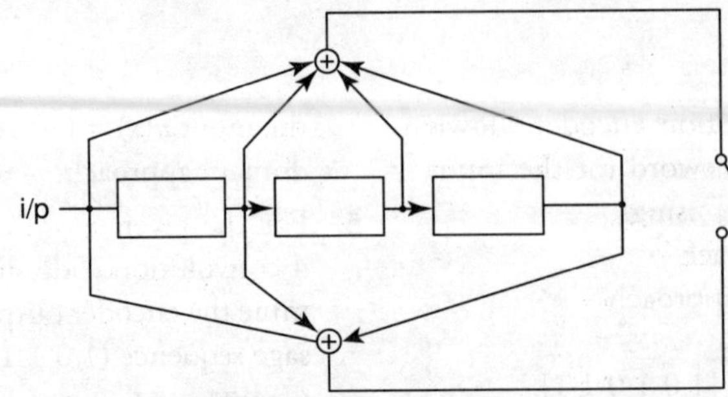

Figure 7.26 | A (2, 1, 3) convolution encoder.

encoded sequence for the input (1 0 1 1 0 1) using matrix approach.

7. For the convolution encoder in the previous problem, find the encoded sequence for the input (1 1 1 0 1 1) using time-domain approach. Verify your answer using transform-domain approach.
8. Consider a (3, 1, 3) convolution code with generator polynomials $g_1 = (1\ 0\ 1\ 1)$, $g_2 = (1\ 1\ 1\ 1)$ and $g_3 = (1\ 1\ 0\ 1)$. Draw its encoder diagram. Also find the encoded sequence for the input (1 1 1 0 1 1 0 1) using time-domain approach. Verify your answer using transform-domain approach.
9. Define
   (a) Free distance
   (b) Minimum distance
   (c) Column distance function
10. Distinguish Viterbi and Stack algorithms for the decoding of convolution codes.
11. Write an explanatory note on
    (a) Turbo codes
    (b) LDPC codes
12. Describe TCM technique in detail.
13. Explain the concept of mapping by set partitioning for a 16-PSK.

Further Reading

[1] Richerd E Blahut, *Algebraic Codes for Data Transmission,* Cambridge University Press: Cambridge; 2003.

[2] Willium E Ryan and Shu Lin, *Channel Codes: Classical and Modern,* Cambridge University Press: Cambridge; 2009.

[3] Tood K Moon, *Error Control Coding: Mathematical Methods and Algorithms,* John Wiley & Sons: New Jersey; 2005.

[4] Shu Lin and Daniel J Costello, *Error Control Coding: Fundamentals and Applications,* Prentice Hall Series, Inc: Englewood Cliffs, NJ; 1983.

[5] Peter Sweeney, *Error Control Coding,* John Wiley & Sons: New York; 1991.

[6] Ranjan Bose, *Information Theory, Coding and Cryptography,* Tata McGraw Hill: New Delhi; 2008.

[7] Simon Haykin, *An Introduction to Analog and Digital Communications,* John Wiley & Sons: New York; 1989.

[8] Shanmugam K Sam, *Digital and Analog Communication Systems,* John Wiley & Sons: New York; 1989.

[9] Ian A Glover and Peter M Grant, *Digital Communications,* Pearson Education: Upper Saddle River, NJ; 2004.

[10] Bernard Sklar and Pabitra K Ray, *Digital Communications: Fundamentals and Applications*, Pearson Education: Delhi; 2001.

[11] Andrea Goldsmith, *Wireless Communications*, Cambridge University Press: Cambridge; 2005.

[12] John G Proakis and Masoud Salehi, *Contemporary Communication System using MATLAB*, PWS Publishing: Boston, MA; 1998.

[13] Rolando A Carrasco and Martin Johnston, *Non-Binary Error Control Coding for Wireless Communication and Data Storage*, John Wiley & Sons: Chichester; 2008.

[14] Leon W Couch, *Digital and Analog Communication Systems*, 5th Ed., Pearson Education: Upper Saddle River, NJ; 2007.

[15] S Benedetto, D Divsalar, G Montorsi, F Pollara, Serial concatenation of interleaved codes: performance analysis, design, and iterative decoding, *IEEE Transactions on Information Theory*, vol. 44, no. 3, pp. 909, 926; May 1998.

[16] S Benedetto and G Montorsi, Unveiling turbo codes: some results on parallel concatenated coding schemes, *IEEE Transactions on Information Theory*, vol. 42, no. 2, pp. 409, 428; Mar 1996.

[17] C Berrou, A Glavieux and P Thitimajshima, Near Shannon limit error-correcting coding and decoding: turbo codes, *IEEE International Conference on Communications*, Houston, TX, pp. 1064–1070; 1993.

[18] A Glavieux (Ed.), *Channel Coding in Communication Networks – From Theory to Turbocodes*. John Wiley & Sons with ISTE Ltd.: Clementi Loop, Singapore; 2007.

[19] WJ Gross and PG Gulak, Simplified MAP algorithm suitable for implementation of turbo decoders, *Electronics Letters*, vol. 34, no. 16, pp. 1577–1578; 1998.

[20] DJC Mackay and RM Neal, Near Shannon limit performance of low density parity check codes, *Electronics Letters*, vol. 32, no. 18, pp. 1645–1646; 1996.

[21] DJ MacKay, Near Shannon limit performance of low density parity check codes, *Electronics Letters*, vol. 33, no. 6, pp. 457–458; 1997.

[22] DJ MacKay, *Good error-correcting codes based on very sparse matrices. IEEE Transactions on Information Theory*, vol. 45, no. 2, pp. 399–431; 1999.

[23] N Miladinovic and M Fossorier, Systematic recursive construction of LDPC codes. *IEEE Communication Letters*, vol. 8, no. 5, pp. 302–304; 2004.

[24] HM Savitha, *Energy Efficient Error Control Techniques for OFDM Systems with their Applicability to Power Line and Wireless Communication Channels*, Research Thesis, NITK: Surathkal; 2014.

[25] Geetha Prakash, *Rateless Codes for Transmission Over Free Space Optics Using Stochastic Models Based on Scintillation Theory and Their Application to Optical Wireless Sensor Networks*, Research Thesis, NITK: Surathkal; 2014.

[26] Bane Vasic. Ivan B. Djordjevic. and Raymond K. Kostuk, Low-density parity check codes and iterative decoding for long-haul optical communication systems, *Journal of Lightwave Technology*, vol. 21, no. 2, pp. 438–446; February 2003.

[27] Po-Yuan Huang, *A Theoretic Study on Three Low-Density Parity-Check and BCH Concatenated Coding Schemes*, Institute of Communications Engineering, National Chiao Tung University: Taiwan; June 2012.

[28] Yifei Zhang and William E Ryan, Toward low LDPC-code floors: a case study, *IEEE Transactions On Communications*, vol. 57, no. 6, pp. 1566–1573; 2009.

[29] H Meliani and A Benidir, *Coding and Decoding Algorithms for BCH Codes*, Al-Ahsa College of Technology, KSA University of Blida: Algeria.

[30] Sarah J Johnson, *Introducing Low-Density Parity-Check Codes*, School of Electrical Engineering and Computer Science, The University of Newcastle: Australia; 2006.

[31] HM Savitha and Muralidhar Kulkarni, Performance evaluation of turbo coded OFDM systems and application of turbo decoding for impulsive channel, *ICTACT Journal on Communication Technology*, vol. 1, no. 3, pp. 175–183; 2010.

[32] HM Savitha and Muralidhar Kulkarni, *Performance comparison of hard and soft-decision turbo coded OFDM systems*, Proc. of 2010 IEEE International Conference on Wireless Communication, Networking, and Internet Security (WCNIS 2010), pp. 551–555; 2010.

[33] HM Savitha, Muralidhar Kulkarni, *An improved turbo decoding scheme for impulsive channel*, Proc. of 5th International Conference on Industrial and Information Systems (ICIIS 2010), pp. 135–139; 2010.

8 Cryptography and Information Security

'There are no secrets better kept than the secrets that everybody guesses.'

–George Bernard Shaw

Learning Objectives

After reading this chapter, you will be able to:

- Understand the need for information security in the communication systems.
- Introduce and define different cryptographic algorithms.
- Detail various encryption and decryption algorithms.
- Analyze different cryptanalysis techniques.

8.1 Introduction

Some communication applications require sending information secretly, in which case we need to hide the actual information content in the message during transmission such that only the intended receiver can properly extract the message. Cryptography is a branch of engineering that deals with encrypting and decrypting the information. A method of converting the message or information to an unreadable form is called encryption, and the process of extracting actual information at the receiver's end is called decryption.

8.1.1 Definitions

1. **Plain text:** It is the actual information which has to be communicated in a secure manner.
2. **Cipher text:** It is the message coded using an algorithm such that no one except the intended receiver can understand the information.
3. **Key:** It is a mathematical value using which a cryptographic algorithm can generate a cipher text from the plain text. Longer the key, better the security.
4. **Cryptanalysis:** The process of analyzing a cryptosystem either for its correctness or its ability to withstand the attacks or to break the system is known as cryptanalysis.
5. **Attacker:** An unintended receiver who performs cryptanalysis in order to break a cryptosystem is called the attacker.
6. **Passive attack:** An attack that tries to read the hidden information in the cipher text, but does not attempt to modify it is a passive attack.
7. **Active attack:** An attack that intends not only to listen to the conversation by an unintended user but also to alter the system or information is an active attack.

8.1.2 Cryptographic Attributes

Before starting our actual discussion on various cryptographic algorithms, it is worth defining some of the basic attributes of cryptography.

1. **Authentication:** Guaranteeing that the person who sent the information is the same who claims to have sent it. In other words, it is the proof of ownership of the message.
2. **Confidentiality:** Making the data secured from the unauthorized entities. In other words, it ensures that the data is free from passive attacks.
3. **Integrity:** Guaranteeing the received data to be the same as the transmitted one. In other words, it is an assurance that the message has remained unchanged during its transmission from the sender to the receiver.
4. **Non-repudiation:** Ensuring protection against the denial of having participated in a communication by an entity.

Any cryptographic algorithm has to ensure these above-mentioned security services.

8.2 Introduction to Number Theory

8.2.1 Congruence

For any three elements *a*, *b* and *N*, we can write

$$a \equiv b \bmod N \quad \text{if and only if } (a - b) \mid N \tag{8.1}$$

In other words, if dividing '*a*' and '*b*' by *N* results in the same remainder, we can say

$$a \equiv b \bmod N \tag{8.2}$$

Properties of congruences:

1. If $a \equiv b \bmod N$, then $b \equiv a \bmod N$.
2. If $a_1 \equiv b_1 \bmod N$ and $a_2 \equiv b_2 \bmod N$, then $a_1 + a_2 \equiv b_1 + b_2 \bmod N$ and $a_1 a_2 \equiv b_1 b_2 \bmod N$.
3. If $a \equiv b \bmod N$ and $b \equiv c \bmod N$, then $a \equiv c \bmod N$.
4. If $a \equiv b \bmod N_1$ and $a \equiv b \bmod N_2$ and if N_1 and N_2 are relatively prime, then $a \equiv b \bmod N_1 N_2$.

To understand the concept better, consider an example of 12 mod 10. To find its value, divide 12 by 10 and find the remainder. This would be 2 in this case. Thus 12 mod 10 ≡ 2. Similarly 14 mod 5 ≡ 4, 256 mod 100 ≡ 56 and so on.

8.2.2 Chinese Remainder Theorem

Suppose that $N_1, N_2, N_3, \ldots, N_k$ are relatively prime numbers and if $n_1, n_2, n_3, \ldots, n_k$ are some integers, then the following simultaneous congruence:

$$y \equiv n_1 \bmod N_1$$

$$y \equiv n_2 \bmod N_2$$

$$y \equiv n_3 \bmod N_3 \tag{8.3}$$

$$\cdots$$

$$y \equiv n_k \bmod N_k$$

will have a solution in unique modulo $M = N_1 N_2 N_3 \ldots N_k$ given by

$$y \equiv (n_1 m_1 M_1 + n_2 m_2 M_2 + \cdots + n_k m_k M_k) \bmod M \tag{8.4}$$

where m_i is the inverse of M_i mod N_i, i.e. $m_i M_i \equiv 1 \bmod N_i$ and $M_i = M/N_i$.

EXAMPLE 8.1

Find the smallest non-negative solution to the following congruences.

$$y \equiv 2 \bmod 3$$
$$y \equiv 3 \bmod 5$$
$$y \equiv 4 \bmod 11$$
$$y \equiv 5 \bmod 16$$

Solution: The given simultaneous congruences can be solved using Chinese remainder theorem. Given

$$n_1 = 2;\ n_2 = 3;\ n_3 = 4;\ n_4 = 5$$

and

$$N_1 = 3;\ N_2 = 5;\ N_3 = 11;\ N_4 = 16$$

The value of M can be found using,

$$M = 3 \times 5 \times 11 \times 16 = 2640$$

Now

$$M_1 = \frac{M}{N_1} = 880$$

$$M_2 = \frac{M}{N_2} = 528$$

$$M_3 = \frac{M}{N_3} = 240$$

$$M_4 = \frac{M}{N_4} = 165$$

The inverse elements for M_i can be obtained as follows:

$$m_1 = M_1^{-1} \bmod N_1 \equiv 880^{-1} \bmod 3 \equiv 1$$

$$m_2 = M_2^{-1} \bmod N_2 \equiv 528^{-1} \bmod 5 \equiv 2$$

$$m_3 = M_3^{-1} \bmod N_3 \equiv 240^{-1} \bmod 11 \equiv 5$$

$$m_4 = M_4^{-1} \bmod N_4 \equiv 165^{-1} \bmod 16 \equiv 13$$

Therefore, the solution for the given simultaneous congruences is

$$y \equiv (n_1\, m_1\, M_1 + n_2\, m_2\, M_2 + n_3\, m_3\, M_3 + n_4\, m_4\, M_4) \bmod M$$

$$y \equiv (2 \times 1 \times 880) + (3 \times 2 \times 528) + (4 \times 5 \times 240) + (5 \times 13 \times 165) \equiv 20473 \bmod 2640 = 1973$$

8.2.3 Fermat's Little Theorem

Fermat's little theorem can be stated as follows:

Statement: For any integer 'a' with a prime number 'p'

$$a^p \equiv a \bmod p \tag{8.5}$$

If 'p' is not a factor of 'a', then

$$a^{p-1} \equiv 1 \bmod p \tag{8.6}$$

Proof: Consider a finite field Z_p which consists of numbers 0, 1, 2, 3, …, $p - 1$.
Consider multiplying all elements of Z_p by an integer 'a' and take mod p on the product such that 'a' is relatively prime to 'p'. That is 'a' and 'p' do not share common divisors.

In other words, consider the following products:

$$a \cdot 0 \bmod p,\ a \cdot 1 \bmod p,\ a \cdot 2 \bmod p,\ \ldots,\ a \cdot (p-1) \bmod p$$

We have $a \cdot 0 \bmod p \equiv 0$.

Clearly, the remaining set of $(p - 1)$ products would result in elements 1, 2, …, $(p - 1)$ in some order, as 'a' and 'p' are relatively prime.

Thus, we can write

$$a \cdot 2a \cdot 3a \cdot (p-1) \cdot a \equiv 1 \cdot 2 \cdot 3 \cdot (p-1) \bmod p$$

$$(p-1)!\, a^{(p-1)} \equiv (p-1)! \bmod p$$

Therefore, $a^{(p-1)} \equiv 1 \bmod p$.

Euler has a proposed a general case of the Fermat's little theorem which can be given as follows:

$$a^{\phi(p)} \equiv 1 \bmod p \tag{8.7}$$

where $\phi(p)$ is the Euler's totient (ϕ) function defined in Definition 1.8 of Chapter 1.

Obviously, for p being a prime $\phi(p) = (p - 1)$ which reduces the theorem to Fermat's little theorem.

8.2.4 Modular Exponentiation

Euler's theorem presented in Section 8.2.3 finds many applications. One such application is to find the value of a larger exponent of a number which is required for some of the cryptographic applications. To make this concept clearer, consider finding a^n mod N for large 'n' which cannot be solved directly. Using the Euler's theorem, we can find the exponentiation a^n mod N by following the steps:

Step 1: Represent N as a product of primes $p_1, p_2, p_3, \ldots$.
Step 2: Find $\phi(p_1), \phi(p_2), \phi(p_3), \ldots$.
Step 3: Find the LCM of $\phi(p_1), \phi(p_2), \phi(p_3), \ldots$, say L.
Step 4: Obviously $a^L \equiv 1 \bmod N$ from Euler's theorem.
Step 5: Raise a^L appropriately and simplify so as to get a^n mod N.

To understand the procedure, consider the following examples.

EXAMPLE 8.2

Find the value of 2^{1010} mod 39.

Solution:

Step 1: Firstly, we need to represent 39 as a product of prime numbers

$$39 = 13 \times 3$$

Step 2: Calculate the totient values for 13 and 3

$$\phi(13) = 12 \quad \text{and} \quad \phi(3) = 2$$

Step 3: Find the LCM of 12 and 2 which is equal to 12.
Thus, from Euler's theorem, $2^{12} \bmod 39 \equiv 1$

Step 4: We can represent 2^{1010} as

$$2^{1010} = 2^{12 \times 84} \cdot 2^2 \bmod 39 \equiv 4 \bmod 39 \ [\text{as } (2^{12})^{\times 84} \cdot \bmod 39 \equiv 1]$$

Therefore,

$$2^{1010} \bmod 39 \equiv 4 \bmod 39 \equiv 4$$

EXAMPLE 8.3

Find the value of $3^{1000000}$ mod 77.

Solution:

Step 1: Firstly, we need to represent 77 as a product of prime numbers

$$77 = 11 \times 7$$

Step 2: Calculate the totient values for 11 and 7

$$\phi(11) = 10 \quad \text{and} \quad \phi(7) = 6$$

Step 3: LCM of 10 and 6 is 30. Thus $3^{30} \bmod 77 \equiv 1$

Step 4: We can represent $3^{1000000}$ as

$$3^{1000000} = 3^{30 \times 33333} \cdot 3^{10} \bmod 77 \equiv 3^{10} \bmod 77$$

Therefore,

$$3^{1000000} \bmod 77 \equiv 3^{10} \bmod 77 \equiv 59049 \bmod 77 \equiv 67$$

8.2.4.1 Modular Exponentiation Using Repeated Squaring Method

Most of the cryptographic algorithms require to calculate a^n mod N. Although Euler's theorem can be used to find the congruence, as seen in Examples 8.2 and 8.3, it would become complex if both 'n' and 'N' are large values. For such situations, the value of the congruence can be obtained using repeated squaring method which is detailed as follows:

Step 1: Represent 'm' bit binary equivalent of 'n' say $[n_{m-1}\, n_{m-2}\, n_{m-3} \ldots n_2\, n_1\, n_0]$. Initialize $\alpha = 1$ and $\beta_0 = a$.
Step 2: If $n_0 = 1$, replace $\alpha = \beta_0$, else $\alpha = 1$. Also make $\beta_1 = \beta_0^2$ mod N.
Step 3: If $n_1 = 1$, replace $\alpha = \alpha \cdot \beta_1$ mod N, else keep α unchanged. Make $\beta_2 = \beta_1^2$ mod N.
Step 4: If $n_2 = 1$, replace $\alpha = \alpha \cdot \beta_2$ mod N, else keep α unchanged. Set $\beta_3 = \beta_2^2$ mod N.
Step 5: Continue the above step for 'm' iterations. Finally, 'α' contains the required result.

EXAMPLE 8.4

Find the value of 2^{55} mod 77 using repeated squaring approach.

Solution:

Step 1: Represent (55) in binary $(55)_{10} = (110111)_2$. Clearly

$$n_0 = 1,\ n_1 = 1,\ n_2 = 1,\ n_3 = 0,\ n_4 = 1,\ n_5 = 1. \text{ Also set } \alpha = 1 \text{ and } \beta_0 = 2$$

Step 2: As $n_0 = 1$, $\alpha = \beta_0 = 2$. Squaring β_0, $\beta_1 = \beta_0^2 \equiv 4 \bmod 77 \equiv 4$
Step 3: As $n_1 = 1$, $\alpha = \alpha \cdot \beta_1 = 2 \cdot 4 = 8 \bmod 77 \equiv 8$

$$\text{Set } \beta_2 = \beta_1^2 = 16 \bmod 77 \equiv 16$$

Step 4: Now $n_2 = 1$. Thus $\alpha = \alpha \cdot \beta_2 = 8 \cdot 16 \bmod 77 \equiv 51$

$$\text{Set } \beta_3 = \beta_2^2 \bmod 77 = 16^2 \bmod 77 \equiv 25$$

Step 5: As $n_3 = 0$, no change in α.

$$\text{Set } \beta_4 = \beta_3^2 = 25^2 \bmod 77 \equiv 9$$

Step 6: Similarly $n_4 = 1$, $\alpha = \alpha \cdot \beta_4 = 51 \cdot 9 = 459 \bmod 77 \equiv 74$

$$\text{Set } \beta_5 = \beta_4^2 = 9^2 \bmod 77 \equiv 4$$

Step 7: Finally, $n_5 = 1$, $\alpha = \alpha \cdot \beta_5 = 74 \cdot 4 = 116 \bmod 77 \equiv 65$

$$\text{Set } \beta_6 = \beta_5^2 = 4^2 \bmod 77 \equiv 16$$

As we are done with all the bits, the process is complete. The value of α gives the required result. Hence, we have $2^{55} \bmod 77 \equiv 65$.

EXAMPLE 8.5

Find the value of $3^{98} \bmod 65$ using repeated squaring approach.

Solution:

Step 1: Represent 98 in binary. That is $(98)_{10} = (1100010)_2$. Clearly,

$$n_0 = 0,\ n_1 = 1,\ n_2 = 0,\ n_3 = 0,\ n_4 = 0,\ n_5 = 1 \quad \text{and} \quad n_6 = 1. \text{ Also set } \alpha = 1 \text{ and } \beta_0 = 3$$

Step 2: As $n_0 = 0$, $\alpha = 1$. Squaring β_0, $\beta_1 = \beta_0^2 \equiv 9 \bmod 65 \equiv 9$

Step 3: As $n_1 = 1$, $\alpha = \alpha \cdot \beta_1 = 1 \cdot 9 = 9 \bmod 65 \equiv 9$

$$\text{Set } \beta_2 = \beta_1^2 = 81 \bmod 65 \equiv 16$$

Step 4: Now $n_2 = 0$. No change in α. Set $\beta_3 = \beta_2^2 \bmod 65 = 16^2 \bmod 65 \equiv 61$

Step 5: As $n_3 = 0$, no change in α.

$$\text{Set } \beta_4 = \beta_3^2 = 61^2 \bmod 65 \equiv 16$$

Step 6: Similarly as $n_4 = 0$, no change in α.

$$\text{Set } \beta_5 = \beta_4^2 = 16^2 \bmod 65 \equiv 61$$

Step 7: Also, $n_5 = 1$, $\alpha = \alpha \cdot \beta_5 = 9 \cdot 61 = 549 \bmod 65 \equiv 29$

$$\text{Set } \beta_6 = \beta_5^2 = 61^2 \bmod 65 \equiv 16$$

Step 8: Finally, $n_6 = 1$, $\alpha = \alpha \cdot \beta_6 = 29 \cdot 16 = 549 \bmod 65 \equiv 9$

$$\text{Set } \beta_6 = \beta_5^2 = 16^2 \bmod 65 \equiv 61$$

Thus, we have $3^{98} \bmod 65 \equiv 9$.

8.2.5 Random Number Generation

Random numbers are widely used in cryptographic algorithms. Majority of the cryptographic algorithms require the usage of random numbers. Thus, generation of random numbers becomes an essential task.

Many algorithms were proposed to generate such random sequences. One such simplest approach is to make use of the following relation to generate the numbers in a random fashion.

$$R_i = K_1 R_{i-1} + K_2 \bmod N \tag{8.8}$$

where R_i is the number generated in the current instance, R_{i-1} is the random number generated in the previous iteration, K_1 and K_2 are constants and N is the modulus value.

The sequence thus generated from the above relation is called *pseudo random sequence.*

8.2.6 Prime Number Generation

There are sophisticated computer algorithms to generate the random numbers. These algorithms generate a sequence of numbers such that one cannot predict or regenerate the same and these numbers thus generated should satisfy the properties of a random number. However, sometimes, we may require to generate prime numbers in a random fashion. In such cases, the random number generators can be used to perform such tasks. The procedure is as follows:

1. Generate a large number 'p' using pseudo random number generator.
2. If 'p' is even, it cannot be a prime number. Thus set $p = p + 1$. Check for the primality for the number so generated.
3. If the test succeeds, consider 'p' as a choice for the prime number; else proceed with the higher values of 'p'.
4. Repeat the above step till a first prime number greater than or equal to 'p' is obtained.

8.2.7 Quadratic Residue mod *p*

Consider a prime field, F_p for $p > 2$. Then F_p consists of the 'p' elements {0, 1, 2, 3, ... $(p - 1)$}. The elements in F_p – {0}, which are square of some numbers are called quadratic residue modulo p.

Take an example of F_5. Clearly F_5 consists of {0, 1, 2, 3, 4}. F_5 – {0} becomes {1, 2, 3, 4}. Consider computing the square of the numbers in modulo 5, starting from 1.

$$1^2 \bmod 5 \equiv 1$$
$$2^2 \bmod 5 \equiv 4$$
$$3^2 \bmod 5 \equiv 4$$
$$4^2 \bmod 5 \equiv 1$$

Therefore, the elements 1 and 4 form quadratic residue of mod 5. In general, any field F_p will have $\left(\frac{p-1}{2}\right)$ number of square elements. Also the entries in the above list are symmetric. Thus to compute quadratic residue modulo p, only $a^2 \bmod p$ for $a = 1, 2, \ldots, \left(\frac{p-1}{2}\right)$ are to be considered.

EXAMPLE 8.6

Find the quadratic residues in F_7.

Solution: Consider the field $F_7 - \{0\} = \{1, 2, 3, 4, 5, 6\}$

Now calculate $a^2 \bmod p$ for $a = 1, 2, 3$

$$1^2 \bmod 7 \equiv 1$$
$$2^2 \bmod 7 \equiv 4$$
$$3^2 \bmod 7 \equiv 2$$

Thus elements 1, 4 and 2 are quadratic residue modulo 7.

8.2.8 Legendre Symbol

For an integer 'a' and a prime number 'p' > 2, we can define Legendre symbol as

$$\left(\frac{a}{p}\right) = \begin{cases} 1, & \text{if '}a\text{' is a quadratic residue mod } p \\ -1, & \text{if '}a\text{' is a quadratic non-residue mod } p \\ 0, & \text{if '}a\text{' is divisible by '}p\text{'} \end{cases} \tag{8.9}$$

EXAMPLE 8.7

Determine the values of the following Legendre polynomials:

(a) $\left(\frac{3}{5}\right)$

(b) $\left(\frac{14}{7}\right)$

(c) $\left(\frac{4}{5}\right)$

Solution:

(a) Clearly 3 is not a quadratic residue mod 5. Also it is not divisible by 5. Thus $\left(\frac{3}{5}\right) = -1$.

(b) 14 is divisible by 7. Thus $\left(\frac{14}{7}\right) = 0$.

(c) 4 is a quadratic residue mod 5. As $2^2 \bmod 5 \equiv 4$. Thus $\left(\frac{4}{5}\right) = 1$.

8.2.9 Jacobi Symbol

Consider an integer '*a*'. Let *N* be a positive odd number (need not be a prime). Now, *N* can be represented using its prime factors as follows:

$$N = p_1^{n_1} \times p_1^{n_2} \times \cdots \times p_1^{n_q}$$

Then the Jacobi symbol $\left(\frac{a}{N}\right)$ can be represented as a product of Legendre symbols as follows:

$$\left(\frac{a}{N}\right) = \left(\frac{a}{p_1}\right) n_1 \times \left(\frac{a}{p_2}\right) n_2 \times \cdots \times \left(\frac{a}{p_q}\right) n_q \tag{8.10}$$

8.2.10 Discrete Logarithms

While working with real numbers, finding the exponent of a number is as hard as finding a logarithm. In other words, it is not easier to find the exponentiation than finding the logarithms. However, it is not true in case of finite fields. Consider an example of a prime field F_p. Finding $a^n \bmod p$ for some '*a*' and '*n*' would be easier using any of the methods of modular exponentiation. But finding a value of *n*, such that $a^n \bmod p$ is given, is not an easy task. This problem is known as *discrete logarithm problem.*

Formally, we can now define a discrete logarithm as follows:

In a group of elements, *G*, let '*a*' be an element in the set. Let '*x*' be another element in *G*. Then the discrete logarithm of *x* to base *a* is an integer '*n*' such that $a^n = x$.

8.3 An Overview of Cryptographic Algorithms

A major goal of any cryptographic algorithm is to provide all security services as described in Section 8.1.2. There are two types of cryptographic algorithms:

1. ***Symmetric key cryptosystem*** in which a single key is used for performing both encryption and decryption.
2. ***Public key cryptosystem*** in which there are two keys, a public key and a private key.

The cryptographic algorithm can be as simple as substituting a message symbol by another. This section gives an overview of the basic cryptographic algorithms.

8.3.1 Substitution Algorithm

Consider a cryptosystem that is used to encrypt the message consisting of English alphabets and a space. A simple encryption algorithm suggests to map each letter in the English alphabet with an equivalent mathematical number. Say A is assigned with 0, B with 1, C with 2, …, Z with 25 and space with 26. Then, the encryption can be done on a letter-by-letter basis using the following relation:

$$C = (P + K) \bmod N \tag{8.11}$$

where C is the cipher text, P is the plain text, K is the key and N is the number of symbols used in the plain text. It is 27 for the present case.

The decoding procedure is exactly the reverse of the encoding procedure. The plain text can be recovered back from the cipher text using the relation

$$P = (C - K) \bmod N \tag{8.12}$$

EXAMPLE 8.8

Obtain the cipher text for the following message sequence using substitution method considering English alphabet along with space. Use a key value of 3.

'ENGINEERING COLLEGE'

Solution: Using the substitution method we can map the message symbols into their equivalent mathematical values as follows:

A = 0	B = 1	C = 2	D = 3	E = 4
F = 5	G = 6	H = 7	I = 8	J = 9
K = 10	L = 11	M = 12	N = 13	O = 14
P = 15	Q = 16	R = 17	S = 18	T = 19
U = 20	V = 21	W = 22	X = 23	Y = 24
Z = 25	SPACE = 26			

We have

$$C = (P + K) \bmod N$$

Substituting $K = 3$ and $N = 27$, we get

$$C = (P + 3) \bmod 27$$

Thus, for each letter in the message an equivalent cipher text can be generated, which is as shown in Table 8.1.

Table 8.1 | Cipher text

Plain Text	*Mathematical Value*	$C = P + 3 \bmod 27$	*Encrypted Message*
E	4	7	H
N	13	16	Q
G	6	9	J
I	8	11	L
N	13	16	Q
E	4	7	H
E	4	7	H

(*Continued*)

Table 8.1 | Continued

Plain Text	*Mathematical Value*	$C = P + 3 \bmod 27$	*Encrypted Message*
R	17	20	U
I	8	11	L
N	13	16	Q
G	6	9	J
SPACE	26	2	C
C	2	5	F
O	14	17	R
L	11	14	O
L	11	14	O
E	4	7	H
G	6	9	J
E	4	7	H

Thus, the encrypted sequence would be 'HQJLQHHULQJCFROOHJH', which cannot be understood without knowing the key.

The decryption process is exactly the reverse of that of the encryption process, and it is depicted in Table 8.2.

Table 8.2 | Decryption process

Cipher Text	*Mathematical Value*	$P = C - 3 \bmod 27$	*Decrypted Message*
H	7	4	E
Q	16	13	N
J	9	6	G
L	11	8	I
Q	16	13	N
H	7	4	E
H	7	4	E
U	20	17	R
L	11	8	I
Q	16	13	N
J	9	6	G
C	2	26	SPACE
F	5	2	C
R	17	14	O
O	14	11	L

(*Continued*)

Table 8.2 | Continued

Cipher Text	*Mathematical Value*	*P = C − 3 mod 27*	*Decrypted Message*
O	14	11	L
H	7	4	E
J	9	6	G
H	7	4	E

Though the simple substitution method of encrypting the information seems to perform well, it is easily prone to cryptographic attack. Using the statistics of the occurrence of the letters in the English alphabet, one can easily hack the key used for substitution. Letter 'E' is more likely to occur in any conversation. Taking this into account, one can easily get the substituted letter for letter 'E' if he/she has the access to a long cipher text. Considering Example 8.1, after having an access to a long cipher text, one can understand that 'E' has been substituted by 'H', as 'H' would be the most occurring letter in the cipher text. Using this information one can calculate the key as 3. Thus, the normal substitution approach is more prone to security attacks and hence not generally used.

An improvement over the simple substitution algorithm is sought and is known as *affine transformation.* The mathematical relations for encryption and decryption are shown in Eqs. (8.13) and (8.14):

$$C = aP + b \bmod N \tag{8.13}$$

$$P = a'C + b' \bmod N \tag{8.14}$$

where a and b are the keys for encryption, $a' = a^{-1} \bmod N$ and $b' = b^{-1} \bmod N$ are the keys used for decryption.

Normal substitution method is a special case of Affine transformation where $b = 0$.

8.3.2 Transposition Method

In transposition method, the message bits are not substituted by another. Instead the position of the message sequence is permuted so that the actual information content is hidden.

EXAMPLE 8.9

Obtain the cipher text for the following message sequence using transposition method considering English alphabet along with space. Use a key value of 5.

'INFORMATION THEORY CODING'

Solution: First, arrange the information in the form of consecutive rows, each containing five letters.

I	N	F	O	R
M	A	T	I	O
N	SPACE	T	H	E
O	R	Y	SPACE	C
O	D	I	N	G

Now read the text columnwise. Thus, the encrypted information becomes

'IMNOONA RDFTTYIOIH NROECG'

In order to decrypt the information, the reverse procedure is used. First, arrange the cipher text columnwise such that there are five columns as the key is 5. Then, read the information rowwise. In the given problem, the cipher text is of length 25. As we require to arrange them as 5 columns, each column shall have five letters.

I	N	F	O	R
M	A	T	I	O
N	SPACE	T	H	E
O	R	Y	SPACE	C
O	D	I	N	G

Now reading them rowwise, we can decode the information as

'INFORMATION THEORY CODING'

8.4 Symmetric Key Cryptography

Symmetric cryptosystems are also known as single key cryptography or private key cryptography. In these algorithms, a single key is shared between the sender and the receiver. The same key is used for both encryption and decryption of the information. Although such algorithms are simple, the strength of the algorithm lies in the distribution of keys between the sender and the receiver.

As the same algorithm is used at both sides, the security assured is dependent on the key used. For better results, key should be changed on time to time basis. However, the smaller the key, easier would be the hacking. Thus the size of the key plays an important role in determining the performance of the system. In early 1990s, a key length of 40 bits was considered to be long enough to assure a certain degree of security. However, the advancements in the processors have now resulted in using a key length of as many as 128 bits in most of the security algorithms. The degree of security requirement varies from application to application. For example, a question paper has to be kept secure till the beginning of the examination, census data of a nation may have to be kept secret for a few months, military strategies have to be maintained secret for years and so on. Depending on the volume of the data to be kept secure and the duration for which the data has to be secured, appropriate key length can be chosen.

There are two types of symmetric key cryptography algorithms, namely,

1. **Block ciphers:** Here the information to be encrypted is divided into blocks and the security algorithms are applied to each block in iterative manner. More the number of iterations, better the security achieved.
2. **Stream ciphers:** Here the information bits to be encrypted are fed in the form of continuous bit stream.

Algorithms discussed in Section 8.3 are symmetric key cryptographic algorithms. The usefulness of the symmetric key cryptographic algorithm lies in the sharing of the secret key in the secured manner. If the key is compromised the whole algorithm fails.

8.5 Asymmetric Key Cryptography

Asymmetric key cryptosystems use two separate keys for encryption and decryption. Here each user will have two keys, a private key that is known only to the user and a public key which is public to all users in the network. The encryption of the information is done by the public key of the receiver. However for the decryption, the private key of the receiver is used. Hence, such algorithms are also called as public key cryptography.

Asymmetric cryptosystems are considered to be better compared to symmetric key cryptography, as an eavesdropper will not be able to decrypt the information in spite of having the cipher text and the public key. Only the intended receiver will be able to read the information using his private key. Thus, the key management process is simpler in public key cryptosystems. However, these algorithms require more computations and hence will take a longer time for encryption and decryption.

8.5.1 RSA Algorithm

The name RSA is derived from its inventors Rivest, Shamir and Adleman. The RSA algorithm is considered to be one of the most popular public key algorithms. Unlike symmetric key cryptosystems, the key cannot be recovered easily from the cipher text.

The RSA algorithm can be summarized as follows:

Step 1: Choose two prime numbers say p and q.
Step 2: Multiply them: $n = pq$.
Step 3: Compute Euler's ϕ function, $\phi(n) = (p - 1)(q - 1)$.
Step 4: Choose a public key 'e' such that GCD $(e, \phi(n)) = 1$. In other words, 'e' has to be relatively prime to $\phi(n)$.
Step 5: The private key of the user can be obtained using the relation

$$d = e^{-1} \bmod \phi(n)$$

Step 6: The set (n, e) becomes the public key of the user and can be used to encrypt the information

$$C = P^e \bmod n$$

Step 7: The set (n, d) becomes the private key and can be used to decrypt the information

$$P = C^d \bmod n$$

One can easily find the product of two prime numbers. However, it is very difficult to factorize the given product into two prime numbers. The computation would be harder for the larger values of p and q. Thus, it is difficult to recover p and q from the given n and, thus, it would be infeasible to hack the private key d even if e and n are known. This is the idea behind the RSA algorithm.

EXAMPLE 8.10

Generate the cipher text for the information 'ME' using RSA algorithm. Consider $p = 5$ and $q = 11$.

Solution: To encrypt the letter 'M':

Step 1: $p = 5, q = 11$.
Step 2: $n = pq = 55$.

Step 3: $\phi(n) = (p-1)(q-1) = 40$.
Step 4: Choose $e = 7$ as GCD (7, 40) = 1.
Step 5: The mathematical value of $M = 12$, thus $C = 12^7 \bmod 55 = 23$.
Step 6: Thus the cipher text for letter 'M' is '23'.

To encrypt the letter 'E':

Step 1: $p = 5, q = 11$.
Step 2: $n = pq = 55$.
Step 3: $\phi(n) = (p-1)(q-1) = 40$.
Step 4: Use the same key $e = 7$.
Step 5: The mathematical value of E = 4, thus $C = 4^7 \bmod 55 = 49$.
Step 6: Thus the cipher text for letter 'E' is '49'.

Thus, the cipher text for the message 'ME' using RSA algorithm is '23 49'.

For decryption the following steps are used:
To decrypt 23:

Step 1: Find the private key d such that $d = e^{-1} \bmod \phi(n)$.

$$d = 7^{-1} \bmod 40 = 23$$

Step 2: $P = C^d \bmod n$. $C = 23^{23} \bmod 55 = 12$ whose equivalent letter is 'M'.

To decrypt 49:

Step 1: Use the same private key $d = 23$.
Step 2: Thus $P = C^d \bmod n$. $C = 49^{23} \bmod 55 = 4$ whose equivalent letter is 'E'.

Therefore, the decrypted information is 'ME'.

8.6 Diffie–Hellman Key Exchange Algorithm

Consider a scenario where two users 'A' and 'B' want to share a secret key for their communication using symmetric cryptography. Let us suppose that the medium through which they can share their key is insecure. Then how do they exchange their secret key without letting any adversary to hack the information over an insecure channel. Diffie–Hellman key exchange algorithm provides a solution for such problems.

Diffie–Hellman key exchange algorithm just assures the users to have their secret key exchanged in a secure manner. This algorithm enables the users to compute a common secret key on their own by just exchanging some public information.

The algorithm can be explained as follows:

Step 1: Both 'A' and 'B' agree upon a prime number p. Let q be a primitive element over the field F_p. Even q is also known to both parties *a priori*.
Step 2: User 'A' selects a secret number K_A such that $K_A < q$ and computes the term $X_A = q^{K_A}$.
Step 3: Similarly user 'B' selects a secret number K_B such that $K_B < q$ and computes the term $X_B = q^{K_B}$.
Step 4: Keys X_A and X_B are made public and are exchanged.
Step 5: Now 'A' computes the secret key as follows:

$$K = (X_B)^{K_A} \bmod q$$

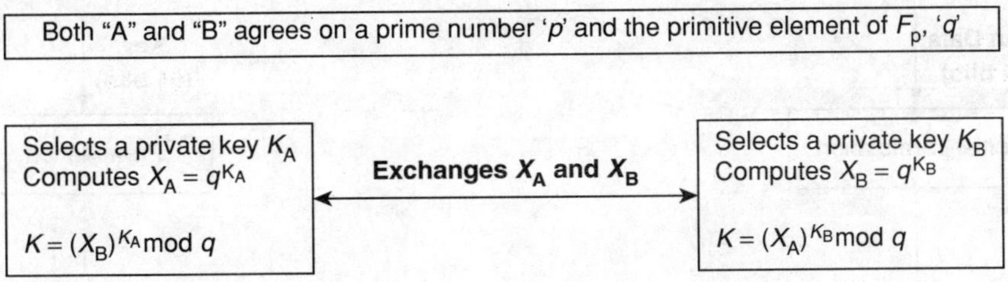

Figure 8.1 | Diffie–Hellman key exchange algorithm.

Similarly, B computes its key as

$$K = (X_A)^{K_B} \text{ mod } q$$

It can be shown that $(X_B)^{K_A} \text{ mod } q = (X_A)^{K_B} \text{ mod } q$. Consider

$$(X_B)^{K_A} \text{ mod } q = (q^{K_B})^{K_A} \text{ mod } q = (q^{K_A})^{K_B} \text{ mod } q = (X_A)^{K_B} \text{ mod } q$$

Thus, at the end of step 5 both parties will have the common secret key without sharing any secret information over the channel. Even if it gets an access to all public information over the channel, it is difficult for an adversary to compute K_A or K_B. This is because of the fact that solving discrete logarithms is difficult compared to exponential operations. Thus, an attacker would not succeed in hacking the secret information for larger values of p.

The Diffie–Hellman key exchange algorithm is detailed in Fig. 8.1.

8.7 Data Encryption Standard

Data encryption standard (DES) is one of the most prominent encryption schemes developed in 1977 by IBM. The DES has been adapted in the National Bureau of Standards. It encrypts the data in blocks of 64 bits using a key 54 bits long. DES is an advancement over LUCIFER, an encryption technique developed by IBM during 1971. LUCIFER used 128-bit key to encrypt the data in blocks of 64 bits. Because of the success of LUCIFER, IBM wanted to improve the algorithm further. Thus, an effort was initiated in reducing the key size of LUCIFER but still achieving better security. This resulted in development of DES. Although DES was considered to be a very powerful algorithm in earlier years, it is no more considered to be very secure. Advancements in processor technologies have made the cryptanalysts to break a 56-bit key of DES in a few minutes. Thus, many algorithms succeeded DES; advanced encryption standard (AES) is one such algorithm which is detailed in Section 8.9.

8.7.1 DES Encryption

The encryption process of DES involves 16 identical rounds. The detailed process of encryption is presented in Fig. 8.2. Although a key of 64 bits is required to be given as the input, only 56 bits of the key are actually used for the encryption process.

Initially, the plain text is permuted to obtain two 32-bit blocks. A set of operations over each of the two blocks is carried out in every round. After the 16th round, the two blocks of 32 bits are swapped. Finally, inverse permutation is carried out to obtain the cipher text of 64 bits.

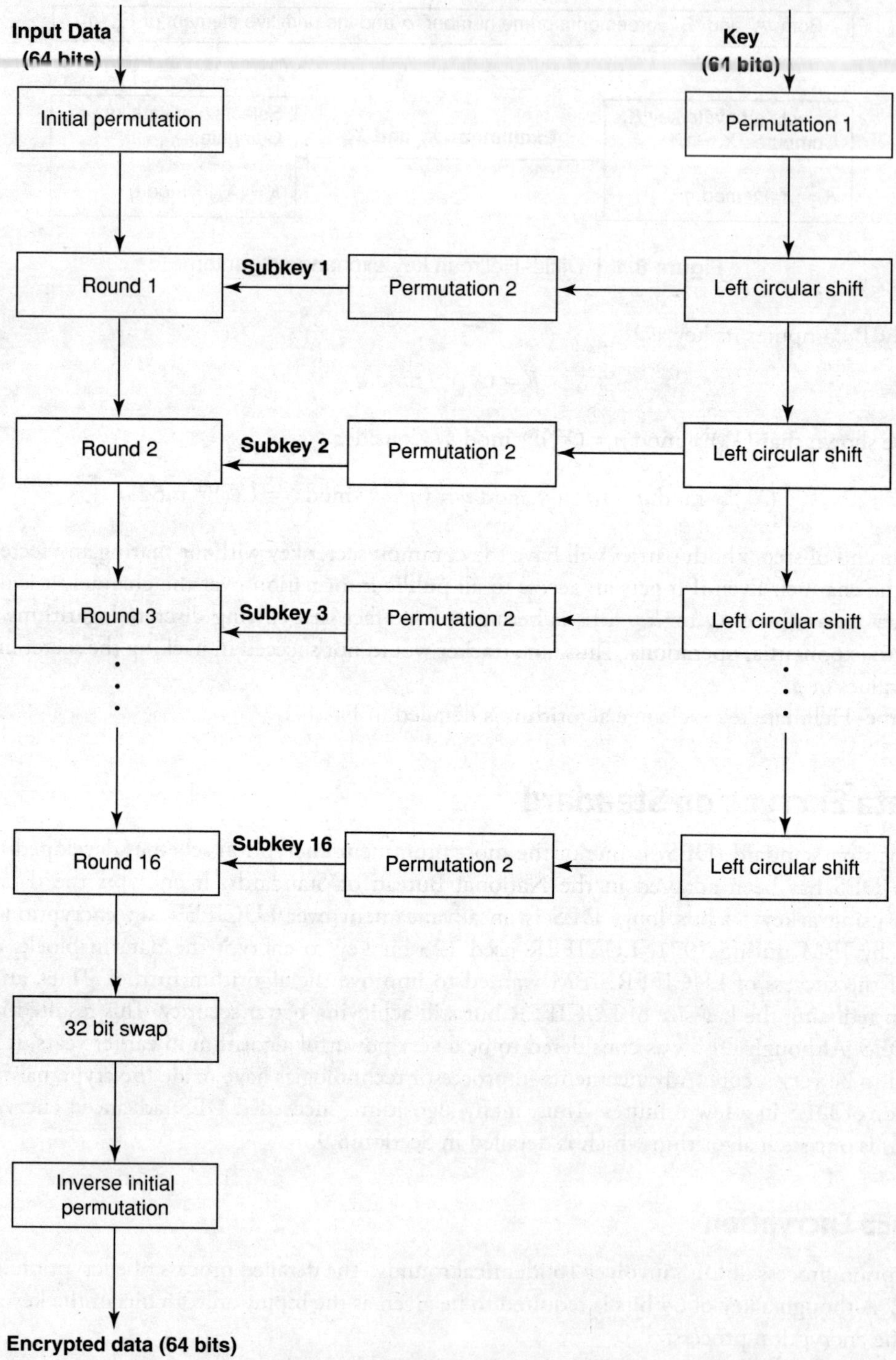

Figure 8.2 | DES encryption process.

Each round of the encryption process of DES involves the following operations:

1. **Key transformation:** In every round, a 64-bit key is reduced to 56 bits by ignoring every 8th bit. Then, 16 different sub-keys of length 48 bits are created for the operation in each round. For each round a different sub-key is used.
2. **Expansion and XOR operation:** The sub-block of 32 bits of data is expanded into 48 bits. Then, these 48 bits are XORed with the 48 bits sub-key generated in each round.
3. **Substitution/Transposition:** Special functional blocks called S-boxes are used for this operation. Each S-box takes 6 bits as input and produces 4 bits as output. Thus, in every round eight S-boxes are required to convert every 48-bit input to 32-bit output. Every 32-bit output of the S-boxes will then undergo a transposition operation.

8.7.2 DES Decryption

The decryption process exactly follows the encryption. The only difference is that the sub-keys have to be applied in reverse manner in each round. In other words, sub-key 16 has to be used for round 1, sub-key 15 for round 2 and so on.

8.8 Triple DES

The degree of protection of DES can be further improved by considering repeating the process of normal DES algorithm for more than one time. One such technique is triple DES in which the DES operations are repeated for three times. Triple DES uses either two or three keys.

8.8.1 Triple DES with Two Keys

Here two cipher keys are used. The algorithm is detailed in Fig. 8.3.

The algorithm involves three steps as follows:

Step 1: Encrypt the plain text with the first key "Key 1" to get the "cipher text 1".
Step 2: Decrypt "cipher text 1" using the second key "Key 2". Let the output be "cipher text 2".
Step 3: Encrypt "cipher text 2" using the first key "Key 1" again, to get the "final cipher text".

Triple DES with two keys is also referred to as "Encrypt–Decrypt–Encrypt" algorithm.

8.8.2 Triple DES with Three Keys

Unlike triple DES with two keys, here three cipher keys are used namely Key 1, Key 2 and Key 3. The functional block diagram of this algorithm is as shown in Fig. 8.4.

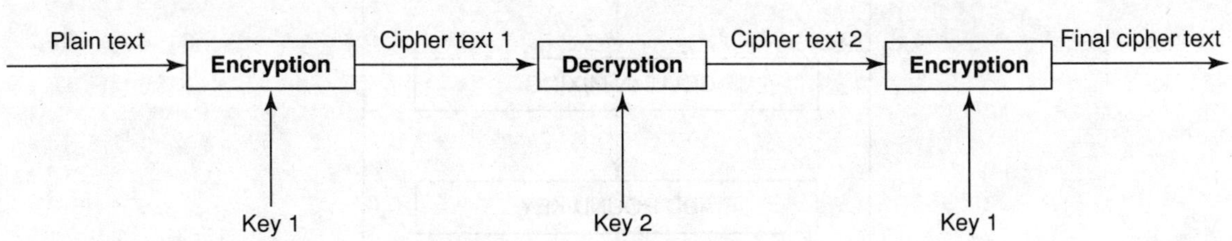

Figure 8.3 | Triple DES with two keys.

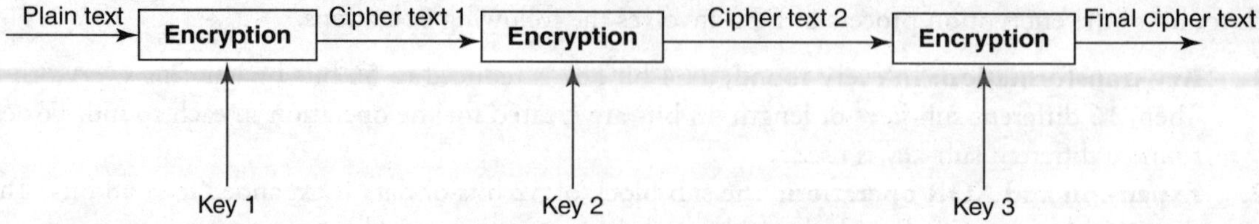

Figure 8.4 | Triple DES with three keys.

Here the encryption is carried out three consecutive times using three different keys. At the receiver end, the decryption also requires three stages, which operates exactly in the reverse manner.

8.9 Advanced Encryption Standard (AES)

The advancements in the processor technologies in late 1990s have made DES to be no longer secure. Thus US government wanted a standard for cryptographic algorithm that replaces DES. Proposals for the algorithms were called worldwide. Finally, the algorithm proposed by two researchers Vincent Rijmen and Joan Daemen, called as Rijndael, was selected as the advanced encryption standard (AES). Among many proposals submitted, Rijndael was considered to be more effective based on the degree of security, cost and ease of implementation.

Normal 56-bit keys used in DES were no more secure. Thus, keys of longer lengths were desired. The proposed Rijndael algorithm uses 128-bit key which would offer a better security against cryptanalysis.

8.9.1 Algorithm

The algorithm uses keys of three different lengths, namely, 128 bits, 192 bits or 256 bits. Also the number of rounds in the algorithm is different for different lengths. There could be 10, 12 or 14 rounds in the algorithm for key lengths of 128 bits, 192 bits and 256 bits, respectively. A general view of the steps carried out in each round of the algorithm is as shown in Fig. 8.5.

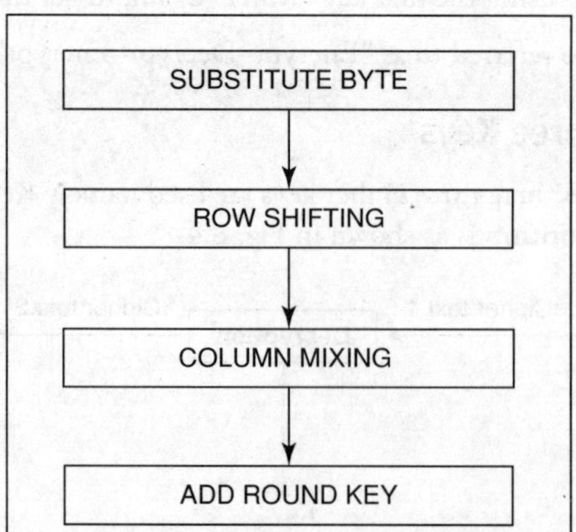

Figure 8.5 | Operations in each round of the algorithm.

The steps carried out in the algorithm are detailed as follows:

1. **Substitute byte:** Here the block of input of 128 bits is passed through the S-boxes, and the text generated corresponding to the S boxes will be given as the input to the next stage of the encoder.
2. **Row shifting:** Here all the rows in the block, except the first one, are shifted for some specific number of times.
3. **Column mixing:** Here four bytes in every column are taken at a time. The mixing is performed to generate four new bytes. Mixing generally implies a linear combination of the contents of the columns.
4. **Add round key:** An 128-bit round key will be added to the corresponding data block, byte wise to generate the cipher block of the current round.

The above four steps are repeated in all rounds of the algorithm except the last one. In the last round, '*column mixing*' step is not present.

Exactly the reverse process is carried out for the decryption.

8.10 One-Way Hash Function

One-way hash function is a mathematical function that accepts the message of variable length as a whole, performs some operation on the same and outputs a fixed length mathematical value called the hash value. Although one can easily compute the hash value of a message using the mathematical relation, it is very hard to recover the message from its hash value. Also, it is very hard to find two different messages to have the same hash value. Hash value of a message can be obtained using the following relation:

$$H = f(M) \tag{8.15}$$

where M is the message and H is the hash value after applying a mathematical operator f.

A hash function can be used for a number of security aspects. It can be used to assure the integrity of the message. This can be explained as follows: Initially, the sender and the receiver have to agree upon the same hash function. At the sender's end, the hash value of the message can be computed and is sent along with the message. At the receiver's end, the same hash function is applied to the received information and the hash value is recomputed. If the recomputed hash value is the same as that of the one computed by the sender, the message is said to be unaltered. The same analysis can be used to check for the authenticity of the information.

8.10.1 Digital Signature

Hash function can be used to sign a document digitally. Steps involved in getting the digital signature of a message are as follows:

Step 1: The sender computes the hash value of the information to be transmitted (plain text).
Step 2: The sender encrypts the hash value with his private key.
Step 3: The sender encrypts both the encrypted hash value and the plain text using the public key of the receiver.
Step 4: After receiving, the receiver applies his private key to the received information and thus obtains the plain text and the encrypted hash value.
Step 5: He then applies the sender's public key to obtain the hash value. Also he applies the same hash function as that of the sender to the obtained plain text and recomputes the hash value.
Step 6: If both hash values are identical, then the receiver gets the assurance that the message has come from the correct sender.

8.11 Cryptanalysis

Cryptanalysis is a process of recovering the plain text from the cipher text without having access to the key. However, the algorithm used for the encryption can be known to the person performing cryptanalysis. The person performing cryptanalysis is known as an attacker and the act of cryptanalysis is known as an attack.

The following are the various cryptanalysis attacks:

1. **Brute force attack:** It is just a trial-and-error method of obtaining the key. Here the attacker tries all possible combinations of the key until he arrives at the correct combination. Although it is simple to perform, it requires enormous amount of time and computational power.
2. **Known plain text attack:** If the attacker knows a part of the plain text and the corresponding cipher text (say last few characters corresponding to a signature or name that can be known *a priori*), he can obtain the corresponding key and hence can decode the information.
3. **Cipher text only attack:** Here the attacker can have the access to the cipher texts for various plain texts. Knowing the algorithm used for encryption and statistics of the language, one can decode the information. For example, the fact that 'e' is the most likely occurring letter in English can make the attacker to find the cipher text corresponding to letter 'e'. Knowing the algorithm and the similar statistics of other letters, one can obtain the key and thus decode the information.
4. **Chosen plain text attack:** Here the attacker may choose a specific plain text and obtain the corresponding cipher text as the algorithm is known *a priori*. This would reveal the information about the key used for encryption and thus the information can be decoded.
5. **Chosen cipher text attack:** It is an iterative approach. The attacker chooses a cipher text to be decrypted and obtains the corresponding plain text. However, this process is repeated till a meaningful plain text is obtained.

Summary

1. Cryptography is a branch of engineering that deals with encrypting and decrypting the information.
2. Plain text is the actual information that has to be communicated in a secure manner.
3. Cipher text is the message coded using an algorithm such that no one except the intended receiver can understand the information.
4. Key is a mathematical value using which a cryptographic algorithm can generate a cipher text from the plain text. Longer the key, better the security.
5. For any three elements a, b and N, we can write
$$a \equiv b \bmod N \quad \text{if and only if } (a-b) \mid N$$
6. For any integer 'a' with a prime number 'p'
$$a^p \equiv a \bmod p$$
7. Euler theorem:
$$a^{\phi(p)} \equiv 1 \bmod p$$
8. The elements in $F_p - \{0\}$, which are square of some numbers, are called quadratic residue modulo p.
9. For an integer 'a' and a prime number 'p' > 2, we can define Legendre symbol as
$$\left(\frac{a}{p}\right) = \begin{cases} 1, & \text{if '}a\text{' is a quadratic residue mod } p \\ -1, & \text{if '}a\text{' is a quadratic non-residue mod } p \\ 0, & \text{if '}a\text{' is divisible by '}p\text{'} \end{cases}$$
10. In a group of elements, G, let 'a' be an element in the set. Let 'x' be another element in G. Then the discrete logarithm of x to base a is an integer 'n' such that $a^n = x$.

11. Cryptographic attributes:
    - Authentication
    - Confidentiality
    - Integrity
    - Non-repudiation
12. Substitution algorithm
    - For encryption, $C = (P + K) \bmod N$
    - For decryption, $P = (C - K) \bmod N$
13. Affine transformation algorithm
    - For encryption, $C = (aP + b) \bmod N$
    - For decryption, $P = (a'C + b') \bmod N$
14. In symmetric cryptosystems/single-key cryptography/private-key cryptography, a single key is shared with the sender and the receiver.
15. Asymmetric key cryptosystems use two separate keys for encryption and decryption.
16. The RSA algorithm can be summarized as follows:

    Step 1: Choose two prime numbers, say p and q.
    Step 2: Multiply them: $n = pq$.
    Step 3: Compute Euler's ϕ function, $\phi(n) = (p-1)(q-1)$.
    Step 4: Choose a public key e such that GCD $[e, \phi(n)] = 1$. In other words, e has to be relatively prime to $\phi(n)$.
    Step 5: The private key of the user can be obtained using the relation $d = e^{-1} \bmod \phi(n)$.
    Step 6: The set (n, e) becomes the public key of the user and can be used to encrypt the information

    $$C = P^e \bmod n$$

    Step 7: The set (n, d) becomes the private key and can be used to decrypt the information

    $$P = C^d \bmod n$$

17. Diffie–Hellman algorithm enables the users to compute a common secret key on their own by just exchanging some public information.
18. The encryption process of DES involves 16 identical rounds.
19. Triple DES is an advancement over DES, in which DES processes are carried out three consecutive times.
20. Triple DES can use either two keys or three keys.
21. AES algorithm uses keys of three different lengths, namely, 128 bits, 192 bits or 256 bits.
22. There could be 10, 12 or 14 rounds in the AES algorithm for key lengths of 128 bits, 192 bits and 256 bits, respectively.
23. One-way hash function is a mathematical function that accepts the message of variable length, performs some operation on the same and outputs a fixed length mathematical value called the hash value.
24. Cryptanalysis attacks:
    - Brute force attack
    - Known plain text attack
    - Cipher text only attack
    - Chosen plain text attack
    - Chosen cipher text attack

Review Questions

1. Define the following:
   (a) Plain text
   (b) Cipher text
   (c) Key
   (d) Cryptanalysis
   (e) Passive attack
   (f) Active attack
2. Evaluate the following values:
   (a) 8 mod 5
   (b) 144 mod 100
   (c) 10 mod 12
   (d) 1 mod 3
   (e) 4 mod 10
3. Find the smallest non-negative solution to the following congruences:

   $$y \equiv 1 \bmod 3$$
   $$y \equiv 2 \bmod 5$$
   $$y \equiv 3 \bmod 11$$
   $$y \equiv 7 \bmod 16$$

4. Find the smallest non-negative solution to the following congruences:

$$y \equiv 10 \bmod 13$$

$$y \equiv 8 \bmod 17$$

$$y \equiv 4 \bmod 5$$

5. Find the value of $3^{10000000} \bmod 65$.
6. Find the value of $2^{1000} \bmod 21$.
7. Find the value of $2^{100C} \bmod 21$ using repeated squaring approach.
8. Find the value of $5^{127} \bmod 77$ using repeated squaring approach.
9. Find the quadratic residues in F_3.
10. Find the quadratic residues in F_5, F_{11} and F_{13}.
11. Determine the values of the following Legendre polynomials:

    (a) $\left(\frac{20}{11}\right)$

    (b) $\left(\frac{121}{11}\right)$

    (c) $\left(\frac{7}{11}\right)$

12. Explain the concept of discrete logarithms.
13. Explain four security attributes with respect to cryptography.
14. Obtain the cipher text for the following message sequence using substitution method considering English alphabet along with space. Use a key value of 8.

    'ELECTRONICS AND COMMUNICATION ENGINEERING'

15. Decrypt the following cipher text using substitution method. Use $N = 27$ and $K = 3$:

    'LQIRUPDWLRQCWKHRUA'

16. Obtain the cipher text for the following message sequence using transposition method considering English alphabet along with space. Use a key value of 3.

    'CRYPTOGRAPHY AND NETWORK SECURITY'

17. Explain RSA algorithm.
18. Generate the cipher text for the information 'ITC' using RSA algorithm. Consider $p = 5$ and $q = 11$.
19. Generate the cipher text for the information 'EC' using RSA algorithm. Consider $p = 7$ and $q = 13$.
20. Explain DES in detail.
21. Write an explanatory note on triple DES.
22. Explain the working principle of a Rijndael algorithm.
23. Explain the process of obtaining digital signature.
24. Define and explain various cryptanalysis attacks.

Further Reading

[1] Neal Koblitz, *A Course in Number Theory and Cryptography*, 2nd Ed., Springer: New York; 2000.

[2] William Stallings, *Cryptography and Network Security*, 3rd Ed., Pearson Education: Upper Saddle River, NJ; 2003.

[3] Ranjan Bose, *Information Theory, Coding and Cryptography*, 2nd Ed., McGraw Hill Education: New Delhi; 2008.

[4] Atul Kahate, *Cryptography and network security*, Tata McGraw-Hill Education: New Delhi; 2013.

[5] Behrouz A Forouzan, *Cryptography & Network Security*, Tata McGraw-Hill Education: New Delhi; 2007.

APPENDIX A

MATLAB Programs

1. Design an information system which gives information every year for around 200 students of E and C branch of NITK. The students can get into one of the following three fields:
   (i) Go abroad for higher studies. State A
   (ii) Join MBA/IAS. State B
   (iii) Join industry in India. State C

   Based on the following data, construct the state diagram of the source model and find the source entropy.

   a. On an average 100 students go abroad every year.
   b. Out of 100 going abroad this year, 50 are reported going abroad next year, while 25 each joined MBA/IAS or industries in India.
   c. Out of 100 remaining in India this year, 50 continued to do so while 50 will go abroad next year.
   d. Those joining MBA/IAS or industry could not swap the two fields next year.

Solution:

```
% Source model
clc
paa = 0.5;
pab = 0.25;
pac = 0.25;
pba = 0.5;
pbb = 0.5;
pbc = 0;
pca = 0.5;
pcb = 0;
pcc = 0.5;
pa = [paa pab pac];
pa1 = -log(pa)/log(2);
pb = [pba pbb ];
pb1 = -log2(pb);
pc = [pca  pcc];
pc1 = -log2(pc);
P = [   1   1     1; -0.5  0.5  0.5; 0.25  -0.5  0];
b = [ 1 ; 0; 0];
a = P\b;
```

```
PA = a(1);
PB = a(2);
PC = a(3);
ha = pa.*pa1;
hb = pb.*pb1;
hc = pc.*pc1;
HA = sum(ha);
HC = sum(hc);
HB = sum(hb);
h = [HA HB HC];
A = a';
H = sum(h.*A)
fprintf ('FOR SOURCE A\n\n');
fprintf ('PA = %f\n\n',PA);
fprintf ('Paa = %f\n',paa);
fprintf ('Pab = %f\n',pab);
fprintf ('Pac = %f\n\n',pac);
fprintf ('The entropy of the source A is %f bit/message-symbol
\n\n', HA);
fprintf ('FOR SOURCE B\n\n');
fprintf ('PB = %f\n\n',PB);
fprintf ('Pba = %f\n',pba);
fprintf ('Pbb = %f\n',pbb);
fprintf ('Pbc = %f\n\n',pbc);
fprintf ('The entropy of the source B is %f bit/message-symbol\
n\n', HB);
fprintf ('FOR SOURCE C\n\n');
fprintf ('PC = %f\n\n',PC);
fprintf ('Pca = %f\n',pca);
fprintf ('Pcb = %f\n',pcb);
fprintf ('Pcc = %f\n\n',pcc);
fprintf ('The entropy of the source C is %f bit/message-symbol\
n\n', HC);
fprintf ('The total entropy of the source is %f bits/message-
symbol', H);
```

2. Write a program to check if a given code is a prefix code.

Solution:

```
a = input (' enter code words and number of bits');
% Input should be of the form [100 3; 00100 5; ...]%

l=length(a);
% Stores the total no. of code words%

num = zeros(1,l);
bits = zeros (1,l);
```

```
flag=0;
b=zeros(1,l);
temp=zeros(1,l);
b=a;
% Loop to store decimal equivalents of the code words in num, no.
of bits in array bits%
for i= 1:l
    temp(i)=0;
    bits(i)= a(l+i);
    a(i)=a(i)+ (10^bits(i));
    while a(i)>0
        r= mod(a(i),10);
      a(i)= fix(a(i)/10);
        num(i)= num(i) + (r*2^temp(i));
        temp(i)=temp(i)+1;
% Array temp stores the no. of bits of each code word excluding
the zeros in the beginning if any
    end
  end
% Loop to sort array num in ascending order%
for i=1:l-1
    for j=i+1:l
        if (num(j)<num(i))
            r=num(j);
            num(j)=num(i);
            num(i)=r;
            r=bits(j);
            bits(j)=bits(i);
            bits(i)=r;
            r=temp(j);
            temp(j)=temp(i);
            temp(i)=r;
        end
    end
  end
% Loop to check for prefix condition%
for i=1:l-1
    for j=i+1:l
        if (num(i)== fix((num(j)/(2^(temp(j)-temp(i))))))
            flag=1;
            break;
        end
```

```
        end
    end
  if (flag==0)
        disp(' the code is a prefix code');
    else
        disp(' the code is not a prefix code ');
    end
```

3. Write a program to generate Shannon–Fano code for a given set of symbols.

Solution:

Shannon Fano code

```
function CODE=sfcode(N,P)
[N,P,CODE] = shannon (N,P);
last=length(N);
count1(last,1)=0;
for i=last:-1:1
fprintf('%d_--->',N(i));
for j=1:length(CODE(1,:))
if CODE(i,j)=='H'
          CODE(i,j)=1;
          fprintf('1');
else
if CODE(i,j)=='L'
          CODE(i,j)=0;
          fprintf('0');
end
end
end
    fprintf('\n');
end
```

Shannon.m

```
function [N,P,CODE] = shannon (N, P) % N-information symbols,
P-probabilities of symbols
total = 0;
last=length(N);
for i=2:last
for j=1:(last-1)
if P(j)>P(j+1)
            temp_pro=P(j);
            temp_sym=N(j);
            P(j)=P(j+1);
            N(j)=N(j+1);
            P(j+1)=temp_pro;
```

```
            N(j+1)=temp_sym;
 end
 end
 end
 for i=1:last
     total=total+P(i);
 end
 if total~=1
     P = 'retype the probabilities';
     CODE=0;
 end
 column=0;
 CODE(last,:)=0;
 CODE=fano(1,last,P,N,CODE,column);
```

Fano.m

```
function CODE = fano(l,h,P,N,CODE,column)
prob_sum1=0;
prob_sum2=0;
if (l+1<h)
for i=l:h-1
       prob_sum1=prob_sum1+P(i);
end
    prob_sum2=prob_sum2+P(h);
       prob_diff1=prob_sum1-prob_sum2;
if (prob_diff1 < 0)
          prob_diff1=prob_diff1*(-1);
end
      j=2;
while (j~=(h-l+1))
              line=h-j;
              prob_sum1=0;
              prob_sum2=0;
for i=l:line
                   prob_sum1=prob_sum1+P(i);
end
for i=h:-1:line+1
                     prob_sum2=prob_sum2+P(i);
end
                   prob_diff2=prob_sum1-prob_sum2;
if(prob_diff2<0)
                     prob_diff2=prob_diff2*(-1);
end
if(prob_diff2>=prob_diff1)
break;
```

```
end
                    prob_diff1=prob_diff2;
                    j=j+1;
end
        line=line+1;
for i=l:line
            CODE(i,column+1)='H';
end
for i=line+1:h
                CODE(i,column+1)='L';
end
            column=column+1;
                CODE=fano(l,line,P,N,CODE,column);
                CODE=fano(line+1,h,P,N,CODE,column);
else
if (((l+1)==h) || (l==h) || l>h)
if ((l==h) || l>h)
    z=0;
else
    CODE(h,column+1)='L';
    CODE(l,column+1)='H';
end
end
end
```

4. Write a program to design a linear block code for the given (n, k).

Solution:

```
% Input Generator Matrix
g=input('Enter The Generator Matrix: ')
disp ('G = ')
disp ('The Order of Linear block Code for given Generator Matrix
    is:')
[n,k] = size(transpose(g))
for i = 1:2^k
for j = k:-1:1
if rem(i-1,2^(-j+k+1))>=2^(-j+k)
u(i,j)=1;
else
u(i,j)=0;
end
end
end
u;
disp('The Possible Codewords are :')
```

```
c = rem(u*g,2)
disp('The Minimum Hamming Distance dmin for given Block Code is=')
d_min = min(sum((c(2:2^k,:))'))
% Code Word
r = input('Enter the Received Code Word:')
p = [g(:,k+1:n)];
h = [transpose(p),eye(n-k)];
disp('Hammimg Code')
ht = transpose(h)
disp('Syndrome of a Given Codeword is :')
s = rem(r*ht,2)
for i = 1:1:size(ht)
if(ht(i,1:n-k)==s)
r(i) = 1-r(i);
break;
end
end
if (s==0)
    disp('No Error')
else
disp('The Error is in bit:')
disp(i)
disp('The Corrected Codeword is :')
disp(r)
end
```

5. Write a program to check whether a given code is a perfect code.

Solution:

```
G = input('Enter the Generator Matrix');
% G = Generator Matrix of the form [P Ik]
[k n] = size(G); dmin = inf;
for i = 1:(2^k-1)
j = dec2binvec(i,k); j = wrev(j);     % j = message vector
C = j*G;
C = mod(C,2)                          % C is Code matrix
if dmin > nnz(C)
dmin = nnz(C)                         % Hamming Weight of the code vector C
end
end
dmin                                  % Minimum Hamming Distance
t=floor((dmin-1)/2)                   % No. of correctable errors
s=0;
for i = 0:t
s = s + factorial(n)/(factorial(i)*factorial(n-i));
```

```
% Total no. of possible error combinations
end
if(s == 2^(n-k)) % Hamming Bound Check:
disp('ITS A PEFECT CODE')
else
disp('ITS NOT A PERFECT CODE')
end
```

6. Write a program to generate the standard array of a (5, 1) repetition code.

Solution:

```
%Generating standard array for a (5,1) repetition code
s= zeros(16,5);
for i= 1 : 5
  s(i+1,6-i)=1;
end
k=7;
for i = 5 :-1:2
      for j= i-1 :-1:1
             s(k,i)=1;
             s(k,j)=1;
             k=k+1;
end
end
      col1=s;
      col2=ones(16,5);
      col2=xor(col2,s);
      disp('column 1 of the standard array is :');
      disp(col1)
      disp('column 2 of the standard array is :');
      disp(col2)
```

7. Write a program to check whether a given generator polynomial is valid or not.

Solution:

```
clear;
clc;
g=input('Enter the generator polynomial:')
k=input('Enter the number of message bits:')
q=length(g)-1;
n=k+q;
x=zeros(1,n+1);
x(1,1)=1;
x(1,n+1)=1;
x1=x;
```

```
m=[1];
for i=0:k
     m=[m x1(1,1)];
    if x1(1,1)==1
    g1=[g zeros(1,k-i)];
    x2=x1+g1;
    l=length(x2);
    for j=1:l
        if x2(1,j)==2
            x2(1,j)=0;
        end
    end
    end
    if x1(1,1)==0
        x2=x1;
        l=length(x2);
    end
    x1=x2(1,2:l);
end
remainder=x1;
quotient=m(1,2:k+2);
if remainder==0
    disp('The generator polynomial is valid')
else disp('The generator polynomial is not valid')
end
```

8. Write a program to obtain generator matrix in systematic and non-systematic forms for an (n, k) cyclic code.

Solution:

```
clear;
clc;
n=input('Enter the value of n');
k=input('Enter the value of k');
c=zeros(k,n);
y=input('Enter the generator polynomial');
%Generates Non-systematic Generator Matrix
for i=1:k
    c(i,i:(i+n-k))=y;
end
disp('Generator Matrix in the non-systematic form is')
d=c
for i=1:k
for j=1:k
```

```
if(i==j)
c(i,n-k+i)=1;
elseif(c(i,n-k+j)~=0)
c(i,:)=c(i,:)+c(j,:);
end
end
end
% Conversion of the Non-systematic Matrix to Systematic Form
for j=1:n
for i=1:k
c(i,j)=mod(c(i,j),2);
end
end
disp('Generator Matrix in the systematic form is')
e=c
```

9. Write a program to generate CRC code for any given input message stream and generator polynomial.

Solution:

```
msg=input('Input Message sequence :');
poly=input('Input Generator Polynomial :');
[M N]=size(poly);
mseg=[msg zeros(1,N-1)];
[q r]=deconv(mseg,poly);
r=abs(r);
for i=1:length(r)
    a=r(i);
        if ( mod(a,2)== 0 )
            r(i)=0;
        else
            r(i)=1;
        end
end
frame = bitor(mseg,r);
x=frame;
y=poly;
disp('The Codeword is');
disp(x);
```

10. Write a program to verify whether the received cyclic code vector is error free or not.

Solution:

```
recievedM =input('Input the received sequence :');
poly=input('Input Generator Polynomial :');
```

```
[q r]=deconv(recievedM,poly);
r=abs(r);
for i=1:length(r)
  a=r(i);
    if ( mod(a,2)== 0 )
       r(i)=0;
    else
       r(i)=1;
  end
end
for i=1:length(r)
 if(r(i)==0)
    z=1;
else
    z=0;
    break;
end
end
if(z==1)
     fprintf('Received vector is error free');
else
     fprintf('Received vector is erroneous');
end
```

11. Write a program to generate a (7, 4) Hamming code and to correct single bit error.

Solution:

```
disp('-------(7,4)Hamming Encoder and Decoder-------')
disp('The (7,4) Hamming code has a dmin of 3.')
disp('Max No of detectable errors : dmin-1=2')
disp('Max No of correctable errors : (dmin-1)/2=1')
disp(blanks(1))
m=input('Enter a message of 4 bits long')
[h,g,n,k]=hammgen(3);
disp('the generator matrix{G}is..')
g
disp('the parity check matrix(H)is..')
h
disp('The encoded vector [parity|msg]is..')
c=mod(m*g,2)
R=input('Enter the received vector with atmost one error');
h_t=h';
```

```
disp('Syndrome vector is..')
s=mod(R*h_t,2)
for i=1:n
    if s==h_t(i,:)
        disp('ERROR IS FOUND AT POSITION ..')
        i
        errpos=i;
        x=1;
    else if s==[0 0 0]
        x=0;
        end
   end
end
if x==1
     disp('The error vector is..')
     E=[zeros(1,errpos-1) errpos zeros(1,n-errpos)];
     E=E./errpos
else disp('The error vector is..')
     E=[0 0 0 0 0 0 0]
     disp ('ZERO ERROR IS FOUND !!')
end
 disp('The Corrected vector is..')
y=xor(E,R)
disp(blanks(1))
```

12. Write a program to obtain the encoded sequence from an (n, k) convolution encode.

Solution:

```
clc, clear;
input_vector = input('Enter the input vector');
g1 = [1 0 0]; % Generator vector 1
g2 = [1 1 1]; % Generator vector 2
disp(['The first generator vector g(1) is', num2str(g1)])
disp(['The second generator vector g(2) is', num2str(g2)])
code1 = mod(conv(input_vector, g1),2); % code vector 1
disp(['The code due to g(1) is', num2str(code1)])
code2 = mod(conv(input_vector, g2),2); % code vector 2
disp(['The code due to g(2) is', num2str(code2)])
% To determine the final code string, obtained by switching
between code vector 1 and code vector 2
for p = 1 : length(code1)
    if code1(p) == 0 && code2(p) == 0
        final_code(3*p - 2) = '0';
        final_code(3*p - 1) = '0';
```

```
        final_code(3*p) = ' ';
    else if code1(p) == 1 && code2(p) == 0
            final_code(3*p - 2) = '1';
            final_code(3*p - 1) = '0';
            final_code(3*p) = ' ';
        else if code1(p) == 0 && code2(p) == 1
                final_code(3*p - 2) = '0';
                final_code(3*p - 1) = '1';
                final_code(3*p) = ' ';
            else if code1(p) == 1 && code2(p) == 1
                    final_code(3*p - 2) = '1';
                    final_code(3*p - 1) = '1';
                    final_code(3*p) = ' ';
                end
            end
        end
    end
end
% To display the final output
disp(['The code vector is', num2str(final_code)])
```

13. Write a program to generate 'H' matrix for a good LDPC code.

Solution:

```
% To generate 'H' matrix for a good LDPC codes of given
clear, clc
% To enter the number of rows
a=input('Enter no of rows (A):');
% To enter the number of columns
b=input('Enter no of columns (B):');
% To limit the no of columns based on no of rows
if(b<=(a+(a*0.5*(a-1))))

% To create an identity matrix of dimension A x A
i=eye(a);
e=a+(a*0.5*(a-1));
   x=i;
for j=1:a-1
for k=j+1:a
        x=[x,i(:,j)+i(:,k)];
%To concatenate identity matrix to temporary H matrix
end;
end;
   t=rand([e,1]);
```

```
% To randomly select the column of temporary H matrix to place in
the final H matrix
for l=1:b
        [c,d]=max(t);
        t(d)=0;
        H(:,l)=x(:,d);
end;

%To display the final output
disp('Generation of H Matrix for good LDPC code');
disp(H)
else
    disp('Generation of H matrix with this dimension not
possible.');
    disp('Maximum possible dimension is A x (A+(Ac2))');
end;
```

14. Write a program to implement LDPC.

Solution:

```
i = [1 1 1 2 2 2 3 3 3 4 4];    % row indices of 1s
j = [1 2 3 1 4 5 2 5 6 3 6];    % column indices of 1s
H = sparse(i,j,ones(length(i),1));    % parity-check matrix H
enc = fec.ldpcenc(H);      % Construct a default LDPC encoder object
% Construct a companion LDPC decoder object
dec = fec.ldpcdec(H);
dec.DecisionType = 'Hard decision';
dec.OutputFormat = 'Information part';
dec.NumIterations = 50;
% Stop if all parity-checks are satisfied
dec.DoParityChecks = 'yes';
% Generate and encode a random binary message
msg = randint(1,enc.NumInfoBits,2);
codeword = encode(enc,msg);
% Construct a BPSK modulator object
modObj = modem.pskmod('M',2,'InputType','Bit');
% Modulate the signal (map bit 0 to 1 + 0i, bit 1 to -1 + 0i)
modulatedsig = modulate(modObj, codeword);
% Noise parameters
SNRdB = 1;
sigma = sqrt(10^(-SNRdB/10));
% Transmit signal through AWGN channel
receivedsig = awgn(modulatedsig, SNRdB, 0); ...
```

```
% Signal power = 0 dBW
% Visualize received signal
scatterplot(receivedsig)
% Construct a BPSK demodulator object to compute
% log-likelihood ratios
demodObj = modem.pskdemod(modObj,'DecisionType','LLR', ...
'NoiseVariance',sigma^2);
% Compute log-likelihood ratios (AWGN channel)
llr = demodulate(demodObj, receivedsig);
% Decode received signal
decodedmsg = decode(dec, llr);
% Actual number of iterations executed
disp(['Number of iterations executed ='...
     num2str(dec.ActualNumIterations)]);
% Number of parity-checks violated
disp(['Number of parity-checks violated ='...
     num2str(sum(dec.FinalParityChecks))]);
% Compare with original message
disp(['Number of bits incorrectly decoded ='...
     num2str(nnz(decodedmsg-msg))]);
```

15. Write a program to choose a codeword from an LDPC encoder of length 8 bits. Introduce an error into the codeword. Use soft decision decoding of LDPC codes based on belief propagation and detect the error.

Solution:

```
clc
% Construct a companion LDPC decoder object
H = [1 0 1 0 1 0 0 0
     1 1 0 1 0 1 0 0
     0 1 1 0 0 0 1 0
     0 0 1 1 0 0 0 1];
H1 = sparse(H);
dec = fec.ldpcdec(H1);
dec.DecisionType = 'soft decision';
dec.OutputFormat = 'Information part';
dec.NumIterations = 1;
% Stop if all parity-checks are satisfied
dec.DoParityChecks = 'Yes';
msg = input('Enter a 4 bit message signal in matrix form\n');
g = [1 0 0 0 1 0 0 0
     0 1 0 0 0 1 1 0
     0 0 1 0 0 0 1 1
     0 0 0 1 0 1 0 1]
```

```
c1 = msg*g;
c = mod (c1,2);
if (c(3) == 0)
    c(3) = 1;
else c(3) = 0;
end
% Construct a BPSK modulator object
modObj = modem.pskmod('M',2,'InputType','Bit');
% Modulate the signal (map bit 0 to 1 + 0i, bit 1 to -1 + 0i)
modulatedsig = modulate(modObj, c)
% Noise parameters
SNRdB = -1;
sigma = sqrt(10^(-SNRdB/10));
% Transmit signal through AWGN channel
receivedsig = awgn(modulatedsig, SNRdB, 0)% Signal power = 0 dBW
% Construct a BPSK demodulator object to compute
% log-likelihood ratios
demodObj = modem.pskdemod(modObj,'DecisionType','LLR', ...
    'NoiseVariance',sigma^2);
% Compute log-likelihood ratios (AWGN channel)
llr = demodulate(demodObj, receivedsig)
% Decode received signal
decodedmsg = -decode(dec, llr)
k1 = find (decodedmsg >0);
k2 = find (decodedmsg <0);
decodfinal(k1) = 1;
decodfinal(k2) = 0;
disp(['Decoded codeword =']);
disp (decodfinal)
% Actual number of iterations executed
disp(['Number of iterations executed =' ...
    num2str(dec.ActualNumIterations)]);
% Number of parity-checks violated
disp(['Number of parity-checks violated =' ...
    num2str(sum(dec.FinalParityChecks))]);
% Compare with original message
disp(['Number of bits incorrectly decoded =' ...
    num2str(nnz(decodfinal-msg))]);
```

APPENDIX B Objective Questions

Multiple Choice Questions

1. Which one of the following statements is not necessarily be satisfied for a group under an operator '*'?
   a. The operator '*' has to be associative.
   b. The operator '*' has to be commutative.
   c. There ha. to be an identity element for the element of G.
   d. Every element in G has to possess an inverse.
2. If all elements of a group can be constructed using an element in the group, such groups are called as
   a. Cyclic groups b. Abelian groups c. Finite fields d. Ideals
3. An element with order $(q - 1)$ in F_q is called as
   a. Generator c. Primitive root
   b. Primitive element d. None of the above
4. The value of $\phi(70)$ is
   a. 48 b. 12 c. 24 d. 12
5. The amount of information conveyed by a definite event is
   a. 0 c. ∞
   b. 1 d. None of the above
6. A source emits four symbols with equal probability. The average amount of information conveyed by the second-order extension of the source is
   a. 2 bits/sym b. 3 bits/sym c. 4 bits/sym d. 8 bits/sym
7. Which one of the following statements is not true?
   a. Efficiency of a source would be maximum if all its symbols are equiprobable.
   b. The average rate of information conveyed by a source is directly proportional to its entropy.
   c. Self-information content of a message can be negative.
   d. Entropy of a source is upper bounded by $\log_2 M$, where M is the total number of symbols emitted by the source.
8. Identify the prefix codes among the following set.
   a. 1, 11, 001, 000 c. 00, 01, 001, 111
   b. 0, 10, 111, 1101 d. 10, 110, 111, 1101
9. Which one of the following algorithms does not require the knowledge of source statistics for coding?
   a. Huffman coding c. Arithmetic coding
   b. Extended Huffman coding d. LZ algorithm

10. Measure of the remaining average uncertainty of the channel input after the channel output has been observed is given by
   a. $H(Y/X)$ b. $H(X/Y)$ c. $H(X, Y)$ d. $I(X, Y)$
11. The joint entropy $H(X, Y)$ is also equal to
   a. $H(Y) + H(Y/X)$ b. $H(X) - H(X/Y)$ c. $H(Y) + H(X/Y)$ d. $H(Y) - H(X/Y)$
12. The channel capacity of a BSC is given by
   a. $C = (1 - h)$
   b. $C = (2 - h)$
   c. $C = (h - 1)$
   d. None of the above
13. Shannon limit on E_b/η for error-free transmission is given by
   a. −1.59 dB b. 1.59 dB c. −2 dB d. 16 dB
14. The Hamming weight of the vector '111 011' is
   a. 4 b. 5 c. 6 d. 1
15. Which one of the following options is a perfect code?
   a. (6, 3) b. (8, 4) c. (7, 4) d. (5, 1)
16. Which one of the following polynomials is a valid $g(x)$ for the construction of a (7, 4) cyclic code?
   a. $1 + x^2 + x^3$
   b. $1 + x + x^2$
   c. $1 + x + x^2 + x^3 + x^4$
   d. $x + x^3$
17. A linear code is said to be a 4 burst correcting code iff
   a. It is capable of correcting all bursts of length 4 or less but not all error bursts of length 5.
   b. It is capable of correcting all bursts of length 3 or less but not all error bursts of length 4.
   c. It is capable of correcting all bursts of length 5.
   d. None of the above.
18. Error correcting capability of a product code is given by
   a. $t = \dfrac{\max(d_{\min 1}, d_{\min 2})}{2}$
   b. $t = \dfrac{(d_{\min 1} d_{\min 2} - 1)}{2}$
   c. $t = \dfrac{(d_{\min 1} d_{\min 2})}{2}$
   d. $t = \dfrac{\max(d_{\min 1}, d_{\min 2}) - 1}{2}$
19. Let C_1 be a (7, 4) linear code and C_2 be a (6, 3) linear code. Then, a product code can be formed with which one of the following (n, k) values?
   a. (7, 4) b. (13, 7) c. (42, 12) d. (42, 7)
20. Which one of the following options was the first class of cyclic codes designed to correct burst errors?
   a. Fire codes
   b. Product codes
   c. BCH codes
   d. Interleaved codes
21. Which one of the following triplets represents a typical convolution code?
   a. (n, k, m) b. (n, m, k) c. (k, n, m) d. (m, n, k)
22. The length of the output for a (2, 1, 3) convolution code for the message $d = (1101)$ is
   a. 12 b. 14 c. 10 d. 16
23. The maximum number of encoder outputs that can be affected by a single input is known as
   a. Constraint length
   b. Code length
   c. Code rate
   d. Column distance function

24. The minimum distance among all pairs of codewords in the convolution code alphabet is known as
   a. Column distance function
   b. Free distance
   c. Hamming distance
   d. Minimum free distance
25. Which one of the following options is not a cryptographic attribute?
   a. Reliability
   b. Authenticity
   c. Non-repudiation
   d. Cryptanalysis
26. The cipher text for the following information:

   "INDIA"

   using substitution method with key 2 is
   a. KPFKC
   b. LQGLD
   c. KQFKC
   d. LQFLC
27. Digital signatures assure
   a. Confidentiality
   b. Integrity
   c. Authenticity
   d. Reliability

State True or False

1. The identity element of a group G is unique.
2. The inverse of an element in a group G is unique.
3. Generator element for a cyclic group is unique.
4. The union of all possible cosets along with the subgroup forms the actual group G.
5. Elements in the conjugacy classes need not be unique.
6. Characteristic of a field is always a prime number.
7. Generators of the cyclic codes are the principal ideals of polynomial rings.
8. Basis set of a vector space is unique.
9. If events A and B are mutually exclusive, then $P(AB) = 1$.
10. The square root of mean is known as standard deviation of random variable X.
11. The amount of information conveyed by an event is inversely proportional to its probability of occurrence.
12. A source conveys maximum information if all of its symbols are equally likely to be emitted.
13. For an nth-order extension of a source S, $H(S^n) = H(S)/n$.
14. Entropy is a symmetric function of its arguments.
15. Markov sources are used to represent discrete memoryless sources.
16. All instantenous codes are prefix codes.
17. All codes satisfying Kraft–McMillan inequality are prefix.
18. The minimum number of bits required to represent symbols emitted by a source is upper bounded by its entropy.
19. Shannon–Fano codes are also known as compact codes.
20. Efficiency of coding can be increased by extending the sources to higher orders.

21. Dictionary-based codes do not require probability of occurrence of symbols.
22. Lossy compression algorithms can achieve higher compression ratios than lossless compression algorithms.
23. Channel matrix is also known as probability transition matrix.
24. The sum of all elements of a channel matrix is 1.
25. Binary erasure channels have two inputs and two outputs.
26. Mutual information cannot take negative values.
27. The maximum rate of error-free data transmission is upper bounded by the channel capacity.
28. Any matrix of dimension $k \times n$ can serve as a generator matrix to generate an LBC.
29. All cyclic codes are linear block codes, but all linear block codes need not be cyclic.
30. Convolution codes are a special case of block codes.
31. Message bits can be extracted from the codeword in systematic codes.
32. For an (n, k) LBC, the product CH^T is always 0.
33. Hamming codes are single error correcting codes.
34. Any polynomial which divides $(x^n - 1)$ can serve as a generator polynomial to generate an (n, k) cyclic code.
35. A linear code is said to be a l burst correcting code if and only if it is capable of correcting all bursts of length $l + 1$ or less.
36. BCH codes are subclass of cyclic codes.
37. Fire codes are subclass of linear block codes.
38. Golay codes are perfect codes.
39. For an (n, k) cyclic code, we can always have an (λ_n, λ_k) interleaved code by simply arranging λ code vectors along λ rows and transmitting them column-wise.
40. Burst error correcting capability of a $C_1 \times C_2$ product code is at least equal to $\max\{n_2 l_2, n_1 l_1\}$.
41. Convolution codes are subclass of linear block codes.
42. Code rate is defined as the ratio of the number of input lines to that of output lines.
43. Generator matrix of a convolution code will be of dimension $k \times n$.
44. The number of input lines in a rate 1/2 convolution coder is twice as many as output lines.
45. The encoded sequence of a convolution code can be obtained by convolving the generator sequence with the input sequence.
46. As $i \to \infty$, the CDF, d_i will become the minimum free distance of the code.
47. Symmetric key cryptosystems use single key for both encryption and decryption.
48. An attack that intends not only to listen to the conversation by an unintended user but also to alter the system or information is known as an active attack.
49. Reliability ensures protection against the denial of having participated in a communication by an entity.
50. Diffie–Hellman key exchange algorithm assures the users to have their secret key exchanged in a secure manner.
51. Affine transformation uses two keys.

Answers to Multiple Choice Questions

1. b
2. a
3. b
4. c
5. a
6. a
7. c
8. b
9. d
10. b
11. c
12. a
13. a
14. b
15. c
16. a
17. a
18. b
19. c
20. a
21. a
22. b
23. a
24. d
25. d
26. a
27. c

Answers to True or False

1. True
2. True
3. False
4. True
5. False
6. True
7. True
8. False
9. False
10. False
11. True
12. True
13. False
14. True
15. False
16. True
17. False
18. True
19. False
20. True
21. True
22. True
23. True
24. False
25. False
26. True
27. True
28. False
29. True
30. False
31. True
32. True
33. True
34. False
35. False
36. True
37. True
38. True
39. True
40. False
41. False
42. True
43. False
44. False
45. True
46. True
47. True
48. True
49. False
50. True
51. True

Index

A

B

C

D

E